Italian Benedictine Scholars and The Reformation

The Congregation of Santa Giustina of Padua

BARRY COLLETT

CLARENDON PRESS · OXFORD
1985

Oxford University Press, Walton Street, Oxford OX2 6DP

Oxford New York Toronto
Delhi Bombay Calcutta Madras Karachi
Kuala Lumpur Singapore Hong Kong Tokyo
Nairobi Dar es Salaam Cape Town
Melbourne Auckland

and associated companies in
Beirut Berlin Ibadan Nicosia

Oxford is a trade mark of Oxford University Press

Published in the United States
by Oxford University Press, New York

British Library Cataloguing in Publication Data
Collett, Barry
Italian Benedictine scholars and the Reformation:
the congregation of Santa Giustina of Padua.—
(Oxford historical monographs)
1. Benedictines—Congregatio Sanctae Justinae
de Padua—History 2. Reformation 3. Learning
and scholarship—Europe—History
I. Title
270.6 BR307
ISBN 0-19-822934-8

Library of Congress Cataloging in Publication Data
Collett, Barry.
Italian Benedictine scholars and the Reformation.
(Oxford historical monographs)
Bibliography: p.
Includes index.
1. Santa Giustina (Monastery: Padua, Italy)—
History. 2. Benedictines—Italy—History—16th century.
3. Reformation. 4. Padua (Italy)—Church history.
5. Italy—Church history—16th century. I. Title.
BX2624.P3C64 1985 271'.1'04532 85-9708
ISBN 0-19-822934-8

Printed in Great Britain
at the Alden Press, Oxford

THIS BOOK IS DEDICATED TO MY WIFE,
PAULA

Preface

. . . la vostra riverenza, la cui mansuetudine m'apri il peto suo il primo giorno che mi vide . . . Ma nella religione, che servite e osservate, non sono pidocchierie

Letter of Pietro Aretino to Don Ambrogio,
from Venice, 11 December, 1537

This work of Italian religious history covers the forty years before Luther's Reformation and fifty years or so after it began. It is an attempt to fill in one of the gaps in our knowledge of the period through the investigation of an order of scholarly Benedictine monks. These monks had once made a lively contribution to the questioning and searching of this turbulent period, but their achievements—and even their names—have now been almost completely forgotten.

Such obscurity appeals to the antiquarian instinct to recover the facts of history, and this alone was sufficient reason for research. However, as the monks of the Benedictine Congregation came to light, they and their theology proved to be of much more than antiquarian interest. Inevitably, a monastic intellectual history involves a detailed analysis of theological writing—much of which may seem impossibly esoteric and specialized to some readers—but theology, when set out in chronological order and placed in historical context, can sometimes be extremely illuminating. Such was the case with the Italian Benedictines. Indeed, the teachings of this relatively small, but learned, order can help us to solve some specific historical problems which have hitherto limited our understanding of what was happening in Italy before and during the Reformation.

There are also other things to learn from the Benedictine monks. Their period of European history saw unparalleled conflict and questioning of authority and values and it was a period of intense speculation about the nature and destiny of man and the good life on earth as well as its fulfilment in heaven. These are perennial questions for the human race, and in our modern world, ridden by technological and social changes, and faced with constant pressures to adapt our lives and to prepare and educate for the future, we may need to be reminded that certain fundamental questions which confront us remain, *mutatis mutandis*, unchanged from one generation to another. These monks, Don Marco, Don Teofilo, Don Isidoro, Don Benedetto, and others, who, five hundred years ago walked in the streets of Padua, Mantua, Venice, Naples, and other cities, were trying to understand something about the nature and happiness of mankind: we of the late twentieth century, also living in troubled and uncertain times, have something to learn from their labours.

They applied their humanist scholarship to Christian doctrine in order to forge a definition of human nature, and in so doing fashioned in themselves a strong sense of humanity. It was this sense of humanity that touched the Venetian writer, Pietro Aretino, who was, like many exuberant sinners, sensitive to such things: in a letter to one Benedictine he summed up his admiration of the whole Congregation: 'Your kind heart was open to me the first day you saw me . . . for in the religion you follow and observe, there is no niggardliness.' What Aretino perceived in the face of that monk who had greeted him in a street in Venice still shines out of the archival and published remains of their letters, sermons, and books. As I came to know these monks well, to be familiar with each man's style of personality and learning, the quirks of personality, the habitual generosity and tolerance, but also the patches of barbed wit and irritation—in short, those things one comes to know about friends—I came to share Pietro Aretino's admiration for such scholarly, humane, and courageous men.

This study arose out of my desire to spend a few years in academic research. Like all postgraduate students, I found myself at first like a miner on the goldfields who begins by prospecting the terrain, then chooses a spot, sinks an exploratory shaft, and if a rich vein is struck, drives tunnels along it. When I began to prospect, I was fortunate to have Dr Oliver Logan of the University of East Anglia suggest that the Cassinese Benedictines might be explored. I sank a shaft amongst the Cassinese writings of the 1520s, found some promising leads, and began to tunnel. Dr Logan was my supervisor for the early stages of the work: his close interest in the topic and his lively discussion stimulated many new lines of investigation and the first chapter, in particular, owes much to his learning. The research then continued at Oxford where it was supervised by Professor Hugh Trevor-Roper, now Lord Dacre, who was at all times a meticulous supervisor, the clearest of teachers, and generous in his encouragement. I shall always be indebted to him, for the development of my research and the writing of this book, and for much else besides.

Of course, all research rests upon a network of help. I am particularly grateful to the staff of many libraries; the Bodleian, Oxford, especially those who work in Duke Humfrey's; the University Library, Cambridge; the British Library; Oriel College Library; the Biblioteca Laurenziana and the Biblioteca Nazionale, Florence; the Biblioteca Comunale, Mantua; the Biblioteca, Universitaria, Padua; the Biblioteca Alessandrina, Rome; the Biblioteca Marciana, Venice; the Biblioteca Apostolica Vaticana; the Baillieu Library and the Education Resource Centre, Melbourne. Financial support was most generously provided at various times by the Bryce and Read Funds of Oxford and the Gladys Krieble Delmas Foundation. Melbourne College of Advanced Education gave me a grant and prolonged leave of absence, to which its vice-principal Dr John Ryan added his personal support. There are many others whose advice and support were valuable during the course of research: George Yule, John Morgan, Bill Kent, Hadyn Mason, Lloyd Evans, Carlo Casarico, Giuliano Ferrari-Bravo, Lorenzo Polizzotto, Christopher Seton-Watson, Richard Collin, John Waterhouse, David Knight, Sheila Pargeter, Warwick du Vé, and my colleagues here in Melbourne. I am also grateful to Oriel College, whose fellows, students, library, and quadrangles provided a stimulating environment in which to work: in particular Jeremy Catto was a constant source of scholarly advice and encouragment. James McConica and Philip McNair, the examiners of this work when it was presented as a thesis, have been generous in their help. Felicity Harris, of Rye St. Antony School, Oxford, and Colin Goodwin of the Phillip Institute, Melbourne, read my manuscript and made many valuable criticisms of both arguments and translations. Henry Mayr-Harting guided the final preparations for publication.

Joy Markwick checked and typed the final draft with the utmost skill.

My final acknowledgement is to my wife Paula, and our five children. They helped my research in more ways than they realize, by practical support, but also by their tolerance, good humour, and general enjoyment of the whole enterprise.

Melbourne College of Advanced Education
July 1984

Contents

Abbreviations

A. et C.	M. Armellini, *Additiones, et correctiones Bibliothecae Benedicti-Casinensis etc.* (2 parts, Foligno, 1735–6).
Bibl. Bened.-Cas.	M. Armellini, *Bibliotheca Benedictino-Casinensis, sive Scriptorium Casinensis Congregationis, alias S. Justinae Patavinae etc.* (2 parts, Assisi, 1731–2).
BL	British Library
Conc. Trid.	*Concilium Tridentinum: Diariorum, Actorum, Epistolarum, Tractatuum Nova Collectio*, ed. S. Merkle *et al.* (Freiburg-im-Breisgau, 1901–).
CSP Venetian	*Calendar of State Papers and Manuscripts, Relating to English Affairs, existing in the Archives and Collections of Venice*, i, ed. Rawdon Brown (London, 1864).
CTE	M. Armellini, *Catalogi Tres Episcoporum, Reformatorum et Virorum Sanctitate Ilustrium e Congregatione Casinensi etc.* (4 parts, Assisi and Rome, 1733–4).
Ord. Cap Gen.	*Congregationis S. Justinae de Padua O.S.B.: Ordinationes Capitulorum Generalium*, ed. T. Leccisotti (Montecassino, 1939, 1970).

I

The Benedictines in
Fifteenth-Century Italy

DURING the fourteenth century Italian Benedictine monasteries, with few exceptions, became notoriously lax in their observance of the rule of St. Benedict. The worship, ascetic discipline, and study which are the ideals of the monastic life, were generally carried out in a perfunctory manner or even totally neglected. Despite sporadic attempts at reform, laxity pervaded monasticism for the greater part of the century, with the result that whilst the monasteries survived as institutions, their inner lives withered, and professions became few. What had once been flourishing houses dwindled to small groups, sometimes only three or four men occupying a large and well-endowed property under the nominal rule of an absentee abbot, and some monasteries had no monks at all. Benedictine monasticism had virtually collapsed; 'ordo monachorum nigrorum in tota Italia pene collapsus est' was the dismissive comment of one contemporary.[1]

The restoration of piety and studies to the Benedictine order was a peculiarly difficult task because it first had to overcome the problem of the appointment of abbots, each one of whom exercised sole authority within his own monastery. A very large number of appointments were made *in commendam*, that is, by exercise of the papal right to nominate and appoint the abbot, who was not necessarily a member of that order, or even a monk.[2] Appointments *in commendam* had once been used to reform and control monasteries, but by 1400 the system was being used to grant financial rewards to curial officials or to sons

[1] L. Barbo, *De Initiis Congregationis Sanctae Justinae de Padua*, ed. G. Campeis (Padua, 1908), pp. 8 ff. There is a description, written in 1434, of decadence in unreformed Benedictine houses, in *Concilium Basiliense: Studien und Quellen zur Geschichte des Concils von Basel*, ed. J. Haller, viii (Basle, 1936), pp. 143 ff. The reasons for decadence are discussed by P. Schmitz, *Histoire de l'Ordre de Saint Benoît* (Gemblous, 1942–56), iii. 3–11, 42–80.
[2] The *commenda* is treated at length in the *Dictionnaire de droit canonique* (Paris, 1924–35), fasc. xvii, cols. 1029–85.

of powerful families, and such 'abbots' were rarely willing to countenance any reforms which might jeopardize their control and enjoyment of the monastery's property.[3] Occasionally, scrupulous abbots were appointed, who initiated reforms, but such reforms were frequently hampered by the resentment of incumbent monks, by legal and financial tangles, or were even reversed by the next abbot.[4]

It was obvious that the removal of the system of *commenda* was the first step in the restoration of the monasteries. Moreover, it was apparent that reform could best be protected and consolidated if individual monasteries were to abandon the Benedictine tradition of autonomous houses and to band together in a 'congregation' with a central authority empowered to appoint competent abbots, limit their tenure of office, move monks from one house to another according to need, direct the building up of libraries, and execute other policies of reform.

An opportunity for reform along congregational lines arose during the first decade of the fifteenth century when Gregory XII indicated that he was willing to co-operate with Venice in the reform of the Paduan abbey of Santa Giustina, which was in a decayed condition, reduced to a handful of lax monks ruled by a wordly abbot. After the abbot's death there were prolonged negotiations between the Papacy, Venice, the city of Padua, and various monastic orders, until, in December 1408, the abbey was given *in commendam* to Ludovico Barbo, a zealous young prior of the Augustinian Canons Regular of San Giorgio in Alga, on the understanding that he would reform the abbey. In 1409 Barbo, with a number of his colleagues, became a Benedictine monk, took possession of the abbey, and established the strict observance of the rule of St. Benedict—not without opposition from the monks already in residence.

Barbo's work proceeded on two fronts. On the one hand he set out to reorganize monastic government, and in this he succeeded brilliantly. In 1419, by which time there were more than 200 monks at Santa Giustina, its chapter entered into negotia-

---

[3] I. Tassi, *Ludovico Barbo (1381–1443)* (Rome, 1952), p. 30; '. . . abati signori. Spesso erano figli di famiglie potenti . . . anche i bastardi del signore.' Tassi says that these 'abati signori' impoverished the monasteries by their extravagance. They included members of the Medici, Gonzaga, Aragona, Carraresi, Farfa, and Graziani families.

[4] For the difficulties faced by the reforming Camaldolese abbot Venier, see V. Meneghin, *S. Michele in Isola di Venezia* (Venice, 1962), i. 24.

tions with other monasteries, and in 1421 four others joined the Paduan house to form the Congregation of Santa Giustina.[5] The Congregation's constitution provided for abbots to be elected annually by the chapter-general, which also appointed a president for the whole Congregation for one year. Each monk made his vows to the Congregation as a whole, rather than to his own abbey, thus enabling men to be transferred from one house to another according to the needs of teaching or administration. This change from Benedictine tradition freed the Congregation from the *commenda* and its dangers, and gave it the basis for a close-knit network of scholarship and piety.[6]

Nevertheless, at first there was some opposition within the Congregation to the abandonment of the traditional Benedictine office of the abbot. During the 1420s there was conflict between those who wished to retain the permanent abbacies and those who favoured Barbo's new system of abbots elected for short terms, and for a period the Congregation divided over the issue. After earnest efforts on the part of Barbo and his

---

[5] The first monasteries to join were the Benedictine houses at Verona, Bassano, Pavia, and Genoa. The commendatory abbots' appropriation of revenue was not hindered and in return they agreed not to interfere with monastic affairs or to dispute the authority of the Congregation's own abbot. There is a good account in J. Cavacius, *Historiarum Coenobii D. Iustinae Patavinae* (Venice, 1606), pp. 197 ff. The associated monasteries were all ruled by the abbot of Padua until 1419, when the order was reconstituted by a bull of Martin V: authority passed from the abbot of Padua to the chapter-general, to which each house sent delegates; the chapter nominated *diffinitors* who then elected a president and four visitors to act as central government of the order; the *diffinitors* also appointed an abbot and officials for each monastery for a term of one year. See T. Leccisotti, 'Sull'organizzazione della Congregazione "De Unitate"', *Benedictina*, ii (1948), 237–43; also W. Witters, 'La Rédaction Primitive des Déclarations et Constitutions de la Congrégation de Sainte Justine de Padue (xvᵉs.)', *Studia Monastica*, vii (1965), 127–46.

[6] Reform, union with other houses, and the formation of the constitution were described by Barbo in *De Initiis*, 8 ff. See also F. G. Trolese, 'Ludvico Barbo, 1381–1443, e la Congregazione Monastica Riformata di Santa Giustina: un Settantennio di Studi', *Fonti e ricerche di storia ecclesiastica padovana*, vii (1976), 35–134, ix (1977–8), 79–188; Tassi, *Ludivico Barbo*, ch. 3; G. M. Picasso, 'Gli Studi nella Riforma di Ludovico Barbo', *Los monjes y los estudios* (Abadia di Poblet, 1963), pp. 295–324; R. Pitigliani, *Il Venerabile Ludovico Barbo e la diffusione dell'Imitazione di Cristo per opera della Congregazione di Santa Giustina* (Padua, 1943), esp. part i; P. Sambin, 'Sulla Riforma dell'Ordine Benedettino promossa da S. Giustina di Padova', with 'Schede per la Biografia di Ludovico Barbo', *Ricerche di storia monastica medioevale* (Padua, 1959), pp. 61–122; *Congregationis S. Iustinae de Padua, O.S.B. Ordinationes Capitulorum Generalium*, ed. T. Leccisotti, i (Montecassino, 1939), pp. ix–liv, 1–189 (the *Ordinationes* of 1424–55). There is an excellent summary of Barbo's life and work by A. Pratesi in *Dizionario biografico degli italiani*, vi (1964), 244–9. Justina was a virgin martyr of unknown date, venerated at Padua since the sixth century at least; G. Prevedello, *Santa Giustina martire de Padova: note biografiche* (Padua, 1972).

supporters, the crisis was resolved in 1431: the traditionalists returned to the Congregation, and the following year Pope Eugenius IV finally confirmed the congregational system of government with its annual election of abbots.[7]

Barbo's other work, the end to which his organizational reforms were the means, was the restoration of monastic piety and learning, and in this work also he succeeded brilliantly. He was fortunate in that his reform took place at the same time as Venice was building up the University of Padua, for the influx of students, both Italian and foreign, made the university one of the most cosmopolitan and intellectually vigorous in Europe. It was a fruitful field for Barbo, whose intellect and piety made a powerful impact upon many students, and of the 200 monks who were professed within the first ten years, most were drawn from the university, including many foreign students.[8]

After 1431 the Congregation entered a period of consolidation of its numbers, reputation, and wealth throughout the entire Italian peninsula. The success of its system and the quality of its monastic life attracted other monasteries—frequently amid an imbroglio of their conflicting intentions and interests—including San Giorgio Maggiore in Venice and San Severino in Naples. Several monasteries were forced into the Congregation, mostly by Eugenius IV, a friend of Barbo and patron of the Congregation.[9] Eugenius gave the monks St. Paul's-outside-the-walls, Rome, and the Badia in Florence, and

[7] I. Tassi, 'La crisi della Congregazione di S. Giustina tra il 1419 e il 1431', *Benedictina*, v (1951), 95–111. The innovations were confirmed by a papal bull of 23 Dec. 1432, *Bullarium Casinense*, ed. C. Margarini, i (Venice, 1650), 46–7, 50–2. During the period of crisis the order acquired St. Paul's-outside-the-walls, Rome, in 1425. G. Penco, *Storia del monachesimo in Italia dalle origini alla fine del medio evo* (Rome, 1961), has a sound account of Barbo's reform, pp. 324–61; also his *Storia della chiesa in Italia* (Milan, 1977), i. 525–37, 557–79.

[8] Picasso, 'Gli Studi nella Riforma', pp. 304–7.

[9] J. Gill, *Eugenius IV: Pope of Christian Union* (London, 1961). Barbo had acted for the Pope at the Council of Basle; Tassi, *Ludovico Barbo*, pp. 82–94. The Congregation was exempted from the authority of the prelates and granted special forms of absolution, indulgences, etc. Details are given in *Pars Prima: Constitutionum Congregationis Casinensis, alias Sanctae Justinae per Directionem Regiminis et Regularis Observantiae dictae Congregationis* (s.l., s.a., but the Bodleian copy has been annotated 'Florence, 1515'), fos. 90^v–91^r; 'Gratiae et Indulgentiae', 2^r–12^v. There is an account of Papal connections in T. Leccisotti, 'La Congregazione Benedettina di S. Giustina e la Riforma della Chiesa', *Archivio della Società Romana de Storia Patria*, lxvii (1944), 451–69. Also I. Tassi, 'Un Collaboratore dell'opera Reformatrice di Eugenio IV: Giovanni de Primis', *Benedictina*, ii (1948), 3–26.

in 1433 he expelled the order of Humiliati from the monastery of St. Peter and St. Paul in Milan and gave it to the monks of Santa Giustina.

Despite bitter and protracted opposition from the deposed Humiliati, the Congregation flourished in Milan, and the way in which they did so serves as an example of their style. They built up numbers, taking care to appoint Milanese abbots and priors. They established a reputation for scholarship, were bequeathed the library of Giorgio Valla, and, being men of quality themselves, moved with ease in, and found favour at, the court of Francesco Sforza. Their exemplary lives gave them a reputation for piety which was greatly enhanced during the plague of 1451 when the monks showed, as they were to do often, a lively concern for society outside the cloister. They worked amongst the plague-stricken poor, and one monk in particular, Don Bartholomew, 'strengthened many with reassuring prayer, and laboured mightily, with love towards his neighbour', until he himself died of the plague.[10]

By 1439 the Congregation was made up of sixteen monasteries and was the largest and most active monastic order in Italy. Barbo's work of reform was complete and his order well established and flourishing. Barbo himself was appointed bishop of Treviso, and reformed that diocese until his death in 1443, but after he had gone his Congregation continued to expand and in 1462 numbered twenty-nine houses.[11] It was clear that congregational reform was entirely successful and the system was adopted at Melk in Austria, at Valladolid in Spain, and in Germany.[12]

The Congregation also became wealthy. The monasteries that joined not only brought with them land and other property, but also provided accommodation, so that, despite its growth, the order was not burdened with heavy building costs.

[10] P. Puccinelli, *Chronicon Insignis Monasterii DD. Petri et Pauli de Glaxiate Mediolani* (Milan, 1655), pp. 6–46, 82–5, 112–13, 116, 118–19. Teofilo Beacqua, abbot in 1466, was a notable scholar.

[11] Lists of the monasteries, with a brief history of each and details of property, taxes, regulations, ordinations, etc., are given in Bibl. Laur. Florence 1826 (1424–63), 1835; Bibl. Naz. Florence, Magl. xxxvii, 320 (1475). A list is published by B. Trifone in *Annales Ordinis Sancti Benedicti, 1909* (Subiaco, 1910), pp. 56–7.

[12] D. Knowles, *Christian Monasticism* (New York, 1969), pp. 137–9. Barbo's episcopal reforms are described in L. Pesce, *Ludovico Barbo, vescovo di Treviso, 1437–1443*, Italia Sacra, ix, x (Padua, 1969), i. 252 ff.

Furthermore, since the Congregation was attractive to educated young men, it recruited mainly from more prosperous families, from whom came gifts and endowments of money and land. Moreover, the piety and learning which attracted novices also attracted lay patronage which appears to have been considerable. Some specific legacies of books and money to buy books are examined in the next chapter, but generally, few details of the order's finances have been brought to light. Almost certainly a study of the assets of joining monasteries, of lay donations, and of the administration of its wealth by the Congregation would illuminate many aspects of fifteenth-century Italy, but that topic is outside the scope of this present volume.[13]

This book is concerned with the intellectual history of the Congregation. Therefore we must ask, what were the religious teachings and practices of this large, close-knit order, and what was the relationship between the monks' piety and their learning? It has been argued, by Pitigliani in 1943, and by Sambin in 1955, that from the beginning the monks of Santa Giustina were strongly influenced by the *devotio moderna*, especially by the *Imitation of Christ*, and by the canons of Windesheim. This argument was based upon the holding of multiple copies of the *Imitation* in Congregational libraries and upon the presence at the University of Padua and amongst Barbo's novices, of students from areas influenced by the *devotio moderna*.[14]

However, other historians have not been convinced of the

[13] Some details of property, income, donations, etc. of the Badia are in the Bibl. Naz. Florence, Conv. Sopp. da Ord., 26–9. There are frequent references to the Badia in P. J. Jones, 'From Manor to Mezzadria: a Tuscan Case Study in the Medieval Origins of Modern Agrarian Society', *Florentine Studies: Politics and Society in Renaissance Florence*, ed. N. Rubinstein (London, 1968), pp. 193–241. Note also L. Ragni, 'La proprietà fondiaria del monastero di San Benedetto in Polirone nei Secoli xii–xiii', *Nuova rivista storica*, an. 54 (1970), 561–80. The monks' relations with lay people are illustrated by the correspondence of Don Domenico of the Badia with the Florentine businessman Bartolomeo Cedini when the latter was visiting Naples in 1450. The monk asked Cedini to procure seeds of the many fruits that Naples has and Florence does not have: later he wrote thanking Cedini for his letters and for the seeds of the *melarancie dolce* (Archivio di Stato, Florence, Conventi Soppressi, 78, 314, fos. 507, 524). Presumably the seeds were planted in the famous 'chiostro degli aranci', which had only recently been completed, giving the name to the cloister. I am indebted to Dr F. W. Kent for this reference.

[14] R. Pitigliani, *Il Venerabile Ludovico Barbo*. Pitigliani holds that the *Imitation* was written by an Italian monk, but his argument is very weak: see P. Sambin, 'Marginalia su Ludovico Barbo', *Rivista di storia della chiesa in Italia*, ix (1955), 249–58.

connection between Venetian spirituality and transalpine devotion, and in 1959 Giorgio Cracco suggested that the general revival of monastic piety in Venice and Padua after 1400 was simply an inchoate religious enthusiasm, a reaction to earlier monastic decadence, and a search to attain a more or less Franciscan style of personal dedication, guided by the Gospel, by the promptings of love, and by the teachings of Bernardino of Siena, Giovanni of Capistrano, and Lorenzo Giustiniani. According to Cracco, this enthusiasm soon became to resemble the Flemish *devotio moderna*, but although it used the *Imitation of Christ*, it nevertheless remained an Italian form of spirituality, whose 'most illustrious harvest' was Barbo's reform of Santa Giustina.[15] The question of sources is further complicated by the probable influence of the Benedictine Rule, which not only guided Barbo's thought, as might be expected, but may even have influenced the *Imitation* as well.[16]

In 1968 Picasso suggested that the themes of the Congregation's early piety were actually drawn from late medieval monastic tradition which was ascetic, liturgical, and Christocentric in nature. Picasso suggested that monastic scholars pursued the imitation of Christ, not in the manner of Flemish or Franciscan spirituality, but in search of 'true man', as a counter to secular humanists who made mortal man the measure of all things. He illustrated his argument with some examples of Christocentric monastic humanism from Congregational writings of the fifteenth century.[17]

[15] G. Cracco, 'La Fondazione dei Canonici Secolari di San Giorgio in Alga', *Rivista di storia della chiesa in Italia*, xiii (1959), 70–81. See also Tassi, *Ludovico Barbo*, pp. 137–9. There is a lucid exposition of the teachings and influence of Giustiniani by Oliver Logan, 'The Ideal of the Bishop and the Venetian Patriarchate: c. 1430–c. 1630', *Journal of Ecclesiastical History*, xxix (1978), 415–50.

[16] See Picasso, 'Gli Studi nella Riforma', pp. 302–3. Tassi, *Ludovico Barbo*, pp. 137–9, makes the point that the Paduan monks were not as mystical or ascetic as the Canons of Windesheim: this would be in keeping with the moderate and sensible tone of the Benedictine Rule.

[17] G. Picasso, 'L'Imitazione di Cristo nell' Epoca della "Devotio Moderna" e nella Spiritualità Monastica del Secolo XV in Italia', *Rivista di storia e letteratura religiosa*, iv (1968), 11–32. Picasso's argument is supported by an early fifteenth-century theological treatise on the dignity of man, written by Bartolomeo Facio, under the strong influence of Antonio da Barga, an Olivetian monk. P. O. Kristeller found it curious and amusing that the first humanist treatise on human dignity should have been inspired from within a medieval monastic ethos; see *Catalogus Translationum et Commentariorum*, eds. P. O. Kristeller and F. E. Cranz, ii (Catholic University of America Press, 1971), 140–75; also P. O. Kristeller 'The Humanist Bartolomeo Facio and his Unknown Correspondence',

Certainly, the Congregation's piety was closely tied to its scholarship, and it is in this connection that we find the key to the order's intellectual history. In his writings Barbo himself seemed to neglect studies, for which he expressed little approval, and even rebuked the idea that a man might become a monk 'addiscere litteras'; nevertheless, as Picasso has shown, in practice studies were approved and carried on within the cloister. After all, Barbo himself was a scholar and the men who gathered around him were cultured and scholarly men. Picasso suggests that when Barbo and his colleagues entered the cloister they did not abandon their scholarship, but set it 'in a new orientation' of piety.[18]

If the Congregation's attitude to study during the first few decades seems ambivalent,[19] from 1444—the year after Barbo's death—the chapters-general showed an unmistakable concern for studies. They issued a series of exhortations and instructions about books, libraries, and teaching, and commenced the annual *mutationes fratrum*, by which learned monks were moved around the Congregation. These steps, treated briefly in the second chapter of this book, were successful, and during this period the Congregation gave itself actively to scholarly pursuits. Moreover, it is clear from the library holdings and surviving writings—including sharp criticisms of scholastic theology—that the monks' scholarship was humanist in nature, grounded in a study of Latin, Greek, and literature, and applied to a study of the Bible, St. Paul, and the Fathers, especially the Greeks, whose rich eloquence they admired.

Such competence in biblical and patristic scholarship must have shaped the Congregation's piety. Whatever its early spiritual sources—Flemish, Franciscan, or 'true humanist'—it seems probable that in the middle of the fifteenth century the monks were still expounding religious themes which they had

---

From the Renaissance to the Counter-Reformation: Essays in Honour of Garrett Mattingly, ed. C. H. Carter (New York, 1965), pp. 56–74; M. Armellini, *Bibliotheca Benedictino-Cassinensis* (Assisi, 1731–2), i, appendix, p. 41.

[18] Picasso 'Gli Studi nella Riforma', pp. 303–10. Barbo was admired and befriended by no less a scholar than Ambrogio Traversari, who, in 1430, presented the Paduan monastery with a copy of one of his translations; see C. L. Stinger, *Humanism and the Church Fathers: Ambrogio Traversari (1386–1439), and the Revival of Patristic Theology in the Early Italian Renaissance* (Leiden, 1977), p. 172.

[19] For the history of Benedictine ambivalence towards learning, see J. Leclercq, *The Love of Learning and the Desire for God*, trans. C. Misrahi (New York, 1974), pp. 13–30.

drawn from those sources, but were now developing and reshaping them in accordance with their scholarship, until eventually those themes were transformed into the specifically biblical and patristic pattern of salvation which, as we shall see, was being taught in the Congregation in the later fifteenth century.

After 1480 the Congregation continued to grow. The number of professions remained steady at about thirty-five per year, until there occurred a sudden rise at the turn of the century during the savage warfare of the invasions; forty-nine were professed in 1501 and eighty-eight in 1507, and altogether there was an average of fifty-five professions per year from 1500 to 1550.[20] In 1505, amid extravagant rejoicing, Montecassino, the mother house of Benedictine monasticism, joined the Congregation, which was thereafter commonly called the 'Cassinese' Congregation. In 1506 the Sicilian Benedictines joined, and in 1515 the accession of the ancient French island monastery of Lérins enabled the order to set up a number of houses in Provence. By 1521, when the first effects of the Reformation were being felt in Italy, the order was at its apogee in numbers, monasteries, wealth, and reputation.[21]

The period from 1480 to 1520 also saw intense scholarly work. Libraries were extended, and many books—biblical commentaries, translations from the Fathers, and devotional works— were written and some were published. In 1487 a visitor to Padua observed that the monastery contained many learned and diligent scholars, although few had academic degrees. By the end of the century the Congregation's libraries were being extended, especially by Abbot Giovanni Cornaro at Venice and

[20] Bibl. Naz. Florence, Magl. xxxvii. 315 (Strozzi Catalogue) 'Catalogus Omnium Monachorum . . . 1409 ad 1595'. (The library catalogue states '1495' in error.) The growth in numbers and the war forced the Congregation to adopt certain changes; Bibl. Comunale, Mantua, 308 (C. II. 13), fos. 218ᵛ–219ʳ, 256ʳ–257ᵛ. See also Leccisotti, *Ord. Cap. Gen.*, vol. i. xxxv, pp. 68–9.

[21] A. Frizzi, *Memorie per la storia di Ferrara* (2nd edn. Ferrara, 1847–50), iv. 161 ff. For the abbot Ignazio Squarcialupi's high-handed exercise of power in the interests of the Congregation, see *I regesti dell' archivio: abbazia di Montecassino* ed. T. Leccisotti, viii (Rome, 1973) 1934, 1964, 2047. By the early sixteenth century there were forty-five larger monasteries in thirty-seven towns, with three nunneries (at Tarascona, Brescia, Milan) and another 145 small branch houses, chapels, etc. There were probably 2,000–2,500 monks, since there were approximately fifty-five professions per year with a lifespan of forty or fifty years after profession: see G. Pelliccia and G. Rocca, *Dizionario degli Instituti di Perfezione* (Rome, 1974), i. 1314–16.

Mantua, and its intellectual life and piety were firmly rooted in biblical and patristic scholarship.[22]

All this was a magnet for able young men inclined towards the monastic life. During the 1480s and 1490s the Congregation attracted a number of good scholars, notably Hilarion Lanterius the Greek scholar, Marco da Cremona the Pauline exegete, and Lucas Bernardus the translator of Chrysostom, but it was during the first two decades of the sixteenth century that there was an influx of especially talented men. Within the space of ten years, from 1507 to 1517, there arrived a brilliant circle of novices who became extremely able biblical and patristic scholars. These men, with their roots in the Congregation's traditions, were in their prime by the time that the Reformation controversies reached their Italian cloisters. It was they who carried their order's theological learning into the turbulent years of uncertainty and controversy from the 1520s until the Council of Trent. However, little is known of the Congregation, or its contribution to the intellectual history of Italy between 1480 and about 1570. This work attempts to fill that gap through an examination of the order's scholarship and definition of its doctrines.

Furthermore, it is to be hoped that the intellectual history of the Congregation will extend our understanding of some other, more general, historical questions. The first of these questions is what kind of theological scholarship existed in Italy on the eve of the Reformation? Was there indeed a pre-Reformation Augustinian or Pauline ethos, as Roberto Cessi has argued, and, if so, did these monks belong to it? And what kind of contribution was made to Renaissance culture by these monastic scholars with their humanist training and fine libraries?[23]

[22] Picasso, 'Gli Studi nella Riforma', p. 319. The visitor was the German Dominican, Felix Faber. For Cornaro see below, ch. 2.

[23] D. C. Steinmetz, *Misericordia Dei* (Studies in Medieval and Reformation Thought, iv; Leiden, 1968), pp. 30–4, has summarized the debate about biblical and patristic (especially Augustinian) studies in western Europe in the period before the Reformation. For the Pauline ethos see R. Cessi, 'Paolinismo Preluterano', *Rendiconti delle sedute dell'Accademia Nazionale dei Lincei*, Series VIII, vol. xii (1957), pp. 3–30. P. O. Kristeller has often pointed to the need for further study of 'the religious element in Renaissance humanism' and its effect upon the Reformation, especially the scholarly labours of the monks, which he describes as 'the true "Christian humanism" of the Italian Renaissance': see his 'Studies on Renaissance Humanism During the Last Twenty Years', *Studies in the Renaissance*, ix (1962), 7–30; 'The Contribution of the Religious

Another question is the relationship between the Congregation and the 'Catholic Evangelicals', or *spirituali*, that is, those Italians who acknowledged some validity in Luther's doctrine of justification by grace alone, but were unwilling to separate from the Papacy, and who sought, unsuccessfully and amid hostility, to reconcile the teachings of the Reformation and Rome? The monks were associated with the *spirituali*, but the nature of the connection is not clear: they were steeped in the Bible and the Fathers, they were familiar with Protestant teachings, they favoured reform of the church, they mingled with, and even instructed, circles of 'progressive' laymen and clergy at Venice, Viterbo, and Naples, they were involved with efforts to negotiate settlements with the Protestants, were mentioned briefly in various inquisitorial investigations, and were connected by ties of friendship or blood with leading *spirituali*: above all, the prime author of the celebrated tract *Il Beneficio di Cristo* was a monk of the Congregation. The monks were Pauline in theology, but they were not Protestant; they were loyal to Rome, but they were not in the main stream of Catholic orthodoxy. They flit like shadows around the fires of controversy, but the details of their contribution from the 1520s to the Council of Trent is obscure.

A third question is the connection between the monks and heretical movements. There are links between the monks and some movements which have been labelled as 'mystical' or 'Anabaptist' or 'Nicodemist'. It is hoped that an analysis of the connections between the Congregation and heresies will enable us to explain at least part of the phenomenon of heresy in Italy during the mid-sixteenth century.

There are two groups of material available to historians. First, there are the printed sources—contemporary publications of monks, eighteenth-century anthologies of the letters and works of individual monks, and modern editions of particular manuscipts and records. Second, there are the manuscript sources—unpublished volumes, tracts, sermons, letters, and library,

Orders to Renaissance Thought and Learning', *American Benedictine Review*, xxi (1970), 1–55, esp. 1–19; *Medieval Aspects of Renaissance Learning* (Duke University Press, 1974), p. 57. As an example of the links between the Benedictines and other scholars see the correspondence between Abbot Bessarion of Naples and the famous Greek scholar, Cardinal Bessarion; Bibl. Laur. Florence, Cod. Ashb. 269, fos. 42–5. See also H. O. Evennett, *The Spirit of the Counter-Reformation* (Cambridge, 1968), pp. 68–9.

administrative, and legal records. Unfortunately, the material is
not complete: a few printed works appear to have vanished
completely, and the manuscript holdings of the important
northern Italian houses were dispersed when the monasteries
were suppressed during the Napoleonic invasions of the early
nineteenth century. Some material was destroyed, some found
its way into Italian libraries, notably at Padua, Mantua, Rome,
and the Vatican, and many valuable manuscripts were sent to
Paris, but the largest collection was gathered by Lord Ashburnham, who purchased them from several sources, not all of them
reputable. In 1884, at a high price and with no questions asked,
the Italian Government bought back the collection from the
Ashburnham family and placed it in the Biblioteca Laurenziana
at Florence.[24]

Despite its gaps, the material presents a consistent picture of a
Congregation which was tightly knit, learned, and distinctive—
distinctive not only in its cultivated ethos and its generous
sympathy for worldly sinners which Pietro Arentino[25] so
appreciated, but much more in its beliefs about the nature and
the salvation of man. Yet, although these teachings were
distinctive, they had their roots, in common with other
contemporary doctrines, in biblical and patristic studies which
enjoyed a revival in the larger religious orders during the
fifteenth century. Therefore, in order to place the Congregation's teachings in the context of other doctrines, it is necessary
to make a brief summary of Italian religious thought at the end
of the fifteenth century.

The Quattrocento saw widespread reform of the monastic
and mendicant orders. An integral part of that reform was the
revival of scholarship, and in the case of the monastic orders this
was strongly influenced by humanism: the monks turned *ad
fontes*, to the authority and the eloquence of the Bible and the
Fathers. One group distinguished for its humanist studies was
the small order to which Barbo had once belonged, the secular
Canons of San Giorgio in Alga. These monks, 'men indeed
gifted with knowledge', as they were described in 1420,
maintained biblical and patristic teachings at S. Giorgio

---

[24] The story has been told by L. A. Ferrai in G. Mazzatinti, *Inventario dei manoscritti italiani della biblioteche di Francia* (Rome, 1887), ii. 549–661.

[25] See below, ch. 5, p. 113.

throughout the century, but they remained a very small order.[26] Humanist studies of the Bible and the Fathers were pursued amongst the Vallombrosians and the Olivetians also, but these too were small orders and little is known about the nature of their studies. The Camaldolese, a much larger order, actively pursued biblical and humanist studies at S. Michele in Isola, the Venetian house of the order, and in the 1430s the Camaldolese general, Ambrogio Traversari, based at S. Maria degli Angeli, Florence, extended these studies throughout the order.[27] However, his order's scholarship barely survived his death and Camaldolese studies declined until the last years of the century, when there was a revival of humanist scholarship at the hands of Paolo Orlandini, a Florentine humanist learned in the Greek Fathers, an ardent Platonist, and a disciple of Ficino.[28] This revival was strengthened in 1513 by the arrival of two Venetian monks of noble birth, Paolo Giustiniani and Pietro Quirini, both close friends of Gasparo Contarini.[29]

The mendicant orders, which dominated university teaching of theology, adhered closely to their traditional syllabi: Scotus for the Franciscans and Aquinas with a revised Aristotelianism for the Dominicans, although after 1524 Dominican scholarship, led by Catjetan, began to include biblical exegesis. Two groups of Augustinians, the Canons Regular and the Hermits, also pursued Thomist studies, using the scholastic Augustinianism of Giles of Rome, supplemented with Aquinas and

[26] G. Cracco, 'La fondazione', pp. 70–81. The praise was that of Pietro Marcello, Bishop of Padua: '. . . viros quidem scientia praeditos', quoted by Cracco on p. 70.

[27] C. L. Stinger, *Humanism and the Church Fathers*; J. Schnitzer, *Peter Delfin: General des Camaldulenserordens (1444–1525)* (Munich, 1926); J. Leclercq, *Un Humaniste ermite: le Bienheureux Paul Giustiniani (1476–1528)* (Rome, 1951); V. Meneghin, *S. Michele*. Traversari translated extensively from the Greek Fathers, including Chrysostom and pseudo-Dionysius, and some of these MSS passed to the Congregation of S. Giustina; see *Annales Camaldulenses Ordinis Sancti Benedicti*, eds. G. B. Mittarelli and A. Costadini (Venice, 1755–77), vi. 210–337; vii. 1–197; P. Ziegelbaur, *Centifolium Camaldulense* (Venice, 1750), p. 107; C. Somigli, *Un amico dei greci: Ambrogio Traversari* (Arezzo, 1964); P. O. Kristeller, *Medieval Aspects of Renaissance Learning*, pp. 155–6.

[28] P. O. Kristeller, *Supplementum Ficinianum* (Florence, 1937), ii. 268, where Orlandini's poem 'Circa le anime separate da' corpi' is quoted. See also E. Garin, *La cultura filosofica del Rinascimento italiano* (Florence, 1954), pp. 213–23.

[29] These cultured Camaldolese were patronized by the Venetian nobility: see Meneghin, *S. Michele*, p. 26, 'Il popolo veneziano e il patriziato, più che nei tempi passati, dimostravano il loro affetto e la loro venerazione per i monaci di S. Michele, come lo provano i lasciti numerosi di questa epoca. La piccola isola era spesso visitata, specialmente dai nobili . . .' Also Cracco, 'La Fondazione', p. 77.

Aristotle. Towards the end of the fifteenth century the Hermits' foremost contemporary scholar, Giles of Viterbo, extended his studies to Plato, biblical exegesis, especially of the Johannine passages, pseudo-Dionysius, parts of Augustine, and later, the Hebrew language. When he became prior-general (1507–18), Giles encouraged his friars to supplement scholastic studies with the pagan writers, and with the Bible and the Fathers, especially texts with a Platonist flavour. Consequently, in the period under consideration the Hermits gave themselves to both scholastic and humanist studies.[30]

The Franciscans were much less responsive to humanist studies. They kept rigidly to the traditional Scotist exposition in both academic and popular writings, and if Konrad Pellikan's description of the Brescian school in 1516 is accurate, their scholarly endeavours were carried out on a factory system. Even in the sixteenth century when the newly formed Capuchin order turned more to the use of the Bible, its exegesis still remained firmly in the Scotist mould.[31]

[30] H. Jedin, *Girolamo Seripando* (Wurzburg, 1937), 2 vols. The English edition is *Papal Legate at the Council of Trent: Cardinal Seripando* (London, 1947). J. W. O'Malley, *Giles of Viterbo on Church and Reform: a Study in Renaissance Thought* (Studies in Medieval and Reformation Thought, v; Leiden, 1968), pp. 157 ff., has some vivid examples of insubordination within the Augustinian order. O'Malley has used and superseded material of F. X. Martin, particularly 'The Augustinian Order on the eve of the Reformation', *Miscellanea Historiae Ecclesiasticae*, ii (1967), 71–104. A study of an earlier period of Augustinian history is K. Walsh, 'The Observant Congregations of the Augustinian Friars in Italy c.1385–c.1465' (Oxford D. Phil. thesis, 1972), ch. 4. F. X. Martin, 'Egidio da Viterbo, 1469–1518' (Cambridge Ph.D. thesis, 1958), 174–84, 358–63, deals with problems that arose from the virtual autonomy of the Lombard Congregation of the Augustinians. In the early sixteenth century the order had 15,000 friars in 1,000 houses in Italy, mostly in the north. See also P. McNair, *Peter Martyr in Italy: An Anatomy of Apostasy* (Oxford, 1967), pp. 84–5, 92 ff., 102–12.

[31] See J. Moorman, *A History of the Franciscan Order from its origins to the year 1517* (Oxford, 1968), pp. 538–43. Moorman says that contemporary Franciscan writing was 'neither distinguished nor original'. The Hebrew scholar, Konrad Pellikan, visited the island school of the Observants at Salò, on Lake Garda, in 1516, where 'quadraginta commorabantur studentes Scoto'. Lecherus published their labours under his name: *Das Chronikon des Konrad Pellikan*, ed. B. Riggenbach (Basle, 1877), p. 58. Presumably Pellikan referred to the commentaries published in Salò in 1517 and Paris in 1520, under the name of Lychetus (Leuchettus in the Paris edition). They were amongst the many commentaries on Duns Scotus published from the 1480s. The principal centre of Franciscan teaching was the Conventual friary of S. Antonio at Padua. Michele Savonarola, writing about 1445, admired the Franciscans whom he esteemed above the Dominicans and Augustinians: see M. Savonarola *Libellus de Magnificis Ornamentis Regie Civitatis Padue*, ed. A. Segarizzi (Rerum Italicarum Scriptores, tome xxiv, part 15, 1902), p. 10. Their biblical teaching was in the scholastic style, 'una cattedra . . . di metafisica';

What kind of piety emerged from the studies of these orders? For our purposes it is convenient to distinguish two types of soteriology. The first type saw the way to salvation as a graded spiritual ascent of man, a *scala perfectionis* through which men progressed, with the aid of grace, to some kind of ultimate union with God. Some exponents of this type, who took up the scheme of late platonist mysticism, thought in terms of successive stages of catharsis and illumination. Others, more patently Christocentric, saw perfection as being achieved by an ascetic self-identification with the humble and suffering Christ; others again saw ascent as a transformation through the divine love, following Bernard's idea of the soul transformed and drawn up the scale of love, beyond encumbrances of the flesh to mystical union with God. All, however, whether teaching an illuminative, ascetic, or affective mode of transformation, thought in terms of ascent and a progression by stages in which self-purification and detachment from earthly things were preliminaries to a growing knowledge and love of God. In such a system the precise function of Christ's saving act might be somewhat ambiguous, and it is not surprising in some writers that the Cross was seen as an example for Christians rather than the instrument of their redemption.

By contrast with the theologies of the *scala perfectionis*, we have 'theologies of the Cross', of which the leitmotif is restoration rather than ascent; that is, restoration of man to God's favour, and restoration of the divine image in man, by virtue of Christ's saving act. In Augustine's *Confessions*, near the end of the seventh book, the two theologies are in essence counterposed: Augustine, led by Platonic philosophy, had a brilliant vision of the ascent to the enjoyment of incorporeal truth, and then, made miserable by the power of sin, impotence, and death, he turned and grasped the Cross, 'the cup of our redemption'.[32] Although it is possible to abstract a Neoplatonist mysticism and other *scala perfectionis* material from certain of his writings, in its fullest

see G. Brotto and G. Zonta, *La facoltà teologica dell'Università di Padova, Parte I. Secoli XIV et XV* (Padua, 1922), pp. 55, 81–2, 90–2, 98. See also B. Pergamo, 'I Francescani alla Facoltà Teologica di Bologna (1364–1500)', *Archivum Franciscanum Historicum*, liii (1960), 361–441, esp. 379–80, 383–6.

[32] *Corpus Scriptorum Ecclesiasticorum Latinorum*, xxiii (1896), *S. Aureli Augustini Confessionum*, pp. 166–8, 'quid faciet miser homo? quis eum liberabit de corpore mortis huius nisi gratia tua per Iesum Christum dominum . . . poculum pretii nostri.'

dimensions Augustine's theology represents an outstanding example of theology of the Cross.[33] Later, it will be argued that the soteriological teachings of the Cassinese Congregation belonged to this category, though they were taken from the Greek Fathers rather than from Augustine.

Of the three varieties of *scala perfectionis* theology, the most popular was the ascetic way of the *devotio moderna*. It possessed little speculative mysticism, but dwelt upon the practical problems of salvation through ardent inward devotion and moral purity. The life of piety was one of withdrawal from the material world, detachment from the body, and ascent to a higher reality through meditation upon the biblical descriptions of Christ's life and death—'Crux Christi in ruminatione passionis fabricanda est'—and through ascetic identification with Christ, until, pure and virtuous, a man becomes changed into the likeness, or imitation, of Christ. Thus the *Imitatio Christi* of Thomas à Kempis (1380–1471) was a *scala meditativa* for the ascent to God, and as such is distinguished by the quality of its counsel, all of which made it a practical programme of spiritual fulfilment for laymen as well as religious.

The teaching of the *devotio moderna*, with its programme of ascent through ascetic withdrawal, drew heavily upon the Bible and the Fathers, especially Augustine, and its writings were studded with quotations from these sources. However, it was biblical and patristic only in a particular sense, for these sources were esteemed for their ardent language and quarried for illustrations and examples rather than for the themes of fall, redemption, and salvation. For example, Zerbolt described salvation as a restoration of the weakened powers of the soul, but despite the use of this Augustinian image, his soteriology was not Augustinian. In his *De Spiritualibus Ascensionibus* he taught that restoration and salvation were achieved by movement up a *scala* of increasing repentance, humility, virtue, and contemplation.[34]

---

[33] Augustine's theology of the Cross was developed in *De Trinitate*, iv. xiii, and in the *Enchiridion*, but it is seen at its most eloquent in the closing words of the *Confessions* where he recalled his mother's death. On this point and on the question of *scalae perfectionis* generally, I am greatly indebted to Dr Oliver Logan.

[34] R. R. Post, *The Modern Devotion* (Studies in Medieval and Reformation Thought, iii; Leiden, 1968), pp. 107–8, 320, 327–8, 536–49. On pp. 318 ff., he discusses the intellectual sources 'esteemed' by the Brethren of the Common Life, and their preference for the 'ardent' writings of the Fathers. See also K. de Beer, *Studie over de spiritualiteit van*

The pattern of salvation in the modern devotion began with man's emptiness and ignorance which man may surmount with the help of grace, until, by following the ascetic example of Christ, the soul was liberated from the flesh, and ascended to God. It was a pattern in which the Cross was seen as the supreme example rather than the unique instrument of man's salvation.

The second theology of ascent was the *scala perfectionis* of illumination, taught by Italian Neoplatonists. In their eyes, man's problem lay in being clouded by the world of sense, and being in darkness, lacking understanding and illumination. Salvation was an ascent through the hierarchy of being, from a dark and base material world to the illumination of the spiritual world. They did not discard altogether the material world (despite Plato's *scala* in the *Symposium*, where each step in the ascent entailed the complete abandonment of lower creation), but retained some appreciation of creation as a reflection of the Creator and almost the only source of knowledge of the unknowable God. Nevertheless they looked upon the world as the base part of the hierarchy of being, and salvation as a process of contemplative ascent (*ascesa al cielo*) through stages of that hierarchy to full illumination. Their emphasis upon contemplation as the instrument of ascent left their teaching with a characteristic vagueness about the significance of biblical doctrines of sin, grace, and the Cross, and sometimes it pushed its protagonists outside a purely Christian framework, towards notions of cosmic harmony and cabbalistic sources of illumination.[35]

Neoplatonists, both theologians and lay writers such as Ficino and Pico, selected and adapted patristic material in order to illustrate their particular *scala perfectionis*.[36] Augustine's theory of

Geert Groote (Brussels–Nijmegen, 1938), ch. 5. Wessel Gansfort (d. 1489) and John Mombaer (d. 1501), both of whom were instructed by Thomas à Kempis, produced *scalae* of ascent to God through meditation and the practice of virtue, using *scalae meditativae*, or spiritual exercises, with some scriptural material for illustration.

[35] See G. di Napoli, *Giovanni Pico della Mirandola e la problematica dottrinale del suo tempo*, Collectio Philosophica Lateranensis, viii; Rome, 1965), pp. 383–8, 393–6, 463–4, 468–79. In Pico's thought the Cross served as a model for inspiration and imitation, together with *testimonia martyrum* and *exempla sanctorum*. *Hominis dignitas* is the central theme, according to di Napoli: Pico understood grace as 'l'energia spirituale di Cristo ad esser trasfusa in noi'; the ascent of man was 'pugna spiritualis', 'via virtutis', 'ascesa al cielo': *Heptaplus*, viii. 1.

[36] The influence of Augustine upon Renaissance Neoplatonists has been described by

the soul as *imago Dei* was commonly employed to argue that the soul follows the principle of *simile fertur in simile* and seeks its own kind in its ascent to God. Seripando's *109 Questiones* and *De summo bono* both adapt Augustine's description of the soul to ascent theology in this manner, and Ficino did likewise.[37] Ficino used the three Augustinian doctrines of *imago Dei*, divine illumination, and the priority of the will, to teach that the soul, aided by grace, struggled to be purified, and to ascend through layers of reality to the illuminated realm of pure spirit, where it achieved union with God.[38] Ficino did not always distinguish clearly between the natural and supernatural, which gave his ascent the appearance of a natural development of the soul and suggested dramatic possibilities of moral perfection. His underlying confidence in the powers of men was based upon the divine potential inherent in the *imago Dei*, and the illuminative powers of God, both ideas he took from Augustine.[39] Thus, although Ficino and other Neoplatonist writers could be called Augustinian in the sense that they adapted Augustinian material to their own schemes of salvation, their soteriology was not that of Augustine, for they barely touched upon his great themes of salvation, sin, grace, Christ, and redemption.[40]

This Neoplatonist doctrine of ascent to God through illumination was one that could be assimilated into a Thomist doctrine of salvation, and this was indeed done by some scholastics about the turn of the century, at a time when they were making greater use of the Fathers. The Thomist doctrine of salvation turned upon its understanding of grace and nature,

P. O. Kristeller, 'Augustine and the Early Renaissance', *Studies in Renaissance Thought and Letters* (Rome, 1956 and 1959), pp. 367 ff. Kristeller does not distinguish between the two approaches to Augustine outlined in this chapter. He notes that Giovanni Pico della Mirandola, Ficino's pupil, also expounded ascent theology, but rarely drew upon Augustine; but cf. di Napoli, *Giovanni Pico*, p. 388.

[37] Jedin, *Papal Legate*, ch. 2. The same argument was used by very many earlier writers, such as Rusbroeck (1293–1381), and Robert Ciboule (1403–58).

[38] Kristeller, 'Augustine and the Early Renaissance', pp. 369–70. Kristeller calls Ficino 'after Petrarch one of the greatest Augustinians of the Renaissance'.

[39] Ibid. pp. 369–71. It should be said that Augustine sometimes alluded to the soul's movement to its proper place, impelled by love, 'pondus meum, amor meus', *Confessions*, chs. 9, 10, 13. Also, in *De ordine*, 2. 11. 21. he described how man may rationally and morally incline his soul away from his mortal state to an immortal and divine condition.

[40] The Neoplatonists' treatment of Augustine is neatly summarized in a remark of G. di Napoli, *Studi sul Rinascimento* (Naples, 1973), p. 292, '. . . per il Ficino la via a Christo passa per Platone e per Plotino; egli trova in Agostino il proprio precursore e il proprio alimento.'

and the central role of the intellect. Because creation reflected the goodness and order of God, there was built into the nature of a man, so to speak, a capacity for intellectual knowledge of supernatural realities and a sense of moral perfection. Consequently man moved towards God through a fulfilment of his own innate nature. The process of salvation was initiated and supported by grace: God infused grace, and when this infusion was willingly accepted by man, it was accompanied by the expulsion of sin. For the Thomists salvation was the fulfilment of an interlocking process of grace and nature, and men were required to strive for intrinsic moral perfection by co-operating with grace.[41]

When Thomist writers drew upon the Fathers, particularly Augustine, they did so in order to illustrate the scholastic doctrine of intrinsic perfection. They applied Augustine's philosophical theories to the soul's capacity to co-operate with grace, to be illuminated, and to ascend to God, but neglected patristic soteriological doctrines of sin, the Cross, and faith. Consequently, whilst Italian Thomists could be described as 'Augustinian' in their origins, their soteriological teachings were based upon ideas of the *scala perfectionis* in Aquinas.[42] A very clear example occurs in the treatise of 1503 on the immortality of the soul by Thomas de Vio, Cajetan.[43] His argument for immortality rested upon the spiritual nature of the intellect and the will, which were described in modified Augustinian terms: he then argued that the divine image of the soul both demanded and made possible its spiritual cultivation, which was an ascent of the soul through asceticism, personal reform, and withdrawal

[41] Clearly this doctrine has semi-Pelagian possibilities but at the Council of Trent the Thomist emphasis upon the gratuity and necessity of grace enabled the Dominicans to rebut charges of Pelagianism: see Jedin, *Papal Legate*, pp. 179 ff.

[42] P. O. Kristeller has drawn attention to the persistent influence of Augustine after the revival of his works in the eleventh century: 'Augustine and the Early Renaissance', 355–72, esp. p. 357: 'Augustinianism survived as an important secondary current, and even the representatives of Aristotelianism preserved many traces of Augustinian influence.'

[43] Cajetan studied philosophy at Naples and theology at Bologna. He lectured in metaphysics at the Dominican school at Padua, where he became Master of Theology at the University. He taught also at Pavia and Rome, where he wrote his *De immortalitate animorum* in 1503 and his famous commentary on the *Summa* of Aquinas. Then, in an attempt to meet the Reformers on their own ground, he turned from this solidly scholastic background to biblical commentaries, on Romans in 1528 (in which he denied that immortality of the soul is demonstrable by reason), and on Ecclesiastes in 1534.

from the world, to levels of illumination and, finally, eternal felicity, which he described in strongly Augustinian language. Therefore, whilst Cajetan's terminology and many of his ideas were Augustinian, his soteriology was still a *scala perfectionis* drawn from Aquinas. Indeed, the fact that a distinguished and progressive Dominican scholar was expounding Augustine in such terms as late as 1503 is an indication of the conservative nature of Thomist scholarship in Italy.[44]

Two other scholastics, Giles of Viterbo and Jacob Sadoleto, similarly used patristic material to expound a Neoplatonist soteriology of withdrawal from the world of sense and ascent to God through illumination. Giles praised the *via negationis* of Dionysius, 'Graecae theologiae unicum lumen', he favoured St. John above other biblical writers, and he attacked Paduan Aristotelians for their study of mere concrete things and secondary causes.[45] His pattern of salvation was withdrawal from the world, moral reform, and progressive ascent through the illumination imparted by biblical, patristic, and even pagan texts. Consequently, he closely studied the Bible, the Fathers, and Greek and Hebrew languages, but in a desire to wring the last drop of illumination from the texts he adopted the bizarre cabbalistic methods of 'secretior theologia', which involved the allegorical and numerological exegesis of every word to reveal the core of higher wisdom—the 'disciplina arcani'—available only to the élite. He even applied the cabbala to non-Christian writers to ferret out the inner core of truth which God in his providence had allowed them.[46]

---

[44] *Opuscula Omnia* (Lyons, 1562), iii, tract 1, 'Se Sex Orationibus Romae Habitas', sermon 4, pp. 186–8.

[45] O'Malley, *Giles of Viterbo*, pp. 22–5, 51–3, 58, 70–1, 143–7. Jedin, *Papal Legate*, p. 31. It seems strange that so long after Valla's researches, Giles should accept Dionysius uncritically. Although an active man of affairs, Giles placed great store by solitude, and believed the religious life, especially the eremetic life, to be best for Christians. For an earlier discussion of the Platonic elements in Giles see J. Paquier, 'Un essai de théologie platonicienne à la renaissance: le commentaire de Giles de Viterbe sur le premier livre des Sentences', *Recherches de Science Religieuse*, xiii (1923), 293–312, 419–36.

[46] O'Malley, *Giles of Viterbo*, pp. 22, 38–9, 57–8. Jedin, *Papal Legate*, pp. 37, 57, has some striking examples of cabbalistic exegesis of Seripando. Since both men were prominent in the order we may assume a general acceptance of the cabbala in Augustinian studies. Giles's admiration for Reuchlin is revealed in F. Giacone and G. Bedouelle, 'Une lettre de Gilles de Viterbe (1469–1532) à Jacques Lefèvre d'Étaples (c.1460–1536) au sujet de l'affaire Reuchlin', *Bibliothèque d'humanisme et renaissance*, xxxvi (1974), 335–45.

The other scholastic, Jacopo Sadoleto, also moved towards humanist and biblical studies, using them in a similar soteriology of ascent. Although he stated his intention of following Augustine's doctrine of grace, he gave little attention to the redemptive function of the Cross. Rather, he described salvation as a process, initiated by man, in which infused grace assisted an ascent from the world of sense to a state of perfection in the spiritual realm of the angels. Thus, what was true of Giles was also true of Sadoleto: both could be correctly called 'patristic' or 'Augustinian', but their use of patristic material was selective and adapted to their Neoplatonist pattern of salvation, and much of Augustine's soteriology was neglected.[47]

The third type of ascent theology, found in both scholastic and humanist writers, was that of union with God through affective experience. Here man's problem is seen as restraint and lack of fulfilment of the kind that is overcome by the experience of divine love and union with God. Amongst the scholastics, the Franciscans blended Bonaventura's emphasis upon love with the philosophy of Scotus. Scotist teaching, in part a metaphysical reaction to Thomism, was based upon a stark contrast between God and his creation, so that the moral law was not written into the nature of man by virtue of his relation to God, but was an arbitrary imposition upon man. The Scotists concentrated, not upon the intellect which understands, but upon the will which obeys the declared laws of God. First God remitted sins, then he infused grace which disposed men to a state of contrition, love, and obedience, but there was no organic connection between the remission of sins and the growth of perfection, as in Thomist teaching. Good works, stimulated by grace, did not in themselves merit salvation, but only in their acceptance as meritorious by God. Thus the relationship between man's interior state and his standing with God was not

<hr>

[47] R. W. Douglas, *Jacopo Sadoleto (1477–1547): Humanist and Reformer* (Cambridge, Mass., 1959). Douglas observes that Sadoleto's attempted synthesis of the Augustinian doctrine of grace with the necessity of works consisted of little more than the grammatical device of linking diverse doctrines with the word 'tamen' (p. 84). Douglas calls Sadoleto's *In Pauli Epistolam ad Romanos Commentariorum Libri Tres* (1535) 'neo-Pelagian'; see the *New Catholic Encyclopedia* (New York, 1967), xii. 846. Even in their later, biblical writings, Giles and Seripando retained certain scholastic definitions; see Jedin, *Papal Legate*, pp. 52–4. Jedin also noted that Seripando's reading did not include any of the Fathers or modern authors such as Erasmus.

always clear. In practice Scotist soteriological writings concentrated upon the dispositions and immediate experiences of man
as he progressively encountered and identified himself with
Christ, and they used the Bible and the Fathers to illustrate that
ascent. Scotist soteriology, despite its sense of the gulf between
God and man, was one of infused grace and progressive
perfection through the responses of the will.[48] This pattern of
salvation carried semi-Pelagian implications which came to the
surface when Italian Franciscan writers of the fifteenth century
applied Scotist theology to popular pastoral writings. The best
example of this genre was the Observant Franciscan Angelo
Carletti's *Summa Casuum Conscientiae*, which first appeared in
1486. It was a handbook on how to live the holy life, a catalogue
of righteous behaviour, which, although formally free of heresy,
suggested that men could make themselves fit for salvation
through the exercise of the will.[49]

The theology of ascent through affective experience was also
taught by Camaldolese monks, notably by Paolo Giustiniani,
the Venetian humanist and friend of Gasparo Contarini. When
Giustiniani became a monk in 1513, he brought with him into
the monastery the Bible and the works of Plato and Plotinus,
Augustine, Jerome, Ambrose, Basil, Gregory of Nazianzus,
Bernard, and Albert the Great. He read the Neoplatonists

---

[48] Methods of prayer and meditation were devised to assist progress in love and
obedience. Raymond Lull, Bianco da Siena, and others in this tradition paid much
attention to all aspects of the indwelling 'divine love' and the 'divine embrace', together
with man's abnegation, illumination, and ascent to God, drawing heavily upon
Neoplatonist elements of Augustine which they adopted to the soteriology of affective
progress. The Franciscans gave Raymond Lull the epithet 'Doctor Illuminatus', and
after his well-earned martyrdom in North Africa in 1316, his works were read widely in
Italy during the fourteenth and fifteenth centuries: most libraries possessed several
copies of his works. See P. Rossi, 'The legacy of Raymond Lull in the 16th century',
Medieval and Renaissance Studies (The Warburg Institute, London, 1961), pp. 182–213.

[49] In order to safeguard against these implications Scotists held to the absolute
predestination of the elect, stressed the necessity of Christ's merits which removed the
obstacles to heaven, and the necessity of grace with which man co-operates for *meritum de
congruo*. See É. H. Gilson, *Jean Duns Scotus: introduction à ses positions fondamentales* (Paris,
1952), p. 329 n. There is also a succinct account by A. H. T. Levi in his introduction to
Praise of Folly and Letter to Martin Dorp (Penguin Books, 1971), pp. 16–21. Carletti's ideas
were reinforced by Scotist stress upon the role of faith as the intellectual acceptance of
church dogma. Luther was so affronted by its implications that he burnt a copy in his
bonfire at Wittenburg in 1520. In Italy it remained the dominant popular work of
scholastic soteriology until the mid-sixteenth century. G. Pou y Marti calls it 'opera
utilissima per i confessori e i moralisti', *Enciclopedia cattolica* (Vatican, 1948), i, cols.
1256–7.

Ficino and Pico della Mirandola and appears to have known early Franciscan writings and Dante, though little of the *devotio moderna*. Using these sources copiously, he described salvation as an ascent from the bodily life to the spiritual life of illumination and regeneration through encountering the love of God.[50] This pattern of salvation through spiritual love was based upon the antithesis between flesh and spirit which Giustiniani drew from various Pauline and patristic texts. Whereas other theologians found in Paul convincing reasons to deny salvation through perfection, Giustiniani's exegesis sharpened the antithesis between flesh and spirit and buttressed his soteriology of the *scala perfectionis* which, however, he expressed in terms of affective experience rather than in a Pauline doctrine of salvation.[51]

After great effort, Giustiniani attained an exalted state of ecstatic, abandoned, passionate love. He tried to persuade Contarini to follow the same route to salvation, but Contarini, true to his Thomist foundations, saw the way of ascent to perfection more in illumination and reason than in affective response: he debated within himself for some time, but finally decided not to follow his friend into the Camaldolese order.[52]

We have seen that Italian soteriology of the late fifteenth and early sixteenth centuries was predominantly of the type that described salvation in terms of an ascent to a state of perfection—by asceticism, illumination, or affective response—and that humanists, and even Augustinian scholastics, adapted the

[50] Giustiniani was a Camaldolese monk from 1513 until his death in 1528. The correspondence with Gasparo Contarini and others is published in *Annales*, eds. G. B. Mittarelli and A. Costadini, ix, appendix, cols. 447–598. Also 'Contarini und Camadoli' ed. H. Jedin, *Archivio italiano per la storia della pietà*, ii (1959), 51–117. Cessi has argued in 'Paolinismo Preluterano' that Christian humanist scholars were disturbed by the disharmony between the secular and religious aspects of their studies, but the argument is imprecise.

[51] Giustiniani's dualism is described in Leclercq, *Un Humaniste ermite*, p. 56; see also pp. 29, 32, 51, 58, 66, 86–7, 107, 111, 128, for a recital of his interior dispositions. For examples of his fussy preparations for total withdrawal from the world see pp. 57–8, 63, 70. Other Camaldolese monks were not convinced that such solitude was necessary for contemplation (pp. 56–7). For the criticism of Cassinese monks see pp. 90–1; for Giustiniani's library pp. 30–3, 47, 54, 56, 127.

[52] Ibid. 62, 89. For their differences see Mittarelli and Costadini, *Annales* ix, cols. 539–50. Camaldolese piety included great frugality, intense liturgical devotion, and affective experiences: see vii, cols. 29–33.

revived biblical and patristic studies to these *scala* patterns of salvation. Consequently, their religious teachings were directed strongly towards the attainment of personal piety and the performance of good works which were both the fruit and the nourishment of piety. Thus, the emphasis upon the attainment of personal piety, a widespread phenomenon in pre-Reformation Europe, in Italy was expressed through 'ascent' theology.

The 'ascent' patterns of salvation laid considerable emphasis upon human effort. Of course this did not mean that a crude Pelagianism was being taught. Merit was not necessarily ascribed to the works of the ascending soul, and in any case the notion of judgement was secondary to the central idea of ascent, whilst a common emphasis upon the necessity of strengthening and saving grace kept *scalae perfectionis* formally anti-Pelagian. Moreover, the influence of Dionysian negative theology retained a sense of the transcendence and sovereignty of God in many writers of this tradition. Nevertheless, it is clear that in 'ascent' theology good works were necessary to salvation. In effect, man contributed to his own salvation, progressively achieving perfection through his efforts in co-operation with grace, so that failure to achieve certain levels of illumination, asceticism, feeling, or works implied insufficient progress towards perfection. This pattern of salvation had a tendency, although it was rarely explicit, to blur the distinction between man's natural and supernatural condition. Seripando came close to such formal Pelagianism in his Platonic writings before 1538, in which he not only failed to differentiate clearly between a natural infusion of divine ideas and supernatural grace, but also drew an analogy between physical light and divine illumination which impeded such a distinction.[53] However, even in writers who lacked such clear Pelagian tendencies, the implications of their soteriology were clear enough: man strives for progress in perfection until he reaches God; whilst the means and strength are given by God, it is man himself who climbs the

---

[53] Jedin, *Papal Legate*, p. 35, also pp. 71–5, 80–1, 83–91. Seripando, who had begun as a Scotist then became a Platonist, took a Pauline position on faith and justification in 1538. He seems to have done so without Protestant influence. Some Dominican theologians eschewed scholastic theology; a notable example was Santo Pagnini, see T. M. Centi, 'L'attività letteraria di Santi Pagnini (1470–1536)', *Archivum fratrum praedicatorum* xv (1945), 5–51, esp. 26, 46.

scala perfectionis and his progress is measured by the inner experiences and by the works that appertain to holiness.[54]

However, whilst good works were necessary to salvation in 'ascent' theology, that necessity was not primarily legalistic in nature, for the merit of good works was not considered to be *meritum de condigno*, meeting a standard of justice requisite for the day of judgement; rather, good works were necessary as a part of the ascent to perfection and union. Amongst Italian theologians the idea of forensic justification was secondary to the idea of ascent, a fact reflected in the detailed guidance, the mild penances, and the sense of comfort, consolation, and encouragement which was to be found in Italian devotional manuals of the period, especially the *Summa Angelica* of Carletti.[55]. It is this that distinguishes Italian piety from that of the north, which under the strong influence of late medieval Occamist theology saw the necessity of works in the context of forensic justification, possessing *meritum de condigno* or *meritum de congruo*.[56]

Protestant theology of the Cross, with its roots in a theology which saw salvation in terms of justification, and with its denial of the saving value of works, had a profound effect upon ascent theology in Italy. It quickly turned the emphasis of Italian spirituality away from the questions of ascent and towards the problem of justification. This change of emphasis was reflected in the great number of biblical, and especially Pauline, commentaries written in Italy after the Reformation, and the simultaneous decline in popularity of the 'ascent' manuals. The new preoccupation with justification produced two separate

[54] Similar ideas of levels of spiritual perfection were apparent in a dispute in 1490 between English Carthusians and Cistercians, concerning the right of monks to move between orders of differing 'religious perfection': *Calendar of State Papers, Venetian*, i. 557, Henry VII to Innocent VIII.

[55] T. N. Tentler, *Sin and Confession on the Eve of the Reformation* (Princeton, 1977), ch. 5, also pp. 30–6, 363–70. P. Heath's review of Tentler suggests that at the parish level there may have been a considerable fear of hell, and that canon lawyers were more legalistic and Pelagian in their teaching then were Tentler's theologians; see *Journal of Ecclesiastical History*, x 103–4.

[56] H. A. Oberman, *The Harvest of Medieval Theology. Gabriel Biel and Late Medieval Nominalism* (Harvard, 1963), chs. 5–7; also *Forerunners of the Reformation, The Shape of Late Medieval Thought* (London, 1967), pp. 1–66, 121–203. When Contarini questioned the saving value of works in his crisis of 1511 his style was scholastic and forensic: he distinguished between reconciliation with God (out of grace) and satisfaction for sin (human works), holding the former to be necessary and the latter meritorious, but not necessary to salvation.

streams of thought in Italy. The first engaged in confrontation with Protestantism, in the course of which a new generation of Roman Catholic theologians hammered out the theology, which eventually prevailed at Trent, of justification through both faith and works. The second stream was that of the *spirituali*. They accepted the validity of Luther's Pauline doctrines of sin and grace on justification, but they were thrown into some confusion about works, for they now doubted whether the good works and piety at the heart of ascent theology were, after all, of any value in man's salvation. Of course, there was no problem for those *spirituali* who became Protestant, men such as Negri, Ochino, and Peter Martyr, for the piety and works they had seen as part of ascent theology they had simply carried over into the Lutheran pattern of salvation as works of gratitude after justification. But those *spirituali* who remained with Rome were faced with a dilemma. Neither their obedience to Rome nor their theological adherence to an ascent to perfection allowed them to discard the necessity of works in reaching a state of justice: on the other hand they were now very conscious of the sinfulness of man and the inadequacy of his works to justify *coram Deo*. Thus the pre-Tridentine *spirituali* were caught between the ascent of man to God and the inability of sinful man to become perfectly just through his works.

However, in addition to the theologies of ascent and justification, the doctrines of *spirituali*, Protestants, and hard-line Romanists, there was another strand in Italian religious history of this period which has barely been recognized. The teachings of the monks of Santa Giustina were quite distinct and different from those of others. Long before the Reformation, the monks taught a pattern of salvation of the 'restoration' type expressed in Pauline terms of sin, the Cross, grace, and faith, mainly using the exegeses of Augustine and Chrysostom: the kind of restoration they taught was not that of guilty and unjust man restored to a state of justice, but rather that of human nature now broken by mortality and suffering both in body and mind restored to life and health. They took these ideas from the Greek Fathers, especially Chrysostom, and from the western tradition, particularly Augustine.[57] Under the pressure of Reformation

---

[57] The monks may also have drawn upon the Victorines, especially Richard of St. Victor, who himself wrote about *imago Dei*. Their works were in Congregational libraries, but there is little direct evidence of their use.

controversy, the monks developed and more clearly defined their traditional teachings, especially those elements derived from the Fathers of Antioch. In consequence they saw the debate over justification through eyes different from those of the Reformation and counter-Reformation theologians. For the monks the religious predicament of man lay primarily not in his guilt, as the Latin tradition taught, but in his mortality and his fear of death, as the Greek Fathers taught. From this it followed that man's salvation lay primarily not in his being justified *coram Deo*, but in his rescue from mortality and the restoration of shattered human nature to health by Christ 'the divine physician'. Therefore, the debate whether man was justified by grace alone, or by grace with works—the irreconcilable antitheses of the conflict—was wrong-headed; it arose from the forensic obsessions of late-medieval theology, missing the true nature of salvation as taught by Paul and explained by Chrysostom. The Benedictine monks held that in the therapeutic pattern of salvation taught by the Fathers of Antioch, free will and works were necessary, not for merit, but as a means of restoring human nature, so that there was no conflict between *gratia sola* and *opera humana*; moreover, fidelity to Scripture, the nature of faith, the doctrine of predestination, and other questions behind the terrible schism of Latin Christian Europe could be resolved by the light of the Antiochene theologians. The monks of the Congregation of Santa Giustine tried very hard to apply their Greek theology to the Latin schism, but they failed. Their intellectual traditions and their attempt, not fully recognized or understood, even by their contemporaries, have been long forgotten. This book sets out to rediscover these learned, unusual, and most humane monks.

II

Studies Within the Cloister, 1480–1520

In this chapter we shall begin the task of defining the theological teachings and studies carried on inside the cloisters of the Congregation after 1480. The question will be approached through an examination of the holdings and acquisitions of monastic libraries, a brief survey of the known teachers from the mid-fifteenth century, and an analysis of texts used in the classroom.

The founders of the Congregation were themselves learned men, but the first few generations of their monks were not particularly noted for their scholarship.[1] However, the Congregation took seriously Benedictine traditions of study, and throughout the fifteenth century steps were taken to foster and direct studies. In 1434 the chapter-general ordered each monastery to draw up an inventory of the books it had acquired 'by donation or written by our brethren', each such book to be considered 'deputatus' to the use of that monastery.[2] In 1444 the Congregation began its policy of moving men from house to house in order to improve studies and discipline: from twenty to thirty transfers were made each year.[3]

There is evidence that by the 1460s the monks were quite active in serious scholarship and in the care and use of their libraries. In 1461 Bernard Placentino, abbot at Padua, arranged the building of a large room to house manuscripts, which were then catalogued.[4] In 1464 the chapter-general

---

[1] L. Blum, *La Biblioteca della Badia Fiorentina e i codici di Antoni Corbinelli* (Studi e Testi, clv; Vatican, 1951), pp. 53–4.

[2] Leccisotti, *Ord. Cap. Gen.* i. 40.

[3] Bibl. Laur. Florence, Cod. Laur. Ashb. 1826. The annual lists of 'Mutationes Fratrum' begin on 50ʳ, when thirty-two transfers were recorded for 1444 between Florence, Verona, Perugia, Padua, Mantua, Venice, Rome, Genoa, Milan, Naples, Siena, and Pavia.

[4] Ferrai, *Inventario*, p. 552. Bucel named 1454 as the year in which the Congregation began to shine in holiness, scholarship, works, and preaching, throughout the entire peninsular, but he gave no details: G. Bucelinus, *Annalium Benedictorum* (Veldkirkius, 1665), ii. 91.

decreed that too many illiterate novices were being admitted to the novitiate.[5] The concern was that the education of other novices was being held back. The following year the chapter-general admonished its brethren 'to spend more time in the reading of holy Scripture than of Cicero and of the Greek poets and literature'.[6] The exhortation reveals not only that the study of classical Greek was well established, but also that the prelates of the Congregation were anxious to apply those Greek studies to Scripture. Very probably the man most responsible for this policy was Don Bessarion of Aragona, a Greek scholar and correspondent of his namesake Cardinal Bessarion. From 1461 to 1469 Bessarion was either president of the Congregation or a *diffinitor*.[7]

In 1472, and again in 1483, the chapter-general issued a strongly worded prohibition of learned works being held for private use, or their unauthorized removal to another monastery, and it commanded all abbots to ensure that there was 'an abundance of appropriate and worthy books so that our brethren may be enabled the more diligently and easily to apply themselves to the study of sacred letters'.[8]

During the same decades the Congregation built up its libraries, particularly at Mantua, Florence, and Padua. The library of the Badia at Florence had been founded in the tenth century, but at the time of its reform and union with the Congregation in the early fifteenth century it was devoid of scholarly books. When the Portuguese abbot Gomez began his long abbacy there he found neither Greek nor Latin works.[9]

---

[5] Leccisotti, *Ord. Cap. Gen.* i. 235. 'Non recipiantur tot novitii illitterati, maxime insufficientes: aliter qui eos admiserint quales fuerint sustinebunt.'

[6] Ibid. 242. 'Hortamur etiam et admonemus ut patres et fratres plus operam dent lectioni sacre scripturae quam Ciceronis, poetarum et litterarum graecarum.'

[7] Ibid. 208, 212, 215, 222, 232, 235, 239, 248, 253, 260. Bessarion was later abbot of S. Severin, Naples, and St. Paul's, Rome, 269, 272, 282. See also *Ord. Cap. Gen.* ii. 1, 2, 67. There were eight *diffinitors* as well as the president: their task was to act as a governing body in the period before the next chapter-general.

[8] Ibid. ii (1475–1504), 30–1: 'Ut autem fratres nostri sacrarum literarum studiis sicuti optamus diligentius atque commodius incumbere valeant, prelatos omnes nostrae congregationis hortamur in Domino, ut paterno officio procurent ut in monasteriis nostris congrua et honesta suppetat copia librorum . . .' In addition to this *ordinatio*, the chapter-general issued an admonition to abbots to supervise the training of monks in grammar and singing (see 33).

[9] Quoted in L. Blum, *La Biblioteca della Badia*, pp. 18–19 '. . . libros latinos pariter et graecos . . .' Blum points out that the wording implies that the monastery lacked works of scholarship rather than liturgical books.

Some works were purchased or bought for the library, but the energetic Gomez made a really splendid catch when he persuaded the Florentine humanist Antonio Corbinelli to bequeath his library to the Badia despite Poggio Bracciolini's protest that the monks were not lettered enough to appreciate the legacy. It was a substantial collection: there were 194 Latin manuscripts of which 105 were of classical authors, principally Cicero and Aristotle, and the remainder made up of the Bible and the Fathers—mainly Ambrose, Gregory, Bede, Augustine—with several works of Aquinas.

There were seventy-nine Greek manuscripts, of which sixty-five were of classical authors, mostly Homer, Euripides, and Plato, and the rest the Bible or the Fathers—including five volumes of different homilies of Chrysostom.[10] The library of the Badia also received fifty-seven Latin and Italian manuscripts when Eugenius IV united S. Maria del Santo Sepolcro with the Congregation.[11] For the remainder of the century the Badia acquired from time to time works given or bequeathed by lay donors or written by the monks themselves.[12] In 1504 the abbot Ignazio Squarcialupi built a new edifice to house the library, and this event served as the occasion for a catalogue of all volumes.[13]

The catalogue for 1504 tells us that the monks had in their possession, and available for their use, a wide range of classical, biblical, patristic, and medieval works. Compared with the libraries of other orders, that of the Badia included rather more biblical and patristic texts and rather fewer scholastic texts;

[10] Leccisotti, *Ord. Cap. Gen.* ii. 53–4, 73–96, 114. When Corbinelli died in 1425, the books went first to a friend who had use and enjoyment of them for life, then to the monks. There is a discussion of Bede's exegesis, his use of Augustine, and his influence upon the homiliary of Paul the Deacon, by Bernard Capelle, 'Le rôle théologique de Bède le Venerable', *Studia Anselmiana*, vi (1936), 1–40, esp. 20 ff. The same volume contains the article of M. Inguanez, 'Il venerabile Beda nei condici e negli scrittori cassinesi medievali', pp. 41–50.

[11] Blum, *La Biblioteca della Badia*, p. 19.

[12] Ibid. pp. 20–1 has examples.

[13] Ibid. p. 14; P. Puccinelli, *Cronica dell' Abbadia di Fiorenza* (Milan, 1664), p. 70. Blum, pp. 27–8, argues that this catalogue was drawn up after 1504, but within the first decade of the century. The catalogue is in the Bibl. Laur. Florence, Cod. Ashb. 151 (2712): Blum has edited and printed the catalogue, 114–72. The Florentine scholar Ambrogio Traversari frequently used Greek MSS from the Badia: G. Mercati, *Ultimi contributi alla storia degli umanisti: fasc. I: Traversariana* (Studi e Testi, xc; Vatican, 1939), pp. 20, 29–33.

nevertheless we can draw no conclusions from the catalogue alone, which can tell us only what was available, and not what the monks wished to study or did study. For this information we must turn next to the rather scanty evidence of the printed works and manuscripts acquired by the monks through their own purchases or copying.

The acquisitions fall into three groups. First, there were works intended for language instructions, a number of Greek and Latin lexicons, dictionaries, and anthologies of Homer, Virgil, and Cicero; there was also a copy of the Milan edition of 1475 of Valla's *De Lingua Latina*. The second group consists of biblical texts and several expositions in the literal style of exegesis. The Badia acquired copies of the Venetian Bibles of 1479 and 1481 (the latter with footnote explanations of Hebrew names), the Gospels in Greek (1482), and the 1495 edition of Lyra's *Biblia cum glossis*, that is with interlinear exposition and marginal concordance. The monks had acquired three editions (1477, 1478, 1480) of Lyra's *Postillae* on the New Testament, his *Expositiones* (Mantua, 1481), and his *Postillae* on the whole Bible (Venice, 1489). There were also commentaries on the Psalms by Turrecremata (Rome, 1476), Gilbert of Holland (Florence, 1485), and Cassiodorus Senator (Basle, 1491). The third group of acquisitions was made up of patristic texts. Between 1474 and 1485 the Badia acquired two copies of the sermons of Ephraem of Syria (Florence, 1478 and 1481), one copy of each of Eusebius of Caesarea's commentary on *Psalms* (1480), Isidore of Seville's *De summo bono* (Venice, 1483), Cassian's *Collations* (Basle, 1485), and two manuscript works of Chrysostom, *Della compunzione del Cuore*, copied in 1474, and *De Laudibus Pauli Apostoli*, copied at the Badia in 1479.[14]

Upon this evidence, it seems probable that the monks' studies after 1470 were concerned with the teaching of languages, biblical and patristic texts, and biblical commentaries, particularly of the exact and literal type represented by Nicholas of Lyra.

[14] This information is taken from Bibl. Naz. Florence, Magl. x 144, *Index iuxta materias distributas codicum mss. ac librorum editorum usque ad annum 1500 Graecorum Latinorum insignis Abbatiae S. Mariae de Florentia . . . compilatus atque transcriptus anno 1737*. This catalogue is not complete, but has the merit of including the dates of several works. The very fine copy of the volume of Chrysostom dated 1474 is in the Bibl. Naz. Florence, Conv. Sopp. E.3.

The contents of the library of Santa Giustina, Padua, show a similar biblical and patristic bent. There is an inventory which was begun in 1453 (when the library contained 466 works), classified according to the quality and value of the manuscript.[15] During the next nine years, to 1462, another twelve entries were made. Then the library received the manuscripts of Palla di Noferi Strozzi, the exiled Florentine humanist who died in May 1462 (entries 479–96). After the acquisition of the Strozzi collection the library continued to grow until by the time of the last entry in the inventory, shortly after 1484, it listed 1,337 items.[16]

The books listed in 1453 included several copies of the Bible in whole or in part, especially the Gospels and the epistles of St. Paul, and biblical commentaries of Augustine, Chrysostom, Ambrose, Bernard, Bonaventura, and Lyra.

There were other patristic works, notably those of Gregory the Great, various works of Aquinas, Boethius, Hugh of St. Victor, Antonius de Butrio, the *Imitation of Christ*, lives of saints, and other devotional works, homilies, copies of St. Benedict's rule and commentaries upon it, the writings of Cicero, Seneca, and Livy. The Bible apart, the most common authors were Bernard and Chrysostom. In ther period between 1453 and 1462 the principal entries were lives of the saints, a commentary on the psalms, a Greek vocabulary, two copies of Chrysostom on Matthew, one in the Greek, the other in Latin. Strozzi's bequest of 1462 brought a number of Aristotle's works, but also copies of the Bible and some works of St. Gregory and other Fathers.[17]

The later entries, those made between about 1462 and about 1484, were of the same kind. Leaving aside practical works such as medical and legal textbooks, doctrinals, and breviaries, there occurred the same mixture of classical, biblical, and patristic texts—mainly Augustine and Chrysostom—with a number of

[15] Museo Civico, Padua, MS 229. The inventory has been printed with an account of the history of the library by L. A. Ferrai in G. Mazzatinti, *Inventario*, pp. 549–661. There is a facsimile of MS 229 in the Bodleian Library, Oxford (MS Facs. d. 140 xerox).

[16] An excellent critical edition of Museo Civico, Padua, MS 229, has recently been published, together with an introduction and a valuable list of MSS from S. Giustina not included in the inventory: Giovanna Cantoni Alzati, *La biblioteca di S. Giustina di Padova. Libri e cultura presso i benedettini padovani in età umanistica*, Medioevo e Umanesimo, xlviii (Padua, 1982).

[17] Ferrai, *Inventario*, items 1–466 (1453); 467–8 (1453–62); 479–96 (Strozzi bequest).

scholastic authors, mainly Aquinas, and a sprinkling of modern works. In short, the library acquired the wide range of works that might be expected in the library of humanist trained monks. However, we can point to some particular entries in this latter period.

After item 811, which was probably written shortly after 1478, seventeen copies of the textbook *Liber Mamortrecti* have been listed.[18] During the same period the library received twenty-four copies of the entire Bible or particular books—especially the epistles of Paul, and also several commentaries of Athanasius and Lyra, and several copies of the *Moralia* of Gregory the Great. The acquisition of these particular volumes indicates that towards the end of the century the monks were paying special attention to biblical studies, not merely the reading of biblical texts, but also the systematic exegetical study of the Bible, especially the Pauline epistles.

There is no similar inventory for the library of San Giorgio Maggiore in Venice, for the only surviving inventories belong the eighteenth century. This is unfortunate because circumstantial evidence suggests that in the later fifteenth century the library was of some quality and that the monks enjoyed a reputation for scholarship. Cardinal Bessarion, the Greek prelate and friend of Abbot Bessarion, decided to bequeath his Greek codices to the monastery, although in the event he yielded to pressure and instead left his entire library to the Signoria.[19] In 1469 the monks were bequeathed property, the income from which was to be allocated to the purchase of books for the

---

[18] Items 812–19, 891, 902, 916, 936; 1013, 1021, 1023, 1050, 1069. *Mamortrectus*, also written *Mamotretus*, *Marmotret* (possibly a corruption of *Mamothreptus*) was a school-book written by Giovanni Marchesito di Reggio c. 1300. It was first published in 1470, and by 1521 there had been thirty-two editions. It contained orthographical, etymological, and grammatical explanations, archaeological information, a glossary of difficult words in the Latin bible, the prologues of Jerome, canonical hours, and 'leggende dei Santi'. Earlier, the work was common in manuscript form: there is a fourteenth-century MS in Monte Cassino, Cod. Cas. 403. It is described in S. Berger, *De Glossariis et compendiis exegeticis medii aevi* (Paris, 1879), pp. 31 ff. The monks also used as a textbook the *Compendium* of Constantine Lascaris, a Greek grammar, first published in Milan in 1480.

[19] There are copies of the celebrated letter of Cardinal Bessarion to Bessarion the monk on the calamities of Christians under Turkish conquest—'Deploranti nuper mihi christianorum hominum calamitates . . .' (1470), Cod. Vat. Lat. 1043, fo. 404; Bibl. Laur. Florence, Cod. Ashb. 269, fos. 42ᵛ-45ᵛ. At the time, Bessarion the monk was abbot of San Severin, Naples. The letter attacks the complacency of the Italians and pleads for Christian unity in the face of Turkish aggression.

library. There were other minor bequests for the library, and in 1520 Raffaele Regio left his entire library of Greek and Latin works.[20]

Rather more can be discovered about the library of the monastery of San Benedetto Po, near Mantua. When this monastery joined the Congregation in 1419 its library held only fifty-six volumes.[21] Under the new order the library was enlarged by the acquisition of ancient manuscripts, by copying, by permanent loans from other libraries of the Congregation, and, later, by purchases of printed volumes. About 1500 it acquired a good collection of fifteenth-century printed works, and the credit for this 'gran raccolta' has been given to the abbot Giovanni Cornaro.[22] Unfortunately no inventories have survived from the late fifteenth or early sixteenth centuries, so that it is difficult to determine which works were acquired during this period. Assessments of the library must therefore rest upon eighteenth-century catalogues, and the collection of nearly 400 volumes which survived the Napoleonic suppression. It is possible to determine whether a particular work was acquired in this period only if there are indications in the work itself: a number of these works will be examined later; for the rest, assuming that works printed in the late fifteenth and early sixteenth centuries were acquired by the library shortly after they were published, it would appear that during this period the library acquisitions of San Benedetto Po were mainly copies of the Bible, especially the Pauline epistles, and works of the Latin and Greek Fathers, mainly Augustine and Chrystostom

[20] The full story of the library and its holdings is in G. Ravegnani, *Le biblioteche del monastero di San Giorgio Maggiore*, Civiltà Veneziana Saggi, xix (Venice, 1976), ch. 1, esp. pp. 24–9, also 76–7.

[21] The story of the monastery and its libraries from its tenth-century foundation is summarized in B. Benedini, *I manoscritti polironiani della Biblioteca Comunale di Mantova* (Atti e memorie, nuova serie, xxx, 1958), chs. 1, 3, 4, also pp. 75–92.

[22] Cornaro belonged to the noble Venetian family. He was professed in 1462, and became abbot at S. Benedetto Po in 1500. He appears to have written nothing of a literary nature and therefore does not appear in Armellini's collection of writers, but he was highly respected within the Congregation. The first edition of the *Chronicon Monasterii Casinensis* (1513) was dedicated to him, as was the compilation of monastic rules by Johannes Franciscus; Teofilo Folengo spoke of him with reverence, see below (this chapter; also ch. 4). The only biography of Cornaro is the rather superficial chronicle of G. Gradenigo, 'Memorie Intorno a Giovanni Cornaro', *Nuova raccolta d'opusculi scientifici e filologici*, ii (Venice, 1756), 265–92. There is a letter of Cornaro to Sanudo, Bibl. Marciana, Venice, MS 4179.

(in Latin) and his followers, such as Chromatius and Remigius.[23]

The ancient monastery of Montecassino joined the Congregation in 1505, and the contents of its library therefore became available to the Congregation as a whole. It was a most valuable acquisition: an inventory compiled between 1464 and 1471 listed about 700 works of theological scholarship. There were 165 bibles or books of the Bible: thirty-two were copies of various epistles of Paul with glosses. There were in addition eighty-two works on particular biblical themes, concordances, and postillae. Therefore nearly a quarter of the theological holdings were biblical in nature, with an emphasis upon St. Paul. In addition, the library contained 184 patristic texts, fifty-six of Augustine, thirty-four of Gregory, and the reminader of Jerome, Ambrose, Bede, Chrysostom, and others.[24] The Paduan monks were delighted that such a collection had passed into their Congregation. They made some effort to retrieve volumes that had been removed from the library, and in 1510 they began restoration and rebuilding of the monastery, including the library.[25] Further south, in Catania, the Congregation had other substantial libraries at the monasteries of S. Maria de Licodia and S. Nicolai de Arenis, but the details of contemporary holdings have not survived. We know only that in 1565 the books at S. Nicolai were utterly destroyed, shredded in an act of deranged vandalism by a young monk. The library was restocked from the northern houses, which sent a number of Greek and Latin teaching texts, biblical commentaries, and other patristic works.[26]

[23] This conclusion is based upon the typescript catalogue of U. Meroni, (1962) which is at the Biblioteca Comunale. See MSS nos. 171, 193, 225, 255, 280, 317, 322, 329, 330, 336, 337, 344, 516.

[24] 'Index librorum' Bibl. Apost. Vat., Vat. Lat. 3961. There is a printed edition of this MS in *Catalogi Codicum Casinensium Antiqui (saec. viii–xv)*, ed. M. Inguanez (Miscellanea Cassinese, xxi; Montecassino, 1941), pp. 17–47.

[25] In 1506, shortly after the union of Montecassino with the Congregation, a book which had been taken from the library many years earlier, was recovered and returned 'per Loysium de Raymo de Napoli': B. de Montfaucon, *Bibliotheca Bibliothecarum Manuscriptorum Nova* (Paris, 1739), i. 215. The process of restoration and rebuilding was begun under Abbot Ignatius Squarcialupi. There is an account of this and a photograph of the foundation stone (laid in 1513) of the sacristry in *Le vicende della basilica di Montecassino*, ed. A. Pantoni (Miscellanea Cassinese, xxxvi; Montecassino, 1973), pp. 87–9.

[26] The episode is recounted in the *Chronicon* of Don Bartolomeo Taverna, who was professed at S. Nicolai in 1541. The relevant passage describes how the 'vesana . . .

In summary we may say that in each of these libraries the monks possessed books appropriate to their humanist upbringing and their monastic vocation.[27] They had available a wide collection of Greek and Latin textbooks, biblical texts, and the Fathers, especially Augustine and Chrysostom. They also possessed some scholastic works, notably Aquinas. In themselves the inventories do not indicate the use made of the books, so that we must be content merely to observe that these works were available to the monks. Nevertheless the inventories are significant, because it is clear from them that the libraries were dominated by the Bible and works given to biblical themes, especially those of patristic writers, both Greek and Latin; in these respects there is some reason to think that the Congregational libraries differed from those of other orders. In contrast with the Congregation's libraries, the Dominicans' library at S. Marco in Florence was dominated by Aristotle, especially his *Physics* and *Ethics*, by Aquinas, Bonaventura, and Antonino, bishop of Florence (*De Casibus Conscientiae*). There were few works of Augustine or Chrysostom, but many of Bernard. This was true of the Dominicans' library at S. Maria Novella also. The Vallambrosian and Camaldolese libraries held copies of Chrysostom's works but not on the topics of Pauline theology. Apart from these two orders and the Congregation, monastic libraries possessed few works of Chrysostom.[28] Moreover, the inventories of the Congregation sometimes indicate acquisitions which (excluding bequests) must have reflected the theological preferences of the monks. Although this evidence is incomplete, the known acquisitions of the last decade of the fifteenth

ignorantia unius monachi juvenis' with the failure of others to intervene, destroyed all the books, 'laceratos, et ad nihilum (nemine prohibente) redactos': it is quoted in F. Tornabene, *Catalogo ragionato delle edizioni del secolo XV e de' manoscritti che si conservano nella biblioteca de' Benedettini casinesi in Catania* (Catania, 1846), p. iv. Also see Armellini, *Bibl. Bened.-Cas.* i. 72–3.

[27] A good example of a humanist textbook is the copy of Homer's *Odyssey* in Bibl. Apost. Vat., Cod. Reginae Suecorum Graeci MS 99. This fifteenth-century MS has themes and main points written in the margins (in a sixteenth-century hand). It belonged to the Congregation's abbey of S. Nazarius, Verona. The conclusions drawn from these libraries' inventories apply to other smaller houses, e.g. S. Pietro, Perugia: see articles of F. A. Ugolini, M. Scaramucci, and G. Battelli, in *Convengo storico per il millennio dell'abbazia di S. Pietro in Perugia*, Bollettino della Deputazione di Storia Patria per l'Umbria, lxiv (Perugia, 1967), 122–57, 226–41, 242–66.

[28] The unpublished catalogues of other libraries are in the Bibl. Laur. Florence, Fondo Conventi Soppressi, and Bibl. Naz. Florence, Fondo Conventi Soppressi.

century, without exception, were copies of the Bible, especially the Pauline epistles, or exegetes of the literary and historical kind, particularly the Greek Fathers.

These conclusions provide the basis for a closer investigation of the use to which the monks put their libraries. What volumes were read, which authors were favoured, and what doctrines were disseminated within the cloisters? Part of the answer lies in the collections of sermons and other readings used in the monasteries. One that has survived is a homiliary of daily sermons from Advent to Holy Saturday, compiled and written in 1466 by Don Peregrinus, a monk of the monastery of Santa Giustina.[29] The volume has sermons for 137 days: they were sermons, said Peregrinus, of 'the most renowned, orthodox, and catholic doctors'. His choice of sermons closely followed that of Paul the Deacon: only pre-scholastic doctors were included; thirty-nine sermons were taken from Augustine, rather fewer from Leo, Jerome, Bede, Chrysostom (including pseudo-Chrysostom) Origen, Gregory, and Bernard. Almost all the sermons were based upon biblical exegesis of the literal historical kind. The marginal comments and instructions to the lector and the good condition of the volume show that it was used for reading aloud at the liturgy, in chapter, or in refectory. Therefore the book was written in order that each day the monks of Santa Giustina might be read a patristic sermon.

At Mantua three manuscript lectionaries have survived which tell us something about the character of biblical studies in the monastery. The first, in a hand of the mid-fifteenth century, consists of readings from old and new testaments,[30] each reading being preceded by a short prologue which summarized the

[29] Bodleian MS Lyall 77. This volume was item no. 568 in the inventory of the library of S. Giustina, see Padua, Museo Civico MS 229, fo. 35^r. It was probably the companion volume to the earlier homiliary from Easter to Advent, no. 234. Sermons in no. 568 were Augustine (39), Leo (16), Jerome (14), Bede (14), Origen (13), Gregory (10), Bernard (7), Ambrose (2), Maximus (2), Jacobus de Voragine (*Legenda Aurea*) (3) John of Salisbury (1), Petrus Chrysologus (1), anonymous *vitae* (2). There were three sermons from Chrysostom and ten from pseudo-Chrysostom, but since Don Peregrinus was not aware of the difference, these authors may be counted as one for the purpose of assessing the preferences and intentions of monks. Marginal insertions are on fos. 8^v, 18^r, 35^v, 39^v, 46^v, 206^r, 258^v, 266^v, 276^r. The MS is printed in *Catalogue of the collection of medieval manuscripts bequeathed to the Bodleian Library, Oxford, by James P. R. Lyall, compiled by Albinia de la Mare* (Oxford, 1971).

[30] Bibl. Comunale, Mantua, MS 395. 'Aliquot libri veteris et novi testamenti'. The manuscript was no. 91 in the library inventory.

passage and gave some historical references. The second lectionary, illuminated and presumably for liturgical use, consists entirely of readings from the Pauline epistles, together with lengthy commentaries. There were ninety readings appointed for the period from Advent to the twenty-third Sunday after Pentecost. Each verse of the epistles was placed beside an expository sermon from Augustine, Chrysostom, Bede, or Jerome, mostly written in the style of literal and historical exegesis.[31]

The third surviving lectionary at Mantua is a copy of Francesco Aretino's translation of Chrysostom's homilies on the Gospel of John: it is a beautifully produced manuscript, written in a late-fifteenth-century hand, before 1505. A repertorium appointed sixty of the eighty-eight homilies to be read on various days throughout the year, as expositions of the particular gospel of the day. One very striking feature of this work is that every homily ends with the formula '. . . gratia et benignitate domini nostri jesu christi'—in later chapters we shall observe frequently the Congregational emphasis upon the grace and the 'benignitas' of Christ. From the nature of these lectionaries it would appear that Pauline theology, historical and literal exegesis, and patristic commentaries, particularly those of Chrysostom, were central to the teaching of the monks.[32]

So far we have established that Congregational libraries of the later fifteenth and early sixteenth centuries made available to monks a wide range of biblical and patristic works and that new

[31] Bibl. Comunale, Mantua, MS 255 (B.V.7) 'D. Paulus: Epistolae cum commentario incerti autoris'. The spine bears the date 1415 but there is no reference in the text to that date: the material suggests a much later date, and the hand (minuscule gothic) was used in the Congregation for liturgical works until c. 1500. The abbreviations and the appearance of the hand suggest mid-fifteenth century. There is a similar lectionary written in 1470, of daily Bible readings at mass, in Italian. The readings include comments which explain old testament passages as simple prophecy and provide the historical context of the new testament readings. Bibl. Naz. Florence, Conv. Sopp. B.5.2582. The catalogue gives the Badia as its provenance, but the MS does not bear the usual inscription.

[32] Ibid. MS 329 (c III 9). The MS bears the title 'Commentarii super Johannis Evangelio: Francisco Aretino', and carries the usual inscription 'Liber est . . . Sancte Justine deputatus . . . Sancti Benedicti de podolirone'. There were others interested in Chrysostom at this time. Urswycke, Warden of King's Hall, Cambridge, from 1485, commissioned copies of the early Fathers, mainly Chrysostom, but also including Augustine and Jerome: J. K. McConica, *English Humanists and Reformation Politics under Henry VIII and Edward VI* (Oxford, 1965), p. 71.

acquisitions were mostly concerned with biblical and patristic studies or were language textbooks. Furthermore, liturgical readings of the Bible suggest a preference for St. Paul and for patristic exegesis, especially that of Chrysostom. However, library holdings and liturgical readings can do no more than indicate the outline of what was taught within the cloister. The next step is to survey the order's early teachers, who taught the men who flourished from about 1480.

Amongst the earlier teachers was Jacobus Astensis of whom it is known only that he was 'abbas pius et doctus' and that he compiled a collection of patristic writings. Rather more is known of Nicholas of Prussia, who died in 1456. He stood out as a man who exerted considerable influence upon his students. In 1463 a former pupil described how his teaching rested upon the Bible and the *Imitation of Christ*: '. . . he read the Bible with so much zeal that he was able to repeat almost all of its passages by heart. Indeed, he read devotional works which are 'able to rouse compunction and the love of Christ: from its first page he always read his Gerson carefully.'[33] Nicholas therefore drew much of his piety from the *Imitation*, and, like the author of that work, he exhorted his monks to mortification and true wisdom, but Nicholas laid much more emphasis upon the grace and goodness of God. His biographer has a story of his gentleness to young men condemned to death and how he preached to them of 'O, the immense mercy of God which wishes nobody to perish'.[34] There are two Fathers, both well represented in Congregational libraries, from whom he probably drew these sentiments. The first is St. Bernard, whose meditation, *De passione Christi*, contrasted the misery of man's condition with the 'beneficium

[33] Vat. Lat. 10907, fo. 142ʳ '. . . Biblia namque tanto studio legeret, ut ex eis fere omnes repetere memoriter sententias sciret. Libros vero devotos qui ad compunctionem et ad amorem Christi incitare possunt: ab exordio sui guersionis a curatione semper legit.' Nicholas also memorized passages from Gregory the Great. Various post-mortem miracles were attributed to Nicholas. Within the Congregation the author of the *Imitation of Christ* was generally held to be Gerson. For Jacobus Astensis see Armellini, *Bibl. Bened.-Cas.* ii. 1; for Nicholas see Armellini, *Catalogi Tres Episcoporum, Reformatorum et Virorum Sanctitate Illustrium e Congregatione Casinensi* (Assisi and Rome, 1733–4), pp. 99–102. See also B. Pez, *Thesaurus Anecdotorum Novissimus* (Augsburg, 1721), ii part 3, 309–40; G. Penco, 'Il Primo Monastero Cassinese di Genova: S. Niccolò del Boschetto', *Benedicina*, xix (1972), 415–30. For the place of the *Imitation* in the Congregation see above, ch. 1.

[34] Vat. Lat. 10907, fos. 139ʳ–140ᵛ 'O, immensa domini clementia quae neminem vult perire . . .'

passionis'; the second is John Chrysostom, whose teaching on sin, mortality, and the 'gratia et benignitas Christi' came to recur in the teachings of almost all the Congregation's writers.[35]

Another influential teacher was Hieronymous Aliotti who, as abbot of SS. Flora and Lucilla, Arezzo, surrendered his *commenda* in 1472 and brought his monastery into the Congregation. Aliotti's ideas were very much in accord with what we have learnt already about the Congregation. First of all, he was a humanist scholar, learned in Greek, a friend of Ambrose Traversarius, and the author of several works of scholarship.[36] He was convinced that the road to salvation began in 'literarum et bonarum artium disciplina', because such studies polished the mind and furnished it with the collected human wisdom of centuries, but, most of all, because they led men to the study of the Bible and the Fathers.[37] Aliotti laid particular emphasis upon the study of the Bible, which he called the 'solid food' of life, especially the epistles of St. Paul: it was 'our treasure which lies within the sacred pages' and it brings to men 'the treasure of Christ himself'.[38] He believed that study of the Bible should be supplemented by that of the Fathers, but for the scholastics—the 'schola philosophorum'—he had no time at all. In 1476 he described vividly how a friend had broken free from a successful career amongst the scholastics in order 'to soar to the wisest foolishness of the Cross',[39] when the man became a monk.

Aliotti's doctrine of the fall was in part the Augustinian notion

[35] e.g. *Il Beneficio di Cristo* (1543), ch. 3, line 84: 'Quest immensa benignità di Dio'. For details see below, ch. 8.

[36] Aliotti was born in July 1412 in Arezzo, of on old noble family. He was educated in his own city and then went to the Academy at Siena from 1425 to 1430. In 1432 he was professed at the monastery of SS. Flora and Lucilla, of which he later became abbot *in commendam*. See *Epistolae et Oposcula G. B. Scarmalli notis etc.*, ed. G. B. Scarmalli (2 vols., Arezzo, 1769), i, pp. xiii–xv; ii, pp. 349 ff.

[37] Ibid. ii. 164–75. Also 143–50. His friendship with Ambrogio Traversari is mentioned in ii. 145. It should be noted that Aliotti took an active interest in political and social affairs: his correspondents included princes, cardinals, and popes. His 'De monachis erudiendis', a defence of studies in the cloisters, against scholastic critics, was written in 1444 and dedicated to Pope Eugenius IV. The MS is in the Bibl. Apost. Vat., Vat. Lat. 1063. Aliotti appeared as a character in Poggio's *Contra Hypocritas*, as a defender of the monastic life.

[38] *Epistolae et opuscula*, ii. 142–4, 173, 'De felici statu religionis monasticae' (1432).

[39] Ibid. ii. 114. '. . . in Gymnasio Senensii magno inter scholasticos florebat ingenio; et ex media philosophorum schola ad sapientissimam Crucis stultitiam evolavit.' For similar sentiments see ii. 109, 153. Also ii. 346 ff., 'Pii Secundi Pontificis Maximi Defensio' (1466). References to patristic studies are made, ii. 144, 148, 173.

that man has become twisted by self-love and concupiscence—which was responsible, said Aliotti, for the greed and dishonour so evident in contemporary Europe.[40] The other element in his teaching was man's rejection of his inheritance and his rebellion and loss of the lordship and freedom that belonged to the pristine state.[41] The juxtaposition of lordship and freedom belonged to Chrysostom and Gregory of Nyssa, who understood pristine freedom in the sense of παρρησία, an open bold confident freedom in speaking, as opposed to the servile, fearful speech of a slave without rights.[52]

Thus Aliotti saw the fallen state as one of degradation from which men could be rescued only by an act of grace, which was the Cross: 'Christ came, as both God and man, and by the wound in his side he has recalled us to our original liberty and restored us to it, and now we are free . . . now we are restored through the blood of Christ.'[43] Later in life, when he had been a monk of the Congregation for five years, his teaching was the same, still based upon the Pauline epistles and still centred upon the 'foolishness of the Cross', which he called the 'beneficium' of Christ.[44] Aliotti laid great emphasis upon faith as the proper response to this 'beneficium'. By faith he meant in the first place firm belief in Christ and the promises of God, and in the second place the zealous pursuit of good works, not for merit, but in order to remove all that is shameful and inappropriate for a son of God. Thus by faith a man accepts his restored status and by faith he is renewed and enters into his inheritance.[45]

These themes of Aliotti occur in both Gregory of Nyssa and Chrysostom: the sense of sin as degradation rather than guilt,

[40] Ibid. ii. 150, 153.

[41] Ibid. ii. 158.

[42] There is a full discussion of the use of freedom in this sense in Gregory of Nyssa in J. Daniélou, *Platonisme et théologie mystique* (Paris, 1944), pp. 110–23. For Chrysostom's very frequent use of the term, emphasizing the right to be free and confident, see *A Patristic Greek Lexicon*, ed. G. W. H. Lampe (Oxford, 1961), pp. 1044–6.

[43] *Epistolae et Opuscula*, ii. 158 'Venit Christus Deus et homo, et per sui lateris aperitionem in pristinam libertatem revocavit nos, atque restituit; itaque liberi iam sumus . . . nunc per Christi sanguinem restitui sumus.'

[44] Ibid. ii. 117 '. . . in primis igitur antequam quicquam aliud adtentemus praestolari debemus finem beneficii Crucis, tamquam rei utillimae . . .'

[45] Ibid. ii. 158–60, also 154, 162. Aliotti laid emphasis upon the need to recall and keep alive the joy of redemption and to avoid becoming lukewarm, ii. 159. '. . . donum Dei, ac beneficia minime cognoscentes, nullas ex corde gratis referunt.' There is a similar passage in the tract *Il Beneficio di Cristo* of 1543. See below, ch. 8,

the rescue achieved entirely by a gift of God, the restoration of liberty given to sons of God, the stress upon faith in the promises of God and faith as the instrument of the restoration of the image of God.[46]

Another teacher in the same vein was Bernard Placentinus, abbot in Venice, Florence, Padua, and Mantua, and six times president of the Congregation, a man 'distinguished in all learning' who 'excelled in sacred and humane letters', who in 1461 extended the library to house manuscripts at S. Giustina, Padua.[47] He was a man of great personal charm and this, together with his scholarship and his pedagogic tracts on the monastic life, made him an influential teacher within the Congregation.[48] The greater part of his writings consisted of practical advice on living peaceably and profitably within the cloister, but there was also a certain amount of theological doctrine, which took the form of meditation upon the Cross and upon faith; he reminded his monks of Paul's teachings and stressed the importance of the Bible, of turning to Christ as to a friend, and as the medicine of man's mortal condition.[49] The 'medicine of salvation' was accepted through faith alone. To illustrate 'true faith' Placentinus chose Mary Magdalene as the exemplar because she sought salvation only with contrition and tears.[50] Thus his doctrine of salvation shows the salient elements seen in other Congregational teachings, namely, salvation achieved by the passion of Christ, and by man's response of

[46] See below, ch. 6, for the commentary on Chrysostom composed by the abbot Luciano degli Ottoni in 1538, which brings out these themes very clearly.

[47] Armellini, *Bibl. Bened-Cas.* i. 106–7. L. A. Ferrai, *Inventario*, 552. Bernard died in 1486.

[48] Bibl. Naz. Florence, MS E.6.2700 'Historia Monasteriorum Congregationis Casinensis', refers to 'commendato da'nostri per la sua mansuetudine e piacevolezza d'animo'. His works included 'Quomodo debeat religiousus in monasterio conversari e de modo orandi', and 'De passione Christi' (in verse). His works survive in the Bibl. Comunale, Mantua, MS 49 (A.II.18); this MS has no attribution, but the contents correspond exactly with Armellini's catalogue of Don Bernard's works. There is also his short biography of St. Auricus, in the Bibl. Alessandrina, Rome, MS 96, part i.

[49] Bibl. Comunale, Mantua, MS 49 (A.II.18), fo. 41ᵛ, where he says that the most valuable part of the monastic office was the 'evangelica lectio cuncta'. In his life of St. Auricus, Don Bernard alluded frequently to Paul and Augustine, and described the conversion of the hermit saint thus: 'vertit atque ad beatum Amicum festinato venit et coram eo stetit', Bibl. Aless. Rome MS 96, part i, fos. 26ʳ, 31ʳ, 31ᵛ. Also fo. 41ʳ, 'medicina salubris'.

[50] Bibl. Comunale, Mantua, MS 49, fos. 78ʳ–79ʳ. Similar sentiments were expressed frequently by Chrysostom.

faith, which consists of contrition and works, and companion-ship with Christ who cures mankind.

The same emphases upon grace and faith are to be found in a group of pedagogic tracts written and used at Mantua in the second half of the century. In 1496 the scribe Don Gregory of Genoa copied out a number of pedagogic tracts, written between 1468 and that year, which may be taken as examples of the teaching given to monks towards the end of the fifteenth century.[51] Much of the material consisted of straightforward advice on perseverance in good works. In doctrine, however, there were three particular ideas: the first was the absence of saving merit in sinful man, the second the benignity of God, the third the necessity for faith in salvation.

A tract written by Giuliano da Ferrara taught that salvation was the gift of the 'benigna gratia' of God, which man must accept by sincere faith:

The interior passion and desire . . . seen in the glorious Mary Magda-lene and in the confidence of the thief and again in the devotion of the centurion . . . The evangelical doctrine . . . is given to us so that we may understand that through pure and sincere faith and a most firm assurance we receive the kind grace of the glorious creator.[52]

In contrast, he said, lack of faith prevented a man from coming to 'la divina largità'.

Another tract described the man of faith as a 'a friend of the Lord', and went on to distinguish between 'the good Christians . . . and the false Christians, who shall be dispatched to the torments of hell'. The distinction rested upon the possession of living faith which characterized the 'good Christians'.[53] Another tract described the fallen state of man as a condition of sickness, whilst salvation was a restoration of health: 'We are soaked in

---

[51] Ibid. MS 63 (A.II.32). The MS consists of a number of tracts bound together, all written in Italian. The scribe, Gregory da Genova, was then an oblate at San Benedetto Po.

[52] Ibid. 130ᵛ–131ʳ, 'lo interiore affetto e desiderio . . . exposito in la gloriosa maria magdalene e in lo fidele ladro et anchora in lo devoto centurione . . . la evangelica doctrina . . . è dato ad intendere che cosi come la pura e sincera fede e firmissima assicurazione che noi riceviamo benigna gratia da lo glorioso creatore . . .' Giuliano da Ferrara was not noted by Armellini.

[53] Ibid. 151ʳ, 'Amico del Signore', 'tutti li fideli amici'; 153ʳ; '. . . nullo esser salvo excepto li boni cristiani . . . e li falsi christiani, inquam, con peccore ferano deputati a tormenti nello eterno e terrible foco infernale.'

the mire: we want to be lifted out of it: let us confess in tears to Jesus Christ our redeemer, so that we may be washed clean of our corruptions by which we are filled and infected.'[54] This collection of Mantuan tracts reflects the Congregational teaching which has already emerged in this chapter; that sin is a state of sickness, and salvation, through grace and faith, is a restoration to health.

Rather less is known about the theological position of the men who taught the Greek language within the Congregation. It seems probable that the language teachers either had been trained in one of the humanist schools, as had Bessarion of Aragona, or were refugees for whom Greek was a mother tongue, such as Don Matthew of Constantinople and Sigismund the Greek; there was also Fabianus Cretensis, professed in 1488, who translated the anonymous *Vita Sancti Eustachii* from Greek into Latin, which he dedicated to Don Gregory Beaqua, abbot at Milan and Venice, and friend of the biblical scholar Brebia.[55] Fabianus undertook this short work in collaboration with the scholarly Don Hilarion of Verona, professed in 1464, who also translated the *Expositions* of St. Dorotheus and was a poet of various themes on salvation, most strikingly the way in which Christ's death 'rescued the human race from the dragon death and takes us with him to heaven'.[56] Other than Hilarion, the only teacher of Greek who left any indication of his theological preferences was Lucas Bernardus, who was professed at Padua in 1495 and was learned in Latin, Greek, and possibly Hebrew. It seems that Don Lucas favoured the Greek exegesis of Antioch,

[54] Bibl. Comunale, Mantua, MS 63, 174ᵛ, '. . . noi nel lubo siamo perfundanti: ne se curemo deglo esser levati et Jesu Christo nostro redemptore dolce lamento fatiamo che ne lavi da nostri defecti de li q(ua)li pleni et infecti siamo.'

[55] This was really a Life of Eutychius: the identities of the two saints were often confused. The original MS, from which several copies were made, is in the Bibl. Naz. Marciana, Venice, Fondo Antico Latino, MS 1809. Details are given in A. M. Zanetti, *Latina et Italica D. Marci Biblioteca Codicum Manuscriptorum*, v (Venice, 1740), 229–301. For Brebia, see below, ch. 3.

[56] Hilarion of Verona died in 1521; Armellini, *Bibl. Bened.-Cas.* i. 224–5. His translation of the Expositions was published in *Monumenta S. Patrum Orthodoxographa*, ed. J. J. Grynaeus (Basle, s.a., but 1569), pp. 195–368, with Greek and Latin texts in parallel. The preface contains a detailed statement of his principles of translation. Armellini gives a full list of his other translations from Greek. The quotation is taken from a poem in Bibl. Apost. Vat., Chigi, I.IV.148, fos. 11ʳ–12ᵛ, 'In super tandem cruce est passus alta / Morte ut humanum genus ab dracone / Solveret secum traheretque caeli / Sedibus alti . . .' Hilarion also translated a work of Hermogenes the Rhetorician: it is published in *Georgii Trapezunti Rhetoricorum* (Venice, 1523), Book v.

for his only translations were from the Greek of Chrysostom's eighty homilies *Ad Populum (De Statuis)* and his *De Laudibus Pauli*. Lucas was skilled, both as teacher and translator, for no less an authority than Pietro Barozzi, bishop of Padua until his death in 1507, wrote to him, commending his careful translation, chiding him for its anonymity and praising his teaching within the Congregation.[57]

Having considered the libraries and the teachers, we now turn to what was taught. The education of a monk was grounded in the ceremony of profession itself, with its symbolic representation of monastic doctrines. According to the rite of the Congregation, the man to be professed was laid out like a corpse before the altar, on a black cloth, with tapers at his head and feet, to signify that men are sinners and born to mortality. Then prayers declared the 'benignissima clementia' and the boundless mercy of God, who calls men so that he may renew them. When the monk was vested with the habit he was reminded that the garment was a symbol of salvation and joy with which God has promised to cloak his people—'the cloak of salvation and the garment of joy, promised to thy faithful people'. We shall encounter again this imagery of being vested with salvation, but for the present it is sufficient to note its presence at the heart of the rite of profession which symbolized the nature of salvation, the breaking free from death to new life, as the officiant cried out 'Surge qui dormis et exurge a mortuis, et illuminabit te Christus: Tunc ipse frater surgat.'[58]

---

[57] Don Lucas of Brescia was professed at Padua on 15 Aug. 1495. *De Laudibus* was published in 1505, and *Octoginta Homilia ad Populum* in 1508, both at Basle, in two volumes. The British Library held a copy of the former work but it was destroyed by bombing during the second world war. The two works were published in *Divi Ioannis Chrysostomi Episcopi Constantinopolitani Opera* (Basle, 'in officina Frobeniana', 1530), iv. 3–29, 324–650. Barozzi's letter is printed on p. 650, '. . . [Congregatio] quam ex plurium tui similium praesentia mirum in modum augeri vides, quia eos tu semper plurimi facere ostendisti.' The *Historia Monasterium Congregationis Casinensis*, a compilation of the late seventeenth century described him as 'Luca Bernardo Bresciano, versato molto nella sacra Scrittura e perito nella lingua Greca e Ebrea.', Bibl. Naz. Florence, MS E.6.2700 (no pagination).

[58] *Missale monasticum s(ecundu)m more(m) (et) ritu(m) Casinensis Congregationis al(ia)s Sanctae Justinae* (Venice, 1515), pp. 303–4. There was an earlier edition of this missal in 1507. The rite was also included in *Regula SS. Benedicti, Basilii, Augustini, Francisci etc.*, compiled by Joannes Franciscus and published in Venice in 1500 and Paris in 1514: 204^v–205^r, '. . . obsecramus immensam tuae largitatis abundantiam . . . vestimentum salutis et indumentum iocunditatis tuis fidelibus p(ro)misisti, clementiam tuam humiliter exposcimus . . .'

After profession the monk's education was pursued in the classroom. A few texts of theological instruction have survived, and we shall examine them briefly. One such manuscript, written in 1479 at the Badia, in Florence, consists of three *opuscula* of Gregory of Nazianzus, Chrysostom's seven sermons *De Laudibus Pauli Apostoli*, a single biography of Paul, and a short account of the martyrdom of Peter and Paul. It seems most probable that this kind of anthology was collected for teaching purposes, as a supplement to the study of the Pauline epistles.[59]

At Mantua there still survives a copy of a work for New Testament studies. The well-used manuscript was written in a clear and careful hand of the late fifteenth century, but before 1505, in the monastery of San Benedetto Po. The epistles are written in full, but the text of each is preceded by two didactic prologues which explain the historical context and summarize the doctrinal content of the epistle.[60] These prologues taught a definite pattern of salvation, predicating first of all that man was caught in sin and impotence, as the Law revealed. The prologue to Romans explained the Pauline argument: '[Paul] in fact established, against the Jews, that no justice resided in the Law, and that all good arose from grace. He then showed in that way that there was no question of Abraham being justified through circumcision . . .'[61]

And in the prologue to Philippians: '[Paul] showed the Law to be as dung and to be no value to salvation.'[62] The teaching is clear: before 1505, in this monastery, the monks of Santa Giustina were being taught that man cannot merit his own salvation.

Various prologues then explain that salvation is achieved only by grace and is a gift out of the love of God for men:

---

[59] Bibl. Laur. Florence, Cod. Conv. Soppr. 27 (2727). The two works of Nazianzenus were the *Apologeticus* and the *Oratio ad Cives*. The latter may have had some influence upon Don Isidora Chiari; see below, ch. 7.

[60] Bibl. Comunale, Mantua, MS 280 (C.I.18). Similar prologues precede Pauline texts in eleventh-century MSS at Montecassino, Cod. 349, fos. 88 ff.; Cod. 552, fos. 56 ff. See the very brief account in *Miscellanea Cassinese* (Montecassino, 1897), Documenti: Biblica, p. 1.

[61] Bibl. Comunale, MS 280, fo. 1ᵛ, '[Paulus] contra iudeos ostendit quidem nullam iustitiam esse legem, et omne bonum ex gratia. Deinde ea ostendit quidem abraam per circumcisionem non esse justificatum.'

[62] Ibid. fo. 63ᵛ, '[Paulus] ostendit legem esse ut stercora et quid non valeat ad salutem.' Similar sentiments were expressed in fos. 63ᵛ, 94ᵛ.

Then [Paul] commends Christ and how his gracious kindness is sufficient for all things.[63]

. . . and he describes the coming of Christ into this world to save sinners, and the certainty of faith in the passion of Christ.[64]

. . . then he declares the humanity and the kindness of Christ in the manner he came.[65]

This doctrine is clear also: the monks were being taught that salvation was a gift of the 'benignitas Christi'.

Next the prologues explained the necessity and the sufficiency of faith in that *benignitas*. In the prologue to the Hebrews: '. . . afterwards, Paul defines faith for them, showing what it is, saying that faith is the substance of things hoped for . . . [then follows references to Hebrews 11].'[66] In the prologue to Galatians it was explained that men must no longer live by the Law, since 'faith in Christ suffices to salvation'.[67] Faith, through which alone men were saved, was manifest in love towards others, and in readiness to bear tribulation patiently.[68] These prologues speak for themselves. The teachings of the Congregation, indicated only in general terms by the library holdings and what is known of the teachers, are here revealed in detail: we begin to catch the precise teaching given in the Benedictine cloisters, and its instruction of monks in the way of salvation according to St. Paul.

Other manuscripts confirm the Pauline bias of the Congregation in the late fifteenth century. At Padua an anonymous treatise reminded monks that men were saved by the work of Christ 'who had offered so great a benefit to the unworthy and undeserving man, indeed, giving to the whole human race a

---

[63] Ibid. fo. 68ʳ, 'Deinde commendat Christum eius beneficia [*sic*] quomodo est sufficientia [*sic*] ad omnia (prologue to Colossians).

[64] Ibid. fos. 80ᵛ–81ʳ, '. . . et dicit Christum venisse in hunc mundum peccatores salvare; de certatione [*sic*] fidei de passione Christi' (prologue to 1 Tim.).

[65] Ibid. fo. 90ᵛ, 'Deinde ostendit de humanitate e(t) benignitate Christi quomodo apparuit' (prologue to Titus).

[66] Ibid. fo. 95ʳ, 'postea determinat eis de fide, ostendendo quid sit dicens: est autem fides substantia rerum sperandarum . . .'

[67] Ibid. fo. 50ᵛ, '. . . fides Christi quidem ad salutem sufficit . . .', referring to 2: 16.

[68] Ibid. fo. 50ᵛ–51ʳ, 63ᵛ, 86ᵛ, 94ᵛ. The prologue to 2 Tim. contains the expression 'omnes qui pie volunt vivere in Christo persecutionem debent sustinere'. This sentiment, together with love of neighbour, was to be found at the end of ch. 5 of the *Beneficio di Cristo* of 1543; see below, ch. 8.

costly gift for all'.[69] Similar expressions were used in a collection
of sermons on the monastic life which were written at S.
Benedetto Po, probably in the 1490s. The anonymous author
exhorted his fellow monks to a constant recollection of the
'beneficium passionis Christi', and the 'liberalitas et largitas
cordis divini', and he urged upon them the necessity of strong
belief in the heart and faith. His sermons drew upon authors well
represented in Congregational libraries—above all Augustine,
Chrysostom, and St. Paul.[70]

Amongst the students of the 1490s was the young Marco da
Cremona. He had been professed in 1488 and almost at once
made such progress in the study of sacred letters that he was
much admired and sought out for his skill in expounding the
scriptures. An inscription in a book in his monastery's library
twice made the point that his scriptural learning was accomplished soon after ('statimque . . . subinde') his profession.[71]
Marco was not only a biblical scholar, but also a practical man,
skilled and experienced in the monastic life and its administration. Presumably, this blend of qualities was the reason that he
was sent with the abbot of Perugia, Don Bartholomew, to
superintend changes in the newly acquired Sicilian houses of the
Congregation.[72] During his time there he wrote an account of his
observations in Sicily, and dedicated the manuscript to Don
Giovanni Cornaro, the ageing Venetian president of the
Congregation, who was venerated by many of the order's young
biblical scholars.[73] After he returned to the north Marco wrote
another work, a 'Vita' of the Blessed Nicolai, the monk whose

[69] Bibl. Univ. Padua, MS 427, fo. 191^{r-v}, '. . . ex amore divino cu(m) recolit quam
b(e)nigne c(er)t(aver)it seu egerit Christus, quanta sibi b(e)n(e)ficia indigno et
imme(ri)to (ob)tulerit, vel pensat g(e)n(er)alia b(e)n(e)ficia o(mn)i g(e)n(er)i
hu(m)ano impe(n)sa . . .'

[70] Bibl. Comunale, Mantua, MS 281, fos. 1^r–146^v, anonymous, with unknown
authors on the monastic life. The teaching draws heavily from the Pauline epistles,
Augustine, and Chrysostom—especially Chrysostom on faith, fos. 104^{r-v}, 112^v–114^v.
These tracts finish with an extract from Chrysostom on the passion of Christ and the
'liberalitas e(t) largitas cordis divinae'. The quotations are from fo. 38^{r-v}.

[71] Armellini, *Bibl. Bened.-Cas.* ii. 90–1. The book in which this encomium was written
was 'Nig.Def.' (Nig(rorum) (Monachorum) Def(ensores)?), book no. 480. The book
number suggests that the volume was placed in the library in the late fifteenth century.
Perhaps it contained post-mortem biographies of monks who had defended the order.

[72] Ibid.: '. . . rerum gerendarum prudentia, ac usu, monasticaeque disciplinae
exemplis excellebat . . .' The two men were at the monastery of S. Martinus de Scalis,
Palermo. Marco died on 20 Jan. 1539.

[73] Ibid. Cornaro died in 1515. Very little material about him has survived.

teachings were discussed earlier. This manuscript has not survived, but it may be assumed that it endorsed Nicolai's use of the Bible and his emphasis upon human weakness and the necessity of grace for salvation.[74] There is ample evidence of Marco's strongly Pauline bias in his later years, but the evidence for his early years is scanty: nevertheless it does suggest that from the time of his profesion, Marco of Cremona was a pious monk and a scholar in the Pauline tradition of the Congregation.

In 1496, at the monastery of San Benedetto Po, a short tract was written, containing a very detailed exposition of contemporary teaching within the Congregation. This valuable work sets out explicitly, albeit briefly, a number of themes which have merely been touched upon elsewhere. The tract began with the observation that man is perverse in will and intellect, and lives blindly ('saipuzando') in perversity and without faith. The author intended to show the way in which 'you must walk to reach the haven of your salvation'.[75] This way he called the 'manna spirituale' of meditation and contemplation. He began with the teaching of Augustine that God's prevenient love stirs the heart of sinful man with the gift of illumination 'sent into the heart of the faithful man by him who wishes to save all . . . through his ineffable sweetness he has disposed and supported your mind with his gifts, to incline you to obey him and to love him with the whole heart . . .'[76] This doctrine, that love of God is a gift of grace, received by men of faith ('li fideli'), was taken directly from Augustine's *De gratia et libero arbitrio*, xviii. 38.

The writer also follows Augustine in teaching that man's free will has the capacity to persevere in love or to destroy it. Consequently a man must 'with sincere faith conform his own will to the divine will'. This raises the question whether a man is able to do good through his free will. This is 'a difficult question' replies the monk to his pupil, but Augustine teaches that grace

---

[74] Ibid.: 'Vitam [*sic*] B. Nicolai Prutenti Monachi S. Justinae.' The MS was formerly in the archives of the Paduan monastery, but was lost at the suppression. It began 'Consueverunt qui alienos mores etc.'.

[75] Bibl. Comunale, Mantua, MS 63 (A.II.32), fos, 175^r–184^r. This tract 'Trattato de meditare e contemplare' is subtitled 'Manna Spirituale'. The fifteen short chapters are in the form of a dialogue between teacher and student.

[76] Ibid. fo. 175^v, 'nota bene . . . le sancte meditatione sono oferte e mandate nel core de li fideli da quello che vole tuti salvare, cioe dio signore redemptore de lo universo . . . per sua inefabile dolceza ha indolata e confortata la tua mente cum sui doni per inclinarla a lui obedire e cum toto core amare . . .'

enables the reason and the will to choose good and so to approximate ('pervenire') to God: for this, perseverance is needed.[77]

The remainder of the tract, though congruent with the Augustinian beginning is a discussion of 'true faith' along lines of Pauline theology which we have seen in other writers of this Congregation, namely, the gift, or 'benefit', of salvation through Christ, the personal relationship of 'true faith', and gratitude and love of neighbour. God's gift of salvation is grounded in his desire for universal salvation. Students must 'note well' how great a love has 'He who wishes to save all men, that is, the Lord God, redeemer of the universe', who has offered salvation to all, as a gift, through grace, 'la divina gratia che tuti vole salvare'.[78] This grace was manifest in the sacrifice of Christ: '. . . through grace he wishes to save all . . . through grace he allowed himself to be humiliated . . . through grace he let himself be betrayed, captured, stripped and crowned with thorns. Through grace he was flogged at the pillar and crucified on a bitter cross.'[79] The gift of salvation, offered to all men, was frequently described as 'tanta benignità' or the 'tanto benefitio' of God, and repeatedly praised—'O quanto e grande questo dono'.[80]

The proper response to such divine kindness, the monk told his pupil, was 'vera fede' understanding and embracing the gift with the whole heart, 'cum tuto coro e potentia'.[81] Only through this response of 'vera fede', are men saved. The monk then elaborated his doctrine. Faith brought intimacy with God, so that man becomes 'filiolo e familiare amico del suo creatore . . . lo benigno Signore . . .'[82] When, through faith, a man became the son and friend of God, he acquired a true fear of God, not a crude fear of an omnipotent deity, nor the mercenary fear of those who wish to avoid hell and gain heaven, but the 'timore filiale' of love: '. . . a man fears God through pure love,

---

[77] Bibl. Comunale, Mantua, MS 63, fo. 176ᵛ, '. . . se non posso fare bene p(er) lo libero arbitrio? . . . Dura cosa hai domandata e dura da declare.'

[78] Ibid. fo. 180ᵛ.

[79] Ibid. fo. 182ʳ, '. . . per gratia tuti vole salvare . . . per gratia lui se volse humiliare . . . per gratia si lasso tradire e pigliare, spudazare e de spine coronare. Per gratia alla colonna fu flagellato e in aspera croce crucifato.'

[80] Ibid. fo. 180ᵛ; also 175ᵛ, 178ᵛ, 179ᵛ.

[81] Ibid. fo. 175ᵛ.

[82] Ibid. fo. 178ᵛ.

as a son fears his father, out of reverence for his parent, not for any reward or because he desires anything to happen. This is holy fear, as David says.'[83] Such a man, continued the monk, becomes 'the son and beloved friend of the loving Creator'.[84]

The man of faith, the student was told, will not wish to sin, being 'held back from sin by his sweetest love' for God. When men do sin, they are guilty of ingratitude for the great gift of God: ' . . . ungrateful creatures, we do not cease from offending him. Through such ingratitude man falls into great misery.'[85] The gratitude of faith is manifest, above all, in love of neighbour. In chapter II of his tract, entitled 'De lo amore de Dio: e de lo proximo', the monk explained that in gratitude for redemption: 'we must bring love to our neighbour and console him, support him and help him in every affliction. . . The Lord created us as brothers, and wishes that we live in brotherly love.'[86] Such care of others was of divine, not human strength: 'Do you not know that Saint Paul said that there is no power if not from God?'[87] Strife, envy, discord, hatred, quarrels must cease: men of faith must care for their neighbour 'come nostro fratello'.[88] All this was in accord with the Benedictine Rule on peace, love of neighbour, and obedience.

There are several observations to be made about this tract. First, it is based entirely on the Pauline epistles. Second, its teaching on fallen man as being in a state of impotence, because he is vitiated in will and intellect, is taken from Augustine. Third, it sets out in some detail a pattern of salvation which is offered to all, which is a 'tanto benefitio' of Christ, which requires 'vera fede' and good works of gratitude: this is the teaching of St. John Chrysostom and the school of Antioch. The combination of Augustine's Pauline theology of the fall and Chrysostom's Pauline theology of salvation is in accord with

---

[83] Ibid. fo. 181ʳ, '. . . teme lo homo dio per puro amore, come lo filiolo lo patre teme per paterna reverentia, non per premio alcuno e che volio consequite. Quest è lo timore sancto che dice david.'

[84] Ibid. fo. 178ᵛ, 'filiolo e familiare amico del suo creatore . . . lo benigno Signore'.

[85] Ibid. fo. 181ᵛ, '. . . ingratissimi che offenderlo non cessiamo, per tale ingratudine cade le homo in grande obscuritade.'

[86] Ibid. fo. 180ᵛ, 'a lo proximo debiamo amore portare et in ogni aflictione consolarlo, subvenirlo e adiutarlo . . . tuti in fraternità ne creati lo signore e come frateli vole che siamo in amore.'

[87] Ibid. fo. 180ᵛ, 'Non sai tu che sancte Paulo disse: non è potentia se non da dio.'

[88] Ibid. fo. 182ᵛ.

what we know of other library holdings, the teachers, and surviving indications of what was taught within the cloisters—and in accord with Benedictine Rule.

These two elements, the Augustinian and Antiochene, are also present in a copy of the monastic rule, written in 1499 with a commentary drawn mainly from Turrecremata and St. Remigius, translated into Italian under the title '*La regola del nostro padre sancto Benedetto*'.[89] The prologue explained that the translation was for the use of monks who could not follow the Latin reading in refectory, and then went on to give a brief exposition of the condition of man and of his salvation. In view of the nature of the work, there can be no doubt that the prologue expressed, in summary, Congregational teachings at the end of the century, and for this reason, it is quoted at length:

As the Apostle said to the Corinthians, we do not know nor are we able to conceive the slightest thing of good. Therefore it is necessary that God himself illuminate the eyes of our mind, clouded by many sins . . . the most high God, through his infinite and ineffable goodness has been pleased always to pour his sweetest blessings upon the sons of men, to whom he gave the power to become sons of himself, to those who believe in his name: but note well that if God gives power to men to become his sons, nevertheless he gives it only to those who believe in his name. Therefore to receive the fullness of this filial joy it is necessary first of all to believe, . . . and after that it is necessary to do good works, as St. James says: faith without works is dead: he says that good works induce a living faith in us . . . therefore with faith let us look into these things saying, O Lord uncover my eyes, that is, the darkness of the eyes of my heart.[90]

---

[89] Bibl. Naz. Florence, II. II. 406. Monks were encouraged to write out the Rule, or some other work, as a pedagogic exercise: there is a splendid example of 'Speculum Bernardi Abbatis Casinensis' produced thus in Florence, c. 1505; Bibl. Naz., Conv. Sopp. G.4.2841.

[90] Bibl. Naz. Florence, II. II. 406, fo. 2ᵛ, 'Come dice lo Apostolo a Corinthi non sappiamo ne possiamo pensare alcuna minima cosa di bene. Bisogno e pertanto che esso iddio illumini gli occhi della nostra mente obtenebrata per li molti peccati. Revela questo domine oculos meos etc. Lo altissimo iddio per la sua infinità e ineffabile bonità s'è degnato largissimente diffundere sempre le sue dulcissime spiratione super filios hominum. Quibus dedit potestatem filios suos fieri. His qui credit [*sic*] in nomine eius. Ma nota che se iddio da potestà agli uomini esser filgiuoli di Dio, non la da però se non ad chi crede nel suo nome. Volere adunque ricevere la plenitudine di questa filiale dilectione e necessario in prima credere si come è scripto . . . et dipoi si conviene fare buone operatione, dicendo sancto Jacobo; fides sine operibus mortua est. Le buone operatione dice inducono in nos fede vicace . . . Quelle adunque fedelemente investighiamo, dicendo Revela domine oculos meos, id est, tenebras oculorum cordis mei.' The opening reference is to 2 Cor. 3: 5.

There was no reference to Christ or the Cross, but otherwise this prologue to the Rule sketched out a pattern of salvation drawn from Pauline theology: in Augustinian terms, man's understanding is vitiated and clouded by sin, and he is helpless, but, following the Greeks, man is rescued by God's mercy and given the power to become a son of God through faith, 'fede vivace', which is in part belief and in part the good works that arise out of belief. This is a pattern which, together with the Greek idea of sin as mortality, we shall encounter often in Congregational writing during the succeeding fifty years.[91]

The Augustinian and Antiochene elements in Congregational thought are also reflected in a collection of patristic sermons copied from ancient codices at Montecassino between June 1507 and May 1512—when the manuscript was in Naples. This 'Spicilegio Cassinese' demonstrates the manner in which the monks of Santa Giustina quickly exploited the library of their recently acquired monastery. The Spicilegio consists of fifty-five sermons and twenty-six extracts for use on Sundays and other festivals; both Latin and Greek sermons were selected, principally from Augustine, Jerome, and Chrysostom. There was only one Bible reading, Romans 8; this chapter's dominant theme of Christ winning back for man all that was lost at the fall—rescue from death and new life as heirs of God—is reflected in the sermons and the extracts.[92]

In this chapter we set out to determine the studies and the teaching which was carried on within the Congregation. The library holdings revealed biblical and patristic interests; the volumes acquired, the texts used for readings, and translations undertaken by monks revealed an emphasis upon the Pauline letters, Augustine, and the Greek Fathers. What has been discovered about the teachers and the surviving manuscripts used for teaching all points to the conclusion that the monks of the Congregation were trained in biblical and patristic studies;

[91] The themes of intellectual corruption, impotence, 'fede vivace', and works, were later used as the principal themes of the *Beneficio di Cristo*. See below, ch. 8.

[92] Bibl. Laur. Florence, Ashb. MS 140. There is a full description of the MS in C. Paoli and R. Enrico, *I codici Ashburnhamiani della Biblioteca Medicea Laurenziana di Firenze* (Indici e Cataloghi, viii. i, fasc. i; Rome, 1887), pp. 111–19. The MS was bound no later than 1517 (fo. ii). There is a medical recipe, dated Mantua, October 1526, on fo. x. Since this recipe may have been brought from Mantua by a transferred monk, its presence does not necessarily indicate that the MS was in Mantua in 1526.

they taught a way of salvation which followed Augustine in dwelling upon the corruption of will and intellect in man, and, much more, they followed Chrysostom (especially in his commentaries on Romans), and the school of Antioch in teaching the mortality of fallen man, the mercy of God in the 'beneficium Christi', and the necessity of 'living faith' which, set in the context of obedience, restores freedom, wholeness, and the *imago dei* to human nature. It was in the context of this kind of biblical scholarship that other, more substantial works were written by monks of the Congregation, and in the next chapter we shall look to these writings.

III

Monastic Writings, 1480–1521

FROM the libraries and the studies of novices and scholars we now turn to more substantial works written by members of the Congregation in the period before the Reformation. The question to be considered in this chapter is whether these writings, most published, a few in manuscript, reflect what we have discovered in previous chapters about the teachings of this order.

The first book to be examined was not, strictly speaking, a work of the Congregation. It was published in Milan in July 1477, eight months before the author, Gabriel Brebia, entered the monastery of SS. Peter and Paul, Milan, in March 1478. Although Brebia was not a monk when he wrote the book, it is clear that he had enjoyed very close connections with the order, for he dedicated the book to the abbot of the monastery, Don Gregorio Beaqua, and he acknowledged the help of Don Urbano, the prior. Moreover, the book was based upon the monastic psalter, and the themes developed by Brebia were congruent with other known biblical commentaries of the Congregation. After the book was published copies were placed in the libraries of other houses of the order. For these reasons we may consider Brebia's work amongst the writings of the Congregation.[1]

The work, which bears no title, described itself as a commentary on the psalms, but was rather a series of extracts from Jerome and from Nicholas of Lyre[2] to which Brebia had added some remarks about the purpose of each psalm and some

[1] Brebia (sometimes spelt Brebbia) was born in Milan, probably in the 1450s. Some biographical details are available in Armellini, *Bibl. Bened.-Cas.* i. 178; A. Wion, *Lignum Vitae* (Venice, 1595), p. 418; Sixtus Senensis, *Biblioteca Sancta* (Frankfurt, 1575), p. 208. Gregory Beaqua had previously been abbot of S. Giorgio Maggiore, Venice. Urbano of Milan was probably Urbanus de Paganis, who was appointed nineteenth prior of SS. Peter and Paul in 1475: he is mentioned in P. Puccinelli, *Chronicon Insignis*, pp. 124–5.

[2] Prologue (iii), '. . . pro maiori tamen parte super Hieronymo et Nicolao iacto fundamento . . .' Brebia may have been using a copy of the *Postillae* of Nicholas published at Rome in 1471–2: this work was the first biblical commentary to be printed.

appropriate prayers.[3] He explained in the preface that his purpose was to bring about 'a clearer understanding of the psalms themselves', and to this end he gave a brief account of Jewish history and customs from David's anointing as king to the captivity under Nebuchadnezzar, an explanation of musical practices, and a glossary of Hebrew and Greek works, explained 'secundum vero litteram'.

Brebia's piety was firmly rooted in the Bible, which he called the source of all religious nourishment because it showed men the coming of Christ and salvation. For this reason he had written this book on the psalms—in which the incarnation, sufferings, death, and resurrection of Christ were prophesied 'figuratively'.[4] That a late-fifteenth-century Italian humanist scholar on the eve of his profession as a monk should be so biblical and Christocentric in his beliefs is itself interesting, but for this study there is further significance in that the themes of sin, grace, faith, and the healing of human nature which we have already found in other writings of the order Brebia was about to join, are discernible in Brebia's own glosses and prayers.

The prologue made it clear that grace was the foundation of his pattern of salvation. 'We are able', he wrote, 'neither to do any good, nor to think any good thought without God.'[5] More specifically, his prayer at the end of the sixth psalm saw the grace of God to consist in the 'benignitas' of the Cross: 'In the compassion which springs from your kindness, you stretched out your arms in suffering upon the Cross, and in your most holy body endured five wounds for the healing of our wounds.'[6] Such

---

[3] The book begins 'religioso monacho et Sapienti viro D. Gregorio . . .'. It is of 340 folios. The British Library copy (IA 26303) belonged to his monastery at Milan. In the preface Brebia acknowledged the assistance of friends at the ducal library, including that of the librarian Giovanni Squasso, whose help with Greek and Latin texts has extended 'dies noctesque Codicibus'. In 1479 Brebia edited Pacificus Novariensis, *Summa de Pacifica Conscientia* (Milan, 1479). The British Library has a copy which belonged to Brebia's monastery, and was no. 489 in the library catalogue. It remains in mint condition, which suggests that this Franciscan work was little used by the Benedictines.

[4] Prologue (viii), 'hi [sc. Jerome and Nicholas] vero psalmos ipsos secundum ipsum figuratum i(d est) Christum exponere nitu(n)t(ur)'. Also (v) for his list of prophecies.

[5] Ibid. (iii): '. . . nec boni aliquid sine eo non solum non operari sed ne cogitare quidem possimus.'

[6] Ps. 6: 'domine Jhesu christe . . . tu(a)e benignitas affectu brachia tua(e) in crucis patibulo expandisti, et sacratissimo in corpore tuo p(ro) n(ost)ris sannadis {sic} vulneribus qui(n)que vulnera pertulisti.' See also Pss. 135, 146.

salvation was a gift, freely given. David was saved, not by his own merits, but by God's generosity:[7] there is no esteem of persons with God,[8] and salvation comes because 'God had sworn so great a benefit to the human race, for which reason it is said that the lord has chosen Sion . . . not out of merit, but out of divine generosity.'[9] Salvation was freely available to all who eschewed worldly wisdom, and to all, without exception, who fear God, and who, like the Magdalene, lie prostrate, weeping, and adoring before God.[10]

At this point Brebia seems to waver on the question whether good works appertain to salvation. His commentary on psalm 138 referred to the cause of predestination to salvation being 'on God's part his generosity and mercy, and on man's part the proper exercise of free will'.[11] The good works do not earn merit, but are foreseen by God, who therefore 'predestined' men to salvation. This was the teaching of Chrysostom and the Fathers of Antioch: moreover, in seeing those works as 'becoming conformed to the image' of Christ, that is, as restoration of human nature, Brebia was again following the teaching of the Greek Fathers.[12] Brebia here only touched upon the tension which exists between the Pauline understanding of grace and the monastic quest for perfection which he was about to undertake: that tension was resolved later by other writers of the Congregation.[13] As far as this book is concerned, we can only observe that he laid emphasis upon biblical themes that were common within the Congregation, especially the teaching that the grace of God was revealed in the 'benignitas' of the Cross.

Similar traits were apparent in a work of Don Michael of Brescia, who wrote a defence of the contemplative life, 'De excellentia vite pure Contemplative', at the Badia of Florence,

---

[7] Ps. 131.

[8] Ps. 127.

[9] Ps. 131: '. . . dues tantum humano generi beneficium iureiurando promisisset. Unde ait: Quoniam elegit dominus Sion . . . non ex meritis sed ex liberalitate divina.' See also Ps. 144.

[10] Prologue (ii)–(iii); Ps. 127; prologue (ix).

[11] Ps. 138: '. . . ex parte dei, e(st) lib(er)alitas et clementia: ex parte vero hom(in)is est bonus usus lib(er)i arbitrii.'

[12] Ibid.: '. . . quos prescivit co(n)formes fieri imaginis filii sui', the latter part of this expression was taken from Rom. 8: 29.

[13] For a detailed examination of the work of Don Luciano degli Ottoni on predestination, God's prescience, good works and restoration (1538), see below, ch. 6.

some time during the 1490s. The manuscript, directed against 'the many who preach to the contrary', asserted that the contemplative life has a natural superiority to the active life, and that human beings possess a natural impulse to enjoy spiritual delights.[14] In support of his argument he referred frequently to passages from the Bible, Augustine, Gregory the Great, and other Fathers, and from medieval doctors, especially Richard and Hugh of St. Victor, in which allusion was made to the superiority of the contemplative life, and the clarity of vision and freedom it gave to the soul.[15]

Michael of Brescia was defending the contemplative life, not against the claims of the secular life, but against the mendicant friars who had mixed contemplation with the activities of preaching and teaching. In particular, his work was aimed at the ecclesiastical and political activities of the Dominican Savonarola and his associates during the period of the Medici downfall and the setting up of the new republic. Michael did not entirely dismiss the mixed life of the friars, and even expressed some admiration for it as a support and stepping-stone to the higher life of contemplation: he simply made the point that they who had chosen the way of Martha, and not that of Mary, had not chosen the better way.[16]

A letter from the Benedictine monk to Savonarola, bound with 'De Excellentia', indicates that the friar had read the work and had made some criticisms, principally on the grounds that Christ himself and the apostles did not lead lives of pure contemplation.[17] This letter was a reply to Savonarola, repeating Michael's earlier arguments with a cool politeness which

[14] Armellini, *Bibl. Bened.-Cas.* ii. 107–8, has some biographical details of Michael, but his date and place of profession are not stated. The MS is at the Biblioteca Nazionale, Florence, Fondo Conventi Soppressi, D.8 (Badia, 2738). On fo. 1[r] there is a reference to 'multi sunt qui contrariam predicant opinionem et acuti nimium in disputando . . .'

[15] 'De excellentia', *passim*, but esp. 24[r]–34[v]. There is a good example on 24[v]–25[r]: 'Et Gregorius sup(er) Ezeckielem dicit q(uam) contemplativa vita amabilis valde dulcedo est.'

[16] Ibid. 17[v]–18[v], 26[r], but esp. 41[v].

[17] This letter is headed 'Michael Brixianus monach(us) ex congregatione s(an)cte iustine veneran(do) Fratri Ferariensi l(ec)tori in co(n)ve(n)tu Sancti Marci ex ordine p(rae)dicator(um) Florentiae.' It is ten folios in length, and mostly given over to a repetition of Michael's earlier arguments. I have been unable to find any reference to this MS or to its author in any study of Savonarola. The most probable date is late 1494 or early 1495. I am much indebted to Dr Lorenzo Polizzotto, of the University of Western Australia, for his comments on this letter.

suggests that behind the attack upon Savonarola there lay a sharp rivalry between the Benedictines of the Badia and the Dominicans of St. Mark's, both possessing scholars and fine libraries—although, when Savonarola eventually fell, he and his condemned colleagues were attended and shriven the night before their execution on 23 May 1498 by three Benedictine monks of the Badia.[18] But Michael had more on his mind than controversy. In a city where political and religious life were enmeshed, and under strain imposed by the downfall of the Medici and restoration of the republic, his defence of the contemplative life was an attempt to remind Florentines of the Augustinian ideal that contemplation was the path to know-ledge of the deeper kind, to wisdom, and, in the end, to love of God.[19]

'De Excellentia' was not original or profound, but it does contain elements which assist our understanding of the intellec-tual tradition of the Benedictine Congregation. In the first place, the testimony of biblical and patristic passages was repeated again and again, as if his repetition of their authority might establish the truth in those uncertain times.[20] Michael's use of the Bible was narrow, his principal text being Luke 11: 42, on the worth of Martha's activity, but the superiority of Mary's contemplation.[21] On the other hand, he referred to a wide range of the Fathers, and supplemented the older writers with Aquinas whenever a telling point could thereby be made against his Dominican rival.[22] In short, Michael largely based his tract upon the Bible and the Fathers, which was only to be expected in a writer of a Congregation whose libraries were, as we have

---

[18] *La vita del Beato Ieronimo Savonarola scritta da un anonimo del secolo XVI*, ed. P. G. Conti (Florence, 1937), p. 177. Savonarola was attended by Don Alessandro and Fra Domenico by Don Antonio: the name of the monk who attended Fra Sylvestro was not given. Of course, the task was one imposed by the Signoria and does not necessarily indicate the sympathies of the Benedictines. The accusation against Savonarola of Angelo da Vallombrosa in 1496 referred to one monk of the Congregation of Santa Giustina who joined Savonarola's 'conventicula, immo sinagoga del diabolo': see R. de Maio, *Savonarola e la curia romana* (vomini e dottrina, 15; Rome, 1969), p. 221. G. Schnitzer, *Savonarola* (Milan, 1931), ii. 144, also refers to the three Benedictines.

[19] 'De Excellentia', 27^v '. . . Augustin(us) in fine de ci(vitate) dei: ibi vacabimus . . .' etc.

[20] Ibid. 2^v–3^r, 10^v–14^r, 23^v–25^r.

[21] Ibid. 41^v, 'Maria optimam partem elegit . . .' etc.: the point is made repeatedly.

[22] Ibid. 8^r, 11^r.

seen, well supplied with biblical and patristic works, and whose students were well trained in those works.

A second element in Michael's work which throws light on the teaching of the Congregation is his treatment of perfection in terms of restoring man to the likeness of God. 'We are created and we live so that we might be like God',[23] he wrote, and by this he meant a reconstruction of the personality—in particular, the healing of the will: '. . . the perfection of the will is . . . making progress towards God . . . when no longer does he wish merely what God wishes . . . he dwells in perfect love so that he is not able to wish anything other than what God wishes.'[24] This view was probably taken from Augustine or Chrysostom, though his allusions to the active role of love and good works in the growth of perfection suggests the influence of the Greek Fathers, as well as the Benedictine Rule on peace and obedience.

At this point Michael was faced with a problem. He was aware of the criticism that whereas love and good works were clearly manifest in the more active life of the Dominican friars, the contemplative life required a withdrawal from good works.[25] Michael dealt with the problem by drawing a distinction between the interior condition of love and the exterior action, and arguing that the contemplative life fulfilled the former. '. . . truly the contemplative life is lived with unreserved love towards God, and for one's neighbour, even if it holds back from exterior action.'[26] This lame argument had been forced upon Michael by his adherence to the role of love and good works in the reconstruction of the personality and the will in order to reach perfection. We have seen a similar pattern of salvation in other Congregational writers, and we shall continue to see it. When Michael of Brescia's teaching is untangled from contemporary controversy over withdrawal from the world and pure contemplation, his pattern of salvation seems to be nothing other than

---

[23] Ibid. 39ᵛ, 'creati sumus et vivimus ut deo similes simus'.

[24] Ibid. 39ᵛ, '. . . ho(min)i sursu(m) cor habenti proficientis in d(eu)m voluntatis e(st) perfectio . . . cu(m) iam no(n) solu(m) vult q(uo)d deus vult . . . in affectu p(er)fectus ut no(n) possit velle nisi q(uo)d deus vult.'

[25] St. Bernard himself was very strongly aware of this problem, e.g. in Sermon 50 of The Song of Songs: Michael refers to St. Bernard on fos. 26ʳ–27ʳ.

[26] 40ʳ, 'Contemplativa v(er)o vita est caritate(m) quide(m) d(e)i et proximi tota mente retine(re) si ab exteriori actione quiescere.' See also 7ᵛ.

common Congregational teaching applied to a particular contemporary debate.

A third element of this work is the sense of a single-minded search for a full, personal relationship with God, which Don Michael expressed in terms of withdrawal from the transitory pleasures of the world in order to pursue the enjoyment of God:

You are not able to see and enjoy how sweet is the Lord—which pertains to contemplative life—except by freeing oneself and ceasing from works . . . as Bernard says, to free oneself for God is not leisure, but rather the work of all works. Truly, this is the pursuit of the heavenly life according to Augustine at the conclusion of his *City of God.*[27]

This search for a personal relationship with God was, of course, drawn from traditional Benedictine monasticism, and was to be found to a greater or lesser degree in most writers of the Congregation, including those who did not advocate the full contemplative life.[28]

There is one other surviving work of Michael of Brescia. About 1500 he wrote a tract in defence of the tradition that St. Benedict had been a priest—a belief that had been defended earlier, probably in the 1480s, by the distinguished abbot Urbanus of the monastery of St. Sixtus, Milan.[29] In the course of a dialogue between two monks of the Congregation, he drew upon Chrysostom for the view that a layman could be a priest by virtue of his sanctity:

[27] Ibid. 26^r–27^r, 'Non potestis videre & gustare q(uam) suavis est dominus. Q(uo)d pertinet ad contemplativam nisi vacando & cessando ab operibus . . . Unde Bernardus vacare deo non est otiosum, im(m)o negotium negotior(um). Est enim exercitium vite beate secundum illud Augustini in fine de ci(vitate) dei.'

[28] The search for personal relationship occurs also in the Benedictine Rule (prologue and ch. 7). Strangely, Michael has overlooked the fact that Bernard and Gregory both favoured the mixed life: see the definitive discussion in C. Butler, *Western Mysticism* (London, 1926), pp. 176–86, 191–7.

[29] This tract is printed in the Venetian edition (1581) of Cardinal Francesco Zabarella's *Consilia Eminentissimi . . . Interpretis D. Francisci Zabarellae Patritii Patavini Cardinalis Florentini*, pp. 189^r–193^v, 'An beatus Benedictus monacorum pater almificus fuerit sacerdos: dialogus interlocutores Michael & Hieronymus, monaci ordinis sancti Benedicti, Congregationis sanctae Justinae de Padua.' The references to Urbanus and other writers occur on pp. 189^{r-v}. Biographical details of Urbanus are in Armellini, *Bibl. Bened.-Cas.* ii. 34–5: probably he was Urbanus de Paganis, the nineteenth prior of SS. Peter and Paul, Milan, mentioned in P. Puccinelli, *Chronicon insignis*, pp. 124–5. Urbanus's tract was entitled 'Defensorium monachorum adversus Eusebium canonicum regularem'. Michael says that Baptista de Caccialupis de Sancto Severino made much use of it in his *Consilium Domini* ('in suo consilio saepius facit mentionem'). I was not able to find this tract of Urbanus.

M(ichael) . . . as Chrysostom says in his commentary on Matthew, every saint is a priest. H(ieronymus) . . . certainly, I know that a righteous layman is in a state of spiritual union with Christ through faith and charity, though not through sacramental power, and for that reason he possesses priesthood for the offering of spiritual sacrifices.[30]

The point was that Benedict's sanctity and his position as abbot—'pastor et pater' invested him with priestly status. In this, Michael took an important stand that we shall encounter again in the writings of the Congregation, namely, the belief that a relationship of faith and love may bring about a level of union with Christ that amounts to a spiritual priesthood: moreover, equally important for our investigation is the fact that Michael drew his argument from the teachings of the Greek Antiochene school, specifically John Chrysostom.

In short, the writings of Michael of Brescia used biblical and patristic material, including that of the Greek Fathers, to expound a concept of sanctification as reconstruction of the will, manifest in love of neighbour, and in search for a close relationship with God. These themes and their sources were similar to other writings of his Congregation—all of them, of course, set in the context of the Benedictine Rule.

*

Another Congregational exposition of the monastic life was also written in the style of the humanist debate on the active and the contemplative life. This exposition was the vigorous poem *De Vita Solitaria et Civili*, published in 1496 at Brescia, together with a *Vita* of St. Bernard. The author was Ottavio Bona, who was professed in 1492, and was known within the Congregation as Philotheus, or, more often, as Teofilo da Brescia.[31]

---

[30] 189ᵛ–190ʳ, '*M* . . . Nam ut ait Chrys(ostomus) super Mattheum, omnis sanctus est sacerdos. *H*. Nolo ut in his immoreris. Scio nempe, quod laicus iustus unitus est Christo unione spirituali per fidem & charitatem: non autem per sacramentalem potestatem, & ideo habet spirituale sacerdotium ad offerendum spirituales hostias.' There follow quotations from Psalms, Romans 12, and 1 Peter.

[31] Biographical details of Teofilo da Brescia are in Armellini, *Bibl. Bened.-Cas.* ii. 184–5. *De vita solitaria et civili* and *De vita et moribus sancti Bernardi* were published in one volume in Brescia in 1496, and a second edition in Cologne in 1510. The latter work has been printed in J. P. Migne, *Patrologiae cursus completus* (Paris, 1855), clxxxv. 551–6. Teofilo dedicated his work to Guidobaldo da Montefeltro, duke of Urbino from 1482 to

De Vita Solitaria et Civili was clearly written for layman as well as religious. It consisted of a dialogue in Virgilian style between a certain Maurus, who has withdrawn from his native city to live in a cave, and his fellow citizen, Pyrrhus, who remained in the active life.[32] Maurus extolled his solitude, with its pastoral joys and his spiritual meditation:

> Here, every grove resounds with lingering harmony,
>> Every field with perfumed flowers laughs,
>> And joyful herbs carpet all the land.
>> . . . Such things recall to me the joys of heaven.[33]

From time to time Don Teofilo returned to meditate upon this theme of the providence of God, but he did not develop it. He was less concerned with contemplation than with preaching the necessity for peace and civic virtue, showing that he fully appreciated the benefits of the active life, which, when well ordered, not only produced 'an excellent life style and the arts of wisdom', but also nourished religious faith:

> For what is better than the city
>> Which preserves the human race, and nourishes
>> The pious hearts of Christ's own folk.[34]

Don Teofilo acknowledged that there were devout and upright men in civic life, and he praised Guidobaldo da Montefeltro, Duke of Urbino, for his personal purity and cultivation and for the justice and wisdom of his rule. But such men were few. Civil life had gone awry, peace was ruptured, and Maurus had fled, or rather, had been driven, to the solitary life by 'mille pericula saevae urbis . . . rudis latratantia vulgi . . . tanta hominum crimina':

1508. A copy of the 1496 edition is in the British Library (IA 31250). Armellini refers to two other works of Teofilo, *Del valor de'Bresciani* and *Discorso del vagare e della certe fede delle anime de'morti*, but I have been unable to find these two works.

[32] The name Pyrrhus alludes to the classical figure, son of Achilles, who acquired a kingdom. Machiavelli used Pyrrhus as an example in the fourth chapter of *The Prince*.

[33] Hic nemus omne vagis resonat concentibus, omnis
Campus odoratis arridet floribus: omne
Gramina laeta solum complent
. . . Talia coelestis referunt mihi gaudia regni. (No pagination)

[34] Quid enim praestantius urbe?
Quae genus humanum servat, quae sancta virorum
Pectora Christigenum nutrit
. . . Egregios mores & Palladis artes.

> . . . compelled to flee unhappy hearth and home
>   To live out life amid the forest wild.[35]

Don Teofilo inveighed against the contemporary miseries of civil life. First, he condemned the invasions of Italy by the French and Spaniards. The conflict was bitter and barbarous, and the land beset with violence, 'the shattered earth trembling with horrifying tumult'. He gave a long list of atrocities. In the humanist style later used more effectively by Erasmus in the *Adages*, Teofilo marked the contrast between animals and the violence of humans.

> Only men grow fat on the blood of their own; only they
>   Labour to make confusion, wounding each other until they die,
>   Alas, the devastation of Italy, so many deaths for nothing.[36]

The other cause of civic misery was the delinquent behaviour of the citizens themselves. They lied, perjured themselves, deceived, robbed, and attacked their fellow citizens:

> Each day brings a thousand dangers to anxious men
>   Who tremble in their hearts: that one dies, from the sword, another
>   By poison, this one suddenly falls from the highest rank. . .[37]

In these ways the peace and order of society was disrupted and suffering caused by unbridled fellows ('infrenes pueros'), each doing as he pleased ('ire per anfractus varios'). Teofilo observed that corruption bred corruption, for as more and more citizens fell into dissolute ways, at length the aberrations of one generation become the habits of the next:

> Little ones learn sordid ways rather than the alphabet,
>   And before their time are taught the speech of lust,
>   . . . neither do they respect the commands of an angry parent.

Thus, concluded Teofilo, through 'the unhappy wretches who

---

[35] . . . misero patriae migrare coegit
Limine & in rudibus vitam producere sylvis.
[36] . . . tremit horrisono tellus quassata tumultu . . .
Soli homines propio grassantur sanguine, soli
Exercent trepidas per mutua vulnera caedes.
Hei mihi, quot clades Italis, quot funera gratiis.
[37] . . . sollicitos per mille pericula ducit
Corde tremente dies, gladio perit ille, cicuta
Alter, & hic celso lapsus de culmine praeceps . . .

lack a rational mind',[38] civic life degenerates into a corrupt condition that cannot be repaired easily. Meanwhile Mauro continued to praise the solitary life as the best way for a man to meditate upon the wonders of God and his creation, and to order himself for the salvation of his soul. Teofilo handles his two contrasting themes with skill: they avoid useless repetition, but rather, develop and gain power by their juxtaposition.

In Don Teofilo we see a Benedictine monk of the late Quattrocento who has entered a traditional debate on the side of the life of contemplation, but in so doing has not only shown considerable practical concern for the peace and the well-being of society outside his cloister, but has also made an effort to analyse the causes and process of disorder and suffering. In short, he used contemplation in order to expound the traditional Benedictine themes of peace and love of neighbour and apply them to contemporary political and social events. In the chapters following we shall see similar applications of the Benedictine 'Pax' in other, later, writers of the Congregation, who also blended piety and social analysis, and wrote for a lay audience.

It is possible that Teofilo Bona taught Teofilo Folengo, the poet, after the latter's profession in 1509.[39] If so, it would have been interesting to know the reactions of the older man to the monastic career of his pupil. However, during the sack of Brescia by the French troops under Gaston de Foix in 1512, Bona was overtaken by the very violence he had denounced. He was then cellarer of the monastery of San Eufemia and responsible for its goods. The troops, in search of loot, captured him and he was tortured, but he refused to reveal the whereabout of the monastery's treasures and he was killed by his interrogators.[40]

Whilst Don Teofilo Bona was writing on civil concord in the 1490s, other monks continued to expound the theological teachings of the Congregation. We have already touched upon MS 280 of the Biblioteca Comunale at Mantua, which gave us a

---

[38] Turpia concipiunt ante alpha & beta tenelli
  Ante diemque modos veneris recitare docentur
  . . . nec irati metuunt mandata parentis
  . . . Heus, infelices animi ration(al)is egentes.
[39] G. Billanovich, *Tra Don Teofilo Folengo e Merlin Cocaio* (Naples, 1948), pp. 39–40. The relationship between the two men is discussed in a long and vigorous footnote.
[40] Armellini, *Bibl. Bened.-Cas.* ii. 184.

glimpse of late-fifteenth-century teachings within the order: that no man is justified through the law, which is as 'stercora', and that all good depends upon grace, that man is saved only by 'Christ, whose benefit suffices for all things', that 'faith in Christ suffices to salvation', and that out of faith arises love of neighbour.[41] During the first two decades of the sixteenth century, as the Congregation grew rapidly in numbers and took in some notable scholars, its published writings continued in the same tradition, with some variations of emphasis—some related the tradition to the institutional life of monks, whilst others concentrated directly upon theological doctrines.

Only two works of this latter period dealt with institutional aspects of the monastic life. The first was an anthology of the rules of Benedict, Basil, Augustine, and Francis compiled by Don Joannes Franciscus, together with some commentaries and his general observations on adherence to the Bible and the teachings of the Fathers. The work was published in Venice in 1500 and a revised edition printed in Paris in 1514.[42] The other work was a manual for monks hearing confessions, written in a legalistic style which was not usual in the Congregation. This was 'Introductorium breve pro monachis deputatis ad confessiones', written at Padua, probably about 1520, by Don Teofilo of Padua. The work, which exists only in manuscript, consists of closely structured advice on the questioning and counselling of penitents, using the seven deadly sins and the ten commandments as a basis, explaining all possible variations of all sins in most circumstances, and indicating when absolutions may or may not be given. There is appended a formidable list of absolutions and another list of plenary indulgences at the disposal of the Congregation, granted by Innocent VIII, Eugenius IV, and other popes.[43]

---

[41] See above, ch. 2.

[42] *Regula S.S. Benedicti, Basilii, Augustini, Francisci, cum vitis, epistolis, expositionibus etc. Coll. et ordinata per Jo. Fr. Brixianum, monachum congregationis S. Justine O.S.B. de observantia* (Venice, 1500, and Paris, 1514), 203ᵛ. The copy of the 1514 edition at Oxford, in the Bodleian Library, was owned by Benedictine nuns near Nuremburg and includes the obituary notices (1529) of two abbesses, sisters of Willibald Pirckheimer.

[43] Bibl. Univ. Padua, MS 1135. The catalogue places the work at c. 1500, but on fo. 115ᵛ a hand other than that of the scribe has written '1520 circiter'. In view of the fact that the author was professed in 1500 the former date cannot be accepted. Biographical details are in Armellini, *Bibl. Bened.-Cas.* ii. 197. The strong exhortations to reconciliation with neighbour occur on fos. 2ʳ, 7ʳ, and *passim*.

The systematic plan for the interrogation and guidance of troubled minds strongly suggests the influence of the popular Franciscan *Summa Angelica*. The work of Teofilo of Padua is almost the only example within the Congregation of writing that mingled Cassinese piety with such legalistic traits. Nevertheless, the underlying piety is congruent with what we have learned of the Congregation's traditions. Passages were inserted from the Bible and the Fathers, especially Ambrose, Chrysostom, Bernard, Jerome, and Bede, the questions asked of the penitent were directed to elicit contrition as much as yield information, and there was considerable emphasis upon 'Pax'— peace, reconciliation, generosity, and works of mercy.

However, during the first two decades of the century there also appeared that other, more substantial, style of Congregational writings which concentrated upon a biblical, Pauline, and patristic pattern of salvation. This was represented by Don Lucas Bernardus, whose translations from Greek to Latin of Chrysostom's *Octoginta Homilia ad Populum* (1505), and *De Laudibus Pauli* (1508) have already been mentioned.[44] In 1518 Don Raphael Justineus of Piacenza, generally known as Raphael Placentinus, published a heroic poem on the life of St. Simeon the Armenian, who had become a Benedictine monk at St. Benedetto Po in the tenth century. The poem, written between 1505 and 1518, interspersed events in the life of the saint with events in biblical, classical, and modern history, the whole written in a style strongly influenced by Dante's *Divine Comedy*.[45] The work was very much a display of the heroic virtues that might be found in the monastic life, the virtues being illustrated with frequent references to biblical texts, especially

---

[44] See above, ch. 2.

[45] Raphael of Piacenza was professed at Mantua in 1477; see Armellini, *Bibl. Bened.-Cas.* ii. 164–6. Raphael's work was published at Cremona 'per Franciscum Ricardum de Luere' on 16 Mar. 1518 under the title *Armeniados*, together with another short poem and some epigrams. The volume was prefaced by a letter to Don Benedictus Regius, abbot of S. Benedetto Po, and president of the Congregation. There is a copy in the British Library (11405 a 39). The autograph MS is at Mantua in the Biblioteca Comunale, MS 194. The use of the term 'Casinensis' on the title-page indicates that the work was written after 1505. A contemporary hand has added at the end of the prologue 'in hoc volumine multa sunt non ut postea in impressis'. Some of Raphael's epigrams are cutting, especially those to Paolo Cortese (1465–1510), which may explain the coolness between Raphael and the much younger Don Gregorio Cortese: see *Gregorii Cortesii Cardinalis*, ed. A. Cominus (Padua, 1774), ii. 190–1.

Pauline passages, and with the Fathers, especially Jerome, Origen, and Chrysostom. There was no detailed exposition of patristic doctrines, but a number of theological allusions suggest the influence of Chrysostom: the fall of man was described in terms of mortal illness, and reference was made to the inability of man to achieve salvation—of both Jews and Christians who strive, like Jews, to do so by their own efforts; Chrysostom's emphasis on faith was praised, and faith itself was described as 'living faith', which is manifest in good works.[46]

The last work to be considered in this chapter was written at the monastery of San Severino Naples, and published 'cum gratia et privilegio decemnali per totum regnum Neapolitanum' in 1521. The author was Don Vincentius Campanus, who had been professed at San Severino in 1508. His book, together with the title of another, now lost, indicates that Don Vincenzo was well versed in biblical studies. The work, published in 1522, was entitled *Fasciculus Myrrhae . . . Expositionibus*: it was a collection of New Testament readings, each accompanied by a passage from the Old Testament, and an exposition, generally the author's own, but sometimes taken from the Fathers.[47] There was a prefatory letter to Don Joannes Evangelista, the prior of the monastery, whom Vincenzo praised for his virtue, study of divine letters, and sense of worship, all of which he illustrated, not without relish, with the text 'inter ubera mea', from the Song of Solomon. The prior had also been professed at San Severino, in 1505, where he was to become abbot. Later he became abbot of S. Benedetto Po, Mantua. He also was a man of some scholarship and well versed in the Bible, and we shall be

---

[46] Biblioteca Comunale, Mantua, MS 194, 110ʳ, 150ʳ for the '. . . morbi ponum . . .', also 18ʳ; 31ᵛ 'Nec Moses genus omne suum, nec fonte piatur/Gratia, nec tonsus crinis ad astra tulit'. A contemporary marginal note reads 'De Judeis christianis et clericis.'; 67ᵛ for the reference to Chrysostom's teaching on faith; 214ᵛ for the necessity for living faith to be manifest in works. The phrase 'Nos ducibus coelo viva locare fides' has the marginal gloss 'fides sine operibus mortua est, ideo hic dicitur viva.'

[47] Don Vincentius de Flumino was professed on 6 Feb. 1508. The 1521 edition of *Fasciculus Myrrhae* is in the British Library (4808 c 34). It does not bear his surname, but Armellini confirms the authorship in *Bibl. Bened.-Cas.* ii. 24, in littera V. The work was reprinted in Naples in 1562 under the title *Collyrium mentis seu commentaria de nominibus Christi*, of which there are two copies in the Biblioteca Alessandrina, Rome (AE a. 86; N a. 146). Armellini refers to another work, *Ad deiparam virginem salutiones pulcherrimae*, also published in Naples in 1562, which he describes as 'ex sacra scriptura delectae'. I have not been able to find a copy of this book.

examining a work of his on the necessity of good works, written against 'li moderni heretici', that is, the Protestants.[48]

In the *Fasciculus Myrrhae* Don Vincenzo continued the Pauline bias we have seen in earlier Congregational writings. The person and the work of Christ, he declared: '. . . is understood to be the man Jesus Christ, the conciliator of God and men, concerning whom John the Evangelist said: God sent his son to be a propitiation for our sins.'[49] This declaration set the theme of the rest of the book, in which the person and work of Christ was placed at the centre of a detailed pattern of salvation, drawn from St. Paul.

Don Vincenzo emphasized the pathological nature of sin. Sin was described sometimes in terms of guilt, but more often in terms of its penalty upon man—mortality, corruption, suffering, and alienation from God: '. . . because by sinning the human race has brought death upon itself, and in this way, through sin, has run into enmity with the creator.'[50] Indeed, the 'myrrh' of Vincenzo's title appertained to human mortality; man lived 'in the darkness and shadow of death', and man was passible—crippled by 'passibilis humanitas' and 'poisoned by sin', so that he was in a wounded condition, 'vulneribus humanis'.[51] In this condition, said Vincenzo, man was unable to heal himself. In his commentary on 2 Kings 4, he described how obedience to the Law could not have liberated men from death: 'The Law led nobody to perfection, for man was not justified through works of the Law . . . in no way could man have been freed from death of the soul through the efforts of man or through the Law.[52] Man was therefore trapped in his state of mortality, suffering, sin, and alienation from God.

But there was a solution, went on the monk, for God desired

---

[48] Armellini, *Bibl. Bened.-Cas.* ii. 35, has details of Johannes Evangelista. His MS of 1545 is discussed below, ch. 9.

[49] *Fasciculus*, Prologus: '. . . mediator dei et hominum homo Christus Jesus intelligitur, de quo ait evangelista Joannes: misit deus filium suum propiciationem [*sic*] pro preccatis nostris.' All quotations are taken from the British Library copy.

[50] 59ᵛ–60ʳ: 'Nam quia humanum genus peccando sibi mortem intulit, sic(ut) propter peccatum gravissimas creatoris inimicitias incurrit'.

[51] 14ʳ: '[crediderunt] in myrrha humanam mortalitatem . . . myrrha vero ad sepulturam pertinet mortuor(um)'; 20ᵛ; '. . . in tenebris et umbra mortis' (51ʳ); also 5ᵛ, 82ʳ⁻ᵛ; 20ᵛ, 74ᵛ; 73ʳ.

[52] 5ᵛ–6ʳ: 'Lex neminem ad perfectum duxit, non enim justificatur homo ex operibus legis . . . nisi deus factus homo fuisset: nequaq(uam) ho(mo) p(er) homine(m) aut p(er) lege(m) a morte a(ni)i(m)ae liberari potuisset.'

that all men be saved—not just some, but the whole world: 'The saviour of the world freed, not only Egypt, but indeed the whole world, from eternal famine, that is to say, from everlasting death and the pains of hell.'[53] Therefore, universal salvation was part of God's plan and was available to all men. Vincenzo said that it was offered to all through grace alone, that is, by the work of the Cross; it was thus he expounded Genesis 30 in terms of Galatians 4. 'Truly, we are redeemed and sanctified by the blood of Christ: like Isaac, we are children of the promise of the free born wife, not of the slave girl, living under grace and not under the Law.'[54] Christ had therefore become a brother of mankind, taking upon himself human passibility, and in an expression repeated often, being 'raised up on the wood of the Cross for our salvation', 'offering himself immaculate to God the Father for our sins, he placated the wrath through his own blood . . . reconciling the human race to God'. It is clear that this monk, writing in a vein already established within the order of Santa Giustina, was expounding the teaching of St. Paul that salvation is by grace alone, through the sufferings and death of Christ.

The next step in his pattern of salvation was to describe the work of the Cross. Sometimes Don Vincenzo, employing the language of St. Paul, used forensic terms such as 'the remission of sins through the blood of Christ',[55] but more often, and with greater emphasis, he described salvation as liberation from the mortality and passibility that had damaged human nature: 'Christ . . . triumphed over the devil and slew death: from the Cross he descended to hell, so that he might lead captivity captive: whom he dragged with great strength from the jaws of death, and took with him to the joys of paradise . . . he overcame not only the pains, but also the power of death.'[56] When death was conquered, so was human passibility, for Christ 'by rising

[53] 11^v: 'mundi salvator no(n) solu(m) Aegyptu(m), ver(um) etia(m) universum mundum ab aeterna fame id est a morte perpetua et inferni cruciatibus liberavit.'

[54] 2^r: '. . . nos aute(m) qui Christi sanguine redempti & sanctificati sumus: secundum Isaac promissionis filii sumus, nati de libera non de ancilla, sub gratia viventes non sub lege.'

[55] 38^v–39^r: '. . . Christi sanguis . . . effunditur in remissionem peccatorum'. Also 40^{r-v}.

[56] 80^v: 'Christus . . . ascendens de diabolo triu(m)phavit et mortem occidit: de cruce autem ad infernum descendit ut captivam duceret captivitatem: qua(m) de i(n)ferni faucibus pote(n)tissime abstraxit, et secum ad paradisi amoena conduxit . . . qui non solum mortis acerbitate(m) sed imperium mortis superavit'.

impassible from the dead . . . became free from death and from suffering'.[57]

These passages show that in using the passage in Ephesians 4: 8 of the Vulgate '. . . ascendens captivam duxit captivitatem: dedit dona hominibus' Vincenzo understood the 'gifts given to men' to mean the rescue from mortality and suffering. For the monk, this was Christ's gift to man, the 'benefit' of the Cross to which other monks of Santa Giustina had so often referred. Moreover the monk saw the saving work of the Cross to be the healing of human nature. As the angel Raphael had healed Tobit, so had God come into the world to heal the human race.[58] Christ 'may truly be called the medicine of God', who 'poured medicine into the wounds of humanity'.[59] In short, that salvation, which was the gift of Christ to mankind, was primarily therapeutic in nature, 'vivifying a lost world',[60] and curing human nature of its mortality and suffering.

Don Vincenzo also expounded a doctrine of faith, which was first of all belief in Christ, who 'liberated from the servitude of the devil those who believe in him'.[61] But faith was more than belief, for it also entailed contrition.[62] Those who thus accepted the gift of grace were transformed by their faith:

By the blood of Christ the hearts of the faithful have melted and are opened to his love and fondness.

By believing in Christ, through newness of life we are made sweet, and we who were alienated, we are made his, in the blood of Christ.

Christians are called 'Christians', because they are born again, from the side of Christ, that is, from his blood.[63]

Those who thus live in faith do so under the 'lex gratiae', and they are 'sons of adoption' as has been promised to men.[64] In this

---

[57] 82[r–v]: '. . . impassibilis a mortuis resurge(n)s: . . . immortalis et impassibilis factus . . .'

[58] 4[v]: 'Sicut igitur angelus Raphael caecum Tobiam [*sic*] sanavit sic dominus in mundum veniens . . . humanum genes . . . a peccatorum caligine expurgavit'.

[59] 73[r]: '. . . medicinam vulneribus infundit humanis'.

[60] 49[v]: '. . . unigeniti filii: qui mundum perditu(m) vivificavit et redemit . . .'

[61] 49[v]: '. . . et populum sibi credentem a diabolica servitute liberavit'.

[62] 14[r].

[63] 51[r]: 'sic Christi sanguine fidelium corda liquefacta et scissa sunt in amorem et affectum suum'; 74[v]: '. . . credendo in Christum novitate vitae facti sumus dulces, et q(ui) eramus lo(n)ge, facti sumus p(ro)p(ri)e i(n) sanguine Christi'; 58[v]: 'Christiani a latere Christi in ei(us) scilicet sanguine renati christiani appellati sunt'.

[64] 90[v].

way the author reached the final stage of his pattern of salvation: man, who had been bound by the penalty of original sin was now liberated from alienation, mortality, and corruption by a gift of grace: when that gift was accepted through faith, human nature was restored to health.

Finally, the work lays emphasis upon the sacrament of the altar as a shield against unbelief: 'it is a defence and a shield against all suggestions of the devil and intrusive temptations of evil spirits'.[65] These sentiments were perhaps taken from the fourth book of the ubiquitous *Imitation of Christ*, in which similar benefits are attributed to the sacrament, but what is significant for this work is that we shall find, in 1543, a very similar exhortation on the value of the sacrament in sustaining faith and gratitude in the *Beneficio di Cristo* of Don Benedetto of Mantua, who had already been professed for ten years when his colleague Don Vincenzo published the *Fascicula Myrrhae* in 1521.[66]

In view of the date at which Vincenzo published his work, we must consider the possibility that he had received his teachings on sin, the Law, grace, and faith from Lutheran sources. We do not know in which month of 1521 it was published, but were it at the end of the year, it is possible that Lutheran works had been imported to Naples and had reached the monastery by, say, mid-1521 in time for the author to digest and use them for his work. Against this rather slight possibility we must put the fact that the earliest known traces of Protestant literature in Naples were in the mid-1530s.[67] Moreover, the fact of publication 'cum gratia et privilegio decemnali per totum regnum Neapolitanum' is a strong indication that no suspicion of heresy was attached to the work.

The text itself furnishes three even more weighty arguments against attributing the monk's arguments to Protestant influence. First, the doctrinal material does not resemble any of Luther's works to that date: the *Commentary on Romans* which does bear some similarity, was not published until 1522. Second, the text contains a number of firm references to the mass and to Mary immaculate: such sentiments, whilst not necessarily

[65] 32ᵛ–40ᵛ, esp. 34ʳ–35ʳ.

[66] See below, ch. 8, p. 181, especially n. 73

[67] P. McNair, *Peter Martyr in Italy: An Anatomy of Apostasy* (Oxford, 1967), ch. 1. However, it is possible that Lutheran literature reached the Cassinese monastery in Naples in 1524: see below, ch. 4.

excluding early Lutheran influence, do suggest that the monk had not become a Lutheran. Third, and most important, the work closely resembles other Congregational teachings. It is therefore unnecessary to postulate Protestant influence, for the book is simply another expression of the theological tradition of the Congregation. Like the other works, this work of Vincenzo bears some resemblance to the soteriological doctrines of the Greek Fathers of Antioch, which, as we have seen, were abundantly represented in the libraries of the order, translated by the monks, used for readings and in sermons and lessons, and reflected in the writings of many monks. We may confidently put aside the possibility that *Fasciculus Myrrhae* is of Lutheran extraction, even though it is a remarkable anticipation of some Lutheran teachings, and recognize it as a part of the Greek patristic element within the Congregation.

At the time when Vincenzo's book was published the Congregation of Santa Giustina had undergone a period of strong development. From about the turn of the century it had grown enormously: there were 529 professions between 1500 and 1509, and in 1505 the Congregation absorbed the ancient monastery of Montecassino. Between 1510 and 1520 there were another 591 professions,[68] and the island monastery of Lérins, in Provence, was acquired. Above all, the Congregation had been fortunate in the intellectual quality of the men attracted to its novitiate, taking into its cloisters a host of bright young scholars—Marco Cropelli and Johannes Evangelista (1505), Gregorio Cortese, Giambattista Folengo, Innocento de'Honoria and Luciano degli Ottoni (1507), Vincentius Campanus and Denis Faucher (1508), Prosdocimus Pignolatus and Teofilo Folengo (1509), Girolamo Lippo (1510), Benedetto da Mantova (1511), Basilio Pleboni (1512), Isidoro Montauti and Mauro Pandulfino (1514), Eusebio Valentino, Prosper Vallinieri, and Hilarion Corbetta (1515), Isidoro Chiari (1517), Angelo Faggio and Onorato Fascitello (1519). These young men, whose intelligence, scholarship, and literary skills were to

---

[68] Bibl. Naz. Florence, Magl. xxxvii, 315 (Strozzi Catalogue), 'Catalogus Omnium Monachorum Congregationis S. Justine, 1409 ad 1595'. The increase began in 1501 where there were forty-nine professions. In 1507 there were eighty-eight; in 1515 seventy-nine. In 1483 there had been 984 persons in the houses of the Congregation—694 monks and 290 others, mostly lay religious (bound by a simple promise but not vows), novices, oblates, etc.

mark them out in the years after 1520, formed a brilliant circle which developed and expounded the teachings of the Congregation after 1520, during the turbulence of the years of the Reformation and the years of changing intellectual climate within the Roman Catholic church.

This conflict was yet to come, but in the meantime, by 1521, we have a picture of a religious order with an established tradition of biblical and patristic scholarship, and expanding in numbers, reputation, and wealth. Side by side with their Pauline exposition the monks continued to manifest a strong sense of their monastic vocation as Benedictine monks, and it is important for us to see their doctrines set in the context of the traditional monastic life. There is a reminder of this juxtaposition in the marginal comments of the copy of the Rule written in 1499 (cited earlier): there is a reference to Cicero's _Offices_, a number of explanatory comments on biblical passages, and references to various patristic works. There were amusing line drawings, observations upon the behaviour of monks in choir and refectory, a mnemonic list of the monastic virtues, and an admonition against sleeping nude.[69]

These marginalia serve as a reminder that as well as being zealous scholars of St. Paul and the Fathers, these men were monks, whose monastic ethos may also be illustrated by the manner in which the monks took possession of Montecassino in January 1505. The long and elaborate ceremony began with a liturgy of the Holy Spirit sung 'devoutly with many tears' and included a _Te Deum_, sermons, processions, the reception of gifts, then a final procession with monks, two by two, singing psalms and hymns, followed by the viceroy of Naples and other notables, whilst through all present there swept a great wave of emotion, said one monk, as if St. Benedict himself were with them.[70] Similar monastic attitudes are revealed in an anecdote

---

[69] Bibl. Naz. Florence, Fondo II. II. 406, fos. 22ᵛ, 30ʳ, 43ᵛ, 45ᵛ, 58ᵛ, 65ᵛ, 75ᵛ, 108ʳ ('note bene che mai, etiam infermi, debbono dormire nudi'), 141ʳ, 146ʳ, 153ᵛ, 160ʳ, 202ᵛ, 220ʳ, 240ᵛ. The poem of Marcus of Brescia (professed 1505), which preceded the 'Chronicon Casinese' in the Venetian edition of 1513, also reflected strong adherence to the monastic life. He called Montecassino 'illa domus, qua sanctior altera non est . . . Humanae Speculum Vitae, Virtutis alumna/Haec est mortales quae facit esse Deos'. Armellini, _Bibl. Bened.-Cas._ ii. 90, Inguanez, 'La prima edizione, p. 137.

[70] Bibl. Naz. Florence, Conv. Soppr. C. 4. 2659. This MS, written in 1535, is a copy of the _Regola_ of 1499. It contains some observations on the acquisition of Monte Cassino and has a few theological additions to the prologue; these are discussed below, ch. 5.

recounted by a Florentine monk who was present at a procession at Montecassino in the summer of 1507. It was a hot oppressive day. There was no rain, but thunder and lightning. Suddenly there was a flash, which struck the novice who carried the cross and then went through the church until it stopped at the altar 'where there are always burning ten lamps in honour [of St. Benedict]'. The novice had been professed only four months, recalled the monk, 'and was like an angel in the flesh'. The scorched boy fell to the ground and called out three times for prayers to St. Benedict. The monks carried him into the infirmary, where thanks to the grace of God and the power of the saint, he recovered, and next morning came to mass as if nothing had happened to him.[71] The details of this anecdote, the procession, the description of the event, the prayers to the saint, the ten sanctuary lamps, all illustrate the way in which the monks adhered to traditional monastic life.

It was within this context that the order gave itself to biblical scholarship. Only two months before the procession at Monte-cassino, the chapter-general reminded 'the brethren who are learned' of their obligation to teach those who were not yet learned. The same chapter exhorted monks to come to perfection through the study of the Bible, thus following in the footsteps of the ancient saints. To that end the chapter required monasteries to attend carefully to their manuscripts, and visitors were appointed to inspect the libraries.[72] Moreover, we have seen that their biblical scholarship was based upon St. Paul. We know that the novices of 1507 not only carried crosses in

[71] Ibid. This anecdote was related to the scribe by a monk who was present at the procession on Sunday 26 June 1507: this monk is identified as 'figlivolo di Matteo degli Albizzi'. (See also P. Meyraert, *Benedict, Gregory, Bede and Others* (London, 1977), pp. 301–3.) There is a critical edition of this MS by T. Leccisotti, 'Montecassino agli inizi del Cinquento', *Benedictina*, ii (1948), 75–94. The description of events is on fos. 226–7 of the MS, 'Un terribil tempor, non piovendo però, ma tonando e ballenando. . . . venne una saecta et percosse uno novitio che portava la croce alla processione: era pure professo di quattro mesi, e era come un angiolo in carne . . . subito cadde in terra e comincio subito a gridare presto, presto, pregate tutti per me san Benedetto e cosi dixe tre volte . . . stanno sempre accesse dieci lampone ad sua reverentia . . . per la gratia di Dio et per meriti del padre san Benedetto. La mattina sequente venne alla messa come se male alcuno non havessi havuto.' Also see T. Leccisotti, 'Documenti per l'annessione di Montecassino alla Congregazione di S. Giustina', *Benedictina*, xvi (1970), 59–91.

[72] 'Regulationes, declarationes, ordinales (1507)', Bibl. Com. Mantua 51 (A II 20), 87ʳ 'in grammaticalibus et cantu sollicite instrufatiant [*sic*] per alios doctor fratres si (h)abilit(er) fieri potest. Quod ut efficatius perfici valeat volumina eis tempus et com(m)oditatem per prelatos et seniores sine detrimento divini offitii ac(c)edi'.

procession, but also studied the Gospel: Denis Faucher, from Arles, became a novice at Mantua in 1507, was professed the following year, 'nurtured for seven years in the study of theology', and emerged in 1515 to be sent to the island of Lérins where he wrote a series of lectures on the epistles of St. Paul.[73] Such a combination, of biblical and patristic studies on the one hand, and monastic practices on the other, had a profound influence on the way in which the monks dealt with the theological controversies of the Reformation period. In the next chapters we shall consider how the monks faced the intellectual questions posed by the Reformation.

[73] 'Annales Provinciae', Bibl. Laur. Florence, Cod. Ashb. 1833, fo. 161ᵛ '. . . in Italiam in Asceterio Divi Benedicti de Padolirone in Agro Mantuano . . . per septennium Theologiae Studiis incubui.'

IV

The Cassinese Tradition and the Reformation

LUTHERAN works were being sold in northern Italy by 1523. In January 1524 papal briefs referred to their presence in Venice, Padua, Brescia, and Verona, and instigated attempts—only partially successful—to prevent their printing and sale.[1] It is certain that at this time the monks of the Congregation were known to have access to Luther's books, for the family of one monk, Don Francesco Negri, made a point of questioning him about the matter. In February 1524 Negri told his brother that the monks were able to read Luther's works, and that they were uncertain about the Lutheran business but generally held that 'the works of Martin were based upon scripture'.[2] The monks not only knew Luther's works, but were also familiar with several men whose interest in theological issues and the reform of the church made them sympathetic to some aspects of Luther's doctrines. Gasparo Contarini was already well known to them and in the midst of his spiritual crisis of 1511 had stayed at the Congregation's Venetian monastery of San Giorgio Maggiore.[3] In 1520 Don Basil Pleboni in Siena and Don Eusebius de Valentiniis in Florence were in touch with Christoper Longolio about corrections to Greek texts. At the time, shortly before his death in 1522, Longolio was staying at Reginald Pole's house in Padua, together with his close friend Marcantonio Flaminio, and was also in correspondence with two other Cassinese monks, Denis Faucher and Gregory Cortese. In turn Cortese, who was

[1] B. Fontana, 'Documenti Vaticani contro l'eresia luterna in Italia', *Archivio della Reale Società Romana di Storia Patria*, xv (1892), 76–87.

[2] G. Zonta, 'Francesco Negri l'eretico e la sua tragedia "Il libero arbitrio"; *Giornale storico della letterature italiana*, 67 (1916), 274–6. The letter, dated 18 Feb. 1524, is in the municipal library of Bassano.

[3] Contarini's crisis and its resolution is described by Dermot Fenlon, *Heresy and Obedience in Tridentine Italy* (Cambridge, 1972), pp. 6–11. Also see J. B. Ross, 'Gasparo Contarini and his friends', *Studies in the Renaissance*, xvii (1970), 192–232.

then reading Lutheran books with a view to their refutation,[4] had connections with Jacapo Sadoleto. By 1523 these men, Contarini, Longolio, Pole, Flaminio, Sadoleto, and others were deeply aware of the questions raised by Luther,[5] and we may conclude that by the end of 1523 the Cassinese monks, certainly those in Padua and Venice, had not only encountered Lutheran teachings, but also discussed them both within and without the Congregation.

The first clear Cassinese response to the Reformation was the apostasy of Francesco Negri. Towards the end of 1524 he left the monastery of Santa Giustina, but stayed near by in the hope of obtaining a licence to formalize his departure, possibly for the sake of his family. He moved about the region for some time (when, according to Zonta, he may have made an Italian translation of Luther's *Appeal to the German Nobility*)[6] and then, in 1529, he went to study with Capito and Bucer in Strasburg.[7] However, Negri's was the only defection at this time, although it is clear that Lutheran ideas had stirred up the Congregation. The chapter-general of 1524 ordered that monks holding Lutheran works must deliver them within three days to their superiors, the works were to be burnt, and nobody was to discuss the doctrines of Luther. The following year the president of the Congregation instructed that 'those who neglect religious ceremonies and follow Martin were in no way to be tolerated'.[8] There were also allusions to the monks' interest in the Reformation: a papal brief of 27 October 1524 referred to monks 'who

---

[4] Bibl. Apost. Vat., Vat. Lat. 7928, fos. 157^r–158^v. The letter to Longolio, dated 27 July 1520 from Florence, refers to Abbot Arsenius, author of several monastic *Acta*, 'Arsenio nostro veterano'. A letter of 23 Apr. 1524 shows that Basil had moved to Mantua. Longolio's correspondence with Faucher and Cortese is printed in *Christophori Longolii Epistolarum* (Lyons, 1563), pp. 82–3. The letter to Cortese indicates a common acquaintance with Sadoleto. Other examples of Cortese's correspondence with Longlio and Sadoleto are printed in *Gregorii Cortesii Mutinensis S.R. Ecclesiae Cardinalis Epistolarum Familiarum Liber* (Venice, 1573), pp. 4–7, 9–14, 59–61, 73–5, 212–13. Also see M. W. Anderson, 'Gregorio Cortese and Roman Catholic Reform', *Sixteenth Century Essays and Studies*, ed. C. S. Meyer, i (1970), 81–2.

[5] Fenlon, *Heresy and Obedience*, ch. 2.

[6] Zonta, 'Francesco Negri l'eretico', pp. 276–8, 283.

[7] G. H. Williams, 'Camillo Renato (c.1500–?1575)', *Italian Reformation Studies in Honor of Laelius Socinus*, ed. J. A. Tedeschi (Florence, 1965), p. 137.

[8] T. Leccisotti, 'Tracce di correnti mistiche cinquecentesche nel codice cassinese 584', *Archivio italiano per la storia della pietà*, iv (1965), 118: '. . . de his qui negligunt religionis ceremonias et sequuntur Martinum nullatenus tolerandis.' The wording suggests that these pro-Lutheran monks did not leave the order.

had fallen into error', and to nuns in the care of the Congregation who had been 'overtaken by error', and instructions were
given that they be corrected and the matter kept quiet.[9] Yet,
despite what appears to have been intense discussion and some
sympathy with Lutheran teachings, there were no other
conversions from amongst the Cassinese.

How, then, did the Cassinese Congregation react to the
questions raised by the Reformation? Part of the answer lies in
the Congregation's traditional study of the Bible, especially the
Pauline epistles, and of the Fathers, especially the Greeks. These
studies were maintained and extended during the early years of
the Reformation, particularly at the hands of Gregory Cortese
and Denis Faucher. Cortese was born of a noble family in
Modena in 1483, and after a false start in the service of Giovanni
de'Medici, was professed at San Benedetto Po, in 1507, to which
monastery he was drawn by 'the learning and sanctity of the
order', in particular by the scholarly abbot at Mantua, his
compatriot, Don Eusebio Fontana. In 1516 he was sent as abbot
to restore the ancient island monastery of Lérins,[10] where he
taught Latin and Greek to novices, built up the library, and
edited and published some of its old manuscripts, so that 'the
people might have them', and developed his own vision of a
monastery as a workshop or powerhouse ('officina assidua')
which could influence Christian society in the same way that the
academy of Varro had influenced ancient Rome.[11]

In 1520 Cortese fell ill and was sent to the monastery at
Genoa, where he studied the biblical commentaries of Origen,
Basil, and Chrysostom. He was deeply impressed by the Greek
Fathers and declared that the Bible could not be understood
without a knowledge of the Greek commentaries. Indeed, from
this time, although he referred often to the Latin Fathers, he
kept his praise for the Greeks, and it would seem that in 1522 he
used the Greek Fathers, especially Gregory of Nazianzus, to

---

[9] Fontana, 'Documenti Vaticani' pp. 85–7.
[10] For the accession of Lérins and subsequent events see H. Moris, *Cartulaire de
l'Abbaye de Lérins* (Paris, 1883, 1905), ii. xxii–xxxv.
[11] Armellini, *Bibl. Bened.-Cas.* i. 183–7; *Gregorii Cortesii Cardinalis omnia quae huc usque
colligi potuerunt*, ed. J. Cominus (Padua, 1774), part i, pp. 13–19. The biographical details
of Cortese are taken from the *Vita*, by G. A. Gradenigo, included in this volume,
pp. 11–51. Eusebio Fontana was professed in Venice, in April 1471, and was first abbot
of Montecassino after the union.

write a defence of papal authority against the Lutherans, and to urge reform of the church.[12] When he applied theological learning to social matters, Cortese did so in the style of Chrysostom and other Greek Fathers, moving immediately from scriptural text to its social application, but in a much more direct way than had Teolfilo of Brescia. In 1522 Cortese wrote to the ruler of his native Modena, quoting Pauline texts and urging the ruler to eschew evil ways and to restore the virtue of the city.[13] Cortese returned to Lérins in 1525, and shortly after was faced with the threat of the French king, Francis I, to expel the Italian monks from French territory. Cortese appealed to the king, again using Pauline theology, this time the text upon which his colleagues had based the doctrine of universal salvation: 'As St. Paul says,' wrote Cortese, 'in Christ there is no Italian or Frenchman.'[14] In 1527 he returned to Modena as abbot, thence to Perugia, and in 1532 to San Giorgio Maggiore at Venice, where he was to draw together his finest 'officina assidua', the circle which included Bembo, Pole, Flaminio, and others. But this was to come later. Long before he went to Venice, from 1516 and throughout the 1520s, Cortese was actively extending biblical and patristic scholarship within the Congregation.

At Lérins Cortese had been assisted by the Frenchman Denis Faucher, who had been professed at Mantua in 1508. Faucher had spent eight years at Mantua, in the study of the Bible,

---

[12] *Gregorii Cortesii Cardinalis* (part ii), pp. 76–7 (letter 41). The letter was probably written in 1521, since Cortese had left Genoa, spent some time in Modena, and was in Rome by May 1522. Here he addressed his letter to Pope Adrian VI urging a thorough reform of the church. See also M. W. Anderson, 'Gregorio Cortese', pp. 81–6. The work on the papacy was a historical assertion of St Peter's presence in Rome (Bibl. Apost. Vat. Otob. Lat., 888). Cortese corresponded in 1538 with Pietro Bembo on the education of monks: see *Opere del cardinale Pietro Bembo* (Venice, 1729), iii. 40.86.

[13] *Gregorii Cortesii Cardinalis*, (part ii), pp. 114–17 (letter 72). At the end of May 1522 the imperial forces had sacked Modena and suppressed the Fregosi faction (with which the Cortese family had connections). Antonio Adorno had then seized the lordship of Modena as Doge, but real power lay in the hands of his more able younger brother Girolamo, to whom Cortese addressed his letter.

[14] Ibid. pp. 162–4 (letter 106). The monks were threatened because their protector, Bishop Agostino Grimaldi, had been in conflict with the crown over a matter of property. The king's chancellor, Bishop Anton de Prat, was strongly in favour of expelling the Cassinese, but he was overruled by Louise of Savoy, mother of Francis, and *regente* whilst her son was campaigning in Italy and during his captivity. On 7 Aug. 1525 she issued letters patent reconfirming the union of Lérins with the Cassinese Congregation.

especially the Pauline epistles, and when he went to Lérins in 1516 he taught Greek and the study of St. Paul. Between 1522 and 1530, he wrote a commentary, 'Praelectiones in omnes Epistolas Divi Pauli', the manuscript of which is now lost.[15] In 1532, when Cardinal du Bellai, Bishop of Grasso, managed to expel the Congregation from the monastery, Faucher returned to Mantua, where he went on teaching Greek and St. Paul. The activities of these two men show that traditional biblical and patristic studies were maintained and even extended within the Congregation during the 1520s. However, these two active teachers have left very few details of their teachings at this time, though we shall see more of them later. It is rather the writings of other monks that reveal in detail reactions within the Congregation to questions raised by the Reformation.

The first Cassinese writer to respond to Lutheranism was Teofilo Folengo, the Mantuan poet, who was professed at Brescia in the summer of 1509, at the age of almost eighteen years. Folengo's passionate temperament was combined with a complex and lively mind which his friends called subtle and his enemies thought devious. His portrait reveals the writer: Folengo clothed in the black habit of a Benedictine monk; his face full and heavy, the nose straight and long, the lips thin, sensual, and slightly pursed, with a touch of amusement, the eyes brown, heavy lidded, and lustrous, suggestive of both shrewdness and humour.[16]

Folengo spent the first year of his profession at Brescia, but when the Venetian territories were under attack by the forces of the League of Cambrai—the campaign that led to the sack of Brescia, the looting of the monastery and the killing of Teofilo Bona—Folengo was moved to the safety of his native city of Mantua. Here he wrote his first work, *Baldus*, a poetic satire upon knightly virtues, human follies, and the social evils of civic corruption and the abuse of power, treated in a manner which owed something to both Erasmus and Ariosto. The work

[15] Armellini, *Bibl. Bened.-Cas.* i. 150–2; *Chronologia Sanctorum et Aliorum Virorum Illustrium ac abbatum Sacrae Insulae Lerensis*, ed. V. Barrali Salerno (Lyons, 1603). The works of Faucher are in part 2 of the volume (which is not distinguished as such), pp. 222–372, under the title *Opera Omnia*. . . . A sixteenth-century copy of Faucher's 'Annales Provinciae', with biographical material and a list of his MSS, is in the Bibl. Laur. Florence, Ashb. 1883. Folio 161ᵛ refers to his 'proelectiones'.

[16] The portrait, by an unknown artist, is at the Biblioteca Comunale, Mantua.

includes several brief theological allusions, but has no definite
religious theme; indeed, the hero, Baldus, moved from child-
hood to maturity, to reach his destiny in a great, empty,
pumpkin—'Zucca mihi patria est.'[17]

In 1525 Folengo and his brother Giambattista both left the
Congregation. The brothers had been amongst those who
opposed the plan of the Florentine abbot Ignazio Squarcialupi
to make the presidency of the Congregation a life appointment.
Opposition to the plan had centred upon the Venetian abbot
Giovanni Cornaro, whom Folengo, in common with Marco da
Cremona and others, admired greatly, and to whom Folengo
had given pointed praise in his revised edition of *Baldus* in
1521.[18] The position of the two brothers took a turn for the worse
when their eldest brother, also a monk, was expelled from the
order after accusations of sexual misdemeanours and theft. The
two monks protested their brother's innocence: later they sought
release from the Congregation. Teofilo went to Cevara and
Giambattista to Venice where he became tutor to the son of the
condottiere Camillo Orsini.[19]

In 1526 Teofilo published *Orlandino*.[20] The work, which
included a witty defence of the Folengo family, entwined
burlesque exaggeration of knightly deeds with satirical criticism
of social evils and clerical laxity, and with discourses on human
waywardness and man's salvation. In his references to salvation
there occur elements of the teaching seen in other Congregational writings. The miserable and sinful state of mankind,
wrote Folengo, could never be overcome by the sophistries,
'sillogismi de altre zanze sofisticar', of Aristotelian theologians,

[17] *Baldus* has been published in a critical edition, *Le Maccheronee*, ed. A. Luzio, 2nd
edn. (2 vols., Bari, 1927–8). There is a very detailed analysis by G. Continelli, *Il Baldus di
Merlin Cocaio* (Città di Castello, 1904). Also see A. Luzio, *Studi Folenghiana* (Florence,
1899), ch. 5. There is an account of Folengo's literary similarities to Erasmus in F.
Schalk, 'Folengo und Erasmus', *Scrinium Erasmianum*, ed. J. C. Coppens (Leiden, 1969),
ii. 437–48.

[18] G. Billanovich, *Tra Don Teofilo Folengo e Merlin Cocaio* (Naples, 1946), chs. 5, 6.
There is a description of this dispute, and of recent writings on Folengo generally, in the
introduction of *Folengo, Aretino, Doni*, tome I, *Opere di Teofilo Folengo*, ed. C. Cordié,
La Letteratura Italiana, Storia e Testi, xxvi, tome I (Milan and Naples, 1977), esp.
pp. xxxiii–xxxvi.

[19] Billanovich, *Tra Don Teofilo*, pp. 108 ff.

[20] The critical edition is T. Folengo, *Opere italiane*, ed. U. Renda, Scrittori d'Italia, i
(Bari, 1911).

but only by the proclamation of the Gospel.[21] This Folengo described in Pauline terms, using an expression familiar to the Congregation 'il beneficio di Cristo':

> O holy, O blessed, O worthy teachers
> to know of Christ his benefit.[22]

This 'benefit of Christ' was available to all men, and it was to be accepted by faith. Folengo was aware that such teaching taken 'from the mouth of some northerner' could be considered heresy, but he was not deterred. Having made the point, he went on to emphasize faith:

> I believe that a tear from the heart
> Of a thief closes hell and opens heaven to him.
> I believe that the Gospel's steadfast rock
> Is none other than pure faith.[23]

These sentiments cannot be taken for Lutheranism. Folengo expressed dismay that through the Reformation 'the seamless garment of Christ has been rent'[24] but, much more significant, other writers of the Congregation, from long before the Reformation, had been placing similar emphasis upon the benefit of the Cross and faith.

Even before *Orlandino* had gone to press, Folengo had begun *Caos del Triperuno*. This tortuous blend of macaronic verse and prose is not a work of prime literary merit, but it very clearly reveals the author's Pauline theology.[25] The title refers to the three stages of Folengo's own development to the age of thirty-six years (as he then was), and to the development and fulfilment of mankind generally. The first of three *selvae* describes how man, made originally in the divine image,[26] has

---

[21] *Orlandino*, 8.84,

> . . . co'l'argomento
> sol d'Aristotel vogliono provare
> quel che con Paolo devono salvare.

[22] Ibid. 3.21:

> o sante, O benedette, O degne scorte
> a consoscer di Cristo il beneficio.

[23] Ibid. 8.75:

> credo che d'un rubaldo una lagrima
> dal cor, lo inferno chiude e il ciel disserra:
> credo che del Vangelo il saldo piede
> altro non sia, salvo la mera fede.

[24] Ibid. 6.46: '. . . di Cristo l'inconsutil vesta squarciata è'.

[25] T. Folengo, *Opere italiane*, ed. U. Renda, Scrittori d'Italia, ii (Bari, 1911).

[26] Ibid. p. 190: 'l'huomo a se fatto simile'.

lost that image: he is now born to die, coming into the world vitiated, 'già devoluta in sterco, fango e sperma', because the 'original sin which was personal in Adam is in the nature of other men.'[27] Man's natural powers are now 'weak and impotent' both physically and mentally. Man cannot understand clearly, for, like a mole, he does not have the illumination given by the sun of righteousness: consequently, man, with his judgement clouded and his senses weak, has lost the capacity to extricate himself from sin by obedience to the Law of God.[28] Therefore, as a result of the fall, human life must endure the penalty of misery and death—'how great the grief, how many the blows'.[29]

Towards the end of the first *selva* Folengo considered the Neoplatonist doctrine of man rising above earthly things and, by a process of purification, ascending to heaven, but he rejected this idea of salvation by ascent because peace cannot be obtained by shedding this world.[30] No one has the power to do this. Salvation is the gift of God, who, because he loves men infinitely, saves them, not because they deserve salvation, but out of his infinite goodness: 'The infinite goodness of God had to come first; now hear what and how great has been his kindness

---

[27] T. Folengo, *Opere italiane*, ii. p. 193–4, 'Peccatum originale, quod in Adam fuit personale, in aliis naturale' (printed marginal note). Also see the use of 'stercus' in the Mantuan MS Bibl. Comunale, 280 (above, ch. 2).

[28] Ibid. p. 191, 'l'human desio . . . le conduce al rete si di legger, ove ne resti presa'.

[29] Ibid. p. 195,

> ma quant'è'l pianto? quante le percosse
> anzi, ch'anchora il misero s' industre
> saper su piedi starsi. Onde ruina
> souvente si . . .

To drive home the point Folengo added in the margin (with some errors) Cicero's 'O, fallacem hominum spem, fragilemque fortunam et inanes nostras conceptiones (contentiones), quae mediocri (medio) in spatio saepe franguntur et currunt (corruunt)' (*De oratore* 3.2.7), and Horace's reminder of death, 'Pallida mors aequo pulsat pede pauperum tabernas/regumque turris' (*Carm.* 1.4.13).

[30] Ibid. p. 213,

> Non t'invagir dunque homo de la terra,
> Anzi contendi . . . salir'in cielo,
> U'sempre t'arda l'amoroso fuoco,
> Riposto d'alma in alma in somma pace,
> Et sotto i piedi ti verdrai le stelle.

However, man who is born in carnal pleasure—Folengo employed a classical allusion to the sea of Venus—will always fall back:

> . . . chi naque in Mare
> trallo dal Cielo in sempiterno Foco.

towards mankind, to remove the shackles of the ancient bondage of damnation.'[31] Man, who is quite unable to fulfil the Law,[32] is rescued by Christ who became 'un miserabilissimo spettacolo' (a Folengian touch) in order to save man. It was a marvellous gift—'tanto beneficio':

O dazzling love, o most burning goodness towards us men, God became man in order to save you, o man; bore the attack in order to defend you, suffered death to give you life . . . behold how he embraces you like a dear brother . . . he has become one of our clan in order to make you lords again. Who could ever comprehend such a gift?[33]

In the third *selva* of *Triperuno*, Folengo again returned to the contrast between 'our modern theologians', with their tangled web of demonstrations and arguments, and the simplicity of the 'santissimo Vangelo', especially that of St. Paul, with its message 'of how great is the divine mercy towards men'.[34] Then he described how the great love of God renewed man and restored him to his former perfection. Man must accept the gift with faith:

> Now I come to free you, hope and believe,
> Hold out your hand, and have no fear, o man . . .[35]

Christ will rescue man from death—'l'empire d'ossa', and renew their minds. Folengo quoted from Bernard of Clairvaux on God's love, and from Basil on the healing of the mind and illumination of the heart. Man, rescued from death, is now renewed, no longer made of clay, but becoming a 'new Adam'. Folengo then finished the work with some lines on the food of the eucharist as a means of that sanctification.[36]

---

[31] Ibid. p. 231, 'l'infinità d'Iddio bontade così a dover avvenire nel principio dispose; or odi quale e quanta verso voi uomoni sia stata di lui la benevolenzia. Lo quale, da l'antico legame di perdizione per scatenarvi . . .'

[32] Ibid. p. 191, 227, 231–2, 349.

[33] Ibid. p. 233, 'O affocato amore, o benivolenzia verso noi uomini ardentissima. Iddio fassi uomo per te salvar, o uomo: offende se, difende te; ancide se, vivificare te . . . vedi come gestisse d'abbracciarti in foggia di caro germano . . . s'ha fatto famiglio per constituirti signore. Or dunque chi renderà mai guiderdone a tanto beneficio equale.'

[34] Ibid. p. 231; 182, '. . . voglia solamente pascersi di contemplare quanta sia verso noi la divina misericordia'.

[35] Ibid. p. 348, 'Or vengo liberarti: spera e credi, porge la man, nè aver, uomo, di tema.'

[36] Ibid. p. 229–30, 352, 357–8, 380. The *Beneficio di Cristo*, published in 1543, has a similar conclusion: see ch. 8 below.

These Pauline sentiments, here abstracted and summarized from a work of great complexity, were not peculiar to Teofilo Folengo. Although he had left the Congregation at the time he wrote *Caos* in 1527, his ideas were entirely in accord with the doctrines we have examined in early Congregational writings; Adam's sin has brought man to a condition of death, misery, and impotence; man is unable to fulfil the law and unable to save himself; salvation is a gift, 'il beneficio di Cristo',: man must accept this gift with faith; human nature is then rescued from mortality and restored to its old perfection. Thus, Folengo's religious themes, although mingled with burlesque, and bearing sentiments that might seem Lutheran, were simply another expression of the traditional teachings of the Congregation. This conclusion is borne out even more strongly by his later writings, to which we shall return later.

In the year in which *Orlandino* was published, another monk was also grappling with the issues raised by the Reformation. He was Gregory Bornato, born in Brescia of a noble family and professed at Brescia in 1508. In 1526, whilst at San Giorgio Maggiore in Venice, Bornato became involved one day in a deep discussion with his nephew on the question of free will, with the monk hotly attacking those who, with 'foolish temerity presume to deny the power of free will'. It is certain that the Benedictines at Venice had considered this question in some detail: we have already seen that some of Luther's books had been bought in Venice and taken to Padua by their colleagues, that Luther's theology had been discussed, that Negri had left his monastery, that there had been suspicions in Rome, that the chapter-general had issued warnings and prohibitions in 1524 and 1525, and that Folengo had made clear allusions to Lutheran doctrines. Indeed, it is possible that the question was alive, not only in Padua, Venice, and Mantua, but in all the major houses of the Congregation by 1526.

Whilst we know that the monks' views on free will were stimulated by Luther, it is equally certain that they were shaped by the writings of John Cassian. The *Conferences* of Cassian were one of the books prescribed by the Rule to be read aloud to the monks after supper, and copies of the *Institutes* were in all Cassinese libraries for which catalogues have survived. Cassian was the abbot who had defended the cause of Chrysostom at

Rome: like Chrysostom, he had upheld the necessity of free will in salvation, and on this matter he opposed his contemporary St. Prosper of Aquitaine, who sought to uphold St. Augustine's teaching on grace and to combat Pelagian tendencies. The teachings of Cassian and his debate with Prosper had been always relevant to the monastic vocation, but were now particularly so in the face of the Reformation issues facing the monks, and were being used by them in their deliberations. There is an early-sixteenth-century manuscript copy of Cassian's *Institutes*, written at San Giorgio Maggiore. At the end there is a brief discussion of the differences between Cassian and Prosper on grace and free will, concluding, with Cassian and with Chrysostom, that by the fall Adam incurred the penalty of mortality, but did not lose his free will, nor have his descendants lost their free will.[37] It was with such teaching behind him that Gregory Bornato defended the role of free will to his nephew in 1526. Since he did not write about this discussion for another ten years (and his written account, with substantial alterations, was published only in 1571) Bornato's beliefs will be discussed later.[38] For the present, his discussion may be taken as evidence that cardinal doctrines of the Reformation were being actively considered by some monks of the Congregation in 1526.

The existence of such discussion was reflected in an ordinal of the 1528 chapter-general, which forbade monks to possess Lutheran books or to discuss Lutheran doctrine. These commands were to be enforced within each monastery by the abbot and others in authority, and individual monks were obliged to lay information against those who spoke to them of Lutheran ideas or who held Lutheran books.[39] However, the prohibition of the direct study of Lutheran theology could not prevent discussion of the themes central to Protestant theology, the crucial questions of the role of free will and the nature of grace and faith, because these themes and questions were also a part of the Congregation's own theological teachings, but the prohibition did act as a catalyst. The common ground between the

---

[37] Bibl. Univ. Padua, MS 833. The MS bears the monastery's catalogue number 334. The anonymous exposition of the doctrines of Cassian and Prosper is on fos. 125^v–129^v.

[38] See below, ch. 5.

[39] 'Ordinatio hoc anno edita 1528, contra sectam luteranam', printed in T. Leccisotti, 'Trace di correnti mistiche cinquecentesche', pp. 118–19.

Cassinese order and the Protestants, earlier a reason for sympathetic consideration on the part of the monks, now became a reason for defining their position on these issues which were dividing western Christendom. From now on there occurred within the Congregation a number of attempts to clarify and to apply the order's traditional teachings to the Reformation debates.

One of these attempts was an early work of the young Isidoro Chiari, later to become one of the Congregation's foremost scholars, a delegate to the Council of Trent and a bishop, Chiari was born in 1495 at Chiari, near Brescia. In June 1517 at the age of twenty-two, he became a monk at Parma, where he remained for several years, until 1527. This was an unusually long stay in one monastery, but most probably it was in consequence of his poor health and to facilitate his Greek studies under Hilarion Corbetta, the translator and exegete of Gregory of Nazianzus.[40]

Chiari's early letters, written during the 1520s, exhibit the self-conscious style of a pious, slightly precious young man. He alluded to Cicero frequently, and adopted the convoluted Ciceronian style which was then fashionable amongst humanists. There were Platonist touches of despair at his soul's imprisonment within the body, but since these philosophical vapours coincided with illness, and since Isidoro was the kind of man who showed detailed interest in his own medical history, they cannot be taken seriously.[41] Those early letters contain only brief allusions to biblical and patristic studies, although as a bright young monk he must have been already immersed in them: certainly he was in touch with other scholars of the Congregation, and is even thought to have taught Reginald Pole at Padua.[42]

---

[40] Armellini, *Bibl. Bened.-Cas.* ii. 49–58; *A. et C.* ii. 64–5; *CTE* 32–4. Also J. G. Gussago, *Biblioteca Clarense* (Chiari, 1822), ii. 12–15, 30. E. Martene and U. Durand, *Veterum Scriptorum et Monumentorum, Historicorum, Dogmaticorum, Moralium, amplissima Collectio*, tome ix (Paris, 1733), cols. 83–4. Armellini says that he was born 'modicis, humilibusque parentibus', Martene and Durand that he was born 'obscuris parentibus'.

[41] *Isidori Clarii . . . epistolae . . . ad amicos, . . . ex autographo descriptas . . . accedunt duo opuscula alia*, ed. J. Olgiato (Modena, 1705), p. 8; see also the letter to his doctor, pp. 31–3. For details of Hilarion Corbetta , see Armellini, *Bibl. Bened.-Cas.* i. 225–6.

[42] Olgiato, *Epistolae*, p. 138; the letter, dated 1524 by Olgiato, but 1529 is more probable, refers to an ancient work which Giambattista of Mantua (sc. Folengo) had brought from Angelo of Genoa to Chiari. See also pp. 3–5, 23, for references to the traffic in books. For the reference to Pole see Fenlon, *Heresy and Obedience*, p. 145 n.

In his twenties Chiari began to emerge as a man of mature scholarship whose writings increasingly discarded the religiosity of his youth and reflected the Pauline and Greek bias of his order. Cicero was not forgotten, but Chiari now concentrated more upon the insights afforded by sacred letters.[43] He was familiar with the writings of Erasmus and agreed with an unknown correspondent that Erasmus was a remarkable man; nevertheless in 1527 he began to voice criticisms which were not specific, but may have been connected with his own exposition of Pauline theology.[44] At the same time his earlier concern with the state of his own soul was gradually replaced by warm attention to his family and friends, and by a pastoral bent which became much more explicit in his later writings.[45]

In 1526 he wrote a commentary on 1 Corinthians 15, which he dedicated to his friend Basilio Pleboni, who was professed at Venice in 1512, but was the same age as Chiari.[46] The work consists of three parts: the first describes the historical context of classical religious and philosophical ideas; the second is a discussion of the nature of the soul, drawing mainly upon Ambrose, whilst the third part is the actual commentary. The style is discursive and repetitious, lacking the concise and vigorous style of Chiari's later years, and for the most part consists of explanations of various phrases used by St. Paul to describe bodily resurrection. There are a number of points of the kind frequently made within the Congregation: he asserted once again the necessity of Greek studies in theology and when he wrote of sin he put forward the common teachings of his order, that man is born in a state of sin and is mortal, that the Law gives knowledge of sin, but man cannot free himself from sin by obedience to the Law, that Christ died for sinful man and by this 'benefit' has liberated the human race from death: '"Through a man came death, and through a man came resurrection of the

---

43 Olgiato, *Epistolae*, p. 70.

44 Ibid. pp. 35–7: '. . . unus, ut ais, in quem exercuerit natura suas vires omnes, et universa bona congesserit . . . ego si inter familiares, quid de Erasmo tuo sum interdum locutus, quod delicatas aures tuas offendere potuisset . . .'

45 Ibid. pp. 37–43, 46–59, 118.

46 Bibl. Apost. Vat., MS Chigiani A IV 83, 'Isidorii Clarii commentationes in cap. xv epistolae prioris divini pauli ad Corinthios, ad Basilium fratrem'. The library catalogue notes that Sixtus Senensis stated this MS to be written in 1526, at Parma in the author's own hand. In citations the original pagination has been used. Basil Pleboni was professed in 1512, and was later abbot at Venice: Armelini, *Bibl. Bened.-Cas.* i. 76.

dead; just as through Adam all men shall die, so also through
Christ all shall live"; the immense benefit of God and a pure
manifestation of love for us men.'[47] In speaking of man's
redemption as a rescue from death and in calling it the
'beneficentia dei' Chiari was interpreting St. Paul as many
others of his Congregation had done, that is, in the manner of
Chrysostom and other Greeks of the school of Antioch.

The commentary was something of a turning-point for
Chiari, for it was a work in which his classical learning shared
equal place with Pauline theology. From now on the Pauline
emphasis and Greek exegesis predominated. In 1527 Chiari was
sent to Torrechiara, but remained under the authority and
scholarly supervision of Hilarion Corbetta, now abbot at
Parma.[48] Guided by Hilarion, Chiari further applied himself to
Greek and Pauline studies.[49] He corresponded with Denis
Faucher, at Lérins,[50] who had recently completed a commentary on the Pauline epistles, with Ambrogio of Ferrara,[51]
translator of Chrysostom, and with Simpliciano de Quadris,
another Greek scholar,[52] with Eusebius de Valentiniis, author of
several tracts on Christological themes,[53] with Angelo di Faggio,
a Hebrew scholar and man of 'ferventissima charitas', whose
works concentrated upon the theme of faith in the Cross,[54] with
Giambattista Folengo and a number of other monks of scholarship and biblical piety.[55]

---

[47] MS Chigiani A IV 106ᵛ (concerning verses 21, 22): '. . . p(er) homine(m) mors
etiam per hominem resurrectio mortuorum. quemadmodu(m) (e)n(im) per Adam
omnes moriuntur, ita et per Christu(m) omn(e)s vivificabuntur. Ingens dei beneficentia
et mera in nostrum genus amoris significatio.'

[48] Olgiato, *Epistolae*, pp. 58, 74. Torrechiara is a small village at the foot of the castle
of the Rossi family, near Langirano, south of Parma.

[49] Gussago, op. cit., p. 23.

[50] Faucher's 'Proelectiones [*sic*] in Epistolam Pauli' was written between 1515 and
1530 at Lérins; Bibl. Laur. Florence, Ashburnham 1833, 156ʳ, 161ᵛ.

[51] Armellini, *Bibl. Bened.-Cas.*, i. 14–15. *A. et C.* 4. P. Schmitz, *Histoire de l'Ordre de Saint
Benoît*, v. 156–7, though the details given by Schmitz are not always reliable. According
to Armellini, Ambrogio translated *Plura opera Santi Joannis Chrysostomi aliorumque
Graecorum Patrum*: I have not been able to find a copy of this work.

[52] Armellini, *Bibl. Bened.-Cas.*, appendix, 11. Simpliciano was professed in 1518. He
was an authority on Scripture, and was sent to the Council of Trent as an observer.

[53] Ibid. i. 159–60. Eusebio's writings include 'In mortem Domini Nostri Jesu Christi':
Chiari gave the same title to one of his poems.

[54] Ibid. i. 22–30. Angelo was the author of 'Quod in cruce Jesu sit gloriandum' and
other works on the same theme. See also Olgiato, *Epistolae*, p. 138.

[55] Armellini, *Bibl. Bened.-Cas.* ii. 23–7.

Chiari's letters to these men referred more and more frequently to the Bible and the Greek Fathers. He expressed enthusiasm for Giberti's 1529 edition of the Greek text of a book of Chrysostom, and shortly afterwards quoted the saint in Greek on a point of interpretation, and he begged Don Ambrogio to send him a copy of Chrysostom's *De Fato*.[56] Towards the end of 1529 he was making a number of passing references to Gregory of Nazianzus. His references to the Fathers are brief, but there are indications that he was meditating certain theological themes which were to emerge in his later writings. Late in 1527, in a letter to his colleague, Vitalis of Modena, he repeated the expression used in his commentary of 1526, describing the Cross of Christ as 'tanta Dei in nostrum genus beneficentia'.[57] A year later he wrote to Simpliciano de Quadris to ask him what Paul meant by the phrase 'God may give them repentance'.[58] Chiari did not elaborate his question, nor do we have the reply, but the question indicates his concern with the nature of grace and faith. One of his poems, although stuffed with classical imagery, managed to blend the Virgilian sense of *lacrimae rerum* with Pauline theology: man was vitiated by original sin, 'the years slip away, and life passes, and the only hope for a secure life lies in Christ who has rescued the human race',[59] whilst another poem described Christ as 'natus nobis . . . orbis terrarum spes'.[60] More significantly, Isidoro saw the salvation of man to lie in the love, wounds, and blood (*cruor*) of Christ, 'vitae fons . . . amans hominum . . . pulcher Jesus . . . noster amor'.[61] Similar sentiments occur in Chiari's last letter to the anonymous protagonist of Erasmus, who was reminded that 'Christ alone must be our comfort and our refuge'.[62]

[56] Olgiato, *Epistolae*, pp. 114–15, 125, 133. This Ambrogio was addressed as 'Ticinensis' that is, from Pavia. I can find no trace elsewhere of such a man: he was most probably Ambrose Ferrarius. Gian Matteo Giberti (1495–1543) was bishop of Verona from 1524.

[57] Ibid. p. 12. Chiari described the eucharist as a means of recalling this divine benefit to sinful man—precisely one of the themes of the sixth chapter of the *Beneficio*. See below, ch. 8.

[58] Ibid., p. 77. The reference is to 2 Tim. 2: 25.

[59] Ibid., p. 99, 'fugaces annos labi, solamque vitae solidae spem esse in servatore humani generis Christo Jesu.'

[60] Ibid., p. 96.

[61] Ibid., pp. 63–4. The letters are undated, but were probably written in late 1528 or early 1529.

[62] Ibid., p. 120, 'unum nobis solatium esse debet, atque perfugium'.

From other letters of May 1529 we learn that Chiari had written a work on predestination and the freedom of the will. Because the manuscript has vanished we do not know its argument, but may presume that it was not Protestant in substance because it was so highly praised by the Greek scholar Abbot Eusebius, who wrote that he found it pleasing and convincing and it confirmed his earlier high opinion and great expectations of Chiari.[62a] Furthermore, as we shall see, Chiari's later writings show that he took his teachings on free will and predestination from Chrysostom. What was special about this manuscript of 1529 (or earlier) is that it was the first known work of a Cassinese theologian to deal in detail with this fundamental question of the Reformation. For this reason it is particularly unfortunate that the manuscript appears not to have survived.

In the summer of 1533 Chiari was sent to Montecassino, en route to Rome as Cortese's assistant for the forthcoming commission of reform. At the same monastery at the same time there was another monk also named Isidoro; this was Isidoro Montauti, a Florentine, a scholar of Latin, Greek, and theology. One or other of the two men bearing the name Isidoro—it is not clear which one though Montauti is more probable—was delighted to be able to work in the ancient library crammed with Greek and Latin manuscripts, where he came across a copy of a work on Christian wisdom ($\lambda \acute{o} \gamma o s\ \alpha \sigma \kappa \eta \tau \iota \kappa \acute{o} s$) by St. Nilus, a disciple of Chrysostom. He translated the manuscript, working in great haste and under pressure because shortly he had to go on to Rome.[63] When he did so, he sent his manuscript to a

---

[62a] Olgiato, *Epistolae*, pp. 3–5, 107–8, 110–14. The MS was entitled 'De Libertate nostra e Praedestinatione'. The letter from Eusebius de Valentiis (Mutinensis) reads '. . . quam mihi valde placuerit, quamque animum expleverit, vicit porro, quae mihi de te semper maxima fuit, opinionem, atque expectionem meam' (p. 111).

[63] Martene and Durand, *Veterum Scriptorum*, col. 85, 'in loci illius biblioteca quamplurima opera tum graeca tum latina . . . quae voluntati meae satis abundeque facere . . . legi et relegi diligenter . . . e graeco latinum feci'. Nilus of Ancyra (sometimes confused with Nilus of Sinai) was a fifth-century exegete in the literary and historical style of Antioch, and the author of several moral and ascetical treatises. Armellini, in *Bibl. Bened.-Cas.* ii. 57, 60–1, and *A. et C.* 65–6, is certain that Montauti was the translator and that the attribution to Chiari is an error. The handrwriting of the MS (Bibl. Naz. Florence, Conventi Soppressi, D.8.2778) is different from Chiari's hand in the MS of his commentary on 1 Corinthians (1526). It is quite possible that Montauti too was sent to Rome at this time, for, according to Armellini, he was adept at handling high negotiations: his translation of an oration of Gregory of Nazianzus is in the Bibl. Apost. Vat., Vat. Lat. 4712.

colleague at the Badia in Florence, Don Ambrogio of Ferrara, the translator of several works of Chrysostom and other Greek Fathers. In a covering letter which reflected the perennial lament of busy scholars, he apologized for the hasty translation which he had intended to put aside, but now offered to Ambrogio and his students for the sake of its doctrine: 'When I heard that your students were strongly pursuing philosophic studies I changed my mind . . . indeed out of the doctrine of Nilus they will make much better and happier progress than they have so far with the works of Aristotle.'[64]

It is not difficult to see why St. Nilus appealed to him. Nilus began with a comparison between sterile academic philosophy and true wisdom gained from Christ—'Christus verus sapientiae doctor'—to whose grace and humanity men must turn for their salvation.[65] Then Nilus continued in Pauline terms to describe how men turn to Christ and become crucified to the world which they renounce, and so conform and fashion themselves ('effingere atque efformare') to the exemplar furnished by the apostles. In his new life the Christian must be prepared to accept difficulties, affliction, anguish, molestation, and persecution; he must avoid giving a bad example to others, eschew litigation (2 Tim. 2: 24), sin and greed (1 Cor. 6: 15), be generous (Mat. 5: 40), live by the word of God (Mat. 4: 4), engage himself in godly, not wordly, conversation, be attentive to the worship of God ('quid sit Dei cultus'), and keep pious thoughts always before him.[66]

The Greek saints' pattern of salvation, with its careful exegesis of St. Paul, its emphasis upon the grace and humanity of Christ, and inward conversion followed by mortification and renunciation, left its mark upon Chiari's later writings, as we shall see shortly. It may have made its mark on other Cassinese writers

---

[64] Martene and Durand, *Veterum Scriptorum*, col. 85, '. . . cum me tempus deficeret, nam prope diem discedere, et Romam venire cogebar . . . at ubi audivi filios tuos in philosophiae studia summis viribus incumbere, mutavi sententiam . . . ex ejus profecto doctrina multi melius ac multo felicius proficient, quam ex Aristotelicis libris hactenus profecerint.' The letter to Ambrose was written from Rome, 18 Sept. 1534. In the MS it can be seen that originally Isidoro had written 'Aristotelicis libris hactenus salemur', but he then deleted 'salemur', because he realized he had made an error. Ambrogio was professed in Venice in 1522. For the high regard in which he was held by Pietro Aretino see below, ch. 5.

[65] Ibid., cols. 87, 126.

[66] Ibid., cols. 91, 94, 123.

too, for Nilus's tract is a description of living faith similar to that set out a few years later in the *Beneficio di Cristo*: the dependence upon grace, the turning to Christ, the signs and fruits of conversion, the mortification of the flesh, the burdens of persecution, and the restoration of the image of God, all linked by a catena of brief biblical expositions.[67] The similarities are sufficient to suggest that this Greek tract was another contribution to that stream of Pauline piety which characterized Cassinese theology.

Meanwhile Teofilo Folengo had just published a poem which was, in effect, a summary of the pattern of salvation that we have seen to be characteristic of the Congregation. In 1527 the Folengo brothers had sought readmission to the Congregation. They were asked to prepare themselves with a period of meditation, and Teofilo to write a religious poem. The two brothers lived alone in an abandoned monastery on the Sorrento peninsula, where Giambattista studied Hebrew and began preliminary work on his biblical commentaries, whilst Teofilo wrote his peom, *L'umanità del Figliuolo di Dio*. The poem, dedicated to the monks of San Benedetto Po, was published at Venice in August 1533, a few months after they had returned to that city and eight months before they were welcomed back into the Congregation.[68]

The central theme of the poem is stated in the preface, 'la somma benignità di Dio verso di noi'.[69] The theme is developed along the lines already sketched out in *Caos del Triperuno*, beginning with an account of original sin and the misery of man. Sin was described as the 'ancient poison' ('invecchiato veleno')[70] which has alienated 'lost mankind' from God:

> From the time that Adam's covetous teeth
> Bit the forbidden apple, and into exile he
> Was thrust amid the misery of this vale
> And all of us do follow in his trail.[71]

---

[67] See below, ch. 8.
[68] There is a critical edition, *Opere italiane*, ed. U. Renda, Scrittori d'Italia, ii (Bari, 1911). Extracts are taken from this edition.
[69] *L'umanità*, p. 5.
[70] Ibid. 4.128.
[71] Ibid. 2.5:

> . . . la perduta gente . . .
> dal tempo che d'Adam l'ingordo dente

Adam's sin had brought to mankind not only alienation from God, but also the penalty of death: moreover, a man's mortality vitiates his personality and inclines him to sin:

> ... Death, that now o'erpours
> The human race a deathly shade
> So that you neither look to heaven, nor it conveys
> Its will to you in heart and mind
> But so great the thrall of tomb and death
> That few men are holy, most are brutish.[72]

Beneath outward happiness, the fact of mortality creates in men an inward despair, aggression, and disorder.[73] This concept of sin as primarily a symptom of broken and corruptible human nature we have encountered in other writers of the Congregation.

The next step in Folengo's pattern of salvation was the proposition that man not only lives in a state of mortality and misery, but is, moreover, trapped in that state. He had 'been made a citizen of heaven', but is unable to attain heaven.[74] At this stage Folengo, like Congregational writers before him, described how man was unable to save himself through obedience to the Law of God. Men obey the Law 'with fear and in servile homage', but underneath, men's hearts were still sinful.[75] Nobody on earth could be reckoned a just man, and it is not possible for sinful man to justify himself, so that in the Law there is only condemnation, and the Law is therefore 'that harsh and haughty Law ... that unrewarding and ruinous tyranny'.[76] All that man could do was to confess his sinful state with fear and shame.[77]

> morse'l vietato pomo, che'n essiglio
> cacciollo di miseria in questa valle
> cui dietro andavam tutti per un calle.

[72] Ibid. 2.24:

> ... Morte ... ch'ora sovraspande
> ... a l'uman seme un ombra pestilente,
> accio non guardi al cielo, accio non mande
> ne suoi desiri a te ne'cor ne mente;
> ma tanti ella nel fondo tien sepolti,
> che belli sono i pochi, e brutti i molti.

[73] Ibid. 3.28. For Ottoni's use of this concept and its Greek origin, see below, ch. 6.
[74] Ibid. 1.20. The image of citizenship, taken from Phil. 3: 20, and also used by Augustine, was used later by other Cassinese writers, notably Chiari and Benedetto da Mantova.
[75] Ibid. 2.35.
[76] Ibid. 2.38; 6.77; 6.79; 7.87.
[77] Ibid. 6.79.

The rescue of man, said Folengo, was possible only by the action of God. This rescue was prefigured by Moses who raised up the serpent in the wilderness—a point which was to be made also by Benedetto da Mantova in 1543. The work of salvation could only be accomplished by the Cross:

> The Law and every prophet pass away . . .
> Neither prophecy nor Law could bring
> As his wounds did, so great a thing.[78]

The work of the Cross was at the heart of his pattern of salvation, and was set out in the opening verses of the first book: 'Christ chose to die and gave life to us', 'he broke the power of hell for us', coming, not as a stern judge, 'but as our brother, our friend and our servant'.[79] Salvation was a gift of Christ, and that gift had been the conquest of death and the cancellation of sins:

> By dying he shall kill Death
> And batter down the gates of hell . . .[80]

Thus Folengo's description of sin was in terms of man's mortality which vitiates the personality, and his description of salvation was in terms of rescue from mortality. Folengo made it quite clear that salvation was a gift, 'the gift that comes from heaven', 'so great a gift', a 'beneficio' given by God because 'so great is the love [his] goodness possesses'. Folengo not only called the Cross a 'beneficio', but again like Benedetto da Mantova, who wrote ten years later, he also spoke of the gift being offered 'with open arms'.[81]

The next stage in his pattern of salvation was man's recognition of his own unworthiness. In contrast to those who

---

[78] *L'umanità*, 3.72–3:
> Passa la legge, passa ogni profeta . . .
> nè di profeta nè di legge possa
> tant'è che le sue piaghe saldar possa.

Also see *Il Beneficio di Cristo*, ch. 2.

[79] Ibid. 1.1–2; 2.28; also 2.47; 2.125; 4.95.

[80] Ibid. 4.58:
> . . . muorendo anciderà la Morte
> e de l'inferno romperà le porte

Also 2.108.

[81] Ibid. 5.59: 'il duon che vien dal cielo'; 9.4: 'tanto duono': 8.80: 'vostro beneficio'; 2.125: 'tant'è l'amor che sua bontà possede'; 10.66: 'Pendea dal legno con le braccia . . .'. See also 2.25.

put their trust in the merit of their good works[82] man should know himself for what he is, 'a great sinner', and then weep and cry for mercy.[83] Contrition leads to faith, by which Folengo meant not intellectual faith, but a trust in the gift of the Cross. This was 'la fede candida e vivace'. He set down three distinct attributes of faith. First he described it as 'the full belief of the heart', which brings illumination to men.[84] Second, he saw good works as a product of the gratitude for the gift of salvation, and therefore as a constituent of the love which belongs to faith.[85] Third, the good works that are born of faith are nevertheless necessary for salvation, because they are the means by which human nature is restored to its pristine condition. This process Folengo variously described as healing, washing, restoring, and vivification—indeed 'vivo' was a favourite adjective—and Christ was repeatedly referred to as 'Il Medico' who restored men by curing the universal illness of 'invecchiato veleno'.[86]

Finally, Folengo emphasized the need to persevere in faith and warned against the dangers of ingratitude. The Jews, he said, had been 'hard and ungrateful to the Donor of such great blessings' and Christians must eschew such ingratitude.[87] In particular Christians were in danger of cutting themselves off from the gift of grace by reverting to the justice of scribes and pharisees, living 'come a giudei' and trusting in works.

> What greater guilt can fall upon man
> Then he should turn his back upon the grace of God?[88]

This theme, as we shall see, was to be pursued by his colleague Benedetto da Mantova in *Il Benefico di Cristo*.[89]

We have seen that Folengo's pattern of salvation was developed and elaborated in his poetry where it lies embedded as an example (albeit expressed in poetry) of Cassinese theology.

---

[82] Ibid. 5.81.
[83] Ibid. 1.6; 6.77; also 1.5; 5.80.
[84] Ibid. 5.25.
[85] Ibid. 4.114; 6.47; 5.33; 5.59; 7.58; 9.54.
[86] Ibid. 4.128; 7.34; 7.109; 10.39.
[87] Ibid. 3.10: 'duro, ingrato fosti al Dator de tanti beni'.
[88] Ibid. 10.63:
    Qual peggior colpa in uomo cader puote
    se poi la grazia volge a dio le spalle?
See also 6.77–8.
[89] *Il Benefico di Christo*, ch. 3.

The details of this pattern correspond with what we have seen was being written by monks of an earlier generation, and—as we shall see—continued to be written by his contemporaries. Folengo himself, in his introduction to *L'umanità*, acknowledged the influence of the older men of the Congregatio upon his religious writings.[90] We may conclude that when Folengo wrote of sin as death and described the miseries of corrupt fallen man, and man's inability to save himself by good works, and when he described salvation as the 'benefit of Christ' by which men are saved through faith alone, the faith consisting of strong belief and good works, that, without justifying man, restored him to this pristine perfection—in all these things he was voicing the principal teachings of the order in which he had been professed, and to which he sought readmission.

However, the theological pattern of Folengo's poetry does more than display congruity with past teaching of the Congregation. It provides, as we shall see in this chapter and the next, a link with the teaching of Folengo's contemporaries. In the writings of a number of these colleagues we shall see precisely the same themes as in Teofilo Folengo, but because his colleagues were scholars rather than poets they developed these themes in a systematic way to deal with the principal intellectual problems of the 1530s and 1540s. In a work of one of those colleagues, Luciano degli Ottoni, we shall be able to observe a particularly well developed example of Cassinese teaching and a clear demonstration of the source of the teachings found in Cassinese writers. Amongst these writers who expounded theologically what Folengo described poetically was Teofilo's own brother, Giambattista Folengo.

When the Folengo brothers rejoined the Congregation in May 1534, Giambattista published a collection of dialogues, *Dialogi quos Pomiliones vocat*, based upon the psalm *De Profundis*.[91] To some extent this work was a defence of their disgraced

---

[90] *L'umarità* pp. 3–4, '. . . non per altro che per ubbedire quegli onorati maggiori miei, Basilio, Teofilo, Leonardo, ed altri prudentissimi vomini . . . sedendomi pure ne la memoria quel loro spesse volte a me donato avviso . . .'

[91] The work was published, together with poems and 'Ianus and Paulum Ursinum' of Teofilo Folengo, under the title *Ioan. Bapti. Chrysogoni Folengii Mantuani Anachoritae Varium poema et IANUS* (In promontorio Minervae ardente Sirio, MDXXXIII). However, the place is fictitious, and the work was certainly published after May 1534, since it refers to the author's return to the cloister. It was probably published in Rome later in 1534.

brother, by now dead, and an attack upon those who had denigrated the Folengo family.[92] However, it was principally a work on salvation and the contemplative life, themes which were treated in a discursive and rhetorical manner as well as with detailed theological argument. In *Pomilione I* Folengo asserted that human nature was created good and wholesome, but was now fallen into total corruption, and unable to cleave to God, and in exile from God: man was, as it were, a shipwreck. Cesare Goffis gathered together these items of theological material and argued that, despite a certain prudence of expression, the work was doctrinally heterodox, and the beginning of what was to be even more heretical opinions, also 'expressed with obvious prudence'.[93] Similarly, he saw heresy behind Folengo's emphasis upon the Cross and upon salvation by grace and sincere faith ('fide nos servari, salutem dari gratuito') his denial of any saving efficacy in works, his emphasis upon the Gospel. These expressions, said Goffis, formed the kernel of his *Pomiliones*, which was to develop later into full heresy. Folengo's reservations about Luther's teaching ('perditione dulcis') and his introductory commendation to God of 'Dei Ecclesiam Haereticis circumventam' were interpreted as signs of his caution.

However, Goffis's conclusions are not entirely satisfactory, for there are two reasons for looking more carefully at the *Pomiliones*. The first reason is that its theological material was not new to the Congregation, but was the teaching which, as we have seen, existed within the order from the later fifteenth century. Throughout the work there was an emphasis upon St. Paul;[94] also upon the Fathers, Chrysostom, and Adamantius amongst the Greeks, and Jerome and Augustine amongst the Latins.[95] When Folengo made his central point on salvation he quoted from Chrysostom: 'Is it not a good message, declared Chrysostom, when both remission of sins and eternal life are promised?'[96]

---

[92] G. Billanovich, *Tra Don Teofilo*, p. 103.

[93] C. F. Goffis, *L'eterodossia dei Fratelli Folengo* (Genoa, 1950), ch. 2.

[94] In *Pomilione I* there occur the expressions '. . . dico igitur cum Paulo', 'Quod facunde in Paulo legimus . . .', and in *Pomilione III* a close knowledge of Paul is put into the mouth of Vittoria Colonna, 'epistolarum est mei familiaris Pauli volumen.'

[95] *Pomilione III*. Admantius was a theologian of the early fourth century, sometimes identified with Origen.

[96] *Pomilione IV*: 'Nonne bonum est nuntium, aiebat Chrysostomus, cum et remissio peccatorum et vita aeterna promittitur?'

Furthermore, Folengo followed his order's teaching when he expounded the nature of salvation. 'Salvation is a gift', he said, and went on to speak of salvation, not only as propitiation for sins, but also as the healing of wounded man and a rescue from the evils of death—themes expounded at length by Chrysostom.[97] Similarly, his references to the inadequacy of the Law and to the necessity of faith expressed the established piety of the Congregation, in which living faith expressed in works was seen as the agent of the renewal of man.[98] In the same way Folengo remained aware of the traditional monastic argument for withdrawal from the world which he was able to express with amusing vivacity.[99] Similarly, if we look upon his doctrine of salvation as an expression of monastic teaching we are able to take seriously his reservation about the Protestants. There is no need to look upon these as mere expressions of prudence: instead we may see them as rebukes to the Protestants for having parted from the Roman church, and an attempt to conciliate and entice them back to 'one doctrine; one church; one way, one temple, one baptism, one altar, and one love.'[100]

The other reason for setting aside Goffis's conclusion is that the work contains the names of certain colleagues whose views must have been perfectly well known to Giambattista Folengo. Because their teachings are known to us in some detail, we shall be able to use them to illuminate Folengo's teaching. Two colleagues, who were also friends, were Luciano degli Ottoni, an exact contemporary of Folengo, and Isidoro Chiari, about ten years younger.[101] In 1534, the same year in which Folengo finished *Pomiliones*, Chiari was engaged upon a lengthy manifesto addressed to the Protestants and setting out a basis for

[97] *Pomilione VI* '. . . fide nos salvari, salutem dari gratuito. Pretio magno comparatum esse hominem. a christi vulneribus vulnera nostra curari. deum factum hominem et eum ipsum advocatum, ac iudicem: fratrem demum benignissimumque propitiatorem . . . mortis nos a malis abducere.'

[98] *Pomilione VII*: 'Finis, inquit Paulus, precepti, est charitas de corde puro, conscientia bona, et fide non ficta. Amor, igitur, Evangelii est terminus.' Also 'Sapienter, igitur, Paulus nihil inquit ad perfectum adduxit lex. Sed unum plane ex lege et Evangelio factum esse, Cipryannus . . . expressit.'

[99] Ibid. 'Perturbationes quidem multae sunt (quis negat?) in curandis rebus domesticis, domi. Sunt molestiae coniugii, sunt filii haud raro inutiles, aut stulti saepe, sunt sexcenta alia tranquillitatem animi perturbantia.'

[100] Ibid. fos. F *VIII*–G *I*, include a sharp, personal attack upon Luther and his movement.

[101] *Pomilione I*. Also see Billanovich, *Tra Don Teofilo*, pp. 120–1.

doctrinal agreement. Folengo's few allusions to the Reformation are entirely in accord with the substance of Chiari's document—which we shall examine in detail in the next chapter—recognizing a certain validity in Reformed doctrines, but seeking to reconcile those doctrines with the teachings of the church of Rome. The other colleague mentioned was Ottoni, to whom *Pomilione I* was addressed: 'ad Lucianum monachum amicum'. In *Pomilione XII* Folengo referred to the need for man to be perfected, and declared to Lucianus 'What could be more miserable than our condition? What could be more sickly, more corrupt, than our will?'[102] Such sentiments should not be interpreted to be crypto-Protestant. On the contrary, the true nature and source of those ideas, which we have seen present for so long in the Congregation, will be revealed and demonstrated clearly in the next two chapters, above all, by that same friend of Giambattista, the scholarly monk Luciano, as he and others began seriously to grapple with the problems raised by the Reformation.

---

[102] *Pomilione* XII: 'Quid quaeso, Luciane, nostra conditione miserius? Quid nostro arbitrio infirmius, corruptiusque?'

V

The Nettle Grasped:
Chiari and Bornato

FOR most of the 1520s and the early 1530s the writers of the
Congregation had skirted around the theological problems
raised by Luther's Reformation. They had maintained their
biblical and patristic studies, but they did not bring their
Pauline theology of the cloister, with its Antiochene bias,
directly to bear upon the Pauline theology of the Reformation.

The first Cassinese monk to grasp the nettle was Isidoro
Chiari. In 1529 he had written his 'De Libertate nostra et
Praedestinatione': that manuscript is lost, but his next attempt
has survived, and indeed was a starting-point for the Congregation's effort during the next twelve years to clarify the issues of
the Reformation and to reconcile the protagonists. In September 1534 Chiari, by now highly regarded within his order,
was sent to Rome with Gregory Cortese, during the interreg-
num between the death of Clement VII and the election of Paul
III, when there was considerable hope that the new pope,
whoever he might be, would convoke a Council to mend the
divisions of Christendom. In this context, in 1536 and 1537,
Chiari wrote an appeal to the Protestants *Ad eos, qui a communi
Ecclesiae sententia discessere adhortatio ad concordiam*,[1] intended to
persuade Protestants that unity with Rome was both desirable
and theologically possible. Chiari was convinced that theologians could agree—a hope common and sanguine enough
when he wrote—but, he observed, discussion was now difficult
because the populace, and even some theologians, had misunderstood theological differences and had turned them into
slogans defended with such obstinate passion that legitimate

---

[1] There were two contemporary editions of the *Adhortatio*, one published in Milan in
1540, and another in Paris in 1545 and 1566. A critical edition was published by J.
Olgiato, *Isidori Clarii . . . Epistolae . . . Opuscula alia* (Modena, 1705), pp. 152–231. The
text was also published by F. Lauchert, *Die italienischen literarischen Gegner Luthers*
(Freiburg-im-Breisgau, 1913), pp. 433–51. Quotations are taken from the Modena
edition.

Christian debate had degenerated into faction and tumult. In religion the mob exhibited 'nothing except hatred and enmity, and zeal for change, and, in short, seeming to want to throw into confusion all authority and divine law.'[2] Intellectual confusion had been destructive of both men's souls and social order. Chiari begged the Protestant divines to consider whether ordinary people really understood their teaching on justification by faith alone: '. . . and do you think that ordinary people understand what you men when you argue, with such force, that the power of justification lies not in works, but in faith, and no sins, except unbelief alone, are able to damn a man, and that all sins may be overwhelmed in a moment by standing firm in faith . . .'[3] Whilst he knew that the Protestant doctrine of liberty from the Law certainly was not intended to encourage antinomian licence, Chiari believed that its theological subtlety ('quid sub hoc paradoxo sapientiae lateat') was being misunderstood, and in consequence 'peribit in tua admiranda scientia frater, pro quo Christus mortuus est.'[4]

To this point Chiari's voice resembled that of other pre-Tridentine Catholic humanists who called for understanding and reconciliation. But now, as Chiari turned to the doctrinal issues, the *Adhortatio* began to unfold as an exposition of Cassinese theology, here being applied to a specific and urgent task. First, he confirmed the authority of the Scriptures and the Fathers. Amidst doctrinal confusion, he said, the only way men could gauge the validity of their arguments was to submit them to the judgement of the church, but by this Chiari did not mean submission to the Curia; he meant the consideration of scholars.[5] Those scholars must be grounded in biblical knowledge,[6] and they must not stray from the ways of the Fathers ('longius a

---

[2] *Adhortatio* 167: '. . . nil nisi odium, inimicitias, novandarum rerum studium spiret, breviterque jus omne, et fas confundere velle videatur.'

[3] Ibid. 157: 'Intelliget vulgus scilicet, quid velles, cum omnes intendis nervos, ut doceas, non ad opera, sed ad fidem justificandi vim pertinere?, et nulla peccata, nisi solam incredulitatem damnare posse, omniaque scelera uno momento absorberi stante fide?'

[4] Ibid. 157, 175: The tone of another reproof suggests familiarity with Luther's *De Libertate*: 'Videte ne vestra haec licentia infirmis sit offendiculum . . . et peribit infirmus in tua scientia frater, propter quem Christus mortuus est' (162). This refers to the closing pages of *De Libertate* where Luther warns of the dangers of misunderstanding liberty and indulging in licence.

[5] Ibid. 166.

[6] Ibid. 171–7.

patrum moribus recessisse'), especially the Greek Fathers: the
three patristic authorities he mentioned were Basil, Gregory of
Nazianzus, and Chrysostom, whose teachings in respect of faith
and salvation he described as learned, excellent, and full of
helpful advice.[7] Adherence to biblical and patristic teaching
could yet mean that out of the present discord God 'might make
us one people'.[8] It was Chiari's intention to apply patristic
teaching, in particular the Greek Fathers favoured by his
Congregation, to the problems of western Christendom. The
fact that those Greek Fathers had long been a staple of
theological study within the Congregation enabled him to
discuss Protestant doctrines from a standpoint at once sympathetic and detached.

Chiari made it perfectly clear that he agreed with the
Protestants' condemnation of scholastic theology—a dislike
which the Dominicans in particular were later to reciprocate
with vehemence. He accused the scholastics of excessive concern
with definitions. It was bad enough, he said, that they were men
of 'puerile fallacies' and given to 'a vulgar dogfight of words',
but, much worse, their doctrines were irrelevant to spiritual
needs and divorced from the insights of the early church: their
religion was little more than 'abstrusam (Deus immortalis!)
philosophiam'.[9] When he came to the divisions between Protestants and Catholics, Chiari was much more perceptive than the
authors of the celebrated contemporary *Consilium de Emendanda
Ecclesia*. He brushed aside the matter of abuses and went at once
to the question of free will as the 'summa causa' and the 'cardo
rerum'. Thus Chiari was to concentrate upon those same
theological questions of the part played in salvation by God's
grace on the one hand and human effort on the other, which had
already been a concern of Congregational writers from at least
the 1480s.

His pattern of salvation began with the inability of sinful men
to save themselves. In vigorous language he condemned those
who thought that they could wipe out their own sins, or 'quod

---

[7] *Adhortatio* 166, 181: '. . . multa succurrisse credenda sunt . . . et praestantiora et
acutiora . . .'

[8] Ibid. 153: 'hodie unus tribus auferetur ex nobis'.

[9] Ibid. 182: '. . . sophistarum importunitatem, et curiosas disputationes, ac super-
fluas, nihilque aliud, praeter jurgia, et lites secum afferentes . . . pueriles fallacias, et
importunam verborum venationem . . .' See also 212–13.

magis insanum est', the sins of others, by human effort.[10] Chiari's Pauline bent was seen most clearly in his defence of monastic life against accusations that it was an attempt to justify self by works: he quoted unnamed authors with approval:

Behold God, I vow this manner of life to you, not because I reckon it to be the way to a just life and salvation, or the justification of sins: indeed this would alienate me from your mercy, it would abound in offence to Christ, my lord, for it would be to deny his merits . . . the lamb of God, who takes away the sins of the world, who washes all in his blood and justifies them. May I not so sacrilegiously reject your grace. I shall hope and trust that these are in him alone, and not at all in myself . . . certainly not in my vows and works.[11]

Chiari was quite clear that 'no human works were of such great merit in themselves that they could render a man just before God'.[12] He fully accepted that the Cross alone was man's way to salvation: 'let him have before his eyes always that blood of God's only son, which was shed for him . . . he knows this much—that all his justification comes from God and Christ.'[13] Therefore he wished only, like St. Paul, to proclaim 'testimonium Dei', that man is justified not by works, but by the grace of the Cross alone: by what he called 'the immense love of God towards us, which was declared in the gift of his son'.[14] This was the 'benignitas' of salvation:

That saving favour and kindness of God, our Saviour, has not appeared out of the good works which we do, but he has saved us out of his mercy, through the washing of regeneration and the renovation of the Holy Spirit which he has poured abundantly into our souls

[10] Ibid. 224.

[11] Ibid. 197: 'Ecce Deus hoc vitae genus voveo tibi, non quod aestimem hanc esse viam ad justitiam, et salutem aut justificationem peccatorum; hoc enim avertat a me misericordia tua; hoc in Christi domini mei redundaret injuriam, cum hoc sit negare ejus merita . . . agnus Dei, qui tollat peccatum mundi, in sanguine suo omnes lavet, et justificet. Non abjiciam tam sacrilege gratiam tuam; expectabo, et praesumam haec in ipso solo, nequaquam in me . . . nedum in vo(t)is & operibus meis.' I have read 'votis' for 'vobis' which is clearly a misprint.

[12] Ibid. 221: 'nulla quidem humana opera tam ingentis sua natura esse meriti ut justum reddant hominem coram Deo.'

[13] Ibid. 221–2: '. . . ante oculos semper habeat illum unigeniti filii Dei pro se effusum sanguinem . . . tantum novit, omnem sui justificationem a Deo et Christo ejus esse profectam.'

[14] Ibid. 180 and 204: '. . . immensam erga nos Dei charitatem in dato filio fuisse declaratam.'

through Jesus Christ, our Saviour, so that, justified by his own grace, we may be heirs according to the hope of eternal life . . .[15]

Thus in 1537 Chiari was expounding without equivocation the doctrine of salvation *ex sola gratia*.

Chiari adhered firmly to the Pauline doctrine that men were 'justified by grace that they might be heirs of life eternal' and argued that this required the exercise of free will and good works. He was distressed that the Reformers drew the conclusion that free will was now irrelevant to human salvation. He recognized the need to avoid the suggestion that 'we contribute in the slightest to our own redemption', but protested that none the less the saints and doctors of the primitive church insisted upon the necessity of works. Men have knowledge and will to be exercised in some way in respect of salvation: this was the 'germanus scripturae sensus': '. . . in innumerable places in scripture, God teaches, summons and exhorts, so that each one of us, to the best of his ability, should struggle, achieve and advance, lest he should let himself down and place his salvation in jeopardy.'[16] St. Paul himself, a champion of justification by grace, had said that each man would render account of his works: this was not to deny grace nor make Christ's death to no purpose.[17]

Then, what was the role of works in the plan of salvation? Chiari grasped the problem firmly. He argued, as Melanchthon had, that works did not merit salvation and they could in any way usurp the work of grace, but they were the necessary accompaniment and manifestation of faith. Therefore the prime task for contending theologians was not to dispute the means of justification, since the Bible and the Fathers agreed that it was the work of grace alone, but to define the nature of faith. Through an exegesis of the word 'faith', following 'superiorum

[15] *Adhortatio* 218–19: '. . . non enim ex operibus justitiae, quae nos fecerimus, apparuit salutaris illa benignitas, et humanitas Servatoris nostri Dei sed secundum misericordiam suam salvos nos fecit, per lavacrum regenerationis, et renovationem Spiritus Sancti, quem effudit in nos abunde per Jesum Christum Servatorem nostrum, ut justificati gratia ipsius haeredes simus secundum spem vitae aeternae.' This use of Paul (Titus 3: 5–7) is similar to that expounded later by Juan Valdés: see below, ch. 8.

[16] Ibid. 177: '. . . illis in locis, qui vix sunt numerabiles, quibus praecipit, invitat, adhortatur Deus, ut pro sua quisque parte enitatur, agat, progrediatur, ne sibi defit, salutis suae satagat . . .'

[17] Ibid. 220–1.

temporum exempla', the necessity of works could be established in a sense that would be acceptable to both Catholic and Protestant theologians.

Chiari's understanding of faith was the same as that seen in other Cassinese monks. Faith began as a response to the grace and goodness of God towards man. It was made up of belief and trust in 'benignitas Dei' and love, and it flooded into the soul in a manner which could only be described with similes from nature: '. . . it is like the blood, which, diffused through the various members of the body, brings life to those members.'[18] In this way faith vivifies man as a result of his conversion to the Cross. Flooded with faith, he performs good works as the outward expression of the inward *affectus* in his soul. This teaching was in substantial agreement with the doctrines of the Protestants.

However, Chiari also went on to assert another doctrine of good works. Like other Cassinese writers, he held that through perseverance in good works the human nature of man is returned to its original divine image. Therefore through works new life is fashioned by faith. The faith that accepts the saving grace of God is also the faith that restores man by a process of sanctification; man, 'liberated by the blood of Christ', responds with 'holiness and justice' undergoing a 'renovatio Spiritus Sancti'.[19]

Chiari set out this doctrine of therapeutic faith along lines similar to those of St. Nilus. Men should keep before them, 'ante oculos', day and night, divine things and not human ambitions. 'In carne extra carnem viverent', as had Christ and the disciples.[20] In this way the works of living faith became the

---

[18] Ibid. 224: '. . . illam esse veluti sangiunem, qui per singula corporis membra diffusus vitam eisdem membris subministrat.'

[19] Ibid. 199, 218–19: '. . . pio ejus cruore de manu inimicorum nostrorum liberati serviremus illi in sanctitate atque justitia.' Also see 181. There are similarities to the teachings of Melanchthon, who distinguished between imputed justice, 'favor Dei' (the benefit of Christ), and justice infused by grace through faith and the Spirit. He saw them as successive stages, beginning as an act of God and continuing as a process of sanctification. However, Melanchthon differed from the Cassinese and the Greeks on the question of free will. Calvin also, from the first edition of the *Institutes*, had a strong sense of man being renovated by the Spirit: see I. xiii. 14–15 (the Spirit as author of regeneration into incorruptible life); III. ii. 31–7 (faith is revealed in the heart by the Spirit); III. iii; IV. xvi. 25; IV. xvii. 1–10, 32–4. Calvin was familiar with Chrysostom from at least 1535: see *Calvin: Institutes of the Christian Religion*, trans. F. L. Battles, Library of the Christian Classics, xxi, xxii (Philadelphia, 1960), i. 18, n. 12.

[20] *Adhortatio* 202.

instrument of restoration to the *imago Dei*, that 'antiquum
bonum' which man would still possess 'nisi peccatum naturam
dissecuisset'.[21] Men ought to imitate closely the form of life of the
apostles and Christ as revealed in Scripture: 'These sorts of men
have clearly disclosed to human beings that they, inasmuch as it
was in their power to do so, recalled and restored human nature
(which was broken and shattered into unnumerable parts) to its
proper condition and to God . . . truly such men are reproduc-
ing nothing but the heavenly condition.'[22] Chiari did not go on
from this point, as his colleagues did, to give the practical details
of behaviour appropriate to living faith. He was to do so in other
works, but for the present his aim was simply to lay the
foundations of a theology that could simultaneously preach
salvation by grace and the way of sanctification, through the
operation of living faith and good works.

It would be tempting to read into Chiari's high doctrine of
faith signs of crypto-Protestantism, were it not for his trenchant
criticism of the Protestants. He disagreed with them on
predestination and the doctrine of faith. He argued that since
predestination had been much debated, from the time of the
Fathers to the present, it could not properly be required as an
article of faith. Moreover, predestination implicitly denied the
validity of free will, which was held by the Fathers, particularly
the Greeks, and most of all, it denied the universal efficacy of the
Cross: this was the same argument that Luciano degli Ottoni
was to advance in 1538 against predestination in his commentary upon Chrysostom's homilies on Romans.[23] We may
conclude that Chiari, so far from being a Protestant, drew his
teaching from the common fund of Cassinese doctrine, based
upon the Greek Fathers.

Similarly, the doctrine of faith as expounded in the *Adhortatio*,
although sympathetic to Protestant theology, did not draw
upon it, but upon teachings derived from the Greek Fathers.
Chiari was at pains to show that 'faith' was not mere belief,
because mere belief could be treated as a work by which

[21] *Adhortatio* 201.
[22] Ibid. 201: '. . . Apostolorum ac Domini formam vivendi accurate imitantur. Hi
vitae hominum aperte declararunt, se disruptam hominum naturam, et infinitas in
partes dissectam, quantum in ipsis est, rursus et ad se ipsam, et ad Deum revocare, atque
colligere . . . nullam hi profecto, nisi coelestem hic imaginem referunt.'
[23] Ibid. 171: See below, ch. 6.

salvation is achieved: '. . . anyone may therefore believe that he is justified for this reason, simply because he has believed, and ascribe it to the merits of his faith that he has merited salvation . . . he shall remain in the same mire when he assigns the reception of salvation to the greatest of the works, that is, to faith, and not to Christ himself.'[24] In other words, Chiari would not even have the doctrine of *gratia sola* compromised by 'faith', just as he would not have predestination compromise the universal efficacy of grace. On both grounds he rebuked the Protestants and showed himself to be more rigidly Pauline than they. Of course, in his own teaching 'faith' was not set in contrast to works, but included works: when he spoke of faith alone, he did not mean faith that alone, in contrast to works, merited salvation, but faith that was the only valid response to the 'benignitas' of God, and that, manifesting itself in good works, was the therapeutic instrument of restoration of man. Thus, although Chiari adhered to salvation 'by grace alone' and 'through faith alone', and was thereby able to appeal to the Protestants, nevertheless his doctrines were quite different from those of the Protestants. Instead, like other Cassinese writers, he took his understanding of St. Paul from the Greek Fathers of Antioch.

Chiari's doctrines of grace and faith also brought him close to the Lutherans in that he perceived priests to be primarily preachers and ministers of the sacrament: 'Let the chief duty of a priest be to see to it that the word of God is disseminated amongst the people, and let that tradition of our Saviour in the breaking of heavenly bread be preserved, so that it might be distributed amongst others.'[25] In this respect Chiari's doctrine resembles that of the only other Cassinese writers to deal with

[24] Ibid. 221: '. . . credant se Fide justificari: credat ergo aliquis, se ob eam causam justificari, quod crediderit, idque fidei suae meritis ascribat, quod salutem sit promeritus (ita enim fere, qui hominem fide justificari audient, interpretabuntur) . . . in eodem cum . . . haerebit luto, quando praestantissimo omnium operum, id est fidei, non ipsi Christo, salutem acceptam referet.' Later, Cranmer was to give the same warning against treating faith as a work by which salvation is achieved. Franciscus Belcarius Peguilio, bishop of Metz, saw the tract as being specifically anti-Calvinistic: he published the *Adhortatio* in his *Concio, sive libellus, adversus impium Calvini ac Calvin ianorum dogma etc.* (Paris, 1566).

[25] Ibid. 193-4: '. . . princeps sacerdotis munus sit, verbo Dei in populum disseminando operam dare, et in coelestis panis fractione servandus mos Servatoris, ut in caeteros fiat distributio.'

the subject, Faucher and Benedetto da Mantova, who also viewed the priesthood in terms of preaching and administration of the eucharistic elements. Moreover, Chiari, like the others, showed his underlying monastic theology, when he related both preaching and the eucharistic food to the process of healing and restoration of the *imago Dei*. In this respect, his eucharistic teaching, which may appear to be crypto-Protestant, reveals itself to be derived not from Protestant sources, but from common Cassinese doctrine based upon the Fathers of Antioch and specifically from Chrysostom on the priesthood.[26]

If Chiari was not a crypto-Protestant, neither did he belong to the school of *duplex iustitia* which flourished briefly, but vocally, in the 1530s and until the failure of the Colloquy at Regensburg in 1541. When Chiari asserted both salvation by grace alone and the necessity of good works, he was not saying that works have some justifying merit, *iustitia inhaerens*, which is supplemented by *iustitia imputata*. Nor was he saying that good works have justifying merit in so far as they are derived from Christ. Nor was he using a mere grammatical juxtaposition.[27] On the contrary Chiari did not see human righteousness in terms of justification at all: like Chrysostom, he saw it simply as the restoration of the *imago Dei*. Once again, we see that despite a great deal of common ground with the *spirituali* and numerous personal connections, the two groups were theologically different.

*

When Chiari finished the manuscript in 1537, he sent it to Contarini, who counselled against publication because of its veiled approval of Melanchthon's doctrine that works are necessary, not for justification, but as outward signs of faith—a

---

[26] See *Il Beneficio di Cristo*, ch. 6, lines 145–63; for Faucher on the priesthood, see below, ch. 7. Neither Chiari nor other Cassinese writers questioned the nature of priestly ordination. Their view of the priesthood clearly follows Chrysostom's *De Sacerdote* on personal sanctity (Book 2), on the sacramental function (Book 3), and on pastoral care and preaching (Books, 3, 4, 5).

[27] The distinction between Cassinese teaching and *duplex iustitia* is explained in chapter 6 below, on Luciano degli Ottoni. For the formula of Bucer and Witzel at Leipzig in 1539, see P. Matheson, *Cardinal Contarini at Regensburg* (Oxford, 1972), p. 8. For the grammatical juxtapositions of Sadoleto see R. M. Douglas, *Jacopo Sadoleto*, pp. 84–6. For the views of Contarini and Pole, see D. Fenlon, *Heresy and Obedience in Tridentine Italy: Cardinal Pole and the Counter-Reformation* (Cambridge, 1972), esp. ch. 3.

position which, as far as it went, was in accord with Cassinese teaching. On the other hand, Chiari's fellow monk, Cortese, was much more appreciative of the arguments and believed that the 'bellissima' *Adhortatio* would resolve the religious conflicts. More than two years later the doubts were put to one side and the work was published in Milan in 1540.[28]

Chiari was not alone in his bold approach to these issues. Marco da Cremona, now growing old, was publicly expounding the biblical texts which he had been studying for forty-five years.[29] In 1535 Reginald Pole saw large crowds being drawn out of the city of Padua and down to the monastery of Santa Giustina to hear his 'powerful and eloquent' preaching upon the epistles of St. Paul.[30] The following year Pole again spoke of his teaching with admiration: '. . . there is no one to whom I more readily listen when he discourses on divinity, as on no subject does he speak more willingly, so that when I hear his words, and those of his companions, who are imbued with the same spirit, I hear nothing but the praise of God.'[31] Pole's words confirm that Marco was not a lone voice, but saying the same things as his brethren. A letter of Contarini, written on 12 June 1537, praised Marco for his success in exciting even the students in a university generally hostile to theology. However, there were others, more zealous than learned, who 'opposed everything he preaches and teaches concerning the greatness of grace and concerning human weakness': they believed him to be a Lutheran and they opposed him with 'vehemence and hot spirit'.[32]

[28] F. Lauchert, 'Der italienische Benedictiner Isodorus Clarius und seine Schrift für den religiosen Frieden', *Studien und Mittheilungen aus dem Benediktiner-Orden*, xxviii (1908), 613–17. Cortese's letter to Chiari was written at S. Benedetto Po, 24 Apr. 1540, *Gregorii Cortesii Cardinalis*, i. 129; see also 132–3.

[29] See above, ch. 2, pp. 48–9.

[30] Armellini, *Bibl. Bened.-Cas.* ii. 90, 'Cum Patavii D(ivi) Pauli Epistolas interpretaretur, frequentissimi ex urbe Auditores ad eum audiendum confluebant ob eximiam nimirum in dicendo vim et efficaciam, miram cum eloquentia et eruditione conjunctam.' Also *Epistolae Reginaldi Poli S.R.E. Cardinalis et Aliorum ad Ipsum*, ed. A. M. Quirini, i (Brescia, 1744), 298. Also see G. de Leva, *Storia Documentata di Carlo V* (Venice, 1867), iii. 344–5.

[31] *Epistolae Poli*, i. 477–9. 'Est enim hic mecum, et fuit jam viginti totos dies Marcus Monachus, qui me etiam huc secum adduxit, quem cum ego libentissime de divinis rebus loquentem audio, tum vero nihil est, de quo ipse libentius loquatur. Quare, cum hujus verba, et comitum ejus, qui eodem spiritu praediti sunt, nihil praeter Deum sonantia audio . . .', letter to Giberti, 10 Aug. 1536.

[32] The letter is quoted in A. Stella, 'La Lettera del Cardinale Contarini sulla Praedestinazione', *Rivista di storia della chiesa in Italia*, xv (1961), 412.

But all this does not mean that Marco was preaching Lutheranism. Any man who preached eloquently in Padua from St. Paul upon divine grace was bound to be suspected of heresy, but in view of his youthful study of St. Paul and the Pauline themes commonly found in Congregational writings, it is most probable that Marco had long ago derived his teaching from within the cloisters in which he had lived for forty-five years or more, and he was teaching, as his brethren taught, that the works of men do not earn salvation. Even one of the Congregation's strongest critics, the scholastic Zanettini, associated the teachings of Marco with those of the other Cassinese monks, particularly Don Luciano Ottoni, whose writings we shall consider shortly.[33] Moreover, it has been established that when Pole encountered and was deeply influenced by the biblical scholarship of Chiari, Cortese, and others at the Congregation's Venetian and Paduan houses in the last months of 1534, at the centre of this influence was Marco, whom Pole himself believed to have 'nurtured him in Christ', with his teachings on grace and works.[34] From the testimony of these two men, one a hostile critic and the other a disciple, and from Marco's personal history, we may conclude that Marco was expounding the same teaching on grace and works as his colleagues in the late 1530s, and indeed, the same teaching he had espoused for the long years of his profession.

At the same time the monastic life continued its steady round. In 1535 a monk at the Badia in Florence made a copy of the Rule and exposition of 1499, giving the prologue an even more Pauline flavour by inserting the word 'adoptivi', making the point that men may become the 'adopted sons' of God.[35] The

---

[33] A letter of Marco's critic, Dionysium Chironissa de'Zanettini, the Observant Franciscan bishop (il Grechetto), is printed in G. Buschbell, *Reformation und Inquisition in Italien um die Mitte des XVI Jahrhunderts* (Quellen und Forschungen aus dem Gebeite der Geschichte, XIII; Paderborn, 1910), pp. 261–2. Zanettini accused the Benedictines of heresy and, in particular, 'mi ricordo un domino Marco, monaco in Padova, stava in Sta. Justine lezeva nel suo monasterio publice, molto favorito del Cardinal Contareno e del Cardinal Polo': to Cardinal Sforza, from Trent, 13 Oct. 1546; Cortese referred to Zanettini in a letter to Contarini, 20 June 1537, *Gregorii Cortesii Cardinalis*, i. 120.

[34] Fenlon, *Heresy and Obedience*, pp. 30–1.

[35] Bibl. Naz. Florence, Conv. Soppr. C.4.2659. The anecdote of 1507 has already been described. Marginalia of the MS of 1499 were incorporated into the text of the MS of 1535. The insertion of 'adoptivi' into the prologue was on fo. 2ᵛ, 'Ma nota che se idio da potesta agli huomini d'esse suo [sic] figluoli adoptivi, non la da però se non ad chi crede nel suo nome.' The MS of 1499 was described above, ch. 2.

monks also exercised some sort of ministry to men outside the monastery, even to those with little appetite for theology. It seems that when the scholarly Don Ambrogio of Ferrara had met Pietro Aretino in Venice, he treated this notorious sinner and most anti-clerical of humanists with a generous courtesy, which, according to Aretino, was a reflection of the Congregation's teaching. He wrote to Don Ambrogio: 'Your kind breast was open to me the first day you saw me, and the reason was this: that in your mind reigned no trace of the friar, so well did you have it under control. For in the religion you follow and observe, there is no niggardliness.'[36] Aretino had a similar high regard for another Cassinese monk, 'the learned best and most reverend Don Onorato Fascitello, that shining light'.[37] As well as being a correspondent of Aretino, Fascitello was a familiar of Contarini, and Pole and his Viterbo circle, including Flaminio. His range of contacts and his learning show that Fascitello was a key man in the Congregation, well before he became a bishop in 1551, but because his writings consist chiefly of poetry given over to wit, classical allusions, and pious generalities, it is not possible to assess his theological beliefs.[38]

Much later, after his death, Fascitello was to be named by Alois as one who had secretly accepted the doctrines of the Reformation.[39] There is no evidence that he did so, and the fact that he was named by the unfortunate Alois in 1564 was probably a reflection of other, later, occasions when the strong Pauline bias of the Congregation aroused suspicions of Lutheranism. In 1536 other accusations were made, this time against Denis Faucher who was now prior of a small house attached to Lérins. There was very little substance to the charge, but the

[36] P. Aretino, *Lettere di M. Pietro Aretino* (Paris, 1609), i. 238ᵛ–9ᵛ. The translation is that of S. Putnam, *The Works of Aretino: Letters and Sonnets* (New York, 1933), pp. 232–4. For details of Ambrogio and his Greek scholarship see above, p. 90.

[37] Aretino, *Lettere* i. 239ʳ⁻ᵛ.

[38] Ibid. i. 239ʳ⁻ᵛ. Fascitello was born of a noble family of Isernia in 1502, and was professed in 1519, on his seventeenth birthday; Armellini, *Bibl. Bened.-Cas.* i. 231–4. His works, mainly poetry, were published in *Honorati Fascitelli Aeserniensis Opera*, ed. G. V. Meola (Naples, 1776). Selections are included in G. Minozzi, 'Onorato Fascitelli da Isernia: la Vita, le Opere', in *Monte Cassino nella storia del Rinascimento* (Rome, 1925), i. 193–294, esp. 208 ff. He was present at the Council of Trent and was made bishop of Isola by Julius III in 1551. He died in 1564. See also L. Primiani, *Note storiche-critiche su Onorato Fascitelli* (Campobasso, 1897). For an example of the connection between Flaminio and Fascitello see E. Cuccoli, *M. A. Flaminio* (Bologna, 1897), p. 73.

[39] Minozzi, op. cit., p. 216, n. 1.

following year the chapter-general of the Congregation renewed its prohibition, made in 1528, of 'libros lutheranos', and private or public discussion of their doctrines.[40] In view of the Congregation's biblical traditions and the monks' appreciation of Lutheran doctrines, it is not surprising that the order was more or less generally under suspicion, or that several monks, whose writings we shall study in later chapters, were directly accused of Lutheran heresy.

On the other hand, the monks' response to the questions raised by the Reformation simultaneously led to suspicions of the quite different, indeed the incompatible, heresy of Pelagianism. In 1537 Don Gregory Bornato wrote an account of the conversation he had had with his nephew in 1526, giving his account the title 'De libero arbitrio'.[41] In this work and presumably in the original conversation, Bornato tackled the problems raised by the Reformation. First, he argued the necessity of free will in salvation, against the teachings of the Protestants; in the second part of the work he set out to reconcile the necessity of free will with the Pauline teachings of Romans 7 on the inadequacy of the will; in the third part he defined the nature of predestination.

In view of the reception given a similar work published in 1538 by his colleague, Luciano degli Ottoni, it is almost certain that Bornato's work was suspected of being heretical, apparently Pelagian, and it circulated only in manuscript. Eventually, after Bornato's death, his family passed the manuscript back to the Congregation, and it was published in 1571 in a form that gives the impression of having been heavily amended by its editor, Don Cornelius Franciscus of Venice. Don Cornelius prefaced the publication with a long and vigorous defence of Bornato as a man learned in the Bible and in the Fathers, erudite, sensible—he was dean of his monastery in 1548—and pious in the Catholic faith. There was a list of eminent men with whom he had been on close terms—all men involved with the questions raised by the Reformation, Pole, Contarini, Marcello Cervini (Pope Marcellus II in 1555), Gian Matteo Giberti, bishop of Verona, Ludovico Beccadelli, former archbishop of

---

[40] *Opera Omnia*, 327–8; Lérins was restored to the Congregation in 1536. Leccisotti, 'Tracce di correnti etc.', p. 119.

[41] See above, ch. 4.

Ragusa. There was also the name of Don Chrysostom Calvini, the Greek scholar, Bornato's teacher for fifteen years, who was now, in 1571, archbishop of Ragusa. There were also letters from two patriarchs of Venice, from Quirinus, dated 8 April 1539, and from Barozzi, dated 20 September 1548, both of whom testified to the orthodoxy and erudition of the original manuscript.[42]

Since this manuscript has not survived, it is not possible to draw detailed conclusions about Bornato's teachings, but behind the editor's hand the main outline of the argument is clear, directed against those who 'with foolish temerity presume to deny the power of free will . . . [claiming] that man is able to contribute absolutely nothing to his eternal salvation'.[43] Bornato's point was that free will was necessary if men were to participate in the divine nature. He quoted from Augustine, Jerome, and Ambrose, but he gave particular praise to quotations from the Greek Fathers, Chrysostom ('magnus ille Chrysostomus'), and Gregory of Nazianzus ('vir ille summus'). Indeed, to this point in the book, the argument was in effect a brief summary of Chrysostom's teaching, especially in the homilies on Genesis and the Gospels of Matthew and John, concerning the freedom of the will to accept salvation and to work towards participation in the divine nature.[44] Then followed an elaborate and lengthy analysis of the nature of the will's freedom, in Aristotelian and Thomist terms. Since scholastic arguments were quite uncharacteristic of the Congregation, and since they add nothing to the preceding argument, it seems probable that the passage was added in 1571, in order to put the Greek teachings on free will—suspected of Pelagianism by many scholastics—in a more orthodox light.[45]

An argument closely resembling that of Chrysostom was also used in the second part of the book in which the necessity of free

---

[42] The history of the conversation of 1526 and the MS of 1537 is given in the volume published at Brescia, 'apud Jacobum Britannicum', in 1571, under the title *De Libero Hominis Arbitrio. Opus vere Aureum pium et Catholicum.* The preface is on fos. 2^r–9^v. For Luciano (degli Ottoni) see below, ch. 6. There is a copy of Bornato's book in the British Library (3833 aa 38).

[43] Bornato, *De Libero* 10^v; also 11^v, 13^v–14^r.

[44] Ibid. 14^r–21^v. The preface includes a passage of similar praise of John Chrysostom, implied in a reference to Don Chrysostom Calvinus, then Archbishop of Ragusa.

[45] Ibid. 12^v–32^v. (The reaction of scholastics to the supposed Pelagianism of Luciano degli Ottoni's translation of Chrysostom in 1538 is discussed below, chs. 6 and 9).

will was reconciled with Pauline teaching on grace. Original sin, said Bornato, was inherited from Adam as corruption of the flesh, suffering, and eternal mortality. Nevertheless, human will remains free, and upon each man, not upon Adam's guilt, lies the responsibility for each man's salvation.[46]

The third part of the book, on predestination, again follows the Fathers on Antioch. Bornato expounded Romans 9: 12, saying that salvation depends upon God's grace, his 'bonitatis excellentia', and not upon human work or merit. It would be blasphemy, he said, to assert that God predestines some to salvation and others to damnation, for God hates nothing that he has made.[47] On the contrary, according to Bornato, God wishes all men to be saved: 'Christ calls all men to himself, invites all, bestows his riches upon all, excludes nobody from the gift of salvation, neither Jew nor barbarian, nor Scythian nor Sarmation, not slave nor free man . . .'[48] Thus men are predestined primarily in the sense that all men are intended to be saved. If a man is prepared to accept that destiny, and become a son of God, and participate in the divine nature, then he fulfils his predestined salvation.[49]

Bornato's teaching on sin, universal predestination, the gift of grace, the necessity of free will, and the restoration of human nature to give participation in the divine nature, all follow the teachings of his order: they also follow, as we shall see in greater detail in the next chapter, the doctrines of St. John Chrysostom, as set out in his commentary on Romans. The resemblances are so strong that we must set aside the recent findings of Prosperi and Ginzburg who, observing what appears to be the Pelagian elements in the book, believed the work to be a combination of humanist sentiment on the dignity of man and common pastoral emphasis on the goodness of God, expressed in terms of negative theology, that is, without regard to precise doctrinal formulation.[50] Instead, the evidence points to Bornato's work having

---

[46] Bornato, *De Libero* 34ᵛ–36ʳ.

[47] Ibid. 47ᵛ–48ᵛ, 52ᵛ–53ʳ.

[48] Ibid. 48ʳ⁻ᵛ 'Christum omnes ad se vocare, omnes invitare, omnibus sua talenta largiri, neminem ab oblata salute excipere, non Iudaeum, non Barbarum, non Scytham, non Sauromatam, non servum, non liberum . . .' See also 49ᵛ–50ʳ.

[49] Ibid. 52ᵛ.

[50] The work is discussed by C. Ginzburg and A. Prosperi in 'Le due redazioni del "Beneficio di Cristo"', *Eresia e riforma nell'Italia del Cinquecento* Biblioteca del Corpus

belonged to the teachings of his own order, based predominantly upon the Greek Fathers of Antioch.

At the same time as the monks applied the Greek themes of
their theology to problems of the Reformation, other men whom
they had influenced began to do the same. Gasparo Contarini
had been a familiar of the monks from at least the time of his
'crisis', in 1510–11, and in those years had studied Greek under
Marco Masuro 'Greco di natione e di dottrina', and then
studied Chrysostom.[51] When Reginald Pole was in Padua, he
also studied Chrysostom, and with Thomas Lupset, searched for
manuscripts to send to Erasmus.[52] In view of what we know
about the Congregation's studies and doctrines and the monks'
active contact with men outside the cloister, and the enormous
influence of Don Marco upon Pole, we may conclude that it was
the monks who had guided Contarini, Pole, Sadoleto, and
others towards a study of the Antiochene Fathers. It appears
that some of these *spirituali* now followed the monks a little way
in the application of Greek theology to the problems of the
Reformation. In 1536 Sadoleto published his commentary on
Romans, an unsuccessful attempt to reconcile the primacy of
grace with the necessity of works. His argument employed the
device of double justification, but it included also Chrysostom's
concept of faith and works as an agent of the restoration of
human nature.[53] Another use of the Greek Father occurred in a
letter of Contarini, written at Easter 1537 to his friend Lattanzio
Tolomei. Contarini described sin as a sickness which required
healing by 'il medico', so that with healed free will, a
'convalescence' of sanctification would establish 'new life' in

---

Reformatorum Italicorum; Miscellanea, I (DeKalb and Chicago 1974), pp. 167–72.
These two historians believe the work to be an expression of humanist thought on the
dignity of man, combined with negative theology, owing little to Reformation or
Valdesian thought.

[51] L. Beccadelli, 'La Vita del Cardinale Gasparo Contarini', *Monumenti di varia
letteratura tratti dai manoscritti di Monsignor Lodovico Beccadelli* (Bologna, 1797), tome i, part
2, p. 11; G. della Casa, *Gasparis Contarini vita*, in *Opere . . . Giovanni della Casa* (Florence,
1707), pp. 100–1.

[52] M. W. Anderson, 'Biblical Humanism and Catholic Reform: 1444–1563'
(Aberdeen Univ. Ph.D. thesis, 1964) pp. 207, 211–14, 219–20.

[53] *Jacobi Sadoleti . . . in Pauli Epistolam ad Romanos Commentaria* (Lyons, 1535) in *Jacobi
Sadoleti . . . opera quae extant omnia* (Verona, 1737), iv. 172–4. Sadoleto's general interest in
Chrysostom is noted by R. M. Douglas, *Jacopo Sadoleto*, pp. 81–90, 265, n. 82. Douglas
suggests that Germain Brice, the French translator of Chrysostom, was not pleased by
Sadoleto's interpretation of the Father.

man. He then explained that the necessity of free will and works was not in conflict with the teachings of Paul and Augustine, for they had been obliged to denigrate works and emphasize grace in order to overcome the excessive confidence in their good works held by the Jews and the Pelagians.[54]

These applications of Greek theology to contemporary problems by acquaintances of the Cassinese were few and slight. But even as they wrote, there was about to emerge from the cloisters a detailed and thorough work which drew together the Antiochene themes of the Congregation and applied them to the Reformation debate. The author was Don Luciano degli Ottoni, the monk to whom Giambattista Folengo had addressed his rhetorical questions. In this chapter we have seen how Chiari and Bornato were the first members of the order to apply their monastic theology to the problems of the Reformation in the hope of clarification and reconciliation. In the writings of Ottoni we shall see the Congregation's theology brought to bear again, with more detailed scholarship and greater strength.

---

[54] A. Stella, 'La lettera del Cardinale Contarini sulla Predestinazione' *Rivista di storia della chiesa in Italia*, xv (1961), 411–41, esp. 427–33.

VI

The Monastic Teachings Clarified:
Luciano degli Ottoni

IN the late summer of 1507 Luciano degli Ottoni of Brescia had been professed a Benedictine monk of the Cassinese Congregation at San Benedetto Po, Mantua. He was one of a new generation of bright young scholars who entered San Benedetto in the early years of the century. Here Ottoni received the usual Cassinese education in Latin and Greek, the Bible and the Fathers. After his general education he specialized in the study of the Greek Fathers, particularly John Chrysostom, whose doctrines were to dominate his theology.[1]

It will be the task of this chapter to give an account of Ottoni's theology, to compare it with the teachings of his colleagues and to identify its sources. We shall see that his theology was a synthesis of the doctrine of the reconcilitation of man to God through grace and the doctrine of man's restoration to perfection through faith and works, which was a distinguishing characteristic of other Congregational writers, who employed precisely the same themes, arguments, and illustrations as did Ottoni. Moreover, his election in 1545 as the Congregation's spokesman at the Council of Trent indicates that the teachings in question were not isolated or aberrant examples, but represented accepted doctrine within the Congregation. Finally, Ottoni's works show beyond all doubt that his sources were identical to those of other Cassinese writers—entirely biblical and patristic, dominated by St. Paul as he was interpreted by John Chrysostom and the Fathers of Antioch.

The humanist cardinal Sadoleto, after a discussion with Ottoni, once told a common friend how much he had admired the monk's 'ingenium, singularemque doctrinam'.[2] The phrase

---

[1] M. Armellini, *Bibl. Bened.-Cas*. ii. 78. Carla Faralli, 'Per una biografia di Luciano degli Ottoni', *Bollettino della Società di Studi Valdesi*, cxxxiv (1973), 34–51.

[2] J. Sadoleto, *Opera quae extant, omnia ad Eloquentiam, Philosophiam ac Theologiam pertinentia* (2nd edn., Verona, 1737–8), ii. 130.

neatly sums up Ottoni's relations with other people. His 'ingenium' brought him friends and acquaintances, both inside the Congregations, whre he was on close terms with a wide range of fellow monks, and beyond the cloister where he was well known to Contarini, Pole, and other Italian proponents of reform as well as a number of laymen.[3] After he became abbot of S. Maria Pomposa in the territory of Ferrara, he gained the confidence and the patronage of Ercole d'Este, duke of Ferrara, for whom he acted as informant at the Council of Trent.

On the other hand, his 'doctrina singularis' attracted some formidable opposition. His only published book, of 1538, aroused the anger of Dominican scholars and eventually was prohibited. A manuscript which circulated at Trent was thought to be touched with Pelagian heresy and induced the emperor's theologian to send a memorandum to the president of the Congregation. Then, paradoxically for a man thought to be a Pelagian, Ottoni provoked the Fathers of Trent to uproar when he expressed apparently Lutheran ideas in a speech, and he was obliged to explain himself and affirm his orthodox intentions. In 1550 again he fell under suspicion when he appealed in person and in writing to the duke of Ferrara in an attempt to keep the heretical ex-monk Giorgio Siculo from the Inquisition and the gallows. It was this episode that led John Calvin to blame Ottoni for all the heretical excesses in Italy.[4] Meanwhile Ottoni's fellow Catholics remained antagonistic towards him. After his death in 1552 his book was placed upon the Tridentine index of 1554 and the index of Paul IV (1559), and the work so thoroughly suppressed that until recently it was thought that no copies had survived. In 1566 the Dominican Sixtus Senensis vilified the writings of 'this foolish and wretched

---

[3] Faralli, op. cit., pp. 40, 46–7. Armellini, *Bibl. Bened.-Cas.* ii. 78. Within the order his friends included Gregorio Cortese (professed 1507), Giambattista Folengo (1507), Denys Faucher (1508), Teofilo Folengo (1509), Benedetto Fontanini da Mantova (1511), and Isidoro Chiari (1517). His friendships covered a wide spectrum of temperament and teaching, from the cautious, conservative Cortese to Benedetto da Mantova and the rebellious Folengo brothers. In monastic politics he was friendly with Ignazio Squarcialupi, the autocratic president who sought to make the presidency a life appointment, and also with Don Ignazio's opponents: E. Menegazzo, 'Contributo alla biografia del Folengo', *Italia medioevale e umanistica*, ii (1959), 392–8.

[4] J. Calvin, *De aeterna Dei pradestinatione qua in salutem alios ex hominibus elegit, alios suo exitio reliquit, item de providentia qua res humanas gubernat* (Geneva, 1552), printed in *Opera Calvini*, viii (Corpus Reformatorum, xxxvi, Berlin, 1870), cols. 255 ff.

little man'.[5] In 1708 Richard Simon wrote a short essay in his defence, but was unable to find a copy of Ottoni's book or even a reference to its author in the libraries of Paris.[6] Thereafter his name and his teachings were virtually forgotten.

Ottoni's book, published in Brescia in 1538, was a translation from Greek into Latin of John Chrysostom's commentary on St. Paul's letter to the Romans. An edition of this work in the original Greek had been published at Verona by Matteo Giberti in 1529, at the same time that Erasmus was editing several other works of Chrysostom.[7] These publications were welcomed by Christian humanists who regarded highly the Greek Father's eloquent moral theology, in which they saw inspiration for church reformers and an antidote to scholasticism. Erasmus praised Chrysostom's emphasis upon charity, his labours 'in the service of Christian piety', and his 'evangelical philosophy'. However, although he lavishly praised the piety and morality, Erasmus confined himself to editorial scholarship, and made little doctinal use of Chrysostom's detailed treatment of the biblical themes of sin, grace, faith, and salvation. Even the ten prefaces he wrote for his editions of Chrysostom contain only passing references to doctrine.[8] Similarly Sadoleto, despite his

---

[5] Sixtus Senensis OP, *Bibliotheca Sancta* (Lyons, 1575), annotation 232, 'ineptus hic et miserabilis homuncio . . . Lucianus Monachus'.

[6] R. Simon (Mr de Sainjore), *Bibliothèque critique ou recueil de diverses pièces critiques* (Amsterdam, 1708), i. 351–61.

[7] Giberti was a humanist scholar and bishop of Verona. He set up the Nicolini brothers, Venetian printers, in his episcopal palace and furnished them with Greek type. In June 1529 they produced an edition of Chrysostom, in 1531 a volume of John Damascene, and in 1532 the patristic anthology of Ecumenio and Areta.

[8] *Desiderius Erasmus: Prefaces to the Fathers, the New Testament, on Study*, facsimiles, ed. R. Peters (Scolar Press, 1970), 'omnes cogit servire pietati Christianae', 'tanta charitatis suavitate condulcat', p. 93; '. . . de dogmatibus Evangelicae philosophiae . . .', p. 95; Erasmus was no more specific in his foreword to the collected works of Chrysostom published in 1530: 'vitae integritas, divinarum literarum amor, iudicii rectitudo, veritatis libera professio . . .' (pp. 153–4). See *Desiderii Erasmi Roterodami Opera Omnia* (Leyden, 1703–6), iii. 1331–46, 1432, 1862; v. 69, 434, 484, 785, 844, 856, 912; vi. 236, 346, 361, 672, 994–5, viii. 2–6; ix. 260. For some evidence of Chrysostom's doctrinal influence upon Erasmus see D. Gorce 'La Patristique dans la Réforme d'Erasme', *Festgabe Joseph Lortz*, i, *Reformation, Schicksal und Auftrag*, eds. E. Iserloh and P. Manns (Baden-Baden, 1958), pp. 233–76. M. W. Anderson has argued that the biblical theology of Erasmus was based upon Chrysostom; see his 'Biblical Humanism and Catholic Reform: 1444–1563' (Aberdeen Univ. Ph.D. thesis, 1964), pp. 145–9, 462–9. However, Anderson's examples are drawn from the later Erasmus, mainly the 1540 edition of the *Annotations*, and in any case are not sufficient to justify his belief that the theology of Erasmus has an Antiochene base. For Erasmus's appreciation of

veneration, barely used Chrysostom's doctrines at all, whilst Giberti himself regarded the commentary on Romans principally as a source of spiritual edification from which it was possible 'every hour to derive fresh blessings'.[9]

Since the Congregation had a long tradition of biblical and patristic scholarship, it was not surprising that a Cassinese scholar, too, should turn to Chrysostom. In particular, the Greek Father's systematic literal exegesis and his preference for St. Paul pleased these humanist monks, especially as he wrote with the eloquence and fervour favoured by Renaissance humanists. Indeed, Ottoni said that Chrysostom's style and his Pauline theology were the reasons he had chosen to translate him: 'I chose John Chrysostom out of them all . . . because he especially had a shining, clear, attractive, flowing, eloquent style, and I believe that he had drunk in and has poured forth the doctrines of Paul, that is, the most Christian of teachings.'[10]

Nor was it surprising that in contrast to Erasmus and others, the Cassinese scholar should concentrate upon doctrine, specifically the question of grace and works. As we have seen, both the problem and Chrysostom's theology had been known to the Cassinese monks for some time. There is considerable tension between St. Paul's doctrine of salvation by grace, with which they were quite familiar, and the strivings for perfection which is implicit in the monastic vocation. In the west after Augustine monastic theologians had always to face the problem of Augustine's sharp antithesis between grace and works. This problem had been an element in the protracted late medieval debate on justification and it was at the heart of the Reformation

Chrysostom's commonplace wisdom, see J. K. McConica, 'Erasmus and the Grammar of Consent', *Scrinium Erasmianum* (Leiden, 1969), ii. 77–99; also A. Prosperi, *Tra evangelismo e controriforma: G. M. Giberti (1495–1543)* (Uomini e Dottrine, xvi; Rome, 1969), pp. 217–20. Prosperi firmly denies that Chrysostom exerted substantial influence upon Italian *spirituali*.

⁹ R. M. Douglas, *Jacopo Sadoleto*, pp. 82 ff. Even when forced to defend himself, Sadoleto made little use of Chrysostom. Douglas, p. 82, quotes Gothein's scathing comment on the paucity of dogmatic material in Sadoleto's commentary. Giberti's remark was made in a letter of 1532, '. . . acquistare ogni hora beneficio nuovo', Prosperi, *Tra Evangelismo*, p. 220.

¹⁰ Preface: '. . . elegi autem ex omnibus Joannem Chrysostomum . . . quod is praecipue sermonem habet nitidum, planum, dulcem, fluentem atque copiosum, et sensus Paulinos, idest Christinaissimos . . . hausisse, ac effudisse mihi videtur.'

debate. During the fifteenth century the Congregation's intensive biblical studies had made the monks particularly aware of the problem. However, Chrysostom had a synthesis of Pauline theology and monastic practice, as the monks well knew, and when Ottoni chose Chrysostom's commentary on Romans, a most apposite work for the purpose, his intension was to defend that synthesis. This his title plainly indicated: *The Commentary of Saint John Chrysostom upon the Apostle Paul's Letter to the Romans: interpreted by Luciano of Mantua, monk of Saint Benedict, with a defence against those who suspect and accuse Chrysostom of having diminished divine grace and having unduly exalted free will.*[11]

Chrysostom's commentary on Romans consisted of thirty-two sermons which covered line by line the sixteen chapters of Paul's epistle to the Romans. Ottoni made a fluent translation into Latin and in order to emphasize the practical moral conclusions he inserted the subheading 'moralia' at the appropriate place in each sermon. He also inserted his own comments in the form of *interpretes*, which varied in length from a few lines to several pages. They were not evenly distributed through the book, for several homilies have none, whilst others have numerous and lengthy *interpretes*. It was the procedure of a man who wished only to draw out and develop certain themes. The themes he considered were those relevant to 'the difficulties and doubts of our times', that is, those that would enable him to render the 'hitherto mutually exclusive' doctrines of grace and works 'harmonious and coherent'.[12]

The intention to defend Chrysostom by demonstrating that his theology 'preserved human liberty, yet in no way diminished grace', took Ottoni into the centre of the Reformation debates.[13] Attempts to argue that the works of human nature could

[11] *Divi Ioannis Christostomi in Apostoli Pauli Epistolam ad Romanos Commentaria; Luciano mantuano divi Benedicti monacho interprete, et in eos, qui eundem Chrysostomum divinam extenuasse gratiam arbitriique libertatem supra modum extulisse suspicantur, et accusant, defensore* (Brescia, 'in aedibus Ludovici Britanici'). Three copies are known to have survived. Two are in Rome: Biblioteca Vaticana (R.G. SS. Padri II 38), from which material has been drawn for this chapter; Biblioteca Casanatense (B.V. 46); one in Paris, Bibliothèque Mazarine (fil. 1070).

[12] e.g. Sermon 4, a vivid homily on purity and concupiscence and the reform of manners, has no *interpretes* at all. His chosen themes, stated in the preface, were predestination, grace, faith, free will, and works, '. . . mutuo tollere videbantur: ita nunc adeo concinnata, et cohaerentia, sunt facta'.

[13] *Commentoria* i^v: '. . . si totum gratiae ascribatur libertatem humanam asservit; nec tamen quicquam gratiae derogavit . . .'

postively contribute to a man's salvation were liable to fall under suspicion of weakening the doctrine of prevenient grace. For this reason the revival of Chrysostom's works was treated with reserve, both by Catholics, especially Thomist Dominicans (who had their own doctrine of salvation as the fulfilment of an interlocking process of grace and human nature, the former arousing and shaping the response of the latter, as man develops and fulfils his innate nature), and by Protestants (who attributed no saving value to human nature at all). Of course, due deference was paid to a saint and Father of the church, but Ottoni, as his modern champion, could expect only to be attacked on several sides.

Ottoni began with aggressive defence. In his preface he asserted uneqivocally that Chrysostom adhered completely to the teachings of St. Paul, which were at the heart of the Bible, and that he himself followed Chrysostom. His fellow monk, Teofilo Folengo, contributed a foreword in which he too praised Paul's epistle to the Romans, 'most profound of all his epistles', for its exposition of God's love for man; then he praised Chrysostom, 'most eloquent of the doctors', 'nourished in Pauline teaching from his youth', for his sure and sound exposition of Paul. Giambattista Folengo appended a short poem which began 'O quam aliis supra est Aura hoc insigne Metallis' ('Amongst metallic elements there is none that matches Gold'). Thus, these three Cassinese monks esteemed John Chrysostom as pre-eminent amongst the Fathers for his exposition of Paul.[14]

Ottoni's own exposition of Paul, like that of Chrysostom, had its starting-point in the doctrine of fallen man. Since Augustine, western theologians had held that in consequence of Adam's original sin the whole human race has inherited Adam's guilt, and furthermore, has lost the ability to lead sinless lives. Therefore man faced a double condemnation, on account of his inherited guilt and also the guilt of his continuing unrighteousness. Accordingly, the path to salvation was understood in terms of gratuitous remission of guilt, and after that the attainment of a state of justice, either imputed or actual. However, Ottoni,

---

[14] Preface. Ottoni also acknowledged Giberti's assistance with various textual problems. The work was dedicated to Giambattista Speciano, 'generali justitiae capitaneo in statu Mediolani, imperalique senatori ac consiliario benemerito'.

following Chrysostom, denied the premiss that men inherited guilt because of Adam's fall:

> no man is condemned, except for his own great guilt, and not merely out of the sin of his first parent.[15]

Chrysostom teaches that original sin does not mean guilt in us, as our doctors teach, but penalty; as if maintaining that it would be quite absurd were the sin of one man to make other men sinners.[16]

The penalty of the fall was not guilt inherited from Adam, but alienation from God and mental and physical corruption, starkly summarized in Ottoni's phrase, 'sufferers, and alienated and exiled from God'.[17] Because the idea is repeated, not only in Ottoni, but also in other Cassinese writings, notably in the opening lines of the *Beneficio di Cristo*, it will be useful to quote Chrysostom's words on this point as they were translated by Ottoni: '[man's] body became mortal and passible and received very many physical infirmities, and so became more sluggish and disobedient.'[18] In short, the consequence of the fall was to deprive man of his original perfection, so that he became mortal and liable to suffering.

Human sin was the consequence of mortality and alienation, for they engendered fear and anxiety, which in turn crippled free will: as if in a sickness, men fell into unjust and evil behaviour, which in turn drove them further into exile: 'we have been born mortal, which implies our being subject to illness and disorder, being prone and inclined to evil, and finally our being enemies of God, rebels and hence damned and exiled from him.'[19] Fallen man is caught in the 'tyranny' of death and sin

---

[15] *Commentoria* 22[r]: '. . . ex omnibus neminem condemnare, nisi ex eorum magna et propria culpa: non ex solo primi parentis errato'. Also 19[r]. This is a fundamental distinction between western and eastern orthodox theology. See J. Meyendorff, *Byzantine Theology: Historical Trends and Doctrinal Themes* (New York, 1974), pp. 143–6. Chrysostom also described mortality as a 'divine remedy' for fallen man, especially in his *Homily on Genesis III*, 18.3. This description does not occur in any later Father, and the Congregation's writers only hint at it.

[16] 42[r]: 'Chrysostomus peccatum originis, in nobis, non culpam, ut nostri doctores, sed poenam asserit esse, tanquam absurdum existimans, si ex unius peccato, alii peccatores efficiantur.'

[17] 77[v]: 'patabiles ac a Deo alienos et exules'.

[18] 49[r]: 'eius corpus mortale factum est et patibile ac plurimos inde morbos accepti, unde et ponderosior et effraenatior.'

[19] 42[v]: 'mortales geniti sumus, q(uo)d morbis et perturbationibus subiecti, quod proni ad malum atque proclives effecti quod denique Dei hostes atque rebelles et damnati et exules ab eo inde eramus . . .'.

which had 'penetrated' the human race in consequence of the fall.[20] The point of this analysis of the fall was that the human condition was not primarily one of guilt and condemnation, but rather one of mortality and damage, so that salvation required rescue from death and restoration of integrity, rather than forensic justification.

The next step in Ottoni's commentary was that man is unable to save himself, nor can his own efforts earn the grace of God to free him from death. Not even strict obedience to the commandments of the Law, given by God to the Hebrews and ultimately to all men, could confer the grace of salvation. On this point Ottoni stayed close to St. Paul. He criticized those theologians who wished 'to oppose Paul diametrically, as they say', and to attribute grace to obedience to the law: 'they try to prove that it has the power to confer grace'.[21] By his belief that man was impotent to merit his own salvation, Ottoni adhered firmly to Paulinist teaching and rejected Pelagian ideas of salvation through works.

In particular, argued Ottoni, those who sought salvation through obedience to the Law misunderstood the functions of the Law, the true purpose of which was set out by St. Paul in Romans 3: 19–20 and 7: 7–13. The first function of the Law was to teach man that he is enclosed by fear and death, and to teach him the nature of sin, so that man may be corrected 'as if in a kind of school'.[22] However, the Law has a second function, in that the knowledge of sin which it gives to men increases the culpability of their offence. Therefore in a sense the Law actually increases sin and condemnation. Chrysostom developed this Pauline theme,[23] and Ottoni followed, saying that it was the function of the Law, not to lessen sin ('peccati regnum diminuere'), but to increase it: 'Paul said that the Law entered in so that the offence might be greater, and Chrysostom

---

[20] 40[r–v]. For Teofilo Folengo's use of this doctrine in 1533, see above, ch. 4.

[21] 25[v]: 'ex diametro (ut aiunt) Paulo repugnare . . . probare nituntur, eam tantae potestatis fuisse; ut gratiam conferat.'

[22] 42[r]: '. . . tamquam in scola quadam '.

[23] 49[v]. An English translation of the relevant Greek passage is to be found in *The Homilies of St. John Chrysostom . . . on the Epistle . . . to the Romans*, tr. J. B. Morris (A Select Library of the Nicene and Post-Nicene Fathers, xi, 1889), p. 193 '. . . not an accuser of sin only, but in a measure, its producer.'

commented that by the coming of the Law the sickness [viz. sin] grew.[24]

Ottoni's treatment of the Law was matched by other Cassinese writers, notably Benedetto da Mantova, by whom the theme was elaborated, though he added nothing not already implicit in Ottoni. Isidoro Chiari also used identical language and placed the topic in the same position within his pattern of salvation as that of Ottoni and Benedetto, that is, between the consequences of sin—which are driven home to the sinner by the Law—and the advent of grace—to which the sinner is guided.

The stage was now prepared for the Pauline doctrine of salvation through grace. Ottoni argued that since man cannot redeem himself by his works, his reconciliation with God can be achieved only by an act of God. The divine initiative was in the Cross of Christ, an unmerited gift of 'divine grace and goodness and benevolence towards men'.[25] At this point he followed the words of Chrysostom and Paul very closely. He attributed reconciliation to the Cross alone, and frequently his interpreters repeated the theme that 'through one man, Christ, justice and life are given to all men', so that 'we are reconciled and restored through the Son'.[26] The Cross broke the power of death and offered new life to men: 'greater than sin is the justice . . . brought into the world through God and grace, which disposes us to a better life and leads us to infinite benefits. Indeed of this life now there shall be no end.'[27] There is no doubt that Ottoni was at one with other Cassinese writers in his belief that salvation was offered through grace alone—a *beneficium*—and not through human merit. Nor is there any doubt that he drew his Christocentric doctrine of grace from St. Paul and from John Chrysostom.

[24] 42ᵛ: 'Paulus ait, lex autem sub intravit, ut abundaret delictum et Chrysostomus subiicit: introeunte lege, morbus accrevit.' Melanchthon also held that the Law reveals sin and terrifies and confounds the conscience, (1 Cor. 15: 56; 2 Cor. 3: 7–8) and that Law increases sin (Gal. 3: 19). See *Loci Communes*, 'The Power of the Law', in *Malanchthon and Bucer*, ed. W. Pauck (The Library of Christian Classics, xix; London, 1969), pp. 77–83.

[25] 40ᵛ: 'divinam gratiam et bonitatem ac erga homines benevolentiam'.

[26] 40ʳ⁻ᵛ: 'per unum homine(m) CHRISTUM iustitua & vita ad omnes pertineat'; 42ʳ: '. . . post modum reconciliati, & restituti per filiu(m) sumus.'

[27] 42ᵛ: '. . . maior est peccato iustitia . . . per Deum et gratiam introducta: quae et vitam nostram in melius dirigit, et ad infinita nos bona perducit. Cuius quidem vitae nullus iam finis erit.'

Ottoni continued in this Pauline vein. Man's proper response to his unmerited reconciliation was the response of faith. The first step in faith was belief in God's grace, but a belief that was much more than intellectual assent. Chrysostom called it a full and unshakable persuasion and Ottoni reiterated the idea of faith as a trusting belief in the grace of God, a belief so strong that it became 'supernatural light' incorporated into the personality.[28]

Ottoni then considered the question whether faith is a gift of God or a work of man. The question was important because it gave him the opportunity to argue that something may be simultaneously the work of God and the work of man. His reasoning was based upon the manner in which grace operates in the soul, by stimulation and interaction:

all men at all times are inwardly disturbed and at the same time challenged by grace, and invisibly flooded and aroused by the inmost ray of its light: in precisely the same way as the rays of the sun stimulate and penetrate and attract the eye, and assist it to see and to fulfil its function . . . Furthermore, we maintain that we are not only excited and drawn by divine favour and grace inwardly, but also outwardly we are stimulated and enticed from many quarters . . . now by preaching and persuasion, now by reading and by the advice of scriptures, now by the advice and rebukes of friends . . . so that it is entirely inexcusable were we not to assent to it. Having said that, we can agree with Chrysostom that faith is a gift of God but none the less our own work.[29]

His argument was that grace intermingled with the responses of faith so that faith was simultaneously the gift of God and a

---

[28] 36^r. Ottoni's translation of Chrysostom's text runs: '. . . et non ait [sc. Paul] credens, sed *certo persuasus*. Talis est fides.' At Trent, in 1546, he used the expression '. . . lumen supernaturale, id est fidei, est dilucidius quam naturale', *Concilium Tridentinum: Diariorum Actorum, Epistolarum, Tractatuum nova Collectio* (Freiburg-im-Breisgau, 1901–), v. 677. He went on: '. . . nam illi non potest subesse falsum.' Gregory the Great had used this imagery.

[29] 29^r (printed 27^r in error): '. . . dico, semper intus pulsanti, et aeque omnes homines invitanti, ac intimo lucis suae radio, invisibiliter perfundenti, ac excitanti: haud aliter q(ua)m solis radius oculos pulsat perfundit, invitat, et adiuuat ad aspiciendum, et proprium videndi munus implendum . . . Dicimus praeterea divino favore et gratia, non solum intrinsecus nos excitari et trahi: verum etiam extrinsecus multifariam provocari et allici, . . . nunc hominibus praedicantibus, et persuadentibus, nunc lectione et scripturis hortantibus, nunc amicis monentibus, et increpantibus . . . ut prorsus inexcusabiles simus non accedentes. His igitur positis una cum Chrysostomo dicimus, fidem et Dei donum esse, et nostrum nihilominus esse.'

response of men. He was sure that the coincidence of grace and works was true Pauline teaching. Faith is 'both the gift of God and nonetheless our own work ... unless it is in our power to believe and reject we completely pervert Paul's teaching.'[30] This description of faith explains the enormous importance Ottoni attached to it, and its recurrence as a dominant theme of his doctrine. Faith served as the essential link between the gratuitous work of the Cross and its fulfilment in men. Faith was the experience of the soul in which God's grace and man's response were coupled: it was therefore a living faith which awakened, vivified, and sanctified a Christian man.

However, a man was free to accept or reject this experience of faith. 'If it be a gift of God', Ottoni wrote, 'nevertheless it is for us to accept or reject it'.[31] Ottoni understood the necessity of free will in a sense quite different from that of contemporary Catholic theologians. He did not predicate the will's capacity to make an active contribution to salvation in the form of merit, but simply its freedom to accept or reject the unmerited gift of salvation. Ottoni expressed his doctrine of free will in one limpid aphorism: 'We are able to refuse; in that consists the freedom of the will.'[32]

The affective language in which Ottoni had described man's response to grace was important to his argument. It had enabled him to argue the coincidence and reciprocity of grace and works. It meant that faith was understood as a total response of the personality, that is, a 'living faith', which, incidentally, was formed and supported in the social context of fellow Christians—a point to which we shall return later. Then, in order to define further the necessity of faith and works, Ottoni described more fully the role of the affect in the process of salvation. His

---

[30] 38^r: '. . . et Dei donum sit, et nostra nihilominus sit . . . vides ut Paulum totum pervertimus nisi nostrum sit credere, atque renuere.'

[31] 30^r: 'Et si donum sit Dei, nostrum tamen est illud admittere aut reiicere.'

[32] 53^r: 'Renuere possumus, in quo consistit libertas arbitrii ': also 29^r (27^v). Of course, the notion of free choice at this point was held by scholastics: Bernard of Clairvaux also held that 'free choice co-operates in the act of consent'. This notion of co-operating grace was developed by Lombard. Calvin rejected Chrysostom's notion of willing acceptance: instead, he used Bernard, rather out of context, to deny that man can freely choose to accept efficacious grace, *Institutes*, II. iii. 10–12, though later he acknowledges an indirect choice—refraining from turning away (*Institutes* II. xvi. 1) See J. Raitt, 'Calvin's use of Bernard of Clairvaux; *Archiv für Reformationsgeschichte* lxxii (1981), 98–121.

theme was that love engenders a different kind of obedience to that which comes of other emotions. He used Chrysostom's distinction between misguided Christians who, like the Israelites, obeyed the Law out of fear and self-interest and true Christians who obey out of faith and love for their Father: 'The Law was given to them: grace and truth was procured for us. We accepted the Law in our hearts: they on tablets of stone . . . we submit to the Law of faith and keep it willingly and freely: they unwillingly obeyed the Law in terror. They with fear and compulsion . . . we with love and faith . . .'[33] True Christians love God; 'we were adopted . . . we loved him as a father'.[34] Therefore Christian obedience flows from personal love for God, who has shown his prevenient love. The same argument was later used by Isidoro Chiari in his *Novum Testamentum* of 1542 and by Benedetto da Mantova in the *Beneficio* of 1543.

Furthermore love engenders not only willing obedience, but also all good works. The love of faith is unconstrained, as Paul said.[35] It gives itself in works:

Such is love . . . blind and indifferent to self, but very perceptive and considerate to all that appertains to the beloved. Once a man is overcome by love he has no longer any concern for himself, his possessions, his honour or his life. He wants only one thing, that he may please, honour, exalt and fulfil his beloved. That is his concern, his zeal and his obsession.[36]

Such works are a constituent of the love which belongs to faith. They are necessary to salvation in the sense that they flow naturally from living faith. Without works there is no living faith, and works cannot be separated from such faith. In this sense works were necessary to salvation.

---

[33] 59[r]: 'Illis lex data est: nobis gratia et veritas facta est. Nos in corde legem accepimus: illi in lapidibus . . . nos volentes et sponte fidei legem subimus et retinemus; illi inviti et territi legem tenebant. Illis timor et vis . . . nos amore et fide.' Chrysostom's distinction is made in sermon 14: Morris, *The Homilies*, pp. 238–41. In the *Beneficio*, ch. 6, unworthy Christians are described as living 'in criminal and servile fear of the Law'.

[34] 43[v]: '. . . in adoptionem asciseeremur . . . tamquam patrem eum diligeremus'.

[35] 70[v] (59[v])–71[r]. There is a marginal reference to ⸆ Cor. 13 and an attack upon scholastic teaching that 'charitas incipit a seipsa, sibi providet primum'.

[36] 70[v]: 'Talis est amor, eiusmodi naturam habet et vim . . . caecus ad propria, et negligens sua: oculatissimus etiam, et diligentissimus ad ea, quae sunt amati. Qui enim amore semel fuerit captus, nulla iam sui cura tenetur: non rerum suarum, non honoris, non vitae solicitudinem gerit: unum id tantum intendit, ut amato gratificetur, ut illum honoret, extollat, amplificet. Haec illi cura est, hoc studium, haec solicitudo.'

The final stage of Ottoni's pattern of salvation was the renovation of damaged human personality. He believed that renovation, rather than judgement, was the way of salvation: '. . . I saw a new heaven and a new earth . . . [God] did not say, it will be purged, or that it would be at peace, but, behold, he was making all things new. Therefore it is not so much that the face of the earth is to be purged, but rather that all things are to be restored and renewed.'[37] The restoration of man was a direct consequence of his reconciliation with God: 'CHRIST has restored those whom Adam ruined and has placed them higher than they were before, provided that they themselves desire and follow him . . . the natural end of man shall be to enjoy God, he is made for this, and to fall from this is against his nature.'[38] That restoration is made possible because men, reconciled and adopted by God, are given 'the gift of the spirit, the abundant source of all goodness'.[39]

In practice, restoration was to be carried out through the exercise of faith and works. Again Ottoni followed Paul and Chrysostom closely in his description of the new life, how the Christian, gratuitously liberated from death, can slough off old attitudes and actions, and grow into a new life, growing in love and doing good works.[40] In this way works play a part in salvation because they accomplish a real and necessary change in man. By the 'mercy and restitution of God' he is 'restored' and 'vivified'. He is gentle, kind, humane, merciful, and a 'treasury of good works'.[41] Where Chrysostom gave a description of the restored person, towards the end of Sermon 10, Ottoni added

[37] 62[r]: 'Vidi coelum novum et terram novam . . . non dixit purgabitur, aut quiescet, et ecce, nova facio omnia inquit. Non igitur facies terrae tantum purganda est sed omnia refundenda ac renovanda.'

[38] 21[v]: 'CHRISTUM restituisse, quos Adam prostraverat: ac in maiori, et altiori gradu eos locasse, quam prius extiterint: modo velint ipsi sequantur . . . et Deo frui naturalis hominis finis erit, ad quem conditus est: ab illo autem cadere, contra naturam erit illius.' Ottoni denied two species of fulfilment, natural and supernatural, because the distinction implied a special intervention of grace for the latter (i.e. election), whereas grace is available to all: see 20[r].

[39] 58[v]: '. . . spiritus donum: bonorum omnium suppeditatio'.

[40] 72[r]: 'Charitas autem ipsa nullam aliam novit mensuram, quam Christum, cuius gratia omnia gerit et optat, ut Paulus exemplo nos docuit.' Also 72[v] and 73[v] for Chrysostom's remark that 'nos generamus per verba Dei . . . generatio non naturae sed divinae promissionis est.' There is a marginal note in a later 16th-century hand, 'regeneratio'. Also 52[v].

[41] 40[v]–41[v], 91[v], 21[v], 36[r], 61[v], 65[r], 74[r], 77[v].

the marginal comment 'A portrait of him who wishes to put on Christ'.[42] In this way the necessity of good works was again asserted by Ottoni. *Opera humana*, already considered to be necessary constituents of love and faith, were now seen to be therapeutically necessary to the healing of man and his restoration to perfection.

It has been observed already that Ottoni understood faith to be formed and sustained amongst other Christians, and not in isolation. Like other Cassinese writers, particularly Benedetto da Mantova and Isidoro Chiari, he emphasized that faith required practical expression in the world.

[The early Christians] our forebears, those first worshippers and followers of Christ . . . with all diligence and zeal used to strive to come to each other, ministering, exhorting, consoling and caring. For this reason many were converted to the faith, because they saw real humanity and love amongst Christians. Indeed Christians not only cared for other Christians, but also many amongst the heathen who were neglected by their own people, but nowadays if the plague comes to any city, everyone runs away, and they keep away from each other as much as possible, so that often more die by hunger than by plague.[43]

This doctrine, with its exhortation to social good works which flow from faith, was characteristic of all Cassinese writers and a direct reflection of Chrysostom's homilies *Ad Populum Antiochenum* on social obligation. This is the furthest point to which Ottoni carried his pattern of salvation.

Finally, we shall examine the vigorous assaults upon opponents with which Ottoni interspersed his pattern of salvation. These defensive postures require our attention because they too embodied themes that were repeated in other Cassinese writings, where sometimes they have been ascribed mistakenly to Protestant influence or to humanist bias.

Ottoni criticized 'Judaizing' Christians, who acknowledged the necessity of grace, but in practice subordinated grace to works as a means of salvation. To trust to obedience was to behave 'like the Jews and in defiance of Paul': 'Certain doctors quarrel with Paul . . . in opposition they strain themselves to

---

[42] 101^v: 'Effigies illius, qui Christum induere cupit'.

[43] 73^r. Benedetto da Mantova has a parallel description of the 'vero cristiano, inamorato di Cristo', who loves and cares for his neighbour. See also Isidoro Chiari's Brescian *Oration* of 1540, ch. 7, below.

prove by every way, and with every argument, that through obedience to the law sin is removed, grace is imparted and much assistance given.'[44] The result was that Christians were behaving like Jews because they lacked confidence in grace: 'Many praise God and abstain from sin more out of fear than for love of God, which in my opinion differs from the Jews very little or not at all.'[45] With these passages Ottoni again attacked contemporary forms of the Pelagian belief that works in some way merit salvation, and in so doing he was defending Chrysostom's and his own Paulinist orthodoxy. Moreover, in this specific criticism of unworthy Christians he was making precisely the same point that appeared in other Cassinese writing, notably the *Beneficio*.

Ottoni also attacked the speculative theology of the scholastics on the grounds that its irrelevant sophistry distracted theologians from the proper task of preaching salvation. However, scholastic theology could not always be criticized with impunity in the late 1530s and he took care to follow the patristic text closely. Chrysostom's second homily had criticized those who defined the Godhead amid 'the dust of infinite reasoning'. Ottoni added his own scorn for 'nostri doctores' who would 'leave nothing undiscussed concerning the nature of God and the Trinity . . . and from that, little man, do you think you can comprehend such hidden and infinite majesty?'[46]

His more serious objection to speculative theology was that it obscured the recognition that God, acting in history, exercises his providence over creation: '. . . from his works it may be known . . . that [God] made all things, governs, sustains, and directs them, and that he cares for all things.'[47] The emphasis upon God's providence—characteristic of the literal style of Chrysostom's biblical exegesis—was the basis of Ottoni's vehement criticism of the doctrine of predestination. He reasoned that since God's providence extended to all men without

---

[44] 34[v]: 'doctores quidam cum Paulo pugnant . . . illi aut contra, et peccata delesse et gratiam infudisse, et multum opis praestitisse legem servandam, omni ratione et via probare nituntur.'

[45] 58[v]: 'multi timore magis quam amore Deum honorant a peccatisque abstinent, qui plane mihi vident a Iudaeis illis parum, vel nihil differre.'

[46] 10[v]; 12[r]: 'Deinde homuncio . . . et illam arcanam et infinitam maiestatem intelligere putas?' This was the insult posthumously returned by Sixtus Senensis.

[47] 11[v]: '. . . quod condiderit omnia, quod eadem regat, sustentet, ac moderetur, quod provideat omnibus . . . cognosci possunt ex illius operibus.'

exception, it could not be a manifestation of God's grace to choose arbitrarily those who are to be saved. On the contrary God willed all men to be saved, not merely some. It was at the heart of God's 'divine grace and goodness and benevolence towards men' that God 'wishes all men to be saved'.[48] On the other hand, if predestination were true,

> it shall be seen that CHRIST did not liberate all men in the way that Adam damned all men. And the sin of Adam shall be stronger and more efficacious than the justice of CHRIST, and the anger of God greater than his love, and death stronger than life.[49]

> Guilt shall be stronger than grace, our loss greater than our profit, death greater than life, and the anger of God greater than his mercy, our damnation greater than our restoration.[50]

This cannot be the case, Ottoni argued, because Paul himself had taught that Christ liberated all men:

> Through one man, CHRIST, justice and life are extended to all men . . . and CHRIST, as far as he is able, regained all men . . . the gift of God, through the grace of one man, floods into more . . . and if death reigned through the sin of one . . . and through one sin all men were condemned, so through the justice of one all men were justified.[51]

In short, the doctrine of predestination was a denial of the universal efficacy of Christ's passion. This was Ottoni's prime objection to the doctrine of predestination. In view of the various interpretations that have been made of Cassinese writings, it is important to observe three things. The first is that Ottoni's objection to predestination did not arise from humanist or Pelagian exaltation of free will, but simply from his Christological doctrine of universal grace. Second, his objection to predestination, despite the emphasis on grace and faith, is a denial of Lutheran, and more especially Calvinist, doctrines of

---

[48] 40ᵛ (margin): [Deus] vult omnes homines salvos fieri . . . '; from 1 Tim. 2: 4.

[49] 2ᵛ: 'Et Christus non omnes liberasse videbitur, quemadmodum Adam omnes damnavit. Et fortius atque validius erit Adae peccatum, quam Christi iustitia; et ira Dei quam gratia: et mors quam vita.'

[50] 40ᵛ: '. . . culpa quam gratia et damnum nostrum quam lucrum et mors quam vita et ira Dei quam misericordia, et damnatio quam restitutio.'

[51] 40ʳ–40ᵛ: 'per unum hominem CHRISTUM iustitia et vita ad omnes pertineat . . . et CHRISTUS, quantum in se est, omnes recuperet . . . donum Dei in gratia unius hominis abundavit in plures . . . et si unius delicto mors regnavit . . . et sicut per unum delictum in omnes homines ad condemnationem, ita per unum iustitiam in omnes homines ad iustificationem.'

grace and faith. Third, his arguments were drawn solely and directly from Paul and Chrysostom.

Ottoni was familiar with scholastic attempts to square God's providence for all men with predestination 'solely by the will and command of God', but he found these attempts unsatisfactory.[52] He believed that the error of western theologians derived from Augustine who, in his zeal to defend the priority of grace against Pelagius, had put forward his doctrine that 'predestination is the prime cause of our salvation and the most potent, or rather, the only cause'.[53] In contrast, the eastern tradition, found in Chrysostom, better understood St. Paul:

... in these matters I used to hold the opinion of Augustine, not so much because it satisfied me (indeed the ideas seem incongruous) as because I did not know how otherwise to understand Paul's words . . . I tell you that only Chrysostom has opened up the meaning of St. Paul to me, untangled the problems, taught and explained the terms.[54]

It was in Chrysostom, Ottoni argued, that the difficulties were resolved, for he was the theologian who successfully synthesized unmerited grace with human works, showing them to be two interacting operations, which together restored man to his original perfection.

What conclusions may be drawn from this book? The pattern of salvation was that of a monk who asserted both the Pauline doctrine of man's reconciliation to God by grace alone, and restoration through a way of perfection, rigorously following Paul and Chrysostom as his sole sources. Moreover, the themes and language of his commentary bore a marked similarity to the themes and language of other Cassinese writings. The similarity suggests an already established community of doctrine within

---

[52] 74^v–75^v; Ottoni attacked Augustine, Lombard, Aquinas, Scotus and Luther. Luther, he said, 'funditus tollit hominis libertatem'; see also 3^v, 20^r.

[53] 2^v: '. . . salutis nostrae causam primam, atque potissimam, vel potius solam existere.' Ottoni was prepared to use the term 'predestination' in the sense of a calling to a particular task or to salvation, or in the sense of God's foreknowledge of man's ultimate destiny. The term is discussed also on 74^v–75^v, with a renewed attack on 'nostri doctores'.

[54] 2^v–3^r: '. . . in eadem cum Augustino sententia mansi, non tam quod illa mihi faceret satis (occurrebant enim absurda praedicta) quam quod aliter intelligere Pauli verba nescirem . . . Chrysostomus, inquam, solus mihi Pauli sensum aperuit, nodos explicavit, verba docuit et explanavit.'

the Cassinese Congregation which was now being clarified by Ottoni.

But how do his teachings stand with regard to other religious movements? His doctrines of grace and faith were not unlike those of the Protestants, and it is apparent why Ottoni was shortly to be accused of Lutheranism. Yet fundamental disagreements over predestination and free will showed that he was not a 'crypto-Protestant'.

On the other hand his doctrines of free will and works bore some resemblance to various forms of Pelagianism, and he was accused of that heresy also. Modern historians have taken up this 'Pelagian' interpretation of the doctrines of Ottoni and other Cassinese writers, and attributed them to their humanist desire to assert the dignity and potential of man against the prevailing religious emphasis upon sin.[55] This explanation rests upon insufficient analysis of Ottoni's doctrine, and does not resolve the paradox of the two contradictory heresies alleged against him. Moreover, his book shows that Ottoni did not accept the Pelagian view that works possessed forensic validity prior to, and independently of, grace. Therefore, it seems that the conflicting accusations of contemporaries, later repeated by historians, that he was crypto-Protestant or neo-Pelagian, were based upon misunderstandings of his teaching.

A more subtle problem is whether he was teaching another form of *duplex iustitia*, in which the justice of Christ, imputed to sinners, supplemented human righteousness. After all, Ottoni had links with Sadoleto, Contarini, Pole, and other *spirituali* who espoused this doctrine. However, here too there are important differences. When Ottoni taught the necessity of works, he did not refer to a growth of inherent justice necessary to forensic justification, for he held God's acceptance of man to be an act of grace independent of the merit of human works.

---

[55] H. Jedin, *History of the Council of Trent*, ii. 118. Jedin makes a passing reference to Christian humanist links with the Benedictine tradition, in respect of biblical studies. The point is developed by Carla Faralli in 'Una Polemica all'epoca del Concilio di Trento: il Teologo e Giurista Domingo de Soto censura un'opera del Benedettino Luciano degli Ottoni', *Studi senesi*, lxxxvii (3rd ser. xxiv, 1975), 400–19. Also C. Ginzburg and A. Prosperi, 'Le due redazioni', pp. 137–204. These two authors consider that Ottoni did not take sin seriously because he valued human free will and 'il tema dell'impeccabilità'. They attribute his supposed near Pelagianism to his being 'intriso di neoplatonismo' for which reason 'reprende il temo umanistico della "dignitas hominis" ', pp. 164, 168.

Freely willed works were necessary only as a constituent of faith and an instrument of restoration: in Ottoni's pattern of salvation, human righteousness did not correspond to the *iustitia inhaerens* of theories of double justification. Nor was there anything to correspond with the doctrine of imputed justice put forward by the *spirituali*—a special application of the merits of Christ to perfect inherent justice. Consequently, in view of the mutual approval expressed by Ottoni and Sadoleto, it should be noted that whilst the two men shared a common aim—to introduce the Greek *altera via* and thereby to avoid the conflict between grace and works which underlay the Reformation debate—their theological positions were entirely different. Thus, the Cassinese monks and the *spirituali* differed in theology, despite their common ground. Much more evidence is needed before we can understand the relationshp between the two groups, but I suspect that they remained separated by the pre-Augustinian theology of the monks, which the *spirituali* did not share.

Ottoni's teaching was not new to the Congregation. For a long time the Benedictines of Santa Giustina had not only concerned themselves with the problems posed by the apparent conflict between the Pauline doctrine of grace and the monastic vocation, but they had also been familiar with the answers to be found in the teachings of the Greek Fathers of Antioch. When Ottoni's work was written it emerged as the most detailed and the clearest exposition of an old dominant theme in the traditional teaching of his order, forced from him under the pressure of hardening conflicts in Europe, political as well as religious. He had clarified the teachings of his order, gathered, ordered, and given them form and a theological cutting edge, and applied them to the task of reconciliation. His book seemed to rally his fellow monks, and from 1538 the Congregation increased its efforts to apply its teachings to contemporary problems, above all, applying its Greek patristic theology to the schism of Latin Christendom.[56]

---

[56] In 1539 the monastery of Santa Giustina, Padua, purchased the newly published fifth tome of the works of Chrysostom, *Divi Ioannis Chrysostomi Episcopi Constantinopolitani homilae xxx ad Populum Antiochenum potissimum habitae Bernardo Brixiano interprete* (Basle, 1539). This volume is still in the library of the monastery. For details of Lucas Bernardo of Brescia see above, ch. 2.

VII

The Propagation of Monastic Doctrines during Years of Crisis, 1540–1543

AFTER Ottoni's book had clarified Cassinese teachings and clearly tied them to the Fathers of Antioch, the monks wrote a number of works that applied Congregational doctrines to the crisis of the division between Rome and the Reformers—by now almost irreconcilable. In 1538 Gregory Cortese published a translation and commentary upon the New Testament, but the work is now lost. Then in 1540 Giambattista Folengo again entered the lists with a commentary on the psalms, published at Basle. It was a work of sound scholarship, in which the psalms were examined phrase by phrase, comparing the Vulgate with the original Hebrew, and expounding the literal meaning, chiefly the prophetic allusions to Christ.[1] However, Folengo also declared his intention of treating with the issues of 'these most troubled times', and this declaration, together with reiteration of his earlier critical allusions to Protestantism, his very frequent references to St. Paul, and the Christological emphasis of his exegesis, all suggest that he was girding his loins to apply his learning to the Reformation crisis, as his colleagues were doing.[2] In fact Folengo only hovered on the edges of controversy, for although the principal themes of Cassinese theology were woven through his philological scholarship, their treatment was brief and their application to controversy elliptical.

Nevertheless, within the limitations of his topic, Folengo made it clear that he was upholding the pattern of salvation taught within his order. He told his readers that human righteousness was imperfect and that it was necessary for God to

[1] *Ioan(nis) Baptistae Folengii Mantuani, Monachi Divi Benedicti, in Psalmos Commentaria, quibus permulta quae hodie passim controversa sunt, tanta pietate gravitateq(ue) deciduntur, ut nullus tam iniquus esse volet, quin se ex harum lectione longe meliorem doctioremq(ue) factum agnoscat* (Basle, 1540). The work considers psalms 1–32, and 120–31 only.

[2] Ibid. 'Typographus lectori', '. . . praesertim hoc tempore inquietissimo . . .'; fo. 2C, 'vana studia, letales haereses, sectas, foedas(q)ue doctrinas'. For his earlier criticism of Protestants see above, ch. 4.

intervene in order to bring righteousness to men.[3] Grace was not given in respect of merits, but was a free gift: 'eternal life was brought freely to mortal men' through Christ: 'the shed blood, that is to say, Christ . . . who alone for the salvation of all, shed his blood most abundantly upon the Cross.'[4] He emphasized not only that redemption lay solely in 'the blood and wounds' of Christ, but also that it was completely gratuitous, a 'donum et beneficium', and a 'benignitas immensa' to the human race.[5]

Folengo also followed his colleagues in his doctrine of faith, which he saw as the acceptance of the gift through which men become 'co-heirs, sons of God through faith'.[6] Faith was made up of, and manifest in, belief, love of neighbour and good works,[7] and through faith men entered into a new life. Thus, he said, righteousness was not imputed to men, but grew in them and transformed them: indeed he wrote almost as if he meant some kind of union with God, of the kind described by his colleague Benedetto da Mantova in the *Beneficio di Cristo*, published three years later.[8]

With such a doctrine of faith, it is not surprising that when Folengo alluded to predestination his remarks were in agreement with the Antiochene arguments of his own *Pomiliones* of 1533 and of Ottoni and other colleagues. 'God knows them to be his, whom through foreknowledge he knew would be his through faith and love, and for this reason blessed and enrolled in the books of life; he knows them, cherishes them, loves them, supports them.'[9] However, Folengo did not go beyond these pious sentiments, nor did he advance a systematic exposition of his pattern of salvation, and the light it might have shed upon 'these most troubled times'. Most certainly he was a scholar and monk in the Cassinese tradition, but in his commentary of 1540

---

[3] Ibid. fo. 14B.

[4] Ibid. fo. 92C; fo. 4D: '. . . aeternam vitam gratis per ipsum [sc. Christum] mortalibus apportatam', fo. 12B, '. . . effundente(m) sanguinem, scilicet Christum . . . qui solus pro omniu(m) salute, sanguinem in cruce largissimum effudit.' See also fo. 69A.

[5] Ibid. fos. 10B, 16A–D, 17A, 23A–B, 24C, 45C, 92C.

[6] Ibid. fo. 79D: 'Fratres hic vocat Christus cohaeredes suos, Dei scilicet filios per fidem.'

[7] Ibid. fos. 1A, 2B–D, 13A, 16A, 93C–D, 123B.

[8] Ibid. fo. 8A: 'a peccato, a morte, ad lucem, ad Deum, ad innocentiam, ad vitam'. Also 14B, 104A. For the passage in the *Beneficio* see below, ch. 8.

[9] Ibid. fo. 2 D, 'Quos novit Deus esse suos, hoc est, quos praenovit per fidem atq(ue) amorem fore suos, ac propterea beatos, & in vitae libro conscriptos, hos ipsos agnoscit, fovet, amat, tutatur . . .' See also fos. 39C, 57A.

he did not assert his Congregation's teachings as strongly as did his colleagues.

In the same year as Folengo's commentary was published, Isidoro Chiari was much more active in applying monastic theology to problems outside the cloister. Chiari was a busy man in 1540: he relinquished his position as prior at Modena, travelled to Maṇtua on Congregational business, became abbot of S. Jacobo da Pontida at Bergamo, and wrote an oration addressed to the citizens of his native city of Brescia. The *Oratio* was a response to the sufferings of the poor during a series of bad seasons capped by a disastrous drought in 1540.[10] It was a conventional condemnation of greed and an exhortation to charity, but its underlying theology was strongly Pauline, with the same emphasis upon the 'beneficentia' of the Cross, the same pattern of salvation, and the same application to social good works that we have observed in other Cassinese writers.

Chiari began with St. Paul, warning his audence that avarice is that 'which Paul calls wisdom of this world', and that they should reject it and embrace the 'wisdom of God', as shown by the light of the Gospel ('evangelicae philosophiae lumen').[11] His exposition of the Gospel was roundabout, starting with its social fruits and working back to the theological basis. He put forward the argument of classical writers, that if all men act out of self-interest, this will cause 'the breakdown of society' and he told the men of Brescia how praiseworthy were the ancient Roman leaders who, eschewing 'wealth, pleasure, and luxury', magnanimously sought the common good.[12] Chiari adopted the familiar humanist simile of earthbound man in order to explain selfish behaviour: there are two aspects ('partes') of man, and the first is that of man unable to escape from his worldly actions, 'deformed . . . able to conceive of nothing good, but always earthbound of necessity'.[13] Amongst the humanist rhetoric lay

[10] *De Modo Divitiis Adhibendo Homini Christiano . . . ad Cives Brixianos, Oratio.* The *Oratio* is published in Olgiato, *Epistolae*, pp. 233–80. For the effects of famine and drought see T. de'Bianchi detto de'Lancillotti, *Cronaca Modense* (Monumenta di Storia Patria delle Provincie Modenesi, vi, vii; Parma, 1868), pp. x, 402.

[11] *Oratio* 216: '. . . sapientia carnis, quam eandem Paulus sapientiam huius mundi appellat, quae stultitia est apud Deum.'

[12] Ibid. 248–9.

[13] Ibid. 250: '. . . nihil sit in homine hac parte deformius, is nihil excogitare egregium potest, sed circa terram semper versetur, necesse est, cogitetque quibus artibus corpus foveat, corpori serviat, et sola, quae per corpus fiant, eique splendorem afferant, judicet appetenda.'

the first threads of his evangelical doctrine of sin, and Chiari quickly moved on to contrast this earthly man with the 'interior man' (a phrase taken from Augustine), whose righteousness was described so well by St. Paul ('sol noster Paulus') as a 'new life' disdaining luxury, seeking only splendour of the soul and caring for the poor.

So far, it was a traditional homily on virtue and charity, doubtless all too familiar to his audience. But suddenly Chiari changed tack, and turned to the Cassinese theme of the restoration of man to his divine image. They, the citizens of Brescia, must realize that Paul says:

you shall be not so much men as gods—after you have begun to profess the Christian faith. He declares, I have told you, it is gods that you shall be, and all exalted sons; for this reason, that you have received the word of God, as the truth itself declares, and this word has shown you the uncertainty and confusion of your own wisdom.[14]

In the style of what were later the opening lines of the third chapter of *Il Beneficio di Cristo* Chiari drew attention to the 'beautiful statement' of St. Paul, and he urged them to fling themselves upon the Lord: 'Begin to embrace [him] . . . throw your care upon the Lord, and he himself will support you'.[15]

Chiari was moving sideways and backwards, as it were, to the centre of his Cassinese teaching, namely the doctrine of the Cross by which men are saved from death and vivified:

But you are dead and your life is hidden with Christ in God, as Paul says. And elsewhere he says . . . Christ has died for all, so that those who live, live not for themselves, but in him who has died and risen again for all. This is a beautiful statement and full of wisdom, indeed, when it says that one man encountered death, for all it shows us that they were then in the hands of death, and to free them he cast down death . . . for he rose for our justification. O great love![16]

[14] Ibid. 257: 'non ut homines tantum, sed ut (postquam Christianam philosophiam profiteri coepistis) deos, ego, inquit, dixi dii estis, et filii excelsi omnes, nempe ob eam causam, quod ad vos sermo Dei factus est, ut ipsa etiam veritas est interpretata, qui incerta atque occulta sapientiae suae vobis manifestavit.'

[15] Ibid. 263: 'incipite complexari . . . jacta in dominum curam tuam, et ipse te enutriet'.

[16] Ibid. 266: 'At vos mortui (ait Paulus) estis, et vita vestra abscondita est cum CHRISTO in Deo. Et alio etiam loco; si unus pro omnibus mortuus est, ergo omnes mortui sunt, et pro omnibus mortuus est CHRISTUS, ut qui vivunt, jam non sibi vivant, sed ei, qui pro ipsis mortuus est, et resurrexit. Pulchra et plena sapientiae

The men of Brescia were exhorted to acknowledge the majesty and the benefit (*beneficentia*) of Christ crucified, and henceforth entirely to orientate their lives to their saviour, 'to look for, to ponder, to carry out, with great effort, those things which are his will'.[17] He told them that when this is done the whole of life—wife, children, family, business, wealth, offices—will be affected by the new relationship, and he reminded them that happiness, as the Apostle says, cannot be found elsewhere than with the name of Jesus and 'in vivante Deo'.[18] The old man will become a new man, fulfilled with joy, because 'charitas Dei manet in eo'.[19] It is this new man who will help 'the brethren' in generosity and kindness, eschewing anger, sharing goods, giving to the poor, and attending to God in all things.[20]

To all these themes Chiari added a final summary, unmistakably Cassinese in nature. Like Folengo, Luciano degli Ottoni, Benedetto da Mantova, and Denis Faucher, he described sin as a sickness which was cured by the Cross and by man's complete response to the Gospel in living faith. He warned his audience that they could walk in new life only if they committed themselves completely to the Gospel. Sin is so deep a sickness, 'morbus tantus est', that it cannot be overcome except by giving the whole heart. They had become deeply aware of the Gospel, he told them.[21] Now they had to go away and ponder the truth of the Gospel.[22]

There is no evidence that the *Oratio* transformed the religious life of Brescia, but it deserves attention as another example of Cassinese doctrine, drawn from Paul and the Greek Fathers in respect of sin, the Cross and new life, and including the traditional monastic theme of whole-hearted perseverence, in this case adapted for the use of laymen. This Benedictine monk, preaching to the Brescians, expounding Pauline theology and applying it to secular life, reveals a vitality amongst the

---

argumentio; cum enim dicitur unum pro omnibus mortem oppetivisse significatio fit, eos jam morti addictos fuisse, pro quibus liberandis ille objecit mortem. . . . nam resurrexit propter justificationem nostri. O charitatem!'

[17] *Oratio* 266.

[18] Ibid. 270.

[19] Ibid. 272.

[20] Ibid. 274.

[21] Ibid. 279–80: 'Bene penitus in Evangelicae lucis familiaritatem dederitis . . .'

[22] Ibid. 274: '. . . ad Evangelicam ego vos veritatem relegabo, cui num habenda fides sit, vos ipsi deliberare.'

Cassinese, characterized by precise theological argument applied to particular issues, in this case a social problem. Like the later *Beneficio di Cristo* of Chiari's fellow monk, Benedetto da Mantova, the *Oratio* was a pastoral tract, written for laymen: both see sin in terms of 'morbus' and the hopeless condition and impotence of unredeemed man, then point to Christ and the Cross alone as the source of salvation. They exhort men to throw themselves upon the Cross and henceforth live in faith, entirely orientated to Christ. Both depict in detail the new life of zealous faith, the social ramifications of Pauline theology, and the restoration of the *imago Dei*, and both exhort perseverence in faith and use frequent brief biblical references to reinforce their argument. Of course, the *Beneficio* was intended as a summary of the whole pattern of salvation, whereas the *Oratio* had a limited purpose, but the similarities with each other, and with Cassinese writings, and the fact that Chiari wrote well before the publication of the *Beneficio*, suggest that the two men were both drawing upon common Congregational doctrines.

In Venice, in 1541, Chiari published a version of the New Testament in Latin.[23] It was not a new translation but appears to have been a revision of the Vulgate, using the Greek text to correct 'innumerable errors', though the supposed linguistic corrections were not enumerated. The work was reprinted in 1542 together with Chiari's revision of the Old Testament, which was influenced in parts by Sebastian Münster's recent translation from the Hebrew.[24]

[23] *Novi Testamenti vulgata quidem aeditio; sed quae ad vetustissimorum utriusque linguae exemplarium fidem, nunc demum emendata est* (Venice, 'apud Petrum Schoeffer', 1541 and 1542). A revised edition appeared in 1557. Richard Simon, the seventeenth-century French scholar, though generally sympathetic to Chiari, criticized the work for its capricious revisions made without reference to other scholarly translations. Simon thought it deserved to have been suppressed for its faulty scholarship rather than for any taint of heresy: see R. Simon, *A Critical History of the text of the New Testament* (London, 1689 and 1692), ii. 111–13. Simon also describes the inquisitorial revision of the earlier editions, particularly the removal of the preface. Another edition was published in Antwerp, 'in aed. Ioannis Steelii', in 1543: *Novum Testamentum brevibus variatum translationum annotationibus illustratum*. This edition contains the 'Haec docent'. There is a copy in the University Library, Cambridge.

[24] The publication of 1542 was entitled *Aeditio Veteris ac Novi Testamenti, quorum alterum ad Hebraicam, alterum ad Graecam, veritatem emendatum est diligentissime* (Venice, 1542). Chiari very probably consulted Münster's *Biblia Sacra*, published at Zürich in 1539 and Lyons in 1540, for he generally followed it in textual questions. Simon, *Critical History*, ii. 112, says that for the Old Testament Chiari once again merely revised faults in the Vulgate, but this time less accurately because he was not a Hebrew scholar. However,

Each book of the Bible was preceded by a commentary, and every author by a *vita* (in the case of Paul, the *Pauli Vita* of Jerome) and each chapter was followed by a scholium. The introductory address admonished those whose scholarship extended only to criticisms of others and accusations of heresy. Their unpleasant activities had forced him, he implied, to put his own name to this translation because 'anonymous writings frequently fell under suspicion of heresy, particularly at this time'.[25]

The 1542 edition contains a second introductory passage, headed 'Haec docent sacra bibliorum scripta', which consisted of a summary of the Christian religion in ten propositions collated from biblical passages. This summary of Isidoro is remarkable as a brief exposition of established Congregational teaching and for its similarity to those passages most probably written by Don Benedetto in the *Beneficio di Cristo*. The first two propositions are those of the first chapter of the *Beneficio*: God made man 'ad imaginem et similitudinem suam', but sin entered into the world and man was subject to 'its tyranny and death'. The next two items follow in substance and style the second chapter of the *Beneficio*: God promised a Saviour to liberate 'believers from sins and the tyranny of the devil', meanwhile the Law was given 'that men might know sin and know themselves to be sinners', which is exactly what Benedetto called the first office of the Law. Chiari taught that the knowledge of sin drove men to thirst for Christ, 'that they might long more ardently for the coming of Christ to redeem them from sins'.[26]

Chiari then turned from the predicament of man to its

Chiari's scholarship was hotly defended by Armellini who said that '. . . Isidorum sub Elia Levita Judeo valde docto, Venetiis Hebraicis Litteris operam navasse', *A. et C.* ii. 65. Also see *Conc. Trid.* i. 207, n. 1. Bishop John Pearson used Chiari in his anthology, *Critici Sacri* (London, 1660). The *Novi Testamenti Vulgata* (Venice, 1541) in the British Library does not contain the 'Haec docent', though it appears that the page may have been cut out. The copy of 1543 in Cambridge University Library does contain this page. For Chiari and Münster, see F. Kaulen, *Geschichte der Vulgata* (Mainz, 1868), pp. 333–6, 488.

[25] *Aeditio*, introduction, '. . . solere hac maxime aetate, ea scripta, in quibus nomen taceretur authoris, in haereses [*sic*] suspicionem venire.'

[26] Ibid. 'Haec docent': 'qui credentes liberaret a peccatis, et tyrranide diaboli . . . qua cognoscerent homines peccatum et se esse peccatores . . . ut ardentius sitirent Christi adventum, qui ipsos a peccatis redimeret.' *Il Beneficio*, ch. 2: 'conoscendo il peccato e disperando di poterci giustificare con le opere . . .' (the title).

remedy. His argument followed the same pattern we have seen in other Congregational writers, namely, Pauline theology as expounded by Chrysostom. The salvation of man was given not as a reward but out of sheer grace:

... not on account of the good works of anyone, for all were sinners, but, and this is the truth, out of the abundant riches of his grace ... he came so that he might reconcile us to the Father, paying the punishment for our sins on the Cross, that he might free us from enslavement to the devil ... that he might bring us sinners to salvation.[27]

Once again Chiari had affirmed that salvation was by grace alone. And now, once again, he moved from his doctrine of grace to the doctrine of faith. Man's proper response to grace is faith, and 'per fidem' comes peace and reassurance. As Ottoni had done in his commentary on Chrysostom, Chiari reminded his readers that faith was not simply a human attribute, but also, in some way which he did not explain, 'faith is truly the gift of God'.[28] With faith, the process of restoration began: believers were given the holy spirit and love poured into them so that the faith through which man embraces Christ then operates in his soul, 'per charitatem'. This 'bonitas Dei' is revealed to men in the Bible so that they might believe, and through belief have life.[29]

In the scholia that followed each chapter of the New Testament Chiari expanded the salient points of this summary, and it is in these scholia that the Pauline Antiochene theology of the Congregation is most clearly seen. First, he argued with vigour that the works of the Law could not bring justification.[30]

[27] *Aeditio*, 'Haec docent': 'non propter bona cuiusquam opera (nam omnes erant peccatores) sed ut verax, abundantes gratiae Suae divitias ... venit ut nos patri reconciliaret, poenas peccatis nostris debitas in cruce persolvendo, et liberaret a servitute diaboli ... ut nos peccatores salvos faceret.'

[28] Nevertheless it is clear that at this point Chiari was following the argument of Luciano degli Ottoni's commentary of 1538 on Chrysostom—that faith was simultaneously a divine gift and a human attribute.

[29] *Aeditio*, introduction: 'Propter hanc in Christum fidem quae per charitatem operatur, justificamur: id est pater ipsius (qui et noster effectus est per ipsum) nos pro filiis et iustis habet, sua gratia non imputans nobis delicta nostra ... utque credentes vitam habeamus in nomine eius ... praeter hoc fundamentum nemo aliud potest ponere.'

[30] Ibid., *Novum Testamentum*, 126: '... ex operibus legis non justificatur ... vide sapientiam Pauli ... non dixit mortuam esse legem, quare maluit dicere, eos mortuos legi'.

In the Law there is only condemnation: 'Certainly the Law does not know grace or pardon, but only exaction . . . indeed the Law is introduced not in order that it might make anyone just, but that it might coerce and accuse the unjust.'[31] Consequently the attempt to justify self by the works of the Law is madness (*insania*) because the Law 'only threatens and punishes'.[32] Under the Law men were servile (*obnoxii*), moribund, and paralysed by sin, 'mortui eramus, vel tamquam paralytici ob peccata'.[33] When the Law was obeyed it was obeyed out of servile fear of retribution: '. . . it is too much like a slave and unworthy . . . to obey divine laws for reward and the hope of recompense. He who serves Christ for these motives is mercenary and is unworthy to be called a son, nor does he deserve to be called Christian.'[34]

Therefore, Chiari argued, the proper end of the Law ('proprium opus legis') was the teaching of the knowledge of sin in order to compel men to turn to Christ. The Law 'tamquam pedagogus pueros regebat'. Like both Ottoni, using Chrysostom, and Benedetto, Chiari mentioned several times 'the knowledge to be sinners, given by the Law', and that 'by the Law . . . we obtain only the knowledge of sin, not liberation from it':[35]

. . . if you have expected to become just through the Law, see in what great danger you put yourselves, for with faith taken away, so is the state of justice taken away, and the promise, those things which go with faith: there only remains anger and vengeance which is the proper work of the Law, for when you hear the Law, then you understand how the Law punishes transgression, therefore it is necessary to trust in faith and grace, if you wish the promise to be fulfilled in you.[36]

---

[31] *Aeditio* 164: 'Lex enim non novit gratiam, vel condonationem, sed tantum exactionem . . . lex enim non ut iustum quemque faciat, lata est, sed ut iniustos coerceat et accuset.' This was part of his scholium on Galatians 3.

[32] Ibid. 163: '. . . nihil unquam vobis aliud attulit, quam minas et poenas'.

[33] Ibid. 126.

[34] Ibid. Vetus Testamentum, 90: '. . . nimium enim est servile, . . . divinis praeceptis operam dare ob mercedem, et spem retributionis. Mercenarii hoc est, et eius, qui filii appellatione sit indignus, neque christianus appellari merito potest, qui hoc animo Christo serviat.' The scholium was of Ps. 118 (119): 112. The entire passage has been scored out in the British Library copy of the 1542 edition.

[35] Ibid. 126–9. The quotations are taken from 128: 'per legem, notitiam esse peccati'; 126: '. . . a lege autem . . . nihil aliud assequimur, quam agnitionem peccati non autem liberationem.' See also ch. 2 of the *Beneficio*, and for Ottoni's views see above, ch. 6.

[36] Ibid. 127, 148–9: '. . . quam promissionem [of justice] si a lege expectatis, videte

The textual evidence alone demonstrates that Chiari's doctrine, like that of Ottoni and others, was based on Chrysostom.

Chiari then expounded the doctrine of grace which was totally efficacious and gratuitous. The Cross cancelled the validity of circumcision and the Law.[37] Christ died so that 'his blood might cleanse'[38] and 'release men from their bondage'.[39] Through their liberation men became sons of God. This was the great 'benefit' of Christ crucified towards men.[40] The Law was now abolished and emptied of its function. In contrast to the condemnation under the Law, sinful man is now freely accepted and loved: 'You are made free from sin, immortal, a son of God, a brother and fellow heir of Christ'.[41] The new condition of man was in no way the consequence of human effort but entirely the work of grace: 'according to grace . . . yes, the grace of God, for rightly, no reward is owed for our works when they are works of God . . .'[42] Chiari's glosses on the doctrine of *gratia sola*, although brief, were so decisive that there could be no question that he accepted the doctrine without equivocation.

As in other Congregational writers, the doctrine of grace alone was followed by a discussion of faith. Chiari used the scholia frequently and at some length to explain his position, for faith was the hinge of his argument in the debate on free will, grace, and works. His definition of faith followed the Antiochene pattern observed in other Cassinese writers. Faith was the point at which grace and *opera humana*—God and man—were coupled. To faith in this sense he ascribed two actions: first, by

quanto vosmetipsos in discrimine constituatis, nam abrogata fide, abrogatur et justificatio, et promissio quae fidem sequebantur: tantum remanet ira, atque ultio, proprium opus legis, nam ubi audis legem, mox intelligis transgressionem, quam lex ulciscatur: necesse est ergo, ut fidei ac gratiae innitare si firmam tibi esse velis promissionem.' (Chiari also considered the disciplinary function of the Law '. . . veluti pedagogum, ut cohiberentur transgressiones, donec deducerentur homines ad Christum', 164.)

37 Ibid. 166. Both Chiari and the *Beneficio* argued that the promise to Abraham overrode the Law given to Moses: the former appealed to Augustine's *Civitas Dei* on the point: 164.

38 Ibid. 218: 'sanguis eius nos emundet . . .'

39 Ibid. 165: 'sicut advenit . . . ut eos, qui peccato erant obnoxii, liberaret'.

40 Ibid. 168: '. . . quanta fuerit Dei erga eos beneficentia . . . ipsos adoptavit in filios', also 192, '. . . benignitas atque humanitatis servatoris nostri Dei apparuisset'.

41 Ibid. 168: '. . . factus es liber a peccato, immortalis, filius Dei, frater et cohaeres Christ.' This passage is part of the gloss on Eph. 1: 3, 'all spiritual blessings'.

42 Ibid. 129: 'secundum gratiam'; '. . . gratia autem Dei: nam recte factis nostris nullum debetur stipendium, cum munera sint Dei', also 46, the scholium on Luke 2.

faith a man apprehended and accepted the saving work of the Cross; second, a man was vivified by faith, so that he lived a new life of hope, love, and good works, all of which worked in him to heal his free will and to bring about a restoration of the divine image.

The first action of faith was to apprehend the gift of grace. Through faith, 'per fidem in Christum', men could accept salvation: 'He who has now embraced faith in Christ, is born again of God, and on that account is a son of God.'[43] Therefore, faith was the only way through which a man could be saved because this was the way he accepted the gift of salvation: 'It is certain that by faith alone, if you believe in your heart and confess with your voice that Jesus is the Lord, you shall be saved.'[44] Since faith required free will in order to accept or reject the gift of salvation, faith was, in a sense, an attribute of man.

At this stage Chiari then began to extend his concept of faith, and to integrate its human aspect with God's grace. The knowledge of faith was greater than mere belief though it had not the certainties of *scientia*: it was a different kind of certainty, the apprehension of unseen realities which enabled 'certa fiducia in Deum', so that living faith experienced its own kind of knowledge:

for all its approach to certainty, knowledge is inferior to scientific certainty which was concerned with the knowledge of causation, and it is above mere belief, which may be shaken by opposition . . . from which faith is free. For it [sc. faith] is indeed certain knowledge, or as is stated here, the apprehension of unseen realities, which here ἔλεγχος is seen to signify.[45]

The Greek noun means 'proof' or 'verification' which can be experienced and known with certainty: at this point Chiari was certainly following Ottoni commentary on Chrysostom.

Chiari was to follow Ottoni further, when he asserted that

---

[43] *Aeditio* 221: 'Qui iam fidem in Christum recepit, ex Deo natus est, et idcirco filius est Dei.' The scholium dealt with the opening words of 1 John 5 on the efficacy of belief. These words are crossed out in the BL copy.

[44] Ibid. 133: 'sola scilicet fide, si enim credideris corde tuo, et ore confessus fueris Dominum Jesum, salvus eris.' These words are also crossed out in the BL copy.

[45] Ibid. 203, concerning Hebrews 11: 'Est enim notitia, quantum ad certidudinem attinet, infra scientiam, quae ex cognitione contingit causarum, et supra opinionem quae adiunctam habet formidinem de opposito illius, quod opinamur, a qua libera est fides. Est enim certa notitia, sive ut hic dicitur, apprehensio rerum non apparentium, hoc enim significare hoc loco ἔλεγχος videtur.'

faith was also a Gift of God—not the scholastic habitual, justifying faith which makes a man inclined to meritorious works, but a free gift prior to works: his faith is not justifying faith, or as the scholastics call it, the gift that makes one pleasing to God, but a gift given gratuitously, which has come to many.'[46] Since faith was a gift of grace, one could assert that man is justified *coram Deo* by faith without turning faith into a work.[47] This doctrine was entirely in accord with Luther's teaching, but its origin did not lie in Reformation writings. The argument and its place in the pattern of salvation was identical to that of Ottoni's exposition of Chrysostom's teaching that faith is simultaneously a gift of God and a response of man, so that faith was inseparably linked with grace on the one hand and man's life on the other, and was therefore the link which coupled God's grace and *opera humana*.[48] This was the basis of the next step in his argument.

The second action of faith was the vivification of man. Man, according to Chiari, was 'obnoxius morti', but was now rescued from death and given life.[49] Now, as he accepts that gift he experiences a new consciousness of assurance, hope, and love, which together make up 'certa fiducia in Deum'.[50] But that faith will manifest itself towards others: 'he who loves the Father will inevitably love those who are also children of the Father . . . let us love our brethren, the children of God, for this is the love of God, and in this we are seen to love God.'[51] Chiari was clear that good works are the sign of the man already accepted by God, and that good works both glorify God and witness to the world.[52] In this sense works are not strictly *opera humana*, but would better be described as fruits of the spirit.[53]

However, for the most part Chiari saw good works as the machinery of the restoration of human nature. Through

[46] Ibid. 148: 'Haec fides non est illa iustificans sive, ut theologi vocant, donum gratum faciens, sed gratis datum, quod multis contigit'. The scholium deals with the 'omnem fidem' of 1 Cor. 13.

[47] Ibid. 127: 'salutem et justificationem . . . sola fides . . . contulit'; 134: 'fidem, per quam justificamur a Deo nostro, et salvatore Jesu Christo'.

[48] For Ottoni's use of Chrysostom on this point see above, ch. 6.

[49] *Aeditio* 130.

[50] Ibid. 203, 192 ('in eisdem tenebris adhuc versaremur'); also 180, 211.

[51] Ibid. 221: 'necesse est, ut qui genitorem diligit, etiam eos diliget, qui ex eo geniti sunt . . . fratres nostros, natos Dei amemus, nam haec est charitas Dei, et in hoc cognoscimur amare Deum.'

[52] Ibid. 127, 212.

[53] Ibid. 166: 'fructum appellat, non opus'.

perseverance in the works of faith, men grew in what was, in effect, the monastic way of perfection. The effect of faith is spiritual growth: 'We men are members of Christ and accepting help from Christ, we grow according to the proportions of our own individual spiritual capacity.'[54] Chiari summed up his doctrine of faith as the instrument of perfection in his gloss on 2 John 4: as a man lives in mortification and the imitation of Christ, God perfects love within him, and restores man to his pristine state:

God perfects love in us that we may have confidence in the day of judgement . . . so that we might imitate him purely and with holiness whilst we have bodily life in the world, and so it happens, that living in this way, we have faith in him and are freed from all fear . . . thus Christ was in the world, spotless and pure, and so we shall be too, or rather, we are.[55]

A corollary of Chiari's argument was the need for simple preaching. He asserted that it was by the Cross, and not by works, that men are saved, and he attacked philosophy and speculative theology.[56] His glosses were biting in their criticism of those 'idiotas et ignobiles homines', whose worldly subtleties were in contrast with the simple scholarship of men like Basil the Great, 'that most learned man who was proud to be the disciple of fishermen'. That expression, 'piscatorum discipulus', was a favourite of Chiari, and later at the Council of Trent he was to use it frequently as a slogan on behalf of biblical studies and against the scholastics.[57]

In another matter Chiari's scholia bore some resemblance to Protestant doctrines. His emphasis upon faith imparted a strong fideist flavour to passages that dealt with the church, so that he

---

[54] *Aeditio* 170: 'Membra Christi nos homines, secundum proportionem privatae spiritualis mensurae, accipientes subministrationem a Christo, crescimus.' See also 129–30.

[55] Ibid. 220: 'perficit Deus charitatem nobiscum, ut fiduciam habeamus in die iudicii . . . ut scilicet imitemur eum pure, ac sancte, dum mundo corpora circumferimus, quo fit, ut ita viventes, fiduciam habeamus erga eum, et omnino liberi metu simus. . . . sicut ille [sc. Christ] erat in mundo immaculatus et purus; sic et nos erimus, vel potius sumus.'

[56] Ibid. 139: 'Nam si sermonis ornatu, et elocutionis vi usi essent, creditum fuisset, hos persuasione potius dicendi, quam veritate nixos, traxisse homines ad credendum, et inanis fuisset crux Christi, cum eius virtuti non ascripta fuisset haec victoria.' The scholium dealt with 1 Cor. 1, 'non in sapientia verbi'.

[57] H. O. Evennett, 'Three Benedictine Abbots at the Council of Trent, 1545–1547', *Studia Monastica*, i (1959), 357.

glossed ἐκκλησία in 1 Cor. 12: 28, as 'the body of the faithful'; 'the members of the household of God are none other than the faithful, they who make up the house of God, that is, the church'.[58] There is some ambiguity in these comments, but in view of the overriding importance he attached to living faith, Chiari could hardly have included mere conformists amongst the 'fideles' who make up the church. Moreover, when he came to the critical passage of Matthew 16, 'super hanc petram etc.', he glossed the passage with the brief but unmistakable interpretation 'super hanc fidei soliditatem'.[59] In other words, in 1542 Chiari's glosses contained the same view of the church as that in the *Beneficio*. Elsewhere I have argued that these passages in the the *Beneficio* were probably written by Flaminio, but whoever wrote them, Chiari's glosses show that they need not necessarily be attributed to Protestant influence, for his ideas plainly came from his Pauline and Greek theology, and from his understanding of faith as the link between *gratia sola* and the monastic way of perfection.[60]

For all these reasons, Chiari's Bible was not well received, and was subjected to Inquisitorial investigation. It was republished in 1557 but without the preface which had referred to the errors of the Vulgate, and without the 'Haec docent'. Later, it was placed on the index of Pius IV.[61]

Chiari's friend Gregory Cortese also prepared a new edition of the Bible—a translation with commentary—published in Venice in 1538, shortly after he had finished his work for the papal reform commission of 1536–7. It is unfortunate that this work has been lost, for despite his very active career, little is known about his theological opinions, though, as we saw in an earlier chapter, he was devoted to the Greek Fathers, especially Chrysostom, and he had made a study of Protestantism. Now, still securely a monk, he became involved in further efforts for reconciliation: although very busy as abbot of San Benedetto Po

[58] *Aeditio* 148: '. . . docet . . . unum nos esse . . . omnes quidem, qui ubique sunt fideles, corpus sunt Christi . . .'; 214 (1 Pet. 4): 'in primis domestici Dei non alii sunt, quam fideles, qui Dei domum perficiunt, videlicet Ecclesiam.'

[59] Ibid. 17. In the BL copy the phrase has been heavily scored out.

[60] Of course, Chiari did not draw the conclusion that separation from the Roman church was permissible; see F. Lauchert, *Die italienischen literarischen Gegner Luthers* (Freiburg-im-Breisgau, 1912), p. 433.

[61] R. Simon, *A Critical History*, ii. 111–13; G. Tiraboschi, *Storia della letteratura italiana*, vii (Modena, 1791), 346–9.

at Mantua in 1538, and abbot of Montecassino in 1539, and again at Mantua in 1540, in the latter year he read Calvin's *Institutes*, set out for the Diet of Worms, looked at the manuscript of *Il Beneficio di Cristo* of his colleague, Don Benedetto da Mantova, and gave his assistance to Cardinal Contarini in preparation for the Colloquy of Regensburg.[62]

Shortly after the collapse of the Regensburg negotiations in July 1541, Cortese was involved in Contarini's last attempt at doctrinal settlement. In Modena, Cortese's native city, members of a learned group were suspected of Lutheran sympathies, and the city was disturbed by uproar in the streets and other signs of religious enthusiasm. Contarini intervened, and after prolonged negotiations, drew up a profession of faith which was intended to accommodate Lutheran beliefs about grace and faith, but to express them in a manner acceptable to Rome. Contarini was assisted by Cortese, who probably negotiated with his fellow citizens and added or reviewed material on free will, works, the eucharist and indulgences.[63]

The formula, *Articuli Orthodoxae Professionis*, was completed in August 1542, shortly after Cortese was made a cardinal, and was signed in Modena by some academicians, and in Rome by a number of cardinals. It was yet another attempt, after the failure of Regensburg, to bring about doctrinal reconciliation, but its articles—particularly those dealing with papal authority, the sacraments, and purgatory, were unlikely to satisfy Protestants, and its success did not extend beyond Modena. It is impossible to distinguish Cortese's contribution to the formula, but his involvement in the affair is in accord with what is known of his work and beliefs—a sympathy for Protestant theology combined with opposition to apostasy and adherence to the teachings of his Congregation.

Another monk was shortly to take a similar stand on apostasy. In August 1542, as the Modena *Articuli* were being drawn up, Bernardino Ochino, the vicar general of the Capuchins, fled over the Alps to the sanctuary of his new-found faith in

[62] M. W. Anderson, *Peter Martyr: a Reformer in Exile (1542–1562)* (Nieuwkoop, 1975), pp. 36–8. Also P. Matheson, *Cardinal Contarini at Regensburg* (Oxford, 1972), pp. 48, 111. For Cortese's views see also above ch. 4, and below, ch. 9.

[63] M. W. Anderson, *Peter Martyr*, pp. 42–3. P. Matheson, *Cardinal Contarini*, pp. 48, 111, refers to Cortese's earlier work as theological advisor to Contarini.

Switzerland.[64] The news of his departure must have been as galling to the Cassinese as to others who still hoped for healing of the breach between Rome and the Reformation. When Ochino wrote to the Venetian authorities in defence of his flight, Don Marco of Brescia, then abbot of S. Vitale at Ravenna, wrote a reply, though neither letter has survived. In turn, Ochino replied to Marco in a work published at Geneva in 1543.[65]

Marco was not unsympathetic to the Reformation, for he held to the same Pauline doctrines as his colleagues. In a sermon he has asserted that salvation was based only upon Christ's death, and that the Cross was 'donum Dei' which saved men: 'through the mercy which {Christ} showed by dying for us, through the blood which he pours out, hanging on the Cross for us'.[66] Man was taken out of his grievous condition and restored 'per crucem et mortem immeritam' of Christ, 'not out of my works, but only by the benefit of your mercy'.[67] However, like his colleagues, Marco adhered strongly to the church of Rome; from Ochino's text it appears that Marco's letter defended the authority of the Pope and the petrine succession, and criticized Ochino for his failure to understand the value of works, and for separating from the church because of its blemishes.[68]

The year 1542 was a time of crisis for Italian evangelicals. The flight of Ochino, followed a few days later by that of Peter Martyr, was a sign of the dilemma being forced upon them. The work of reconciliation was no longer a virtue, and began to carry the smell of treachery: Contarini told Ochino that even he believed himself to be in danger because he had not opposed the Protestants strongly enough on the article of justification.[69] The

---

[64] P. McNair, *Peter Martyr in Italy*, pp. 277 ff.

[65] *Responsio Bernardi Ochini senensis ad Marcum Brixiensem* (Geneva, 1543). There is a copy in the Bibliothèque Publique et Universitaire, Geneva (Bc 2506). There are references to the episode in R. H. Bainton, *Bernardino Ochino esule e riformatore senese del Cinquecento 1487–1563* (Florence, 1940), pp. 50, 54, 56, 72. For details of Don Marco of Brescia see Armellini, *Bibl. Bened.-Cas.* ii. 89–90. Marco probably taught Teofilo Folengo, see G. Billanovich, *Tra Don Teofilo*, p. 32. Also see K. Benrath, *Bernardino Ochino of Siena* (London, 1876), p. 145.

[66] Bibl. Apost. Vat., Urb. Lat. 1501, 'Homilia super Joannis xiii ante die(m) festu(m) paschae', fos. 9^r, 16^v, 33^r: '. . . per misericordia(m) qua(m) exhibui(t) moriendo pro nobis, per sanguinem quem effundi(t) in cruce pendendo pro nobis . . .'

[67] Bibl. Univ. Padua, MS 152, fos. 107–8, 119: '. . . acceptum fero, non autem meis ex operibus, verum tui tantummodo misereritis [*sic*].'

[68] Ochino, *Responsio*, B.5^r, also B.3^r, B.4^r–v, B.7^v, B.8^r, C.2^r–C.3^v.

[69] Ibid. B.5^r.

new virtue was militancy, and before its bold face the peace-makers amongst the evangelicals looked increasingly like unrea-listic appeasers, and increasingly they were being forced to choose between obedience and heresy. But for the Benedictine monks the problem was different: for them the debate between faith and works had been long resolved, and their theology rested upon a synthesis which could not admit the intellectual validity of the quarrel between Rome and the Reformation. For them the split in Latin Christendom was the product of Latin theology, and they held the remedy—taken from the Greek Fathers—in their hands. For them there was no question of apostasy; their only course was to uphold their monastic theology and its Antiochene roots in the face of growing suspicion and hostility.

Despite the changing climate of opinion, the monks held their ground and continued to profess their doctrines. In 1542 Denis Faucher was again prior of the house at Tarascona, near Arles. He found the job a heavy one, for he was directing biblical and patristic studies and at the same time supervising a convent in which bright young women learned Latin and Greek, and 'studied seriously the holy scriptures and works of the holy Fathers'.[70] Moreover, Faucher was in poor health, troubled by accusations of Lutheran tendencies, and not a little flustered by the more aggressive young nuns in his charge, but he found time in 1543 to compose a tract for the clergy of Arles on the subject of the priesthood.[71]

The importance of this topic to the Congregation arose from their Pauline theology, which not only rendered them open to the suspicion of Protestant views in this as well as in other matters, but also confronted the monks themselves with the

---

[70] *Opera* 276–7. The letter was written to Cortese, from Tarascona, 9 February 1542, 'fingers numb with great cold'. For his convent school see 277, 310, 340, '. . . young women destined to the service of God ought to study Greek at the same time as Latin, seeing that it is necessary for them to meditate upon scripture in the heart and not to mouth it like magpies and parrots as is so common . . . and to study seriously the holy scriptures and works of the holy Fathers.'

[71] The tract, *Sermo ad Clerum Arelatensem*, is printed in the *Opera* 265–9. For references to Lutheranism see 267, 282, 293, 325–6, 'nulla tam falsa doctrina est, quae non aliqua vera intermisceat'. For his difficulties with nuns see especially 310–11, with Faucher's complaint about a confrontation with one of his students, '. . . canina facundia multis verbis mecum de se et sorore sua egerat . . .' (with bitchy loquacity she carried on at me about herself and her sister).

question of the part which the priesthood played in salvation. In this address, Faucher set himself the task of asserting the necessity of the priesthood, in obedience to the monks' own priestly vocations as well as obedience to Rome, without denying salvation by grace alone, for he was speaking to his fellow monks as much as to his audience.

The tract began by asserting the dignity of the priesthood, which was upheld by the quality of the priest's life and the example by which he guided his flock: 'Feed them', he told the clergy of Arles, 'by your virtues and with your good examples.' Priests must not be greedy or ambitious—a point well made in a diocese whose bishop was both—for greed and ambition were not merely a scandal to the church, but also an affront to Christ's sacrifice.[72]

When Faucher turned to the sacramental functions of the priest, he spoke only of the eucharist. He reminded his audience that the eucharistic mysteries were derived entirely from the Cross and that it is Christ who gives the sacramental food at the hands of priests. He laid such strong emphasis upon the offering of the High Priest that the priestly function of the clergy seemed little more than 'the right to administer'. At the heart of his address was the exposition of the Cross as the sole source of sacramental benefits. After a reminder to the clergy that 'potestas nulla est nisi a Deo' he went on to say that in the eucharist 'Christ, the true and high priest offered himself, an immaculate victim, to God for our sins'.[73] There was no discussion of transubstantiation, nor any suggestion that priests possessed sacerdotal sacramental power which helped men to achieve salvation. Rather, he depicted priests as pastors whose task was to bring men to the Cross, and to help them grow in sanctity through teaching, reconciliation and through administering the sacraments.[74]

Faucher's address tried to explain the work of priests within

---

[72] Ibid. 265–6. There is a similar passage in *Il Beneficio di Cristo*, published the same year, see Caponetto, *Beneficio* 53–4. Jean Ferrier was coadjutor bishop of Arles from 1499 to 1521, then bishop until his death in 1551.

[73] Ibid. 266: 'Christus . . . sacerdos summus ac verus semetipsum pro peccatis nostris obtulit hostiam immaculatam Deo . . .'

[74] Ibid. 251, 266–7. Melanchthon is similar in part: he acknowledges 'the benefits of the mass and the power of the eucharist', but is opposed to elevation of the priesthood: see *Loci Communes*, 'Human Laws', and 'Participation in the Lord's Table', *Melanchthon and Bucer*, ed. Pauck, pp. 70, 145–7.

the pattern of salvation taught by the Congregation, combining both salvation by grace through faith and the monastic way of perfection, concentrating upon the way of perfection and showing how priests administer, teach, guide, set an example, and generally act as pastors. It was not only in accordance with Cassinese doctrines, it was also perhaps intended as a doctrine of the ministry that might be accepted by both Rome and the Reformers. It showed the pastoral nature of the office of a priest, and made it wholly subordinate to the Cross, which may have pleased the Protestants, and it asserted the dignity and necessity of the priesthood (though not the sacramental power), which may have been acceptable to the Catholics.

Faucher's tract was an attempt to resolve one of the problems of divided western Christendom, but it did not reach a wide audience, and, indeed, probably reached few people other than the clergy of Arles. On the other hand, a tract of a colleague and friend of Faucher, published also in 1543, received the widest acclaim, and it is to this tract that we shall now turn.

VIII

Benedetto da Mantova and the
Beneficio di Cristo

WE have seen that the writers of the Cassinese Congregation of
Benedictines held in common certain doctrines drawn from
their biblical and patristic studies, in particular from the
Antiochene exegesis of the Pauline epistles. In this chapter what
has been discovered about that teaching will be applied to a
much debated Reformation tract which was published in its
second edition, in the autumn of 1543, in Venice 'apud
Bernardinum de Bindonis'. This small book was entitled *Trattato
utilissimo del beneficio di Giesu Christo crocifisso verso i Christiani*.
Written in lucid and vigorous Italian, it described the fall of
man, his sin, redemption through faith in the gift—the 'beneficio'—of the Cross, and the nature of the Christian life. Clearly it
was a work of rhetorical preaching intended for a wide
audience, and in this respect it was entirely successful. A number
of prominent churchmen approved the work for its spirituality
and encouraged its propagation. Vergerio, the bishop of Capo
d'Istria, estimated confidently that 40,000 copies had been sold
in the six years it was available to the public. On the other hand
the Dominican Lancelotto Politi (Ambrogio Catarino) immediately claimed that the book was a compendium of 'errors and
Lutheran deceits'. It was burned in Naples, denounced in
Verona, and included in della Casa's Venetian index of
prohibited books in 1549. Thereafter it was suppressed with
such thoroughness that it seemed all copies had been destroyed,
until, in 1843, one was discovered at Cambridge.[1] The discovery

---

[1] There is a modern critical edition, Benedetto da Mantova, *Il Beneficio di Cristo, con le
versioni del secolo xvi, documenti e testimonianze*, ed. S. Caponetto (Corpus Reformatorum
Italicorum, 1972). The circumstances of the original text's publication and its
suppression are described by Caponetto in his 'Nota Critica', pp. 469–532; by P.
McNair, *Peter Martyr in Italy*, pp. 42–5; and by D. Fenlon, *Heresy and Obedience*, pp. 74–85.
The history of the debate is given by Ruth Prelowski, 'The Beneficio di Cristo, translated
with an introduction', *Italian Reformation Studies in Honor of Laelius Socinus*, ed. J. A.
Tedeschi (Florence, 1965), pp. 23–94. Also M. Rosa, 'Il Beneficio di Christo:

initiated debates, which still continue, upon the authorship of the tract, its theological sources, and its place within Italian Reform movement generally.

In 1566–7, during his trial for heresy, Pietro Carnesecchi told the inquisitorial tribunal that the *Beneficio* had been the work of two men, of whom 'one began it and other finished and polished it'. Don Benedetto da Mantova[2] began the tract whilst he was at the Cassinese monastery of S. Nicolo de Arenis in Sicily, from 1537 to 1541, and the man who finished and polished it was Marcantonio Flaminio, a humanist poet and friend of Don Benedetto. Very probably, Flaminio carried out his revision of the manuscript in Florence in 1541, and a now extinct first version of the work circulated between late 1541 and 1543.[3]

As for the theological sources, the themes and much of the language of the *Beneficio* reproduce the teachings of Juan de Valdés. Valdés, a Spaniard, was a humanist and biblical scholar and something of a mystic. He held a position at the papal court, but after the death of Clement VII, in 1534, he retired to Naples. Until his death in July 1541, he gathered around him a group of disciples, amongst them the impressionable Marcantonio Flaminio.[4] Valdés taught that man, doubly burdened with original guilt and the acquired guilt of personal sin, could not be justified through his own efforts, but only by the gratuitous gift of Christ's righteousness, which he called the 'beneficio di Cristo'; man's response was to understand and accept this gift and then to manifest his salvation by good works. Valdés emphasized inner fervour but was weak on biblical exegesis. His sources are

Interpretazioni a Confronto', *Bibliothèque d'Humanisme et Renaissance*, xl (1978), 609–20. The tract is seen in a wider context in P. F. Grendler, *The Roman Inquisition and the Venetian Press, 1540–1605* (Leiden, 1977), pp. 82, 84, 105–6, 125.

[2] E. Menegazzo, 'Contributo alla Biografia di T. Folengo (1512–1520)', *Italia medioevale e umanistica*, ii (1959), 378–9. In 1978 the same author produced many family details of Benedetto, notably that he was closely related to the Gonzaga family, 'Per la Conoscenza della Riforma in Italia. Note d'Archivio', *Atti e memoire dell'Accademia Patavina di Scienze, Lettere ed Arti*, xc, part 3 (1977–8), 193–216, especially 205–10.

[3] Caponetto, *Beneficio* 460, 481–96; Fenlon, *Heresy and Obedience*, pp. 78–81; S. Caponetto, 'Benedetto da Mantova', *Dizionaria biografico degli italiani*, viii (Rome, 1966), 437–41. The president of the Congregation in 1543 was Don Innocentius de'Honoria da Novara, formerly abbot of S. Giorgio Maggiore, Venice, who had also been abbot at Ravenna, and in Sicily where he spent six years (he was abbot at Messina in 1541); Caponetto, *Beneficio* 430, 490; 'Nomina Omnium Monachorum', Bibl. Naz. Florence, Conv. Sopp. da Ord., Badia, 4, fos. 126–7.

[4] McNair, *Peter Martyr in Italy*, p. 98.

not clear, for he did not acknowledge them, apart from the Bible, but his teachings can be seen to have affinities with those of Luther, Calvin, and other Protestant theologians, with Spanish *alumbrados*, with Erasmus, and with Italian *spirituali*.[5] Whether the paternity of his ideas lay with some or all of these men, or with his own original thought, remains uncertain despite the labours of recent biographers.[6] On the other hand the proliferation of his ideas is easier to trace. In particular the *Benefico* has so many textual similarities to the works of Valdés, and Flaminio was such an ardent disciple, that there can be no doubt of his influence. For these reasons the *Beneficio* has been considered generally to be the product of his evangelical circle at Naples.

However, at the same time a number of historians expressed unease with the idea that the *Benefico* was purely of Valdesian inspiration. They felt that it had a strong Protestant flavour and some suggested Protestant origins. In 1961 their suspicions were confirmed when Tommaso Bozza discovered that the tract incorporated, by translation or paraphrase, whole passages of the 1539 edition of Calvin's *Institutes*. In later works Bozza argued that Benedetto da Mantova had read this edition of the *Institutes* when copies first reached Sicily in 1540, and there, in Sicily, inspired by Calvin, he had composed the *Beneficio*: in 1542 Benedetto had travelled to Viterbo, where he had given his manuscript to Flaminio, who had merely polished the style using some expressions, including the title, from the works of Valdés. In short, Bozza argued that the *Beneficio* was written by a Benedictine monk turned Calvinist, and that it was Calvinist in substance and had little in common with the teaching of Valdés.[7]

---

[5] J. C. Nieto, *Juan de Valdés and the Origins of the Spanish and Italian Reformation* (Geneva, 1970), pp. 106–12, 126–7, 134–9, 188–94, 323–6. The main Spanish influence upon Valdés was Pedro Ruiz de Alcaraz. Calvin laid emphasis upon the Spirit and the growth of new life in justified man in the *Institutes*, I. xiii. 14–15; III. ii. 31–7; III. iii; IV. xvi. 25: IV. xvii. 1–10, 32–4.

[6] In addition to Nieto's work see J. N. Bakhuizen van den Brink, *Juan de Valdés réformateur en Espagne et en Italie* (Geneva, 1969); C. Ossola, 'Tradizione e traduzione dell' "Evangelio di San Matteo" di Juan de Valdés', in *Eresia e riforma nell'Italia del Cinquecento* (Biblioteca del Corpus Reformatorum Italicorum, Miscellanea I, 1974), pp. 7–68. Ossola argues that Valdés was aware that his teaching was new, but he was unable to abandon old attitudes to good works.

[7] T. Bozza, *Introduzione al Beneficio di Cristo* (privately printed, Rome, 1963); *Nuovi studi sulla Riforma in Italia, I Il Beneficio di Cristo*, Uomini e Dottrine, xxii (Rome, 1976).

Bozza's discovery was interpreted otherwise by Salvatore Caponetto, who argued that, passages from the *Institutes* notwithstanding, the theology of the *Beneficio* was not Calvinist. It differed from Calvin in the doctrines of knowledge, the capabilities of fallen man, the ethical value of the Law, the visible church, double predestination, the doctrines of baptism and the eucharist. Moreover, some passages taken from Calvin were actually paraphrases of Augustine. Caponetto believes that the *Institutes* were merely a 'precious instrument of work' from which the author had taken illustrative material. The 'heart and substratum of the work' were the doctrines of Valdés, with which both Benedetto and Flaminio were familiar.[8]

Yet another suggestion has been put forward by Dermot Fenlon, who agreed with Bozza that the *Beneficio* was substantially a Calvinist work with Valdesian additions, but who saw no need to postulate, as Bozza had done, Don Bendetto's conversion to Calvinism in Sicily in 1540 or 1541. Instead, Fenlon argued, both the Calvinist and Valdesian elements were the work, not of the monk, but of the revisor, Flaminio, who was familiar with the works of both Calvin and Valdés, whose works, in any case, have much in common.[9] Fenlon concluded that Flaminio had revised Benedetto's original manuscript so thoroughly that 'the main lines of the work (not just the form) . . . the real originality of the work derives from Flaminio'. As for the monk, Benedetto da Mantova' 'his contribution to the final product is historically indeterminate'.[10] In this chapter I shall argue that this is not the case and that the contribution of the monk is recognizable.

In 1974 Adriano Prosperi and Carlo Ginzburg put aside the questions of authorship and sources and turned their attention to the evolution of the manuscript and the printed text.[11] They suggested that Benedetto's original manuscript had been written as a work of late medieval Benedictine piety, was revised by Flaminio, and circulated amongst *spirituali* at Naples, Rome, Viterbo, and Verona, by 1540. This revised manuscript was then seen by the Dominican Catarino, who criticized its heretical

[8] Caponetto, *Beneficio* 476–9.
[9] Fenlon, *Heresy and Obedience*, p. 70; McNair, *Peter Martyr in Italy*, p. 47.
[10] Fenlon, *Heresy and Obedience*, p. 81.
[11] C. Ginzburg and A. Prosperi, 'Le Due Redazioni', pp. 137–204.

tendencies along the lines later set out in his *Compendio* of March 1544, and in response to this criticism Flaminio rewrote the *Beneficio*. This new version is the *Beneficio* of 1543 which we have now. By comparing Catarino's detailed criticism in the *Compendio* with the final version of the *Beneficio*, Prosperi and Ginzburg concluded that Flaminio had added chapters 5 and 6, and a small part of chapter 4, using a great deal of material from Calvin.[12]

The two historians observed that the earlier part of the chapter, the 'strato anteriore', included certain themes that were also present in the writings of other Benedictines. These included trust in the mercy of God, universal predestination, and healed free will, and the treatment of these themes clearly differed from both Reformed and Valdesian theology. They concluded that the themes were representative of fifteenth- and sixteenth-century Italian piety, a widespread 'pelagianismo diffuso', particularly found amongst Benedictine writers, and unrecognized until the Reformation debates brought it to light. The heart of this first version of the *Beneficio* was 'dolcezza', the 'dolce dottrina' that salvation was accomplished by belief. Far from being a masterpiece of the Reformation, it was a work of sophisticated Pelagianism which used the Fathers to bolster its form of piety.[13] The following year the authors developed their two arguments, that the *Beneficio* appeared in two editions, and that Benedetto wrote the first version, of four chapters, expounding the 'via larga alla salvezza', the Pelagian 'tradizione sotteranea nell'ordine benedettino', whilst Flaminio wrote, or rewrote, the fifth and sixth chapters in the Augustinian manner. These latter chapters, they say, are like a mask, covering, but conserving, the original shape.[14]

In a lengthy article written in 1975 Paolo Simoncelli agreed that the text developed in response to Catarino's criticism, but denied that it was composed of disparate theological traditions.[15] He denied that differences between the text of 1543 and

---

[12] Ibid. pp. 142–7.

[13] Ibid. pp. 177–82.

[14] A. Prosperi and C. Ginzburg, *Giochi di Pazienza: Un seminario sul Beneficio di Cristo* (Turin, 1975), pp. 14, 62–3, 183. Their argument was criticized by V. Vinay in his review in *Zeitschrift für Kirkengeschichte* (1976), pp. 406–7; also Bozza, *Nuovi studi*, pp. 387 ff.

[15] P. Simoncelli, 'Nuove Ipotesi e studi sull'Beneficio di Cristo', *Critica storica* (New series, 2, 3, 4, 1975), pp. 144–212.

Catarino's reference implied the existence of an earlier, different text: on the contrary, he claimed, from the beginning the *Beneficio* was a tract of Protestant theology, and he quoted passages from Calvin and Melanchthon to show that the themes of trust, free will, and universal election, which Prosperi and Ginzburg thought 'Pelagian', were compatible with the evangelical nature of the tract.[16] He argued that Catarino wrote two criticims of the *Beneficio*. First he read it in manuscript form, recognized its heretical flavour and then wrote his *De Perfecta Iustificatione* (1541) in order to provoke his evangelical opponents into a clearer statement of their position—to flush them into the open as it were—by accusing them of holding that mere belief effected salvation and being unconcerned with works. Simoncelli suggested that Flaminio reacted to these accusations with anger and, using Calvin's *Institutes*, vigorously expounded a doctrine of certitude and the necessity of works of gratitude, at the same time making aggressive, partisan distinctions between true Christians ('noi') and those false Christians who attributed saving value to their works. According to Simoncelli, these passages were added 'per risposta a questo Padre Politi [sc. Catarino]'.[17] Thus, Simoncelli saw the *Beneficio* as an evangelical tract which, in response to the provocations of Catarino, became aggressively Protestant at the hands of its revisor, Flaminio. At the end of his long article, Simoncelli recommended as 'not without validity' Fenlon's thesis that the virtual author of the *Beneficio* was Flaminio, whose revision had transformed the tract into an evangelical banner, woven from Reformed and Valdesian sources.[18]

In 1975 M. Rosa, though sceptical about the 'two editions', hypothesis, acknowledged two different parts to the tract. Rosa said that the first was quietist and ascetic, a form of interior piety based upon the *Imitation of Christ*, the other doctrinal and theological, based upon Melanchthon's exposition of justification by faith alone. These two 'filoni', Rosa says, were entwined to give a dual nature to Italian Evangelism, and its debates on faith and works.[19]

---

[16] Simoncelli, 'Nuove Ipotesi', pp. 197 ff.

[17] Ibid., pp. 195–6. The phrase is taken from a letter of Priuli to Beccadelli, dated 1 May 1542; the letter was quoted by Bozza and is printed by Caponetto (*Beneficio* 431).

[18] Simoncelli, 'Nuove Ipotesi', pp. 211–12.

[19] Rosa, 'Il Beneficio di Christo: Interpretazione a Confronto', pp. 614–16.

In this chapter I shall analyse the text of the 1543 edition in the light of other Cassinese writings. Since we know that Don Benedetto wrote the first draft, any close resemblances between the text and writings common to other Cassinese writers may be presumed to be the work of Don Benedetto, and the remnants of his first draft. By such application of the Congregational teachings to the text, the respective contributions of Benedetto and Flaminio may be elicited and the boundaries of their work traced within the text. It will then be possible to establish the nature of this first draft, whether it was an example of traditional quietist and mystical piety (as Rosa says) or Pelagian piety (as Prosperi and Ginzburg say), or whether, like other Cassinese teaching, it was Pauline teaching drawn from the Greek Fathers of Antioch. I shall argue that the text of 1543 was indeed the work of two authors, and that the text reflects their different approaches to Pauline theology—Benedetto's derived from his order and ultimately from the Greek Fathers, Flaminio's derived from Valdés, Thomas à Kempis, and, later, from Calvin. Moreover, as we shall see, Flaminio's contribution was made in two distinct stages—the first the polishing of Benedetto's manuscript, and later, the addition of partisan Calvinist material.

The key expression used in the tract's title, 'the benefit of Christ' is derived from St. Paul's idea that the death and resurrection of Christ is a gift to mankind. The idea was expounded by later writers, principally Augustine, Chrysostom, and Bernard of Clairvaux. In the fifteenth century the term 'benefit' was employed by Thomas à Kempis and Paul Giustiniani and, of course, by the monks of the Congregation, who used it extensively in their Pauline theology. Amongst the reformers it was first used by Melanchthon, who may have taken it from a philological footnote in Erasmus's *New Testament* of 1516,[20] and it was also used by Valdés. Since Don Benedetto and Flaminio would have been familiar with the term and its Pauline implications, no firm conclusion can be drawn from this use of it.

The first chapter of the *Beneficio* consisted of a mere forty-eight lines, headed 'On original sin and the misery of man'. The

[20] Caponetto, *Beneficio* 473.

chapter introduced in summary form the three salvation themes which were to be developed in later chapters—man's original perfection, his fallen nature, his restoration. Man, who was made in the image and likeness of God, immortal, without suffering, and holy, lost original perfection when, through Adam, imperfection entered the human race. Thereafter, men were physically and mentally corrupt, in their minds 'unjust, lying, cruel, impious, and hostile to God', and in their bodies mortal and subject to suffering.[21] This fallen condition of man was described in extreme physical terms as a kind of congenital gangrene which completely corrupted the whole of human nature', 'a destructive and deadly . . . pestilential illness contracted through the contagion of our first parents'. In these words we see the definition of sin perceived as a condition of inherited disintegration rather than a state of inherited guilt. Congruent with this pathological concept of sin, the last lines of the chapter described salvation in terms of healing and restoration, 'to be freed from this mortal illness and to return to that first innocence, regaining the image of God'.[22]

What were the sources of the doctrine of the fall set out in the first chapter? There is a superficial resemblance to Calvin's doctrine, but as Caponetto has pointed out, the *Beneficio* has a much more pessimistic view of fallen man than has Calvin, for whom the effects of the fall were adventitious, not essential.[23] Caponetto's observation is valid: Calvin appreciated the natural righteousness of man, merely denying the capacity of the vitiated will to merit justification, whereas the *Beneficio* saw fallen man as 'completely corrupted': 'There is no language that could express a thousandth part of our calamity, that we who were created by God's own hands, have lost that divine image and have become like the devil, acquiring his nature and

---

[21] Caponetto, *Beneficio* 13–14: '. . . perdette quella imagine e similitudine divina . . . divenne ingiusto, mendace e crudele, impio e inimico di Dio; e in quanto al corpo, diventò passibile e suggetto a mille incomodi e infirmità . . . Insomma, questa nostra natura per lo peccato di Adamo tutta si corruppe . . .' For the most part, my translations follow those of Prelowski.

[22] Ibid. 15, lines 39–49. This notion of the restoration of the *imago Dei* in man, which we have seen in other Congregational writings, was vividly described by Chrysostom as a restoration, through faith, 'like fire in our souls', to 'the image of the heavenly, fresh coined, bright and glittering, as from the furnace-mould': *The Homilies of St. John Chrysostom . . . on the Gospel of John* (Library of the Fathers, Oxford, 1848), p. 85.

[23] Caponetto, *Beneficio* 13, n. 3; 14, n. 5.

identity.'[24] This was the language of a theology of sin and salvation quite different from that of Calvin. Calvin's *Institutes* saw fallen man as guilty and condemned in the face of God's justice, whereas the first chapter of the *Beneficio* depicted sin in terms of disintegration and death as opposed to wholeness and life. The doctrines of Calvin were unlikely to have been the inspiration for the first chapter of the *Beneficio*.

On the other hand there is a clear connection between the first chapter and the writings of Valdés, since the opening lines incorporated paraphrased material from Valdés.[25] The question is whether the substance of the chapter has been taken from Valdés or whether his writings have merely been used to illustrate the chapter. In this case there is reason to suppose that the elegant phrases taken from Valdés are merely illustrative.

In earlier chapters we have seen that within the Congregation of Santa Giustina a pathological concept of sin had long been taught, together with the corollary that salvation was a process of healing and restoration. Moreover, Benedetto's contemporaries, Denis Faucher, Isidoro Chiari, Gregorio Bornato, Giambattista Folengo, and others also taught it. In 1527 and again in 1533 Don Teofilo Folengo described the condition of fallen man in almost the same words, as a loss of the divine image, an inherited state of corruption—'sterco, fango'—which clouded the mind and kept man trapped in sinfulness, victim of the 'morbo' of the 'invecchiato veleno' and able to be cured only by Christ the 'Medico gentil'. In particular, Benedetto's friend, Luciano degli Ottoni, in his translation and commentary upon Chrysostom's *Homilies upon Romans*, of 1538, had expounded the Greek Father's account of the fall as a condition of morbidity and alienation, describing fallen men as 'patibiles ac a Deo alienos et exules'.[26]

These men had been colleagues and fellow scholars of Benedetto for about thirty years before the *Beneficio* was written. The similarity of their teachings and the fact that such doctrine was commonly taught in the Cassinese Congregation, suggests that the first chapter was indeed written—at least in part—by the Cassinese monk Benedetto da Mantova, who derived his

---

[24] Ibid. 14, lines 25–30.
[25] Ibid. 13, n. 3.
[26] See above, ch. 6.

ideas from within his own order. It is less clear whether the Valdesian phrases used at the beginning of the chapter were written by Don Benedetto or added by his reviser, Flaminio, as a vivid and elegant introduction. However, since there is no direct evidence that Benedetto was a disciple of Valdés, whereas we know with certainty that Flaminio was a most ardent disciple, and moreover, a man with an eye for literary form, it seems probable that the Valdesian phrases in the first chapter were inserted by Flaminio.

On the other hand, the substance of Valdés theology has not been used in this chapter. Valdés concept of sin was predominantly Anselmian and forensic in nature. He held that men inherited Adam's guilt and condemnation, which they compound with guilt acquired through their own wilful depravity. When he spoke of loss of *imago Dei*, physical passibility, and mental wickedness, the emphasis lay upon man's punishment and loss of free will, in contrast to the monks' Greek patristic understanding of these terms.[27] Thus, whilst the language of Valdés coincided in part with the language of the Cassinese, this did not signify coincidence of doctrine. It was rather an overlap of terminology—which enabled Flaminio to use some of Valdés's writings on guilt to illustrate a Cassinese tract on damaged humanity.

The second chapter turned to the process of salvation, in which the first step was man's recognition of his morbid condition. In order to 'persuade men of their misery' God gave to men the Mosaic Law: 'God gave us the Law so that we would recognize our sin, and despairing of our ability to justify ourselves by works, would have recourse to the mercy of God and the justice of faith.[28] First, the Law commanded men to love perfectly both God and fellow man, 'with joy and readiness of heart', but when confronted with this commandment men realized their inability to fulfil it, and so they became aware of their sin. This was the first of the five offices of the Law—to act as 'a mirror', 'to make sin known'. The second office of the Law

---

[27] Nieto, *Juan de Valdés*, pp. 302–3; also pp. 130, 274, 297–9; *Diálogo de doctrina christiana*, ed. B. F. Stockwell (Buenos Aires, Mexico, 1946), pp. 37–8, 148; *Alfabeto christiano*, ed. and trans. B. B. Wiffen (London, 1861), pp. 20–6, 106; *Divine Considerations* (Sacred Treasury, London, no date, but probably 1905–6), Consid. 6, 11, 34, 98. This edition is a reprint of Nicholas Ferrar's Oxford edition (1638).

[28] Caponetto, *Beneficio* 16.

was to make sin grow ('fa crescere il peccato'), by which it was meant that the prohibitions of the Law stimulated concupiscence, thereby driving men deeper into sin, so that they might the more be aware of their impotence.[29] In the remaining offices of the Law there was a shift in emphasis from the awareness of sin to the guilt of man and the wrath of God, that is, from the Law's pedagogic to its punitive function: 'The third office of the Law is to reveal the wrath and judgement of God, who threatens wrath and eternal punishment to those who do not fully observe his Law.'[30] The fourth office of the Law was to terrify man by the 'wrath and anger of God who threatens death . . . because he fears that God will chastise and punish him severely'.[31] The fifth office was that the Law thus compelled men to go to Christ as their advocate and mediator.[32]

Caponetto has shown that the part of the chapter that describes the offices of the Law is a paraphrase of the *Alfabeto christiano*, written by Valdés in 1536. Valdés's treatment of the Law concentrated almost entirely upon the Law's provocation and its punitive functions and very little upon its pedagogy, describing how the Law confronts men with the meaning of sin, and then 'works wrath . . . fear and dismay . . . and error, alarm, and conflict of affections . . . to fear the judgement of God'.[33]

On the other hand, the first and second offices, in which the Law has merely a pedagogic role and is not an instrument of terror, closely resemble Cassinese writings on the Law. In 1533, in his *L'umanità del Figliuolo di Dio*, Don Teofilo Folengo had said that it was when men realized their inability to become inwardly perfect through obedience to the Law, and recognized their condition of wretchedness and sin, that they turned to grace for salvation.[34] The same teaching was seen in Ottoni's translation and commentary upon Chrysostom's *Homily on Romans*, published in 1538. Ottoni, following Chrysostom, held that the functions of the Law were first to teach the nature of sin, and second, by the explicit definition and prohibition of wrongdoing, to increase the culpability of sinners. In 1542, a year

---

[29] Ibid. 16–17, lines 20–32. The increase of sin is treated in Gal. 3: 19.

[30] Caponetto, *Beneficio* 17, lines 32–4.

[31] Ibid. 17, lines 39–43; from 1 Cor. 15: 56; 2 Cor. 3: 7–8.

[32] Ibid. 17–18, lines 45–53.

[33] Ibid. 16, n. 1; *Alfabeto* 32–4. His image of the mirror was taken from Calvin.

[34] See above, ch. 4.

before the publication of the text of the *Beneficio*, Isidoro Chiari's *Novum Testamentum* also asserted that the function of the Law was 'that men might know sin, and themselves to be sinners'.[35] Since this teaching was expressed within the Congregation before the *Beneficio* was written (and in the case of Folengo and even earlier writers, before Valdés had written anything on the topic), it is clear that the 'pedagogic' part—though not the 'punitive' part—of the chapter was derived from within Benedetto's own Congregation, from its teaching based upon Chrysostom. After all, Benedetto had been a member of this closely knit order for thirty years before he wrote his tract, and he was known to be on intimate terms with his scholarly colleagues, especially Ottoni.

If this interpretation is correct, the earlier part of the chapter, including the first two offices of the Law, was originally written by the monk; then it was polished by Flaminio, disciple of Valdés, using Valdesian words and phrases, and the chapter extended by the addition of material from Valdés on the punitive offices of the Law.[36] Clearly, the biblical material in these two chapters came from Benedetto. Moreover, the revisions and additions of Flaminio reflect Valdes's virtual absence of biblical exegesis.

The third chapter moved the argument on to salvation by grace alone. The enormous emphasis placed upon this doctrine has led some historians to regard the *Beneficio* as Italy's masterpiece of the Reformation.[37] However, I shall argue that in separate parts of the third chapter the central doctrine of grace has been treated in two different ways. First, it was described in the Cassinese manner as rescue from death and the restoration of perfection, which is available to all men, but the latter half of the chapter (lines 102 to the end) described it, as did Protestant and

[35] See above, ch. 7.

[36] This conclusion suggests the possibility that the Benedictines were a source for Valdés's teaching. Whilst it is probable that much of his teaching was heavily influenced by Calvin, it is also quite possible that part of his teaching on the Law—the part that resembles the teaching of Chrysostom—was derived from the scholarly monks of Santa Giustina, who, after all, were well versed in patristic theology whilst Valdés was not. For the influence of Calvin upon Valdés see McNair, *Peter Martyr in Italy*, 47; Nieto, *Juan de Valdés*, pp. 199–201; for Valdés's lack of patristic knowledge see pp. 126–7, 188–91.

[37] The expression 'il vero capolavoro della Riforma Italiana' was used by A. Casadei, 'Fanino Fanini da Faenza', *Nuova rivista storica*, xviii (1934), 173.

Valdesian teaching, in terms of justification through the remission of guilt and the unmerited imputation of righteousness.

The chapter's title—'That the remission of sins, justification and our whole salvation depends upon Christ'—was probably composed by Flaminio. It could be taken as a neat summary of Cassinese teaching, with its juxtaposition of two aspects of salvation: the two themes were developed in the first sentence: Christ came 'so that he might free us from the curse of the Law, reconcile us with our God, make our will capable of doing good works, heal our free will, and restore to us that divine image which we lost.[38] Therefore the 'tutta la salute nostra' of the title was in the first place an unmerited reconciliation with God, and in the second place a healing of damaged human nature and the restoration of the divine image in men. Consequently, Christ was described as the restorer of mortal, damaged man, 'the most kind physician', 'through him we have been given eternal life and death has been slain'.[39] This summary does not accurately reflect Valdés, whose emphasis was upon guilt, justification, and the acquisition of personal justice. On the other hand it is an exact summary of the teachings of the Congregation which we have encountered in this study.

The text then passes on to the doctrine of universal salvation, that is, that God's saving grace applied indifferently to all men, not merely to the elect: 'God granted a general pardon to the whole human race. This pardon is enjoyed by all who believe in the Gospel.'[40] In the four pages that made up the first half of the chapter, universal salvation was described twice, and on both occasions it was seen as a consequence of the universal efficacy of the Cross.

This doctrine was found in the writings of both Valdés and Cassinese monks, but the latter is the more probable source. Valdés mentioned the doctrine in the form of a lengthy but theologically vague parable of a king's general amnesty.[41] In contrast, Cassinese writers gave the doctrine a particular and critical place in their pattern of salvation and expounded it

---

[38] Caponetto, *Beneficio* 19, lines 2–5; also lines 26–8.
[39] Ibid. 19–20, lines 22–3, 36–7.
[40] Ibid. 22, lines 78–80.
[41] *Divine Considerations*, pp. 443–57, the epistle dedicatory to Giulia Gonzaga.

vigorously. Teofilo Folengo, his brother Giambattista, Chiari, Faucher, and Ottoni emphasized that universal salvation was a consequence of the absolute grace of God, and of the efficacy of Christ's passion, which extended to the whole world. Ottoni went further in his commentary on Chrysostom, using the doctrine of universal salvation to make a prolonged attack upon scholastic and Reformation doctrines of predestination, and to argue that all men are by grace offered salvation and must therefore by an act of will accept it.

In our chapter on Luciano degli Ottoni we saw that such teaching, a synthesis of grace alone and free will, drawn from Greek exegesis, led the Cassinese to be suspected, at the same time, of Lutheran and Pelagian heresies.[42] The supposed Pelagian element is present at the beginning of the third chapter of the *Beneficio*: ' . . . let us run into his arms with the footsteps of living faith.' Catarino had seized upon this as 'errore pelagiano', and went on to remark that 'questo è contra la lor posizione, che vilifica l'opere . . . '.[43] This neat demonstration of the contemporary misunderstanding of the Greek theology of the Cassinese suggests two conclusions. First, the earlier 'Pelagian' part of chapter iii, characterized by universal salvation, was derived from Cassinese sources, with the Valdesian phrases being imported by Flaminio in the course of his revision. Second, these Benedictine teachings were not Pelagian, as Catarino (and more recently, Prosperi and Ginzburg) alleged, but were simply one aspect of the Greek theology of the Cassinese monks.

In contrast, the latter half of the chapter contains a quite different definition of salvation. From line 102 to the end there is a concentration of highly forensic language in which salvation was seen primarily as a cancellation of guilt:

What an abominable thing it is, if we who profess to be Christians, and who understand that the Son of God has taken all our sins upon himself, and has cancelled them all with his most precious blood by allowing himself to be chastised for us on the cross, still claim that we want to justify ourselves, and to seek the remission of our sins with our

---

[42] See above, ch. 6; also below, ch. 9.

[43] The *Compendio d'errori e inganni luterani* is published in Caponetto, *Beneficio* 343–422. The quotation is taken from p. 357. For Catarino's distinctive doctrine of original sin see L. Scarinci, *Giustizia primitiva e peccato originale secondo Ambrigio Catarino, O.P.*, Studia Anselmiana xvii (Vatican, 1947).

own works. As if the merits, the justice, and the blood of Christ are not sufficient to accomplish this . . . [44]

The unmerited cancellation of guilt means that men can now 'apply this satisfaction of Christ . . . enjoy the remission of sins through his justice . . . become good and just in the presence of God'. Thus they stand 'before the tribunal of God . . . clothed in the justice of Christ'.[45] The concluding lines of the chapter summed up the concept of salvation as the remission of sins and the imputation of justice *coram Deo*: '. . . let us firmly hold that we are just, not through our own works but through the merits of Christ . . . confident that the justice of Christ cancels all our injustice, and makes us good, holy and just in the sight of God.'[46]

This kind of forensic theology was not characteristic of the Cassinese tradition, but it was to be found in the teachings of Valdés and in the 1539 edition of Calvin's *Institutes*, both of which were familiar to Flaminio.

It would appear that chapter iii treated the doctrine of salvation by grace alone in two different ways. The obvious explanation would seem to be that the chapter was written by two men and that one was the Cassinese monk, and the other the disciple of Valdés and of Protestant theology. Therefore we must disagree with the idea of a single authorship of the *Beneficio* put forward by Bozza, who saw it as a Calvinist work written by Benedetto alone, and by Fenlon who saw it as a blend of Valdesian and Calvinist teaching, written by Flaminio virtually alone. We have shown that the chapter contains more than a blend of Valdés and Calvin, for it was composed of two radically different, though not exclusive, concepts of salvation. One was justification by grace through faith, in which the influence of both Valdés and Calvin is apparent. The other was restoration by grace through faith: this later concept was to be found in Valdés, but in an attenuated form, mere exhortations to piety, well written but vague, often tied loosely to his theological argument, and, despite the language of restoration, having

[44] Caponetto, *Beneficio* 22–6, esp. lines 102–9.

[45] Ibid. 24, lines 130–3; 25, lines 176–7. The metaphor of clothing is used often in the *Beneficio*. It is briefly mentioned in Valdés; see Prelowski, op. cit., p. 55, n. 7, Caponetto, *Beneficio* 25, n. 12. An obvious source for both men was the Cassinese rite of profession (see above, ch. 2), but ultimately the image is derived from the New Testament, especially Luke 15: 22; Col. 3: 10.

[46] Caponetto, *Beneficio* 26, lines 205–8.

much in common with Calvin's doctrine of human righteousness after justification. Consequently the passages in the third
chapter which expound restoration appear to come, not from
Valdés, but from the monastic theology of the Cassinese order.
The implication is that the chapter was the work of two men, the
one writing in the Cassinese tradition, the other a disciple of
Valdés and Calvin. This conclusion has the advantage that it
conforms exactly to the clear evidence of Carnesecchi that
Benedetto composed the work and Flaminio revised it, preserv-
ing the theme, but rewriting it according to his own ideas.[47]

The fourth chapter ('On the effects of living faith and the
union of the soul with Christ'), dealt with faith.[48] Once again, as
we shall see, the subject has been treated in two different ways.
One theme expounded faith in the Cassinese manner as an
instrument of restoration, whilst the other taught justification
by faith alone and not by works.

The first theme followed almost exactly the pattern laid down
by other Cassinese writers. The first step in restoration was
man's acceptance of the benefits of the Cross. In the preceding
chapter the act of acceptance had been depicted briefly in vivid
affective language, 'let us run into his arms with the footsteps of
living faith'.[49] Now, in the fourth chapter, the act of response was
again stressed: 'Whoever accepts and believes this good news
really has the true faith and enjoys the remission of his sins; he is
reconciled with God . . . he enters into God's kingdom.'[50] As in
Ottoni's work, the point is made that the first step in the
restoration of man is his act of acceptance of the unmerited gift
of grace, which in turn brings certitude: '. . . your certainty
consists in the true living faith, with which God purifies the
hearts, as St. Peter says.'[51] This description of certitude is
identical to that of other Cassinese writers, especially Ottoni,
who took from Chrysostom the idea that certitude was a full and
unshakable persuasion, a trusting belief which is a constituent of
faith.[52]

---

[47] Caponetto, *Beneficio* 459–60, 464 (docs. 42, 50).

[48] For the distinction historical faith and true faith, and its use by the northern
Reformers, see Prelowski, op. cit., p. 67, n. 2.

[49] Caponetto, *Beneficio* 19, lines 8–9.

[50] Ibid. 30, lines 82–5.

[51] Ibid. 30, lines 77–8.

[52] See above, ch. 6.

In common with other Cassinese writings on faith, certitude was succeeded by an experience of reciprocal love, an experience which, as it were, coupled divine grace and human response. In the *Beneficio* also, reciprocal love had been touched upon in the description of salvation at the beginning of chapter iii. Now, in the fourth chapter, the teaching was reiterated:

this extremely firm and spirited trust in God's mercy expands and stimulates our heart, directing it towards God with the sweetest affections and filling it with most ardent love . . . this holy trust, which never lacks divine love, is generated in the heart by the Holy Spirit, who is imparted to us through faith.[53]

Still following the sequence found in other Cassinese writers, the text then moved from faith's certitude and love to its good works. However, in this part of the chapter we find not the Cassinese doctrine of works as an agent of restoration, but two paraphrases of Valdés's own doctrine:

Justifying faith is a work of God in us, through which our old man is crucified, and we are all transformed in Christ, so that we become a new creature and very dear children of God. It is this divine faith which inserts us in the death and resurrection of Christ and consequently mortifies our flesh.

This same faith unites us with God and makes him live in our hearts and clothes our soul with himself . . . to humility, meekness, obedience to God, charity and all the other perfections, through which we regain the image of God . . . the true Christian, (that is, one who holds himself just through the justice of Christ) . . . stirred and impelled by the force of divine love, offers himself eagerly to all holy and Christian works and never ceases to act well.[54]

Although the passages refer to 'transformation' and a 'new creature', the terms mean only the turning to a new life of righteous behaviour inspired by faith in justification. This was the doctrine of Valdés and Calvin, a teaching to which the monks were sympathetic as far as it went, though it did not go as far as their own doctrine that *opera humana* were an instrument of restoration and perfection. A consideration of the major works

---

[53] Caponetto, *Beneficio* 32–3, lines 151–7.

[54] Ibid. 42, lines 389–94. Valdés wrote often of mortification, but most clearly in Consid. 17. Chrysostom's teaching is to be found in his other works, e.g. 'it is, on the one hand, God's part, to give the grace, on the other, man's to supply faith', *The Homilies of St. John Chrysostom . . . on the Gospel of John*, 85.

of Valdés, above all the *Alfabeto*, from which these passages were taken, shows that when he spoke of regaining the image of God he meant that after justification a Christian should live righteously, eradicating actual depravity and personal guilt. Valdés saw works in a forensic role as a means of attaining a state of personal justice following the unmerited remission of sins through the Cross. But this was quite distinct from the Cassinese doctrine, drawn from the Greeks, that through works the damaged personality was reconstructed and restored to perfection. Assuming that originally Benedetto had written of works along the lines of other Cassinese writers, we may conclude that when Flaminio rewrote Benedetto's text 'according to his own ideas', he modified the Cassinese theology on this crucial question of the works of faith, by the insertion of paraphrases from the *Alfabeto*.

But why should Flaminio have modified the Cassinese doctrine of works? There is one particular reason. In 1538 Luciano degli Ottoni in his commentary on Chrysostom had defended the Greek Father's synthesis of salvation by grace alone and the necessity of *opera humana* to restore human perfection, but Ottoni's work had aroused suspicions that in speaking of faith and works he was guilty of Pelagianism.[55] We have seen that the early chapters of the *Beneficio* retain traces of the original author's Cassinese 'Pelagian' doctrine, but when we come to the specific treatment of works in the fourth chapter, we find inserted Valdesian paraphrases free of the Pelagian implications of which the monk had been accused. The conclusion is that Flaminio used Valdés to rewrite the teaching on works, removing the element of supposed Pelagianism.

The treatment of faith, manifest in certitude, love, and works, was then succeeded by a passage on the mystical union of the soul with Christ—the 'unione dell'anima con Cristo' which had been referred to in the title of the chapter. In this passage, the soul, its faith, and Christ are all merged into one, 'diventano una cosa stessa'.

This most holy faith embraces Christ and unites him with the soul, and all three, that is, faith, Christ, and the soul, become one and the same thing. In this way the soul merits whatever Christ has merited, and

---

[55] See below, ch. 9.

therefore St. Augustine says that God crowns his gifts in us. In St. John's gospel, Christ himself testifies to his union with the soul through faith . . . we become one with Christ and as he is one with God so we are also one with God through Christ. Oh the stupendous glory of the Christian who through faith is allowed to possess those ineffable things that the angels long to see.[56]

This strongly affective statement of mystical union has puzzled scholars because it is out of keeping with the Valdesian and Calvinist doctrines of the *Beneficio*.[57] However the puzzle evaporates if the description of mystical union is attributed to Don Benedetto, and not to Flaminio's Valdesian and Calvinist teaching. In so far as Calvin was prepared to use the term 'union' at all he meant 'an indwelling of the Christ in our hearts', whilst Valdés meant an influx of the Spirit and a 'clothing', that is, a life lived in imitation of Christ.[58] On the other hand, the passage does accord with the Cassinese notion of a progressive restoration, through faith, of fallen man. More-over, as for other Cassinese writers, faith is the instrument of this process, and union is the culmination of faith, for 'questa santissima fede abbraccia Cristo e lo unisce con l'anima'.[59] Thus, both in theological argument and in style, the passage on union reads like a triumphant conclusion to a Cassinese devotional treatise, and a natural end to the chapter.

However, the chapter as it was printed extends for another seventy-two lines. These additional lines, returning to the doctrine of justificaton by faith and to the denial, expressed in aggressive partisan language, that works contribute to salva-tion, represent such a marked change in style and theological content that after the passage on mystical unity, they read as a counter-climax to the chapter.

In order to elucidate the significance of those seventy-two lines it is necessary to examine briefly all passages in the fourth chapter that appear to be additions to the original Cassinese pattern of salvation. These additional passages fall into two groups. First there are those, for the most part paraphrases from

[56] Caponetto, *Beneficio* 46, lines 494–513.
[57] Ibid. 46, n. 46; Prelowski, op. cit., p. 70, n. 1.
[58] Calvin, *Institutes* III.ii.10; Valdés, *Divine Considerations*, Consid. 73, 86, 100, 109; *Alfabeto christiano*, ed. Wiffen, pp. 17–19.
[59] Caponetto, *Beneficio* 46, lines 494–5.

Valdés and Luther, which illustrate the Cassinese Pauline teachings on grace and restoration. The chapter begins with a loose paraphrase of Luther's analogy of the marriage of Christ and the Christian, based upon Ephesians 5: 21–33. Luther's analogy has been here developed into one of complete identification in whch man becomes 'a participant in the divine nature'—an Antiochene expression used by the writers of the Congregation. This arrangement of Lutheran and monastic material suggests that Flaminio introduced the Lutheran paraphrase in order to illustrate Benedetto's monastic notion of growth, perfection, and union. There followed a similar arrangement in which Valdés's parable of the king's edict, which forgave all rebellious subjects, but which could be efficacious only for those who believed it, was placed in the middle of what otherwise would be a complete statement of the Cassinese doctrine of universal grace, a general pardon for the whole human race, and release from the bondage of death, in which men may have perfect confidence.[60] Both these passages, one from Luther and the other from Valdés, have the appearance of insertions used to illustrate the Cassinese pattern of salvation, and presumably they were introduced by Flaminio in his revision of Don Benedetto's first text.

There follows a group of quotations which support that other view of salvation which is more clearly derived from Valdés and Calvin: a catena of biblical and patristic quotations from Paul, Augustine, Origen, Basil, Ambrose, and Bernard, all upon the theme that justice *coram Deo* is imputed and not achieved by works.[61] These quotations were followed by a number of paraphrases from Calvin, Luther, and Melanchthon, all attributing salvation to the imputation of Christ's justice, which cloaks guilty man:

... it is necessary that we clothe ourselves with the justice of Christ through faith, and hide ourselves under the precious purity of our first-born brother if we want to be accepted as just in the presence of God. This is certainly true, for if we appear before God without being clothed in the justice of Christ we will certainly be judged as completely unjust and worthy of every punishment; but if on the other

[60] Caponetto, *Beneficio* 31–2, lines 114–32; also 30, lines 88–9; 32, lines 146–50.
[61] Ibid. 33–9, lines 167–320.

hand, God sees us adorned with the justice of Christ, undoubtedly he will accept us as just and holy and worthy of eternal life.[62]

It was this forensic theme that came to a vigorous conclusion in the final seventy-two lines of the chapter, forming an abrupt anticlimax to the preceding passages on mystical union. These final lines expounded the doctrine of justification aggressively, sharply separating those who include works as part of their pattern of salvation from those ('noi') who do not:

. . . one can clearly see the difference between us, and those who defend justification by faith and works. We agree in that we also uphold works, affirming that justifying faith cannot be without good works, whilst they say that those who are justified by faith do works which can truly be called good. We differ in that we say that faith justifies without the aid of works . . . [63]

This doctrine, held by Calvin, Valdés, and by Flaminio and a number of Italian *spirituali*, must be distinguished from the Cassinese doctrine that works play a part in salvation through the restoration of perfection. A few Cassinese-like phrases were retained, but the concentration upon forensic justification, the sense of separation of the justified from those who rely upon 'human prudence', and the aggressive style, all indicate that these seventy-two lines did not belong to the original draft of Benedetto, but were added by Flaminio, probably in a later revision.

In our examination of chapter iv, I have sought to identify two separate doctrines of the 'viva fede' which are entwined throughout the chapter. The first is the Cassinese doctrine of faith as an instrument of restoration and perfection, set out in the same pattern as that of other Cassinese writers. This recognizable core of the Cassinese teaching on 'viva fede' has been illustrated by material taken from elements of Luther and Valdés that were congruent with Cassinese thought: also the monastic doctrine of works has been modified. This polishing and revision was the work of Flaminio. The second doctrine of faith treated salvation in forensic terms as the unmerited remission of sins and justification, not by works, but by grace, through faith. Its intellectual sources were, on the one hand

---

[62] Ibid. 38, lines 281–9: Caponetto refers to the connection with Calvin, discovered by Bozza; see n. 23.

[63] Ibid. 467, lines 513–20.

Reformation theology, especially that of Calvin, and on the other hand Valdés's writings which considered salvation in similar terms. Almost certainly, this second doctrine of faith was added by Flaminio, the ardent disciple of Valdés and Calvin.

The fifth chapter renewed the discussion of faith and works under the catching title 'How the Christian clothes himself with Christ'.[64] The chapter contains very little of Cassinese origin, but its principal sources were all familiar to Flaminio, which suggests that he was the author rather than the revisor of the chapter. However, the text deserves a brief examination because it clearly reveals the influence of the *Imitation of Christ*, and because the structure and style of the chapter may clarify the way in which Flaminio revised and polished the *Beneficio*.

The opening section expounded the doctrine of justification by faith, using the imagery of clothing: 'the Christian adorns and covers himself with the innocence of Christ and all his perfections. Then he presents himself before God, the Lord of the universe, relying on the merits of Christ . . . believing that this heavenly garment makes us pleasing and acceptable to God.'[65] In this vivid and poetic passage Flaminio has once again explained faith and salvation in Calvinist and Valdesian forensic language of guilt remitted by unmerited grace.

Then followed a second use of the image of 'clothing', 'the other way of clothing oneself with the image of Christ, which we call patterning'. Christ 'was given to us by the Father as an example that we would always follow, moulding our life so that it may be an image of the life of Christ.'[66] This imagery was accompanied by exhortations to be clothed with new life, by living in imitation of Christ, in humility and charity. There can be no doubt that Flaminio took his inspiration from the *Imitation of Christ*, which he admired intensely, praising it, in a letter written in February 1542, as the pre-eminent guide to Christian living for men who had been justified by faith. The two uses of the image of 'clothing' both echo the Benedictine rite of profession. They may even have been used deliberately to link Calvin, the *Imitation*, and monasticism.[67]

[64] Caponetto, *Beneficio* 52, 'Come il cristano si veste di Cristo'.
[65] Ibid. 52, lines 8–17.
[66] Ibid. 53–4, lines 52–4.
[67] Ibid. 55, n. 7. Caponetto does not refer to this letter, which was written to Carlo Gualteruzzi on 28 Feb. 1542: it is printed in *Opuscoli e lettere di riformatori italiani del '500*, ed. G. Paladino (Bari, 1913), i. 72–3. The rite of profession is described above, ch. 2.

At the same time his description of good works in imitation of Christ has an emphasis, greater than in Thomas à Kempis, upon the social nature of works, the obligation to 'give my goods and my life for the love and welfare of my neighbour'.[68] Of course, Flaminio may have been influenced by similar teachings in Luther's *De Libertate Christiana*, in Calvin and in Valdés, but it is possible that he was also acquainted with this theme in Cassinese writings, particularly those of Chiari and Ottoni, who drew directly from Greek patristic sources. The Cassinese translation of the tract of St. Nilus's *De Christiana Philosophia* (1534) has a description of living faith, with details—accepting affliction, eschewing greed, litigation, and sin, being generous, all with brief biblical refences—remarkably similar in style and substance to the corresponding parts of chapter five. Ottoni's translation of, and commentary on, Chrysostom's *Homily on Romans* had drawn upon the Greek Father to emphasize that since Christians were 'redeemed by divine grace and goodness towards men', they were to 'clothe themselves with Christ' ('Christum induere'), 'loving others and doing good things', 'ministering, exhorting, consoling, and caring'. Then again, in 1540, Abbot Chiari had reminded the citizens of Brescia that the 'evangelical doctrine' of the 'beneficentia' of Christ's Cross demanded a living faith manifest in generosity, kindness, and a 'sharing of goods' with their 'brethren', the poor.[69]

The exposition of the two 'clothings' comes to an end at the semicolon in line 120. At this point the chapter might well have ended, for beyond it there is a complete change of tack for the final forty-three lines. The topic is still the status and new life of a Christian, but whereas before the semicolon it was described in terms of justification and the imitation of Christ, after the semicolon the topic is treated in a partisan manner, describing how 'gli uomini del mondo', 'falsi cristiani', attack, torment, persecute, and kill 'veri cristiani', whose faith none the less is strengthened by such ordeals: they are separated out from 'the world' by their suffering, their true adoration of God, and their final victory.[70] So marked is the change in style at this point that

[68] Caponetto, *Beneficio* 54, lines 68–9. Prelowski, op. cit., 74, n. 7, refers to similar sentiments in Luther.

[69] For St. Nilus, see above, ch. 4; for Ottoni, ch. 6; for Chiari, ch. 7.

[70] Caponetto, *Beneficio* 57, lines 127 ff. These sentiments, on willingness to suffer, and the distinction between true and false Christians, resembles the substance, though not the style, of Chrysostom's tract *On the Providence of God*, chs. 12–22.

all translators have replaced the semicolon of the 1543 edition with a full stop at this point.[71] Moreover, these final lines contain the first of the major paraphrased passages from Calvin's *Institutes*, on the certainty of divine assistance in time of tribulation.[72] The change in substance and style, and the insertion of a paraphrase from Calvin all suggest that these forty-three lines were written separately from the rest of the chapter, and presumably were added at the same time as the similar partisan passage at the end of the fourth chapter.

From these observations it would appear that chapter v was written by Flaminio in two stages. The main part of the work continues and brings to a conclusion the twin themes of faith and works: in earlier chapters it was possible to distinguish between Don Benedetto's text, as revised by Flaminio, and Flaminio's own additions, but in this chapter there is very little of Cassinese doctrine—only, perhaps, the influence of teaching on social obligations—whilst the text strongly reflects Flaminio's Calvinist and Valdesian views. For this reason we may conclude that the main part of the chapter was entirely Flaminio's own composition, written at the end of the revision of Benedetto's original manuscript.

Then, in contrast, the final lines of the chapter read like a separate piece, an appendix of aggressive retaliation, a tail with a sting. This passage is like the end of the fourth chapter, and, as we shall see, the whole of the sixth chapter, in marked contrast, in style and substance, to the earlier part of the work. In these final lines we see a second revision, a spirited counter-attack to criticisms of the first edition, such as has been postulated by Ginzburg, Prosperi, and Simoncelli.

The sixth and final chapter of the *Beneficio* expounded the same theology and was written in the same style as the tail-pieces of the fourth and fifth chapters, that is, it was not a revision of Cassinese piety, but a partisan diatribe which drew heavily upon the *Institutes* of Calvin. The title of the chapter is 'Alcuni rimedi contra la diffidenza'. The four remedies of Luther were

[71] Caponetto, *Beneficio* 130, line 130 (anonymous French translation of 1545); also 246, line 124 (the Croatian translation of 1563 of Consul and d'Alessandro); 317, line 132 (the English translation of A.G. in 1573); Prelowski, op. cit. 76. Edward Courtenay's English translation of 1548 begins a new sentence at the next semicolon, see Caponetto, *Beneficio* 188, line 130.

[72] Ibid. 57–8, lines 150–8; also 58, n. 10.

given: prayer, the memory of baptism, the use of holy communion, and the recollection of predestination. Prayer was
described very briefly as a petition for belief, then the chapter
moved immediately to its principal task, the defence of justification by grace alone. Baptism was described as a 'clothing' with
Christ's justice, so that sins 'are not imputed to us by God'.
Similarly, the eucharist is a 'sign and a pledge' that although
men 'merit a thousand hells and eternal death', and are 'sinful
and condemned', they are given 'remission of sins through the
blood of Christ'.[73] In this way discussion of the sacrament served
as a vehicle for Calvin's doctrine of justification, following the
1539 edition of the *Institutes*.[74] The exposition of the eucharist
carries no reflection of the Cassinese teaching on the restoration
of human nature. Furthermore, the passage that deals with the
eucharist as a sign of unity, resting upon paraphrases from
Calvin, describes such union, not as the mystical union with
Christ as in chapter iv, but as the 'peace, union, and fraternal
charity' which ought to obtain between Christians.[75]

This chapter is distinguished from earlier chapters also by its
treatment of predestination. Those whom God has chosen are
'predestined to eternal life', because 'God from eternity has
given them eternal life': they are the 'true Christians' as against
the false Christians who persecute them.[76] The treatment of
predestination in this chapter is taken directly from Calvin, and
contrasts strongly with the monastic and Greek patristic
doctrine of universal salvation found in the third chapter.

The chapter then turns to a consideration of the certainty
with which salvation may be known. The question of certitude,
a common topic in late medieval theology, is here answered with
a vigorous defence of the doctrine of predestination. Using
passages from the *Institutes* and some minor points from Valdés,
it is argued that the Spirit of God gives knowledge and certainty

---

[73] Ibid. 60, lines 20–4; 61, lines 65–6; 63, lines 104–15. In a letter of 1527 Isidoro
Chiari referred to the 'beneficentia' of Christ, the weakness of man, and the use of the
eucharist to confirm faith (Olgiato, *Epistolae*, p. 12). Chiari's approach, however, was
not tied to justification.

[74] Caponetto, *Beneficio* 61–2, lines 70–94. In note 8 Caponetto has given Calvin's text.

[75] Ibid. 65–8, lines 164–225. Ch. 6 has one passage which reads like a monastic
comment on 'la messa' (lines 145–63). These lines may be an interpolation into an
otherwise Calvinist chapter although they are not incompatible with Calvin, not even
the passage on the 'soul drunk . . . with sweet and saving liquor'.

[76] Ibid. 69–72, lines 228–312.

to the minds and hearts of predestined men, 'like a seal that authenticates and stamps those divine promises in our hearts'.[77] Once again the difference between this chapter and the greater part of the earlier chapters is clear, for this chapter is a firm and spirited defence of Calvin's doctrine of predestination. The remainder of the chapter is a defence of Calvinist doctrine against allegations that predestination removes the obligation of good works and gives licence to sin.[78]

Finally the chapter, and the book, end with a brief summary:

We have arrived at the end of our discussion, in which our principal aim has been to praise and exalt . . . the stupendous benefit that the Christian has received from Jesus Christ crucified, and to demonstrate that faith of itself justifies, meaning that God receives as just all those who truly believe that Jesus Christ has satisfied for their sins. However . . . good works cannot be separated from this faith, which alone justifies.[79]

As a summing up of the sixth chapter and its Calvinist doctrines of predestination, justification, and faith; this final paragraph is accurate, but as a summary of the whole book it is manifestly inadequate, for it makes no reference to the themes of renewal in the preceding chapters. It is obvious that this conclusion refers to the arguments of the sixth chapter, and not to those of the book as a whole.

Therefore, we may conclude that the sixth chapter, together with the endings of the fourth and fifth chapters, differs from the rest of the *Beneficio*, being a tract for the exposition and defence of Calvin's doctrines of predestination, the Spirit, faith, and works. It is here that we find the direct paraphrases from the *Institutes* (mostly from Book III.ii) on faith and certainty. Some pieces from the Bible, the Fathers, and Valdés have been used to illustrate the argument, but the argument itself is dominated by Calvin, in marked contrast to the earlier part of the *Beneficio*. The language is partisan and aggressive, whereas in the earlier chapters there is neither controversy nor polemic: its frequent exhortations to gratitude, moral obligations, and righteous behaviour entirely lack the affective piety and the warm language of earlier chapters. It would appear that having

---

[77] Caponetto, *Beneficio* 72–81, lines 312–559.
[78] Ibid. 81–3, lines 560–608.
[79] Ibid. 83, lines 608–24.

revised Don Benedetto's Cassinese tract, Flaminio added, probably at a later date, a postscript different in intention, argument, and style.

We are now in a position to draw some conclusions about the *Beneficio* as a whole. On the presumption that Carnesecchi spoke the truth when he said that the prime author was a Cassinese monk, the work has been examined in the light of other writers of the same Congregation. Those writers all exhibited a remarkable similarity of doctrine: all turned their scholarship to the Bible, especially St. Paul, and to the Fathers, especially Chrysostom; all taught a similar pattern of salvation, describing the fall in terms of mortality and decay, and asserting the necessity of grace alone in order to reconcile man with God, and then to restore the *imago Dei* in man through good works. The greater part of the *Beneficio* treats the same themes in the same way. Where there has been deviation from the monastic doctrine, or its embellishment with congruent passages from Valdés, Luther, or some other source, then the hand of Flaminio is readily discernible. Thus, behind Flaminio's polished revision, embroidered with interpolations from the Reformers, the outlines of Benedetto's original manuscript are still visible, in the first two chapters, the first half of the third chapter, in parts of the fourth chapter, and in the middle section of the fifth chapter.

This conclusion has a number of implications. Interpretations of the *Beneficio* as a Valdesian work must be modified, for it is, in the first place, a tract of monastic theology based upon the exegetical methods, the literary style and, above all, the theology of salvation of the Greek Antiochene Fathers, especially Chrysostom. This theological basis, hitherto unrecognized, explains the presence of certain passages which have been considered anomalous in an evangelical tract. Moreover, setting the text against Cassinese doctrine has enabled us to distinguish between the two revisions of Flaminio: the first was a mere revision and polishing of Benedetto's original work; the second a series of substantial additions in vigorous defence of Calvinist theology. This second revision, different in substance and style from the earlier part, was perhaps the response to Catarino's criticism which Prosperi and Ginzburg have postulated. The *Beneficio* is really two separate works. The first was a monastic treatise on sin, grace, faith, and restoration, written by the monk and polished by the poet, who was familiar with the Congregation and its theologians, but who was also a disciple of Valdés and sympathetic to Reformation theology. The second work, entirely the work of Flaminio, was his later exposition of justification by faith alone according to the teachings of John Calvin.

Don Benedetto's original manuscript was neither Protestant nor Pelagian; nor was it mere medieval mysticism caught up in the remorseless religious conflicts of the late 1530s and the early 1540s. Indeed, why should Don Benedetto, a close friend and colleague of men heavily involved in the now quite desperate attempts to achieve reconciliation in the face of hardening divisions, have written a tract merely expressing, almost anachronistically, late medieval piety, or (to take the opposing interpretation) putting forward Protestant doctrine? In fact, his teaching was drawn from his order's Pauline and Antiochene doctrines. Therefore we may ask whether perhaps Benedetto intended his work of piety to be a work of reconciliation, expressing in devotional terms what his colleagues, especially Chiari and Ottoni, had done in matters of doctrine.[80] If Benedetto's manuscript were one of the several Cassinese writings in search of reconciliation with the Protestants, then his intention is reflected in the way Flaminio set about the first revision of the manuscript. Flaminio inserted Lutheran material—not too much and not too intrusive—in a way which would have skilfully augmented any intention that Benedetto may have had of showing that Protestants and Catholics might be reconciled through the Greek theology of his order. After all, as Menegazzo has shown, Flaminio had close and continuing relations with the monks of the Congregation, and must have known their theological tradition and their irenic intentions.[81] Moreover, if this were the case, the support given the tract by Cortese, Morone, Pole, Vittoria Colonna, Giberti, and others, becomes more understandable: it is possible that they approved it, not only for its piety, but also because it was at heart a tract of reconciliation. Here perhaps, in literary collaboration, is

---

[80] Caponetto, *Beneficio* 479, makes a similar suggestion about the irenic intentions of the tract.

[81] Menegazzo, 'Per la Consocenza', pp. 210 ff.; also E. Cuccoli, *M. A. Flaminio* (Bologna, 1897), p. 73.

another element in the relationship, which is still not clear, between the Cassinese monks and the *spirituali*.

There is one other question raised by the findings of this chapter. Since the underlying Cassinese theology placed heavy emphasis upon the Pauline themes of sin, grace, and faith, and since Flaminio had close connections with the order, it is possible that Flaminio's own Pauline emphasis had been earlier imbibed from the monks: if so, when he read Luther, and encountered Valdés, and through him the writings of Calvin, he must have been aware of the common ground between the monks of Santa Giustina and the Reformers, not only the Bible and Pauline theology, but also Calvin's sense of new life and transformation, which appears to have been drawn from the Greek Fathers.[82] Indeed it is possible that when Flaminio came to write the last sections of the text in 1543, the partisan, Calvinist passages, he may have felt that this common ground of Pauline theology justified his extension from the doctrines of Benedetto and other Cassinese monks and Chrysostom, to those of Calvin.

---

[82] Calvin, *Institutes*, trans. Battles, i. 18, n. 12; R. S. Wallace, *Calvin's Doctrine of the Christian Life* (Edinburgh, 1959), pp. 23–7, 103–11, 148–69. The French edition of 1545, *Du benefice de Iésu Christ*, translated by the Calvinist Claude Le Maistre of Lyons, was bound with his translation of Chrysostom's sixteenth homily on the woman of Canaan: see Caponetto, *Beneficio* 506.

IX

The Crisis at Trent

THE furore that arose over the publication of *Il Beneficio di Cristo* in 1543, and the work's swift suppression, must have alarmed the Congregation, for in the spring of 1544 the chapter-general renewed the *ordinatio* of 1528 against 'the Lutheran heresy', ordering that cells be searched and a strict watch be kept for 'libri suspecti'.[1] It was necessàry to be on guard in the uncertain religious climate after the *Beneficio*. There had been denunciations and public burnings, and although Don Benedetto's co-authorship of the tract was not officially revealed until Carnesecchi's confession of 1566, the monks themselves, and some lay friends, knew that the Congregation was involved, whilst some ecclesiastical officials were obviously suspicious. The fact was that the monks could no longer preach their doctrines with the old confidence, for the divisions had hardened and those who sought to reconcile the antagonistic ideologies of western Christendom were now facing a new intolerance.

Nevertheless, in June 1545 the Congregation embarked upon a course which was to bring it into open theological conflict in the cause of reconciliation. At S. Benedetto Po the chapter-general chose its representatives to speak 'in the name of all' at the forthcoming Council of Trent. The three men chosen were Luciano degli Ottoni as chief spokesman, Isidoro Chiari, and Crisostomo Calvini.[2] At the same time Ottoni was elected to his

---

[1] Leccisotti, 'Tracce di correnti Mistiche Cinquecentesche nel Codice Cassinese 584', *Archivio Italiano per la Storia della Pietà*, iv (1965), 119. In Venice in 1554 Chiari published yet another biblical translation, *Canticum canticorum Solomonis*.

[2] *Conc. Trid.* i. 206, '. . . tutta la loro congregazione . . . ha eletto gli detti tre da venire in nome di tutti al concilio.' Calvini, a Calabrian, was professed in 1530, at the age of thirty-six years. He was learned in Latin, Greek, and Hebrew, and became abbot at Gaeta in 1545. He spoke from time to time at Trent, but made no major speech. In 1560 he succeeded Ludovico Beccadelli as archbishop of Ragusa; Armellini, *Bibl. Bened.-Cas.* i. 117–19; *A. et C.* i. 31; *CTE* 13–14. In 1548 Calvini directed the adoption of the Cassinese constitution by the Congregation of Melida, which united the Benedictine houses of Dalmatia.

first abbacy at the small abbey of Santa Maria Pomposa, near Ferrara:[3] in view of his competence as a theologian and his incompetence in practical administration, it is possible that he was given the abbacy so that, as an abbot, he would be able to attend the Council.

When the three abbots arrived at Trent on 18 June 1545, Ottoni wasted no time in making known the Congregation's theological position.[4] Almost at once he circulated, in manuscript, a dialogue on free will which soon came into the hands of Massarelli, secretary to Cardinal Cervini.[5] Massarelli thought the dialogue 'very foolish' and virtually heretical.[6] He gave the manuscript to Cervini, who was at first unwilling to take any action, but finally wrote to the president of the Congregation about it.[7] The manuscript then passed to Domingo de Soto, a Dominican theologian to Charles V and head of the Council's commission on heretical writings, who was engaged at the time on a study of Ottoni's book of 1538.[8]

In January 1546 de Soto announced that after 'careful consideration of a book which was not orthodox by a certain abbot', he had found three errors. The first was Ottoni's denial that there were fires in hell, but when questioned Ottoni had replied that he referred to 'corporeal fires'. The second error was Ottoni's belief that unbaptized infants died without punishment. This teaching was a corollary of his denial that Adam's guilt was inherited and the new born were guilty and liable to punishment. The third error, that 'our good works are the reason why God predestines us', was de Soto's version of

---

[3] E. Menegazzo, 'Pomposa nella congregazione benedettina riformata di S. Giustina poi cassinese', *Convegno Internazionale di Studi Storici Pomposiani*, i (1964) 236, 241–2. By 1545 the monks had abandoned the unhealthy site at Pomposa and were living at S. Benedetto, Ferrara. Note that Massarelli referred to the Cassinese monks as being of 'St. Paul', a reference to their church of St. Paul-outside-the-wall, Rome, and he wrongly called Ottoni abbot of Pontida, *Conc. Trid.* i. 587.

[4] *Conc. Trid.* i. 206; H. O. Evennett, 'Three Benedictine Abbots at the Council of Trent, 1545–1547', *Studia Monastica*, i (1959), 346–7.

[5] *Conc. Trid.* i. 215. Massarelli called the work 'il dialogo del libero arbitrio'. It is not known whether more than one copy existed. No copy is known to survive. Cervini was Cardinal Santa Croce, one of the three presiding legates. In 1555 he became Pope Marcellus II.

[6] Ibid. i. 224, 226, 229. The expressions were 'ineptissimum', 'quello mi pareva circa haeresiam'.

[7] Ibid. i. 267.

[8] Faralli, 'Una polemica', pp. 401–2.

Ottoni's belief that the term 'predestination' simply referred to God's foreknowledge of man's good works and ultimate destiny.[9]

It is clear that de Soto reckoned Ottoni to be espousing Pelagian ideas. In a work published in 1550 de Soto said that when Ottoni taught the necessity of *opera humana*, he had gone so far as to deny the priority of grace, whilst Sirleto, a close friend of Cervini, crudely interpreted Ottoni to have said that all the Greek Fathers taught that man was saved by works alone.[10]

Thus, even before the Council had begun, Ottoni acquired one reputation for heresy, as a Pelagian. However, he was later to earn quite a different reputation as a crypto-Protestant, in the course of speeches delivered during the Council's debates upon justification in October 1546, when he spoke 'pro se et suis collegis abbatibus' on the subject of faith and the certitude of grace, advancing trenchant arguments which Massarelli described as 'argumenta Lutheranorum'.[11]

Whilst de Soto was still scrutinizing Ottoni's writings, another exposition of Congregational doctrine appeared in the late summer of 1545, written by the abbot of San Severino, Naples, Don Joannes Evangelista Bononia, for Giovanna d'Aragona, the duchess of Tagliacozzo, and sister-in-law of Vittoria Colonna.[12] Don Joannes, professed forty years earlier at St. Severino, was a man of some standing within the order. He was the man to whom Vincentius Campanus had dedicated his *Fasciculus Myrrhae* of 1521: in 1525 he was appointed prior of

---

[9] *Conc. Trid.* i. 380, 'Soto era in grande cogitatione sopra il libro d'un certo abbate quale non è cattolico, per quanto lui ha visto . . . aliqui dubitant ignem esse in inferno corporeum . . . gli infanti che muoiono senza battesimo non patiranno pena alcuna. Il terzo quod bona nostra opera sunt causa quod Deus praedestinet nos, quasi dicat sine mera voluntate Dei etc.'

[10] De Soto, *In Epistolam divi Pauli ad Romanos commentarii* (Antwerp, 1550), pp. 20–1. *Conc. Trid.* i. 380 n. Ginzburg and Prosperi consider that Ottoni did not take sin seriously because he valued human free will and 'il tema dell'impecabilità'. They attribute his supposed near Pelagianism to his being 'intriso di neoplatismo' for which reason 'reprende il temo umanistico della "dignitas hominis"', 'Le due redazioni', pp. 164, 168.

[11] *Conc. Trid.* v. 472–3. The episode is described below, pp. 201–2.

[12] Giovanna was the wife of Asconio Colonna from whom she separated in February 1535, although she remained very close to her sister-in-law Vittoria. Thereafter she probably had connections with the *spirituali* of Naples and Viterbo. She also accepted the attentions of Jesuits who tried unsuccessfully to persuade her to return to her husband, and in 1549 she asked Loyola to send her a spiritual adviser. The existence of this tract shows that she was still undecided about her religious beliefs in 1545.

Montecassino, and in 1538 he was given a papal brief to reform a disorderly monastery of the Hermits of St. Jerome.[13]

Presumably, it was after the publication of *Il Beneficio* that the duchess sought his advice on matters of salvation, faith, and works. He protested his inability to answer her satisfactorily, but lest she be led astray by 'alcuni libri macchiati' then circulating in Italy, he wrote the tract for her.[14] It was written in guarded terms and with frequent references to the authority of the Roman church, the sacraments, and the necessity of works, as though to reassure the duchess—and doubtless, any inquisitive reader—that he was a steadfast monk.[15] His intimate style and homely illustrations resembled the *Beneficio*,[16] but the tract did not possess the structural coherence of the earlier work, the main theological points being expounded almost at random by Don Joannes.

Nevertheless his tract was an exposition of the traditional teachings of the Congregation. In his description of fallen humanity Joannes used a phrase remarkably similar to one in the first chapter of the *Beneficio* when he told Giovanna that we must first become 'aware of our own misery and weakness'. Man is unable to do, or even to think, anything good, and therefore cannot be saved through mere obedience to the Law or through rites. Such belief would be presumptuous—an 'amazing effrontery'—and the monk reminded the duchess of the Pauline statement that no man can glory or hope in his own justice, but only in the justice of God.[17] But if salvation was not a reward for good works, whence came salvation? Don Joannes answered with the expression that his Congregation had long since drawn from the Greek Fathers: salvation lay 'solo in la misericordia e

[13] Armellini, *Bibl. Bened.-Cas.* ii. 35. For the *Fasciculus* see above, ch. 3. The papal brief is printed in B. Fontana, 'Documenti Vaticani Contro l'Eresia', *Archivio della Società Romana di Storia Patria*, xv (1892), 161–3.

[14] The tract is entitled 'Trattato di quello che concorre alla giustificatione'. There are two MS copies. The earlier copy, probably autograph, is in the Bibl. Apost. Vat., Ottob. Lat. 896, fos. 1ʳ–39ʳ: this copy has only the first nineteen chapters, and the final three chapters are missing. The other copy is in the Bibl. Aless. Rome, 90 II A: it is complete, but written in a later hand.

[15] Ottob. Lat. 896, especially fos. 6ʳ–8ᵛ.

[16] Ibid. fos. 10ʳ–12ᵛ. Christ is twice depicted as a generous king, and once as a hardworking husband.

[17] Ibid. fos. 11ʳ (for similar expressions of the misery and infirmity of man see Caponetto, *Beneficio* 15, 19, 14ʳ–15ᵛ, 23ʳ–27ʳ.

benignità di Dio', and he drove home his point with a catena of references to St. Paul's Epistle to Romans.[18]

The proper response of mankind to the saving 'benignità' 'tal beneficio', 'quale gran beneficio', of God was faith, and because it was in this matter that misunderstandings and heresies arose, the monk stated his intention to instruct the duchess carefully in the doctrine of 'true faith'.[19] In so doing he repeated the teachings of Ottoni's commentary of 1538 on Chrysostom. The first component of faith was acceptance, that is, to believe that salvation came through grace and faith and not by works.[20] The importance of belief did not mean that works were irrelevant to salvation, as was taught by the 'poor heretics', and even by some who claimed to be Catholics.[21] On the contrary, works were also a component of faith, for they were the fruits of 'la fede viva': they were a means of accepting salvation and of perfecting man. In this, Don Joannes reflected Chrysostom's understanding of works as both a consequence of grace and an instrument of restoring human nature to its former perfection.[22] Good works were necessary, not as a cause of justification, but as an instrument of sanctification, and those who failed to appreciate this were ignorant of patristic teaching on the necessity of works. The good works of monks and pious laymen were a means of the restoration of human nature, particularly the healing of the will, until in the end men came to participate in the divine nature.[23]

Joannes was very anxious that his position be not misinterpreted. He vigorously attacked the Protestants and also Catholics who thought that salvation by grace and faith alone precluded the necessity of works. Indeed, these 'simulating Catholics were worse and more dangerous than the open heretics', despite their learning and upright lives.[24] He urged the duchess to look to the church, to find strength in the mass and

[18] Bibl. Aless. 90 II A, fos. 229^v–230^v.

[19] Ottob. Lat. 896, fo. 9^r, 'la confessione della vera fede'; 3^r.

[20] Ibid. fos. 11^v–12^r: '. . . la gratia et remissione dei peccati o vero giustificatione farsi a tutti per la fede del Nostro sig(no)re, et niente essere le nostre opere'; see also 1^v.

[21] Ibid. fos. 22^r–23^r.

[22] Ibid. 23^{r-v}, 27^v–28^v, 31^{r-v}, 35^r; also 18^r, 12^{r-v}.

[23] Ibid. fos. 4^r, 34^r–35^r, 36^r–38^r. (For the healing of the will see Caponetto, *Beneficio* 19.)

[24] Ibid. fo. 11^v, 'Li simulati Catolici: quali sono peggiori e più pericolosi che manifesti heretici.' Also 6^r–8^r, 9^v, 22^v–23^r, 27^v, 53^v.

priestly absolution, and he defended the doctrine of purgatory.[25] Above all, he repeated frequently the necessity of works as the proper response to grace, illustrating the relationship between grace and works with a royal story of the kind used by Valdés and Benedetto da Mantova: a king freely grants equal plots of land to built houses, but the nature of the building depends upon the recipient. Yet, as often as he described the necessity of works he also reminded the duchess that works themselves did not save, and that she must avoid the pride and presumption of Pelagian doctrines by adhering firmly to Pauline teaching. The very last words of his tract were a final reminder that works, although necessary, could not merit salvation.[26]

In 1546, whilst the three abbots were preparing for the debates at Trent, Giambattista Folengo produced yet another work, a commentary on the first epistle of John. The book was published in Venice by Aldus Manutius, and was dedicated to Reginald Pole.[27] In the prologue Folengo alluded to the unhappy state of religious debate which had split into two camps—the proponents of grace and those of free will—with no reconciliation between the two views.[28] Nevertheless Folengo did not deal directly with this question, for his ambitions were primarily pastoral: 'I chose to write these few words certainly not with literary vituperation, but in defence of the generosity of CHRIST.'[29] His text fulfilled his intentions: he expounded the epistle phrase by phrase without overt argument and with scholarly exhortation to piety, but it was piety centred upon 'liberalitas Christi', in accordance with the traditions of the Congregation.

Folengo's glosses described sin in terms which have become familiar to us. Sin was the consequence of Adam's fall, bringing alienation from God, sin, and the penalty of death—*tyrannis mortis*—to the human race.[30] His theology was that which his

[25] Ibid. fos. 9ᵛ, 15ʳ, 19ʳ, 22ᵛ, 27ᵛ, 53ᵛ. Also, Bibl. Aless. 90 II A, fo. 234ʳ.

[26] Ottob. Lat. 896, fos. 12ᵛ–13ᵛ; Bibl. Aless. 90 II A, fos. 231ʳ–243ᵛ.

[27] *Commentaria in Primam Epistolam D(ivi) Io(annis) Baptista Folengio Monacho Mantuano Auctore* (Aldus, Venice, 1546). It was published 'Cum privilegio Pauli III Pont. Max. & Senatus Veneti, ad annos decem'.

[28] Ibid. 2ʳ.

[29] Ibid. 5ᵃ: 'Haec pauca, non quidem in literarum vituperationem scribere libuit, sed in defensionem liberalitatis IESU CHRISTI.'

[30] Ibid. 14ʳ, 16ʳ, 70ʳ, 79ʳ, 86ᵛ, 88ʳ, 96ᵛ.

order had drawn from the Greek Fathers, especially Chrysostom, and his words reflected those of Ottoni.[31] Folengo also told his readers that it is a mistake to believe that man may free himself from the mortal illness of sin, for the works of the Law did not avail to salvation: to believe otherwise was a Pelagian delusion. In careful language, glossing 1 John 1: 8 ('If we say we have no sin we deceive ourselves') Folengo remarked with gentle sarcasm: that 'a very great thing is the confidence of those men who assert themselves to be clean from the filth of sin'.[32]

Folengo was equally gentle when he insisted that salvation could come only from God, through the 'benefit' of the Cross:

The apostle [John] clearly lays it down that man is in no way able to exist and to live in the light, that is, cleansed from sin and from the darkness and foulness of sin without the Father and his Son, by whose blood and death truly all our sins are wiped away . . . truly, the benefit and the gift, which we have received ought to be traced back to the most efficacious blood of Christ, which washes us from every sin.[33]

'Truly, you are justified freely by faith'[34] he told them, 'and in this way the chirograph of death is cancelled'.[35] Folengo also expounded the next step in Cassinese teaching, that the efficacy of the Cross is universal and that the blood of Christ was shed, not for a chosen few, but for the whole world, confounding the argument of Jews, heretics, and hypocrites who believe that the grace of God is reserved for them.[36]

The book also reflected the Cassinese doctrine of faith. Faith was first of all acceptance of the 'beneficium Christi'. Not to

[31] See above, ch. 6, especially Ottoni's 'patibiles ac a Deo alienos et exules'. Folengo, however, did not press the distinction between penalty and guilt.

[32] Folengo, *Commentaria* 14ᵛ: 'Maxima ea est hominum illorum confidentia, qui a peccati sorde se mundos praedicant'; also 13ᵛ, 15ᵛ, 70ʳ, 78ᵛ–79ᵛ, 130ᵛ–131ʳ.

[33] Ibid. 13ᵛ: 'Aperte definit apostolus haudquaquam posse dici in luce esse & vivere hominem, hoc est a peccato peccatiq(ue) caligine, & foeditate purgari, absque Patre, atque illius filio, cuius sanguine ac morte nostra adeo omnia sunt abstersa crimina . . . quidem beneficium ac donum efficacissimo cruori JESU CHRISTI qui nos emundat ab omni peccato, referri acceptum debet.' Also 3ʳ, 12ᵛ, 14ᵛ ('beneficium et munus'), 37ʳ⁻ᵛ, 50ᵛ, 66ᵛ ('. . . divinae charitatis erga homines . . . immensa Dei charitas erga genus humanu(m)'), 86ᵛ, 87ʳ, 95ᵛ, 98ʳ, 111ʳ, 132ʳ (where prior grace and calling are described as 'the fount of justification and the beginning of salvation'), 134ᵛ, 139ʳ.

[34] Ibid. 131ʳ.

[35] Ibid. 81ʳ. Cf. Caponetto, *Beneficio*, 25: 'el chirografo . . . è stato scanzellato'.

[36] Ibid. 24ᵛ: 'Non pro nostris autem tantum, fuit scilicet expiatio filius Dei, sed etiam pro totius mundi . . . fateamur CHRISTUM universale(m) fuisse victimam et expiationem.'

accept would be shameful, whilst those who do accept receive the power to become sons of God, that is sons by grace through faith, to whom God is truly a father.[37] In a sense, faith is a gift of God, but when man responds to grace, then faith also becomes a human attribute. Folengo's term was 'concentus'—the harmonious blending together of grace and human will 'as it were a marvellous and divine harmony between the grace of God and human will . . . bridegroom and bride, God and soul, mercy and misery, death and life. O, surely a mystery and a marriage . . .'[38] Here was Chrysostom's doctrine of faith as the link between the grace of the Cross and its fulfilment in man, the coupling between God and man which had been expounded so clearly by Ottoni.

According to Folengo, good works arose naturally out of such faith, and were an integral part of it.[39] In the style of his colleagues, Folengo described frequently, and at length, the social manifestation of works: care for one's neighbour, enemies forgiven, perseverance in the face of adversity, unflagging zeal (of the proper kind), a scorn for fraud, hypocrisy, and wordly honours, and above all, generosity, which reflects—as Chrysostom taught—the generosity of God.[40] Such good works were, as Chrysostom said, the gift of God, but they were also the works of man, not justifying him, but giving new life and restoring old mortal human nature to its former health.[41] Works enabled man to put on ('induere') Christ, to 'put on nothing other than Christ . . . the immense benefit of this garment . . . from the blood and death of Christ'. Here, once again, was that old and familiar monastic imagery of clothing with perfection in order to become perfect: 'to put on the heavenly image' was the therapeutic process which restored man to the image of God and unity with God—which was the point of Gregory Cortese's remark to

---

[37] Ibid. 10ʳ, 19ᵛ, 37ᵛ, 50ᵛ–51ʳ, 87ʳ, 131ʳ.

[38] Ibid. 106ʳ⁻ᵛ: 'Verum tantae est erga homines bonitatis pientissimus Pater . . . unde concentus quidam mirabilis et divinus inter Dei gratiam et arbitrium humanu(m) ab his auditur . . . succinunt harmonia et sponsus et sponsa, Deus et anima, misericordia et miseria, mors (ut sic loquar) et vita. O certe mysterium, connubiumq(ue) . . .'; also 15ᵛ, 111ʳ–112ʳ, 139ʳ. Also 131ʳ: 'sic dato gratis beneficio, teq(ue) per gratiam innovato, iam te vult suum esse tuo in negotio cooperatorem.'

[39] Ibid. 14ʳ–15ʳ, 37ʳ, 60ᵛ, 78ʳ, 108ᵛ.

[40] Ibid. 8ᵛ, 9ᵛ, 14ʳ, 15ʳ, 29ʳ–31ᵛ, 35ʳ⁻ᵛ, 43ᵛ–46ʳ, 50ᵛ, 78ʳ, 89ʳ–90ʳ, 96ʳ–101ᵛ, 102ʳ, 118ʳ. Chrysostom's reference to divine and human generosity is mentioned on 102ʳ.

[41] Ibid. 7ᵛ, 14ᵛ, 15ᵛ, 27ᵛ, 60ᵛ, 65ʳ, 70ʳ, 86ʳ⁻ᵛ, 104ʳ. The reference to Chrysostom is on 79ᵛ.

Cardinal Morone that when he dressed in the morning he vested himself with the 'benefit of Christ'.[42] This was the culmination of Folengo's pastoral exposition, just as it was the culmination of the traditional Congregational teachings in which it was rooted.

*

Those teachings were about to be put to the test, at Trent, in a final attempt by the Congregation to reconcile Catholic and Protestant theologies. The opening sessions of the Council dealt with the Bible and biblical studies. In March 1546 Chiari spoke against the proposition that a vulgate translation of the Bible adopted by the Council would be 'indettata' by the Holy Spirit and therefore authoritative. He sought to refute this opinion by the use of historical narrative, with a detailed account of various translations and their use by the see of Rome and others, referring to Origen, Augustine, Jerome, and St. Gregory. He opposed the attempt to claim exclusive authority for Jerome's translation, pointing out that since St. Jerome himself plainly states that no interpreter has spoken with the Holy Spirit it would be a peculiar thing to attribute divine assistance to him who denied that he had it. He suggested that the Council should simply authorize a new revision of the Vulgate in accordance with the original texts and forbid further translations.[43] During April the abbots spoke on various details of the proposed canon of scripture, and unsuccessfully opposed the idea that tradition ought to be received 'pari pietatis affectu', that is with equal reverence to scripture.[44]

---

[42] Folengo, *Commentaria* 107ᵛ: 'Nihil aliud quam CHRISTUM induunt ac referunt . . . Id sane ingens huiusce vestimenti beneficium . . . CHRISTI nimirum cruore ac morte'. The sentiment is repeated often; see 77ʳ, '. . . coelestem imaginem, ut eam appellat Paulus, induere'; 96ᵛ, '. . . ad vitam qua in Deo beatissimam transferimur. Vide porro quid benignissimus asserat magister.' There is an exposition of restoration and unity on 69ᵛ–70ᵛ; 86ᵛ: '. . . siquidem redintegrata Dei imagine per CHRISTUM in homine, cessit peccati lex' etc. See also 13ᵛ, 14ʳ⁻ᵛ, 19ʳ, 23ʳ, 24ʳ, 28ᵛ, 87ᵛ, 107ᵛ. For Cortese's remark see Caponetto, *Beneficio* 454, 488. For the imagery of clothing see also p. 179 above.

[43] *Conc. Trid.* i. 507, 537, 541, 543; P. Sarpi, *Istoria del Concilio Tridentino* (Florence, 1966), i. 193. For the complicated question of rights and privileges at the Council see Evennett, 'Three Benedictine Abbots', pp. 343, 347–9. The three abbots had only one decisive vote; *Conc. Trid.* i. 16, 362, 431; ii. 412–14; iv. 543–4; x. 300–3.

[44] *Conc. Trid.* v. 53. In the vote of 1 Apr. 1546, thirty-three voted in favour of 'pari pietatis affectu' (including Franciscans, Augustinians, Dominicans, Carmelites); eleven in favour of 'similis pietatis affectus', and three in favour of 'reverentia debeatur' (Mortelli, the bishop of Fiesole, Pate, the bishop of Worcester, and Chiari).

Chiari was particularly enthusiastic about the proposal that biblical lectureships should be established in all cathedrals and monasteries. It was hoped that such lectureships would dominate studies in these places, restore the Bible to the centre of Christian intellectual effort, and also serve as a basis for lay religious education. These were ideas that Chiari had himself held for more than a decade. On 20 May 1546 he spoke in favour of the proposals, dwelling upon the importance of biblical studies, particularly their value for monks, in contrast to the sterile and provocative scholastic studies. His speech drew a furious reply from Fra Domingo de Soto, the Spanish Dominican inquisitor of suspected books, who had just completed his criticism of Chiari's colleague, Ottoni. De Soto argued that scholastic philosophy provided the means to study the Bible and to defend the church from Protestant criticisms. Moreover, added de Soto pointedly, theology was properly the business of the mendicant orders and not of monks who ought to get on with their devotions and leave theology alone. Both sides gathered considerable support, and the debate waxed in warmth and quality: '. . . and so, all the Fathers debated the two questions, fully and with discernment, and until this debate no session had reached such a level of doctrine and profundity.'[45] As Evennett observed, scholasticism was almost forced upon the defensive: the Cassinese abbots must have felt some pleasure at the mark they had made upon the Council.[46]

It seems probable that Chiari was asked by the legates to preach a sermon at the session set for 29 July 1546, and that he composed a long sermon 'De Gloria'. The session was postponed and the sermon put aside, but later it was published together with his speeches at Trent.[47] The sermon, presumably composed

---

[45] Evennett, 'Three Benedictine Abbots', p. 355; *Conc. Trid.* i. 60 '. . . adeoque per omnes patres, docte diffuse et discrete haec duo [sc. the two questions] pertractata sunt, ut nulla congregatio hactenus facta fuerit huic in doctrina et gravitate similis.'

[46] Evennett, 'Three Benedictine Abbots', p. 355. Eventually biblical lectureships were made compulsory, but without defined precedence over other studies, so that, in effect, institutions could continue to arrange studies as they pleased.

[47] *Isidori Clarii Fulgin(ensis) Episcopi Sententia de Iustificatione hominis, in conventu Patrum Tridentini Concilii, dicta* (Venice, 1548). The sermon is printed in two parts, as 'De Gloria . . . oratio prior', fos. 22ʳ–30ᵛ, and '. . . oratio posterior', fos. 31ʳ–36ʳ. Three speeches and extracts from 'De Gloria', are published in J. Hefner, *Voten des Abtes Isidor Clarius vom Trienter Konzil* (Würzburg, 1912). Evennett, 'Three Benedictine Abbots', pp. 351–2, has an account of Hefner's work with some criticism of his interpretation.

early in July, opened with the ritual declaration that true glory was to be found only in the search for truth, and then set about a reassertion of Chiari's old themes. In contrast to true glory was the false glory sought by men who paraded their learning to satisfy vanity or to carry a flag for some school of thought. Such behaviour is not the way to truth, but a source of strife. It was the same warning that he had made to the Protestants in his *Adhortatio* of 1534, that men are not led to Christ by the arguments of contoversy, nor by tangled intellectual subtleties, but by the simple knowledge of Scripture. Of course, Chiari himself was not altogether free of provocation and subtlety, but his point was well made as a warning to the Fathers of Trent, that intransigent scholasticism at this point could only harm the Christian religion.[48]

In July 1546 the debates on justification began. On 13 and 22 July Chiari put the Cassinese view. He prefaced his argument with the tart observation that once the doctrine of justification had been easily understood: '. . . not only learned men, but also boys and working girls could understand it, but now so obscure is the understanding of it, that the world's most distinguished Christian scholars, who have gathered here, applying the utmost effort, are seen to have great difficulty in finding it.'[49] He blamed human reasoning and calculation ('habenas humanae intelligentiae'), for the fact that Christian teaching was now in a mess ('obscurissima'), to the great harm of ordinary people. 'We have forgotten that we are disciples of fishermen' he told his audience, and said that he himself would draw his doctrine only from the plain words of Scripture.[50]

He intended to expound the basic facts of the Christian religion, 'faith, justification, grace, and free will', which, he said, was no easy thing to do these days when justification was a matter for contention and the fruits of faith were dissipated.[51] He

[48] Hefner, *Voten des Abtes*, p. 40, has a vivid account of Chiari's attack on the scholastics.

[49] Ibid. p. 7. Adriano Prosperi concludes that few of the prelates at Trent actually read the Reformers' works. Instead, this was done by a small group of professional theologians skilled in controversy, who prepared brief summaries for the others. Prosperi believes that this 'filter' strongly diminished the chances of understanding and rapport at the Council: 'Lutero al Concilio di Trento', *Lutero in Italia*, ed. L. Perrone (Turin, 1983), pp. 97–114.

[50] Hefner, *Voten des Abtes*, p. 8.

[51] Ibid. p. 8.

began with the assertion that men are justified through the death of Christ, whose merits are attributed to us.[52] Justification is the remission of sins given freely, 'iustitiam gratis donari per Christum',[53] and it is accepted by faith, 'gratia per eam, quam diximus, fidem justificationem homini subministrat'.[54] The point was reiterated several times throughout the speech, accepting the doctrine of *gratia sola* without any of the reservations to be found amongst the scholastic speakers or adherents of double justice. Chiari was speaking for the Congregation as a whole, for whom grace was grace, totally gratuitous and in no way due to human nature.

Yet grace cannot come to a nature wholly unprepared to receive it: grace must be accepted by free will. When Chiari asserted the validity of free will, he, like Ottoni, meant simply the freedom to accept or refuse the gift of God, not the ability to contribute to one's salvation which was the error of those whose concept of salvation was legalistic (he may well have had the proponents of *iustitia duplex* in mind also).[55] The Cassinese monks, drawing upon the Greek Fathers, saw free will simply as liberty, 'which we attribute to the will, in that man assents to the gifts offered by God and does not reject them'.[56]

He then turned to *opera humana*, arguing that grace and the restoration of man were not separate, but two aspects of the one process of salvation, and that good works, born of gratitude, were also part of that process. Thus, there can be no separation of 'our works' and 'grace working in us', for grace and works are coupled by faith. Chiari had neatly introduced Greek patristic theology into the deliberations of Trent: '. . . when a man's sins are remitted and he is renewed inwardly (this is what is meant by 'justification'), the soul cannot but be filled with the most excellent resolutions, framed in truth and uprightness, and

---

[52] Ibid. p. 9: 'Censeo prius declarandum et sacrae scripturae auctoritatibus ostendendum merita ipsa [i.e. of Christ] ad iustificationem adiungi nobis.'

[53] Ibid.

[54] Ibid. p. 13; also p. 9.

[55] See above, ch. 6, pp. 136–7.

[56] Hefner, *Voten des Abtes*, p. 10: '. . . id autem est libertas, quae vocatur arbitrii, ut oblatis a Deo donis homo assentiatur eaque non aversetur . . .' Chiari quoted at length the lament of Prov. 1: 24–6, 'Quia vocavi et renuistis'. Massarelli summarized Chiari's point thus, 'Deus movet et nos assentimur nostro libero arbitrio voluntati Dei', *Conc. Trid.* v. 331.

attracting the name of good works'.[57] The Lutherans considered only the imputed righteousness of God and not works could justify man, whilst their opponents held that in some way the works of man justified him before God, but in the pattern of salvation that Chiari was presenting to the Council on behalf of the Congregation, good works which were part of faith and new life, sweeping into man, referred not to forensic values and judgement, but to growth and restoration.[58]

It followed that the operation of free will and works was to be described not in legalistic terms of justification and acquittal, but in affective language: the benefit of God towards man was the kindness of a father and friend, faith was like the life in the shoots of a vine or like fire in a sword from the forge. Faith surged through him, 'flooding in through veins and body', like the blood which vivified his body, and by it his human nature was restored to health.[59] Chiari was now hammering at the heart of Cassinese theology—that human salvation consisted less in acquittal from guilt than in restoration to health, that there was no dichotomy between grace and works, and that through the works of faith human nature is restored to its former glory, by the inward force of faith, pulsating to the exterior, like blood and spirit.[60]

On 22 July 1546 Chiari spoke again, this time expounding the Pauline necessity to work out one's salvation in fear and trembling. He drew a distinction between the mental condition of belief (sufficient, for example, for a man at the point of death to be 'ex fide adoptus') and the 'working out of salvation' which was necessary in the course of life. When faith was lived, it entailed gratitude and perseverance in good works and the

[57] Hefner, *Voten des Abtes*, p. 11; '... cum remittuntur homini peccata et interior innovatur homo (hoc enim est justificari), non potest tunc anima pulcherrimis cogitationibus, quae vere sunt recte factae, quae et bona opera vocamus, non esse gravida.' See also pp. 14–15.

[58] Ibid. p. 12: '... ita definire possumus, ut justificatio sit innovatio interioris hominis, dum ei per fidem in Christum remittuntur peccata et charitas Dei in cor illius per spiritum sanctum effunditur.'

[59] Ibid. pp. 9–10, 12, also *Conc. Trid.* v. 332: '... nisi infundatur per venas et per corpus, nihil faceret, sic fides ...'; 331: 'Sic fides: ea iustificamur, si corpori virtutum illabatur.'

[60] Hefner, *Voten des Abtes*, pp. 10–11, 'Ea ipsa, quae agente in nobis eadem gratia agimus, nostra etiam appellare prohibemur ... eadem ergo opera, dum justificando Deus hominem innovat interiorem, a justificante gratia non sunt separata'. See also pp. 9–13.

restoration of perfection. When he sat down, he was applauded. His task had been a difficult one, for he was proposing a synthesis of grace alone and the necessity of works, not to merit, but to restoration, and he was applying this pattern of salvation, drawn from the Greek Fathers of Antioch, to the theological quarrel of Latin Christendom, but despite the applause, his arguments were not well received, nor always understood, by the Fathers of Trent.[61]

In September 1546, after a summer break, the Council discussed the nature of faith and the certainty of grace. The Congregation's tradition was represented by its chief spokesman, Luciano degli Ottoni, on 7 October. At first, Ottoni exhibited his 'Pelagian' aspect, by arguing that righteousness is truly a work of man. Instead of using the Thomist description of 'the justice of God which is in us . . . since we accept it from him', Ottoni preferred to use the language of his 1538 book, in which he had defined faith as simultaneously the gift of God and the work of man. Accordingly, he called the justice of God that 'which is in us although we accept it through him'.[62] Ottoni's meaning is not quite clear, but it does seem probable that he was trying to prepare the ground for the teaching of his commentary of 1538 that both certitude of grace and good works were integral components of the living faith by which men were restored to original perfection.

His 'crypto-Protestant' views on grace and faith began to emerge during the discussion on chapter 10 of the draft decree on justification. The decree declared that a man was cut off from the grace of justification by mortal sin, not necessarily accompanied by loss of faith. The separation of faith and works thus implied was in contrast to Ottoni's own pattern of salvation, in which faith and works were inextricably linked, and faith was the source of all good works. With a touch of sarcasm, Ottoni

---

[61] Ibid. pp. 17–19, Chiari referred principally to Rom. 10: 10, and to Phil. 2:12. He also used the analogy of the status and obligations of citizenship to represent the rescue and sanctification of the soul. On 17 Aug. 1546 the three abbots gave a written statement to the President, 'De Potestate Credendi', probably written by Ottoni, *Conc. Trid.* v. 409, 477–8.

[62] *Conc. Trid.* v. 475, '. . . iustitia (Dei) quae in nobis est . . . quoniam ab ipso illam accepimus' [the Thomist formula]; '. . . quae in nobis est quamque [*sic*] per illum accepimus'. Evennett, 'Three Benedictine Abbots', p. 361, suggests that Ottoni had double justification in mind. However, this is not likely in view of the teaching of his book in 1538, which was not seen by Evennett.

invited the Council to agree that loss of faith was the root of all
sins:

> ... good works flow from faith as Paul tried to teach the Hebrews ... if
> good works flow from faith and are born out of faith, does it not follow
> that evil works spring from lack of faith ... does not Paul himself testify
> that men fell because of unbelief? ... we fall by lack of faith alone,
> irrespective of all evil works. Therefore, tell me, are we going to make a
> decree to the contrary, that we fall on account of sins alone,
> irrespective of our soul's lack of faith? They [sc. Christ and Paul] reject
> works: we shall reject faith.[63]

This argument against the separation of faith and works, and
the high value placed upon faith, were identical with the
doctrines expounded in his book of 1538. Also, they are very
similar to the themes of other Cassinese writers, and since Ottoni
was speaking for his Congregation 'in nome di tutti', the
doctrine may be taken as that of the Congregation. The doctrine
was rejected by the Council.

The same pattern of salvation was brought to bear during his
next speech, on the implications of faith. The question was
whether a man might know with certainty whether he possessed
the grace of God, such as the Lutherans asserted. First, Ottoni
drew a distinction between knowledge and the belief of faith:
faith does not possess the same kind of certainty as knowledge,
and knowledge does not have the certainty of faith.[64] Therefore
they must be distinguished. Faith has its own certainty which
cannot be separated from it:

> It does not seem to me to be very important whether we say simply 'to
> believe' or whether we augment it by saying 'to believe with certainty':
> for faith and certainty mutually arise from each other, and in so far as
> we are certain, to that extent we believe, and when we believe, at the
> same time we are certain ... therefore when it is said that certain belief
> or certain faith is necessary, they must be understood as the same

---

[63] *Conc. Trid.* v. 476, '... bona opera fluunt a fide ut Paulus ad Hebr(aeos) probare
conatur ... si bona opera inquam fluunt et oriuntur a fide, cur non etiam mala ab
infidelitate prodibunt ... Nonne Paulus ipse testatur, propter incredulitatem eos
cecidisse ... ex sola infidelitate nos cadere, opera mala omnia excludentes. Ergo,
inquam, nos e contra dicemus, ex solis peccatis nos cadere, infidelitatem penitus
excludentes? Ipsi reiiciunt opera, nos fidem reiiciemus.'

[64] Ibid. v. 477–8: 'Certum est enim, fidem stare non posse cum certitudine. Quare nec
scientia cum certitudine fidei. Separanda est igitur fides a scientia.'

thing, and likewise when it is said that great, or true, or living faith is necessary.[65]

Sometimes, he went on to argue, the experience can be so intense that men may experience an absolute certainty 'on account of spiritual abundance and sweetness and the living water which they feel and experience within themselves'.[66] Once again these sentiments were substantially those expressed by other Cassinese writers, and by Ottoni himself in his book of 1538, namely that living faith was the central religious experience and the pathway to salvation.

On 23 November Ottoni spoke again on the subject of faith. This time he repeated, rather more aggressively, his belief that faith cannot be separated from works. The scene was recorded by Massarelli in his diary:

> . . . using the arguments of the Lutherans he tried to demonstrate that faith is lost through sins, and faith is not able to stand with sin. Faith, therefore, is not able to coexist with sins. And when the President, the most Reverend Cardinal del Monte, asked him to say what he believed to be the truth of the matter, he replied that Christian faith is not able to remain in a sinner, and whosoever sins loses his faith, since faith is not able to remain with sins . . .[67]

Del Monte's interruption did not inhibit Ottoni and he turned boldly to the subject of the certitude of grace. He argued that a man might know with certainty that he possessed the grace of perseverance, and even that he would have eternal life:

[65] Ibid. v. 478 : 'An autem dicamus simpliciter credere vel cum additamento certo credere, non admodum mihi referre videtur: nam fides et certitudo se mutuo consequuntur, et eatenus certi sumus, quoad credimus, et eo usque credimus, quousque certi sumus . . . cum ergo dicitur, certo credendum esse vel certam fidem esse necessariam, pro eodem haberi debet ac si dicatur, magnam fidem et veram et vivam esse necessariam.'

[66] Ibid.: '. . . ob affluentiam et dulcedinem spiritus et aquam vivam, quam in se sentiunt atque degustant'.

[67] Ibid. v. 659: '. . . per peccata tamen fides amittitur et fides non potest stare cum peccato, quod probare conatus est per argumenta Lutheranorum. Fides igitur non potest stare cum peccatis. Et cum a R.mo. cardinale de Monte praesidente interrogaretur, ut diceret, quid in eo in veritate ipse sentiret, respondit, quod fides Christiana non potest stare in peccatore, et qui peccat, fidem amittet, cum fides non possit stare cum peccatis . . .' In terms of scholastic theology the question was whether sin can coexist with supernatural faith when this is not *fides formata*, i.e. faith active in love. In effect, Ottoni denied the distinction between the two. Evennett thought his statement 'well on the way to Lutheranism', op. cit. 365. Jedin, *History of the Council of Trent*, ii. 291, said that Ottoni 'clearly sided with Luther'.

Concerning the certainty of grace, a just man may be able to believe that he will certainly have eternal life, since John says 'he who believes shall have eternal life'. And if this is true, it follows that someone is able to know that he is amongst the predestined, because if he believes, he believes with certainty that he is going to have eternal life, that he is amongst the predestined etc.[68]

In terms of Chrysostom's theology and the doctrines held by other Cassinese writers, the arguments of their spokesman were not exceptional. The teaching was patristic and monastic in origin and owed little or nothing to Luther. But, delivered in these circumstances, and presumably with characteristic vivacity, Ottoni's words provoked an uproar, the assembled Fathers of Trent shouting as one, 'omnibus patribus uno ore acclamantibus', their condemnation of heresy.[69]

The following morning Ottoni made a personal statement. He declared that he was a loyal Catholic and explained that he had spoken of *fides* in the sense of *fides formata*, that is, faith informed by love. (He might have added, but did not, that it was the only sense in which he understood faith.) Finally, he rebuked his detractors for the noise they had made.[70] The equivocal nature of the apology suggests that it was an act of prudence, not recantation, and his later brief interventions and his correspondence show that he continued to hold to his opinions.[71]

[68]   *Conc. Trid.* v. 659, 'De certitudine gratiae . . . iustus teneatur credere, se certo vitam aeternam habiturum, cum Ioannes dicat "Qui credit, vitam aeternam habebit". Et si hoc est verum, ergo quis posset scire, se esse in numero praedestinatorum, quia si credit, certo se habiturum vitam aeternam credit, se esse in numero praedestinatorum etc. Quod illico ab omnibus patribus uno ore acclamantibus est reprobatum.'

[69]   Both Evennett and Jedin have drawn attention to similarities between Cassinese and Scotist theology. The former suggested that the role of *dilectio* was of Scotist origin, op. cit., p. 370. However, this seems to be unlikely, considering the monks' use of biblical and patristic material. Jedin noted the Cassinese agreement with the Scotist 'certitudo cui non potest subesse falsum', *History of the Council of Trent*, ii. 288–92. This phrase had been used by Ottoni in his description of faith in 1538, but whereas Ottoni meant that certitude was a constituent of faith, the Scotists meant the complete assurance that grace had been conveyed by a sacrament. Thus the Scotist faction and the Benedictine abbots both voted in favour of *certitudo fidei*, but for different reasons. On 7 Oct. 1546 Ottoni was engaged in argument with two ministers-general on the question whether certitude of grace can be proved from Scotus, *Conc. Trid.* i. 105, 929.

[70]   Ibid. v. 659–60, 24 Nov. 1546. Massarelli referred to Ottoni as 'qui heri in voto suo notatus fuerat de haeresi'. In *History of the Council of Trent*, ii. 290–1, Jedin says that Ottoni took refuge in a tautology: however, this fails to recognize Ottoni's rich doctrine of faith.

[71]   The same day, 24 November, Ottoni opposed the removal of 'gratis' from the Canon, *Conc. Trid.* v. 659, 680–5. After the decree on justification was passed, Ottoni

However, after this fracas it was clear that Cassinese doctrines could not hope to succeed, and Ottoni said very little else for the remainder of the session.

The episode had effectively put an end to the Congregation's intervention in the debates on justification. The attempt had failed. Ottoni was bitterly disappointed, as his letters to the Duke of Ferrara reveal,[72] but his colleagues must have been equally unhappy. In fact Chiari had prepared an alternative speech, presumably in case Ottoni was unable to speak, and this undelivered speech was equally forthright.[73] It argued that salvation was not primarily a quest to attain a state of justice, but a 'salutis beneficium', a gift of grace out of which comes faith, works and restoration—'coming to the measure of the full stature (as Paul says) of the life of Christ'. Chiari had proposed to assert that certitude of grace was derived from a man's filial relationship with God, and that the assurance of a father and friend stood despite a man's shortcomings.[74] The undelivered speech was to have summed up all this in a passage reminiscent of the early chapters of the *Beneficio*, and, like that tract, drew upon Basil, Hilarion, and Gregory the Great, saying that he who returns to God, however deep his sins, is received back as a son into the friendship of a beneficent father.[75]

But the speech was not delivered, and indeed after 23 November the three abbots contributed very little else to the Council. They and the Congregation—and their opponents—knew that their attempt to interpose Congregational teachings had failed, and their doctrines had been rejected. The final decrees on justification took almost no account of what they had said.

The monks had been hopeful, but their failure cannot have been altogether unexpected, for their theology was quite out of

wrote in unhappy terms to the duke of Ferrara that it was 'fatto tutto nel modo che hanno voluto li dottori Scolastici'. He prophesied, 'sono certo che col tempo si ne pentiranno', *Conc. Trid.* x. 776, 877 (3 and 14 Jan. 1547).

[72] *Conc. Trid.* x. 552, n. 4; 805, n. 3.

[73] Hefner, *Voten des Abtes*, pp. 22–33; Evennett, 'Three Benedictine Abbots', pp. 366–9.

[74] Hefner, *op. cit.* pp. 25–6, 28, '. . . usque dum perveniamus ad mensuram plenae (ut ait Paulus) aetatis Christi'; '. . . aeternae salutis beneficium a Deo accipiamus'.

[75] Ibid. p. 32. On p. 28 there is an interesting trace of Chiari's collaboration with Ottoni in his description of the scholastics' supposed opposition to biblical theology, '. . . ex diametro (quod aiunt) oppositis sententiis . . .' The same phrase was used for the same purpose by Ottoni in his commentary of 1538 on Chrysostom.

place in a dispute that turned upon legalistic Latin concepts.
Because the Greek, pre-Augustinian elements in their doctrines
led them to describe salvation as man's restoration rather than
his forensic justification, the monks largely avoided the presuppositions common to antagonists of the Reformation debates.
But, although it bypassed the central deadlock of the Reformation conflict, Cassinese theology had little chance of preventing
the religious division of western Christendom. Its few tracts,
books, and sermons, and even the speeches at Trent, made
almost no impact upon the official teachings of Protestant and
Catholic theologies. The attempt to remedy a western schism
with Greek theology was a misunderstood and lost cause.[76]

Failure at the Council of Trent took the steam out of the
Cassinese Congregation, and over its subsequent history there
hangs an air of anticlimax. Of course, the old teachings
remained, and continued to be expounded in books and tracts,
but from the beginning of 1547 the Congregation lost both the
sparkle and the hard edge of its scholarship. It sustained a
particular loss when Chiari was elevated to the see of Foligno in
January 1547, only a few weeks after Ottoni's last major speech.
Chiari was an exemplary bishop: he reformed his diocesan
clergy, inviting the Jesuit Silvestro Landini to spend some
months in the diocese to advise him. He attempted a number of
social reforms, and particularly tried to reduce prostitution and
to care for the poor, he organized the distribution of alms, and
he showed unfailing courtesy and compassion, especially to the
poor and even to unemployed youths ('ah, poverelli') who
insulted him in the street. He continued to write sermons and we
shall hear more of them later,[77] but at Foligno he was more or
less cut off from his Congregation, and whilst he continued to

---

[76] Reusch says that Ottoni was one of those Italians who put forward a pre-Augustinian doctrine of grace with Luther in mind. 'Der Verfasser [sc. Ottoni] . . . der 1546 in
Trient war, gehörte zu den italienischen Theologen, welche mit Rücksicht auf Luthers
Lehre den Thomisten gegenüber die Gnadenlehre der voraugustinischen namentlich
der griechischen Väter zur Geltung zu bringen suchten', H. Reusch, *Der Index der
verbotenen Bücher* (Bonn, 1883) i. 400. Also see R. Simon, *Bibliothèque critique*, pp. 353–4.
Simon said that Ottoni and other learned Italians believed, and he, Simon, concurred,
that 'le seul et veritable moyen de détruire l'hérésie de Luther était d'appuyer les
sentiments des Pères Grecs', but that their efforts were in vain. He said that Ottoni's
intemperate attacks upon scholastics 's'éleva contre lui une infinité de Théologiens qui
firent condamner son Livre'.

[77] See below, ch. 11.

preach the old doctrines, he was no longer an active protagonist for them. He appears to have been happy to go to ground after the events of 1546, and gave himself fully to his pastoral obligations.[78]

At the same time the Congregation became the object of ill-defined suspicions of heresy. In January 1546 Pier Paolo Vergerio, Bishop of Capodistria, was staying at San Benedetto Po, where he wrote a paraphrase of the psalms and a tract on dying. His patron, Cardinal Ercole Gonzaga, thought the works to be Lutheran, but endeavoured to protect Vergerio. One day the doorkeeper at the monastery imprudently showed an agent of the Inquisition to the bishop's room and Vergerio was handed a summons to attend an inquisitorial tribunal. Vergerio was very angry indeed and treated the messenger with an outraged haughtiness which indicates the difficulty of dealing with heresy in high places, but three years later the suspicions were verified when Vergerio embraced Protestantism and went into exile.[79] A certain amount of residual suspicion must have stuck to the Congregation during this period, and in October 1546 the Franciscan bishop, Dionisio Zanettini, a rabid vigilante, made it plain that he thought the Congregation to be a hotbed of Lutheran heresy.[80]

---

[78] Armellini, *CTE* 34; F. Egger, *Idea Ordinis Hierarchico-Benedictini* (Constantia, 1717), ii, p. 263; L. Jacobilli, *Vite de' santi e beati di Foligno* (Foligno, 1628), pp. 105–12. The inclusion of Chiari's biography in this hagiographical work seventy years after his death suggests popular veneration. B. Ulianich, 'Scrittura e azione pastorale nelle prime omelie episcopali di Isidoro Chiari', *Reformata Reformanda: Festgabe für Hubert Jedin* (Munster, 1965), i. 610–34; A. Marani, 'Il Clario e la residenza dei vescovi', *Brixia Sacra: Memorie storiche della diocese di Brescia*, a.vii (1972), 114–21. G. J. Gussago, *Biblioteca Clarense* (Chiari, 1832), ii. 5–95. Chiari had Silvestro Landini in his see for some months at the end of 1548. He approved highly of the intellectual qualities of the Jesuits: L. Pastor, *The History of the Popes*, ed. R. F. Kerr (London, 1912), xii. 80, 89. For an account of Venetian policies towards religious dissenters and the hardening of attitudes after 1547, see A. Santosuosso, 'Religious Orthodoxy, Dissent and Suppression in Venice in the 1540s', *Church History*, xlii (1973), 476–85.

[79] The episode, together with notes on Vergerio's friendship with Pietro Aretino, is described in P. Paschini, *Pier Paolo Vergerio il Giovane e la sua Apostasia* (Rome, 1925), pp. 107–13.

[80] Letter of Dionisio Zanettini ('Il Grechetto'), Bishop of Chironissa and Melopotamos, to Cardinal Guidascani Sforza, from Trent, 13 Oct. 1546. The letter is printed in G. Buschbell, *Reformation und Inquisition in Italien um die Mitte des XVI Jahrhunderts* (Paderborn, 1910), pp. 260–2. Zanettini had three Benedictines, the three abbots at Trent, on his list of prelates whose attitude to heresy he considered to be lax and dangerous—Chiari, Calvini, Ottoni; see A. J. Schutte, *Pier Paolo Vergerio: The Making of an Italian Reformer* (Travaux d'Humanisme et Renaissance, clx, Geneva, 1977), p. 210 n. Zanettini was also intensely suspicious of Don Marco of Padua.

Rather more precise suspicions are suggested by the diary of Massarelli, secretary to the Council of Trent. In December 1548 he was at Padua, asking questions about Don Benedetto da Mantova, from whom he received sundry letters during the next few months. Massarelli gave no details, although he said that the monk requested him 'to write to the general of his order'. On 3 May 1549 it was noted that Benedetto had been detained at Padua (there was a marginal comment 'Videtur suspectus fuisse') and that Cardinal del Monte wrote to the Congregation in support of him.[81] Nothing seems to have come of the matter, probably not only because Benedetto enjoyed the support of the man who shortly became pope, and because he was perhaps related to the Gonzaga family, but also possibly because it was recognized that his contribution to the *Beneficio* was not Protestant in character.

However, the Congregation was not entirely thrown on the defensive. In 1549 Giambattista Folengo published another commentary on the psalms in which he touched frequently upon his Congregation's traditional teaching.[82] He asserted that through the fall man suffers infirmities and the penalty of death, and has lost his similitude to God—though not completely, for there still remains free will. Yet man cannot use his free will to achieve perfection through obedience to the Law. On the contrary, the Law could not lead to perfection at all. Its function was pedagogic, for, as 'Paul declares, the divine law teaches us the way to perfection'.[83]

Folengo's dominant theme was that salvation is a gift of God's

---

[81] *Conc. Trid.* i. 817, 818, 825, 836, 839. For Benedetto's family connection with the Gonzaga see Menegazzo, 'Per la Conoscenza', pp. 205–10. The letters of support suggest that the Congregation was making its own investigation, as was its privilege from 1528; see Caponetto, *Beneficio* 494. For the growth of religious intolerance see A. Santosuosso, 'Religious orthodoxy, dissent and suppression in Venice in the 1540s', *Church History*, xlii (1973), 476–85.

[82] *In Psalterium Davidis Israelitarum Regis et Vatis Divinissimi, Ioan(nis) Baptistae Folengii Mantuani Monachi Cassinatis Commentarii . . . ex ipsa Hebraica Veritate Confecti et Absoluti* (Basle, 'per Mich(aelem) Isingrinium, 1549). The work included and completed Folengo's *Commentary* of 1540 (see above, ch. 7). It included a dedicatory epistle to Ercole Gonzaga, and a letter to Folengo's brother, Nicodemo, dated December 1542. There was also a preface written in 1543 by Don Anastasius Ubertus, who was made bishop of Imola in 1552. The work was reprinted by the publisher in 1557, and it is to this edition that reference is made.

[83] *In Psalterium* 10A–B, 49C, 204D, 64D,' [Paulus] asserit divina(m) legem nos ad salutem instruere'. Also 389C, 379B–C.

'misericordia erga hominum genus immensa'. The 'benignitas erga homines', an idea which he expressed again and again,[84] was manifest in 'the infinite benefits brought to the human race by the Cross and death of the son of God'. Salvation was by grace alone, and 'without Christ there could be no salvation'.[85] Through 'the most immense power' of the Cross, said Folengo, 'all damnation has been removed from this world, death destroyed and sin annulled'.[86] Thus the justice which man himself could not achieve had been given by an act of grace. At times Folengo's exposition seems to be almost Lutheran: '. . . the justice of God is the immense fullness of the divine goodness, which . . . by his own blood and death . . . set free the human race into the liberty of the sons of God.'[87] However, Folengo understood *iustitia Dei* to refer also to sanctification: 'God freely imparts justice to us, and purity of hands, that is, bestows innocence of life'.[88] Moreover, in accordance with Cassinese tradition Folengo held that grace was extended to all people, as 'a father's love and universal charity for all men'.[89]

Folengo also followed Cassinese teaching on faith as being first of all belief and trust that Christ was indeed 'humani generis amantissimus', whose 'immensa misericordia' was manifest in the Cross. Such acceptance was simple and did not demand theological speculation. Folengo used precisely the same passage from Chrysostom as had Ottoni in 1538: 'As Chrysostom declares, God does not ask those who hear him to be wearied, or to search with excessive curiosity . . . but only to accept and believe.'[90] Faith itself was a gift of God, and man's acceptance of

---

[84] Ibid. 306D, 235B, also 1A, 6C–D, 24A, 47D, 62C, 72D, 88A, 155B, 223B, 235B, 256A, 264C, 342B–D, 356C, 357D, 439A, 442C.

[85] Ibid. 24A, 'de infinitis beneficiis humano generi a cruce & morte filii Dei exhibitis'; 66C, 'nulla salus esse queat sine Christo'.

[86] Ibid. 66D, 'e mundo omnis est sublata perditio, extincta mors, ac abolitum peccatum'; also 438A.

[87] Ibid. 80B: '. . . iustitiam Dei, hoc est, immensam divinae bonitatis amplitudinem, qua . . . proprio cruore & morte, hominum genus . . . in libertatem filiorum Dei vindicavit.'

[88] Ibid. 55A: '. . . meritum non extollit quidem, sed nos potius ad co(n)siderandam Dei erga homines benignitate(m) provocat. Deus enim, qui gratis iustitiam nobis impartit, ac manuum puritatem, hoc est, vitae innocentiam elargitur.'

[89] Ibid. 79C, 308A: 'Amor . . . patris, atq(ue) universalis ad omnes charitas'; also 26A, 204A.

[90] Ibid. 204A–B: '. . . ut inquit Chrysostomus, non oportet audientes multum defatigari, aut curiose nimium indagare . . . sed tantum excipere & credere.'

this 'donum Dei' was a human action which coupled man to God. Acceptance was accompanied by certitude, and both were nourished by the Scriptures, which could be understood even by unlearned women and youths.[91] Thus the Law had become redundant, because salvation was now available to all believers, who were all freely forgiven and justified through faith in the Cross. 'Love and faith', said Folengo, with striking imagery, 'have their nest in the wounds of Christ'.[92]

Still in the Cassinese tradition, Folengo held works to be an essential part of faith. Works spring from faith; they are necessary to it yet in no way detract from the work of Christ.[93] With good works comes new life, which is manifest in purity of life, in love of neighbour, and in perseverance, even to death (for Christ's own faithful people suffer).[94] These things were all part of the response of gratitude for the astonishing divine kindness of Christ: to respond otherwise would be sinful ingratitude.[95] Finally, through the works of faith God 'recalls, restores and recreates' the soul:

the similitude of God so greatly obscured in us through the sin of Adam . . . through the righteousness of faith . . . with Christ as the cause, is able to be reshaped, and we are able to grow as we progress in faith. Then truly, with Christ in whom we are transformed by love, it shall be brought to perfection in the final resurrection.[96]

Folengo was reasserting his Congregation's teaching of the restoration of the divine image in man. The human race, he said was 'renewed with a new kind of justice' and partook of the divine nature, so that, in a phrase which repeated Chiari's assertion to the men of Brescia, 'we are made gods through Christ'.[97]

[91] *In Psalterium* 62C–D, 66D, 204A, 255C, 304B–C, 314–15, 349D, 357D, 383–4. At the Council of Trent, in his speech on 13 July 1546, Chiari made a similar reference to the understanding of the unlearned.

[92] Ibid. 153A–B, 233D, 438D: 'In vulneribus igitur Christi, in quibus suum habent nidum amor & fides . . .'; also 233C, 304D, 312D, 356–8, 438D.

[93] Ibid. 12C, 89B–C, 287C, 348–9, 357D, 383C–D.

[94] Ibid. 41A–C, 301A–B, 356C.

[95] Ibid. 264C–D, 349B.

[96] Ibid. 62D: 'restituit, revocat, & in aeternum renovat'; also 308D; 49C–D, 'Similitudo enim Dei in nobis adeo per Adae peccatum perlanguit . . . per iustitiam fidei . . . opera(n)te Christo, reformari potest: ac dum de fide in fidem ambulamus, augescere. Tum vero cum Christo in quem per amore(m) transformamur, novissima in resurrectione perficietur.'

[97] Ibid. 331D: 'renovandi erant, novum iustitiae genus in Christo'; also 349A–B; 66C, 'dii facti sumus per Christum.' For Chiari's use of this expression see above, ch. 7.

Folengo also said that the church was the house ('aedes') of salvation, and that church, Gospel, and Christ are one.[98] Of course, it was prudent to say such things, but doubtless he meant them. Cassinese monks had always spoken thus. They were also loyal to the Roman church, and Folengo was simply making an effort to reaffirm his order's teaching within a church that had, only three years earlier, declined to accept those teachings.

After the failure at Trent, other changes came over the Congregation, one of which emerged in two tracts written by Denis Faucher in 1548 and 1549. Faucher had returned to Lérins in 1544, where he had edited an edition of *Instructio ad Monachos Sancti Fausti* of St. Hilary, and continued to supervise the studies and devotions of the able nuns of Arles. For one of those nuns, Delphine Tornatoria, he wrote two tracts, *De Reformatione Mentis*, in 1548, and *De Meditatione Passionis Christi*, in 1549.[99] Together, the two works were another exposition of the pattern of salvation traditionally taught by the Congregation. Faucher began, as usual, with the argument that man was made in the image of God: he adopted Augustine's belief that the threefold qualities of the soul—will, intellect, and memory—reflect the Trinity, but he followed Gregory of Nyssa in placing almost all the emphasis upon the will and the emotions.[100] The image of God was deformed, but not destroyed, by sin, which was also described in Augustinian terms as an implanted egocentric preoccupation of human nature with itself ('incurvata siquidem et in se reflexa cum se a Deo averterit').[101]

Like Benedetto da Mantova, he saw the consequences of the fall in the miseries of mankind, in suffering, death, political turmoil, and personal unhappiness. Men are trapped in their misery and sin, enemies of God ('inimici nimirum crucis Christi'), yet are blind to their sickness. Using the language of the Greek Fathers Faucher described sin in the familiar terms of the penalty of damage and mortality suffered by human nature, 'tam immensum et tam inveteratum morbum'.[102]

[98] Ibid. 307–8, 331C–D, 377C.
[99] The two tracts are printed in V. Barrali Salerno, *Chronologia Sanctorum*, ii. 220–48, 249–54. (For references to the 'collegium virginum' and its higher studies see above, ch. 7.)
[100] Ibid. ii. 226–8, 247.
[101] Ibid. ii. 226–8.
[102] Ibid. ii. 228–9, 241, 255–6, 269.

The only remedy, Faucher told Delphine, was the grace of the Cross: this alone was the means of salvation. It was the gift of God's love towards the human race, the 'beneficium Dei', 'tam ingens beneficium', 'ingens erga nos divinae charitatis dignatio'.[103] By the Cross, men are snatched to safety from the powers of death and hell, the penalty of passibility and death is removed, and the 'ancient sickness is healed' by Christ, who is the 'custos ac medicus' of the human race.[104]

Having insisted that salvation is by grace alone, Faucher went on, in the Cassinese fashion, to describe faith. The first attribute of faith is the soul's recognition of its own sickness—the point made by Benedetto in the first two chapters of the *Beneficio*. When the sickness is recognized, then men will look for the doctor: in this understanding they are guided by the holy scriptures.[105] Faith is also belief and trust in the promises of God. To some extent, such faith was a gift of God, but it was also man's freely willed acceptance of the gift. From such a faith, with its divine and human aspect, good works flowed naturally, and as faith healed man's free will so did the good works flow more freely.[106] Through these good works man is made a son of God through faith, and is restored to his pristine integrity. The wretched Protestants ('pestes illas') were mistaken in thinking that salvation by grace alone denied the necessity of works, for works were necessary as the instrument of healing and restoration. Through living faith, day by day, men were restored to perfection.[107]

Perseverance is necessary 'ut Dei beneficium non aspernandum potest', and failure to persevere is not only a sign of ingratitude, but is also a self-inflicted wound because it means that a man is not restored to health. Faucher told the nun to use her monastic vows as the 'protection of righteousness' and an 'instrument of good works' so that she might remain steadfast.[108] He seems to suggest that tribulation and temptation are the signs of a true Christian, and certainly his understanding of

---

[103] Barrali Salerno, *Cronologia Sanctorum* ii. 228, 241, 249–51, 253–4. Also see ii. 316 (letter to Delphine, 1551).

[104] Ibid. ii. 250–1, 255.

[105] Ibid. ii. 228–9. (For similar passages in the *Beneficio* see above, ch. 8.)

[106] Ibid. ii. 246–7, 250, 261, 315–16. See also Caponetto, *Beneficio*, 6–7, 30.

[107] Barrali Salerno, *Chronologia Sanctorum*, ii. 235, 246–7.

[108] Ibid. ii. 228, 230, 235, 255, 264, 315.

living faith and works had no place for lukewarm Christians, or mere conformists, or monks who are lazy, or lack love 'tam frigido corde'.[109]

This whole process of good works, perseverance, and restoration, he summed up in the characteristic Cassinese phrase, 'to put on Christ' ('Christum induere').[110] This was the way of all Christians, 'omnium Christianorum vocatio';[111] it was not merely for monastics, though they had certain advantages. In all this, Faucher was in accord with his Congregation's theology which had never been intended only for the cloisters.

However, when Faucher moved from the restoration of *imago Dei* to a description of the concomitant union with Christ, his pattern of salvation began to adopt strongly emotional tones. 'O, happy soul', he wrote, 'who, burning with ardent desires calls unceasingly to the Lord'.[112] His enthusiasm was ecstatic: the 'will was inflamed with divine love', the soul 'dissolved into Christ with utter love', and was 'drunken with divine love'.[113] At this point, Faucher's doctrine of faith was stretched beyond the constraints of the Congregation's traditional sober biblical scholarship, moving away from its focus upon grace and restoration towards an idea of faith as a strong emotional experience. Faucher's description of the union with God of a soul ravished by passionate love, has the language of emotional faith tinged with the eroticism of the Song of Songs: 'May you hear what the Lord your God speaks within you . . . what could be more ravishing, O daughter, than to hear intimate words uttered to your heart by Christ Jesus—words no man may utter—while all inside you melts into love of the Spouse from Paradise.'[114]

What are we to make of Faucher's tracts of 1548 and 1549? Clearly, his pattern of salvation was based upon the teachings

[109] Ibid. ii. 250, 256–7, 336.

[110] Ibid. ii. 228, 247.

[111] Ibid. ii. 227.

[112] Ibid. ii. 265, 'O, felix anima . . . ardentibus desideriis aestuans non cessat clamare ad Dominum.' See also ii. 247, 315–16.

[113] Ibid. 247, '. . . inflammata divino amore voluntas'; 259, '. . . tota in eum . . . per amorem liquescit'; 317, 'divino inebriata amore . . .' See also ii. 229, 248, 251, 253, 261, 265, 315–18.

[114] Ibid. ii. 232, 'Audias quid loquatur in te dominus Deus tuus . . . quid suavius, filia, . . . quam ut ad cor tuum Christum Iesum arcana verba loquentem audias quae non licet homini loqui . . . tota in amorem coelestis sponsi liquefacta'; also ii. 248.

which the Congregation had drawn from the Greek Fathers and which he himself had followed since his profession in 1508. Yet these tracts of 1548 and 1549 had veered away from the confident scholarly expositions that distinguished Congregational writings before the Council of Trent, towards subjective emotional warmth and excesses of piety. In this man at least, Cassinese theology was drifting from its strict biblical and patristic base: it was losing its balance and becoming prone to exaggeration.[115] The traditional terminology of the Congregation was being employed to build up subjective devotion, moving from scholarly exposition to learned enthusiasm. It is difficult to say to what extent the failure at Trent and a loss of confidence contributed to Faucher's tendencies, but in the next chapter we shall examine another example of distortion of the Congregation's teachings—the case of the heretical monk, Giorgio Siculo.

[115] There is a similar trait in a prayer before eucharistic celebration, written by Don Basil of Naples at San Severino in 1549, and placed at the end of an anonymous 'libellus' (on various subjects) which was transcribed by him. The prayer refers to Christ as 'salvator misericors, clementiss(imu)s ac benigniss(imu)s, o veriss(im)e amator . . .' etc. Bibl. Apost. Vat. Chigi, B IV 53, fo. 67ᵛ.

X

Giorgio Siculo:
Monastic Doctrine Exaggerated

Don Giorgio Siculo, one of the more audacious heretics of post-Reformation Italy, was born Giorgio Rioli in the village of San Pietro, near Catania, possibly in 1516 or 1517. He was professed in the Cassinese house of San Nicolò L'Arena on 24 February 1534, where he remained until at least September 1539.[1] It is quite possible that during this time the young Giorgio was taught by Benedetto of Mantova, who arrived at San Nicolò in August 1537 and remained there until the spring of 1542.[2]

There is no definite record of Siculo's movements after September 1539[3] until some time in the late 1540s, when he experienced a vision of Christ, who appeared to him so vividly and so near that his body could have been touched by the monk. The vision spoke to Siculo and delivered into his hands the true interpretation of scripture.[3a] Afterwards Siculo began to

[1] Caponetto, *Beneficio* 462 n., 485.

[2] Ibid. 485, 'Per circa tre anni il giovane catanese completò la preparazione sotto la guida del decano di Mantova, dal quale sarà stato spinto allo studio della sacra Scrittura e iniziato forse alla dottrina valdesiana. Da questa il passo al radicalismo spiritualistico e al nicodemismo è breve.' This suggestion of Caponetto is not convincing. It has been shown earlier that biblical studies were already at the centre of Cassinese training, and it has been argued that the doctrines of the Cassinese monks, including Benedetto, were drawn from the Greek Fathers, not from Valdès. Therefore, whilst it is probable that Benedetto exerted some influence on the young monk, we cannot assume that what Benedetto taught, and Siculo received, at San Nicolò was anything other than traditional Cassinese theology and spirituality.

[3] Ibid. 462 n. At Ratisbon in 1542 Morone, Bishop of Modena and papal nuncio gave 20 scudi to one 'Georgio Sicelio'. It is possible that the monk had been sent on an errand to Morone by Gregory Cortese, who was involved in negotations. Caponetto thinks it probable that the man was Siculo.

[3a] J. Calvin, *De aeterna Dei praedestinatione* 258–9: 'Nebulo hic Christum sibi apparuisse, et totius scripturae ab illo se interpretem constitutum mentitus . . .' Calvin was probably sent this information together with a summary of Siculo's book, by the duchess of Ferrara or by the Protestant minister Giulio da Milano. See D. Cantimori, *Eretici italiani del Cinquecento* (Florence, 1939), pp. 60, 62 n. Cantimori quotes from Francesco Pucci's account of the vision. Siculo may have seen and been impressed by the paintings of Giulio Romano in the Palazzo del Té, Mantua; through mainly erotic, they made strong use of dazzling light to produce visionary effects. Romano was Raphael's principal assistant, and in fact completed Raphael's *Transfiguration*.

expound the doctrines he had received, which, as we shall see later, both resembled and differed from common Congregational teachings. His fellow monks were divided in their responses. A few took an interest in this intelligent and articulate young man: amongst them were Isidoro Chiari, Luciano degli Ottoni, and Benedetto da Mantova, and under the tutelage of these men he wrote his first work, a commentary on the ninth, tenth, and eleventh chapters of Romans, in which he expounded his ideas on predestination and justification.[4] However, other monks were not impressed by Siculo's vision, and were less tolerant of his personality and probably of the way in which he handled monastic theology. There was some kind of quarrel and he left the cloisters.

Siculo wandered across the Po valley, still calling himself Don Giorgio, and preaching his revealed doctrine. In 1548 or 1549 he visited Bologna, where he waited to deliver Christ's message to the Council when it resumed deliberations. At Bologna he preached in an excited manner to small groups of devout citizens and scholars from the Collegio di Spagna, some of whom were impressed by his exposition of biblical themes, in particular the vice-rector, Juan Delgado, with whom he became friendly. In 1549 he was in Ferrara where his preaching attracted well-to-do people and teachers from the Studio.[5] Then in 1549, or possibly early 1550, Siculo left the Po valley and went up into the foothills, to Riva di Trento, probably drawn by the imminent return of the Council to Trent. At Riva he preached a sermon every day throughout Lent of 1550 in the principal

---

[4] This work was published in Bologna in 1550 by Anselmo Giaccarello under the title *Espositione nel non decimo e undecimo capo della Epistola di San Paolo al li Romani*. I could find only one copy of this work which is in the library of Duke University, North Carolina, USA. No other historian has used this work or even referred to it. A deposition of Nascimbene Nascimbeni, at Venice in 1570, refers to the book as *De justificatione*, and says it was translated from Sicilian into Italian by Benedetto and into Latin by Ottoni; see Caponetto, *Beneficio* 462–3. Such translation seems quite feasible, since the *Espositione* only slightly deviates from Cassinese teaching, and translation would not imply Ottoni's approval of heresy.

[5] Siculo's connection with Delgado and other Spanish scholars has been demonstrated clearly by Adriano Prosperi, 'Un gruppo ereticale italo-spagnolo: la setta di Giorgio Siculo', *Critica Storica*, iii (1982), 337–51. C. Ginzburg, *Il Nicodemismo: Simulazione e dissimulazione religiosa nell' Europa del' 500* (Turin, 1970), p. 175: 'Due note sul profetismo cinquecentesco', *Rivista storica italiana*, lxxviii (1966), 188 n. 19; L. Berini, 'Ancora sul libraio-tipografico Pietra Perna e su alcune figure di eretici italiani in rapporto con lui negli anni 1549–1555', *Nuova rivista storica*, li (1967), 404.

church of the town. According to his own account, these forty sermons were delivered with faith and sincerity, and afterwards people were seeking him out and begging him to preach again.[6] He says that his sermons were an exposition of his doctrine, and perhaps his sermon notes were the basis of the rambling and repetitious *Epistola . . . alli cittadini di Riva di Trento* which he published later in 1550, together with the Italian version of his earlier treatise on Romans.[7] In the summer of 1550 he went to Ferrara, where, in September, he was arrested and imprisoned as an impenitent heretic, and in May 1551 condemned and hanged.[8]

Siculo's fate seems far removed from the scholarly cloisters in which he spent his formative years, but despite the incongruity it is possible that there were connections, and that Siculo's heresy was not entirely plucked from the apparition, but perhaps was embedded in the Greek patristic scholarship of his Congregation. In order to see if this were the case we shall examine his two surviving works in detail.

In the *Espositione*, the earlier of the two works, Siculo set out to 'demonstrate more clearly than has been done before the true meaning of the ninth, tenth, and eleventh chapters of Paul's epistle to the Romans'.[9] Despite Siculo's intention, there was very little new in his work. On the contrary, it was made up of themes which were commonly taught within the Congregation. The central theme, an attack upon the doctrine of predestination in the sense of special election of particular men, was taken almost entirely from Ottoni's commentary of 1538 on

---

[6] *Epistola* 121^v–122^r. The sermons were preached in 'la pieve', '. . . io fui recercato con istanza e grandamente pregato . . .'

[7] *Epistola di Giorgio Siculo servo fidele di Jesu Christo alli cittadini di Riva di Trento contra il mendatio di Francesco Spiera, e falsa dottrina di Protestanti*, published by Anselmo Giaccarello, of Bologna, in 1550. There are copies of the *Epistola* in the library of the University of Bologna, the British Library and the Duke University Library, North Carolina.

[8] A. Rotondò, 'Per la storia dell'eresia a Bologna nel secolo xvi', *Rinascimento*, xiii (1962), 153–4; also Cantimori, *Eretici italiani*, p. 59.

[9] *Espositione* 2^r. The frontispiece includes the etching of a man with a flaming brand, fighting off a hydra-headed, winged serpentine devil; underneath is the motto 'Affectus virtute superantur'. The opening words of the text address it to 'signor dottor Alfonso', who was described as a man of 'honesta e Christiana mente'. The work, of only thirty-two folios, has a repetitious, loping style which suggests that it was compiled from sermon notes. It was written first in Sicilian dialect, with numerous biblical quotations in Latin, and was probably put into Tuscan by Benedetto da Mantova: See Caponetto, *Beneficio* 462–3.

Chrysostom. Siculo argued that by the term 'predestination' Paul did not mean the gratuitous election of particular men to salvation, but that God had ordained from the beginning that all men, without exception of persons, should believe and obey and thus be saved. The term had been used to impress upon the Jews that God's mercy and grace was not given to them by right, either as the carnal descendants of Abraham, or for their obedience to the Mosaic Law, but that from the beginning God had ordained that it should be given to all the spiritual sons of God who believed and obeyed as he had ordained: 'The holy scriptures . . . testify to the salvation and the general grace of his divine majesty to all his believing and obedient people . . . preordained to receive the holy spirit and to attain their heavenly inheritance.'[10] This theme of universal grace as opposed to particular election was commonly taught in the Congregation, notably by Ottoni. Shortly after Siculo's profession, both he and Benedetto da Mantova, Ottoni's friend, were at the monastery of San Nicolò L'Arena. When Siculo travelled north he then fell under the tutelage of Ottoni himself. Presumably it was from these men that he received the doctrine of universal grace, which they in turn, like other Cassinese scholars, had taken from the Antiochene Fathers.

The manner in which Siculo expounded the central theme closely resembles the teaching of his Congregation. Their scholars had a long tradition of literal and historical exegesis of biblical texts, and copies of the Pauline epistles used for teaching novices were glossed with such brief explanations.[11] Siculo, too, began with a preliminary discussion in which he attempted to describe the historical context and the significance of Old Testament figures, 'in order to understand better the mind of the Apostle', and 'the true meaning' of his terms.[12] He followed the Congregational scholars who taught that the faith of Isaac and Jacob in the promises of God foreshadowed Christian faith

---

[10] *Espositione* 8^r–8^v, 10^v, and 17^v: 'le divine scritture . . . testificano la salute e la gratia generale di sua divinà maiestà sopra tutte le sue credenti e obedienti creature . . . preordinati a conseguire il spirito santo e la celeste heredità.'

[11] See above, ch. 3, the *Breve Commentarium in Psalmos etc.* (Milan, 1477), of Don Gabriel Brebbia. The teaching of novices is discussed above, ch. 2, especially the prologues to the Pauline epistles in the Mantuan text Biblioteca Comunale, MS 280.

[12] *Espositione* 10^v.

in the Gospel, whilst Ishmael was the figure of those who, although not legal heirs, acquire a heavenly inheritance.[13]

The first step in Siculo's pattern of salvation, the description of sin, also clearly reveals Cassinese influence and its Greek basis. The consequence of Adam's fall he described as 'mortality and utter ruin'; that is, the inheritance of sin was not guilt but 'participation in Adam's mortality'.[14] He did not deny that men bear guilt—on the contrary—but asserted that guilt is personal and not transmitted from original sin:

> . . . our reprobation and damnation in hell shall not be for the sin of our first father Adam, nor because we lack divine grace . . . but because we do not wish to believe in the holy Gospel, or to live, or to walk according to the divine will and pleasure . . . the son shall not bear the iniquity of the father . . . but it is the soul that has sinned that will perish.[15]

Having denied original guilt, Siculo scorned the idea that God could choose some men to unmerited salvation and leave others to unmerited damnation, 'leaving men in utter ruin and the flames of hell because of the sins of their father, Adam'.[16] In a previous chapter it was shown that this teaching—that man inherited Adam's corruption and mortality, but not his guilt—was derived by the Cassinese from the Greek Fathers of Antioch.

From the same source Siculo defended the potency of free will in fallen man, giving us another glimpse of the teachings he had received in the cloister. He asserted that it was a dark heresy:

> . . . to say, with that arch-heretic Manichaeus that there is no free will in us. What cursed and dreadfuly blasphemous heresy, condemned by Chrysostom and many other Catholic and Christian doctors. But alas, nowadays in the Catholic and Christian religion there is so often

---

[13] Ibid. 2^v–4^v.

[14] Ibid. 14^r, 20^v–21^r.

[15] Ibid. 21^r–21^v: 'la nostra reprobatione e infernale damnatione non sarà per il peccato del nostro primo padre Adamo, né per mancamento della divina gratia . . . ma perchè non vogliamo . . . dar credito al santo Evangelio, né vogliamo vivere, né camminare secondo il beneplacito e voluntà divina . . . filius non portabit iniquitatem patris . . . sed anima quae peccaverit ipsa morietur.'

[16] Ibid. 29^v: '. . . lassare nel'interito di perditione e fiamme infernali per il peccato del loro padre Adamo.'

taught and defended that same cursed heresy of Manichaeus in support of particular predestination.[17]

The defence of free will, the specific mention of Chrysostom, and the allusion to both Protestant and scholastic upholders of predestination—all to be found in the writings of Ottoni and his colleagues—confirm that the source of this passage was the Congregation.

When Siculo turned to a closer consideration of works, we find, once again, Cassinese doctrines, but also the first signs of deviation. Like his brethren, he stressed that the works of Mosaic Law could not merit salvation, which came 'through God's grace alone and through Christian justice, and not through the merits and justice of the Law'.[18] The Cassinese writers, following the Greeks, interpreted the rejection of the Law as a rejection of the idea that salvation was a reward for merit. However, Siculo was interpreting the rejection of the Law to mean that whilst 'justice of the Law' cannot merit salvation, nevertheless 'Christian justice' can do so. Thus Siculo held the idea of salvation by merit, and merely replaced good works under Jewish Law by good works under Christian Law. It was an argument he was to develop in his next treatise, and it was to give his teaching its distinctive heretical content.

The next step in his pattern of salvation was the central theme of universal grace, which has been mentioned already. Salvation, he said, came by 'the bloody death and triumphant resurrection' of Christ, which was available to all mankind, 'without any respect and exception of persons'. Thus, 'Christian redemption is not particular, but general without any exception of person'.[19] That 'salvation and general grace of his divine majesty over all his believing and obedient creatures' could be accepted through 'the free will which is in all rational creatures by general grace'.[20] This doctrine could have come only from

---

[17] *Espositione* 24ᵛ: '. . . dire con quello grande heretico Manicheo, che in noi non è libero arbitrio. Qual maladetta heresia è grandemente bestemiata, e vituperata da Crisostomo e molti altri Catholici e Christiani dottori. Ma ohime che oggidí nella catholica e Christiana religione è talemente confessata e defenduta simile maledetta heresia di Manicheo, in confirmatione della particolare predestinatione.'

[18] Ibid. 27ᵛ: '. . . per sua sola gratia e Christiana giustitia e non per li meriti e giustitia della legge.'

[19] Ibid. 14ᵛ, 9ᵛ, 7ᵛ, 16ʳ, 24ʳ: 'Christiana redentione non è particolare, ma generale, senza alcune eccettione di persone.'

[20] Ibid. 17ᵛ, 24v: '. . . libero arbitrio in tutte le creature rationali per gratia generale.'

Ottoni and his colleagues, who, in turn, had taken it from the Greek Fathers.

Then Siculo passed to his doctrine of faith, in which, for the second time, we encounter teaching monastic in origin, but given emphases that alter the substance of that teaching. The life of faith, he said, began with conversion, 'turning with heartfelt penitence and obedience to the Gospel'.[21] Siculo described faith entirely in terms of obedience, by which he meant believing the promises and following the commandments of God—a definition of faith which fell short of that found in other Benedictine writers. Siculo did suggest that faith is accompanied by illumination of the holy spirit, but even in this idea he parted from his colleagues, matching the visitation of the spirit with the punishment of unbelievers: 'To believers he sent his holy spirit of sanctification and divine regeneration, so that they might become sons of the living God, but to the unbelievers he sent spirits of darkness and of error so that they might not have any further light of the Gospel of the glory of Christ.'[22] When he described the fulfilment of faith he continued to use Cassinese vocabulary, speaking of regeneration, vivification, and the inheritance of the 'living sons of God'.[23] However, his use of these terms was invested with a forensic significance peculiarly his own. The goal of Christian life was expounded entirely in terms of a state of justice achieved through obedience to divine laws, and the judgement given when all 'is revealed before the tribunal of Christ'. Then, the unbelievers would be 'heavily punished for their unbelief', but the obedient sons of God would be rewarded by salvation.[24]

Siculo imitated his teachers, especially Ottoni and Chiari, in another way, by the insertion into his narrative of outbursts against those who taught the doctrine of particular predestination. He mentioned by name only the Protestants, but his

[21] Ibid. 16ᵛ–17ʳ.

[22] Ibid. 16ᵛ: 'Alli credenti gli mandava suo sancto spirito di sanctificatione e la divinae regeneratione, aciò doventassero figliuoli di Iddio vivente, ma alli increduli gli mandava spiriti di caligine e di errore, aciò non havessero più alcun lume del Evangelio della gloria di Christo.'

[23] Ibid. 4ᵛ: '. . . gli credenti del suo santo Evangelio dovevano per virtù di quello renascere vivi figliuoli di esso vivente Iddio, per poter leggittimamente heredità e la sua celeste heredità, attestando l'Apostolo che dice . . .' (here follows Titus 3). See also 5ʳ, 8ᵛ.

[24] Ibid. 22ᵛ; also 5ᵛ, 6ʳ, 9ᵛ, 24ʳ–24ᵛ.

criticisms were also directed against the scholastics: 'Openly and without fear of God they deny the grace, mercy and truth of salvation which the living God promised through his divine scriptures without any exception of person.'[25] The errors of 'i predestinatori' were first that they believed all men to be condemned by the inherent guilt derived from Adam, and second that God was unjust and cruel enough to rescue only particular men from the punishment of that guilt: 'not understanding the mind of the apostle, they who teach predestination say . . . that God has given grace to one part [of the human race] and left the other part in its mortality and corruption.'[26] Other Cassinese writers rejected the first of these supposed errors of predestination because it presumed that the legacy of the fall was guilt rather than mortality, and the second because it denied the goodness ('benignitas', 'beneficio') of God. In contrast, Siculo's objection to both was more legalistic:

the scriptures tell us that we men shall cancel ourselves out of the divine book, not because of the sin of our father Adam, nor because divine grace is not given to us, but on account of our own impenitence, our unbelief, and because of our actual sins which we commit against the divine will without fear of God.[27]

In short, Siculo objected to predestination because that doctrine failed to recognize punishment—the just punishment of personal guilt.

What then are we to make of the *Espositione?* We may conclude that it came from the Cassinese teaching that Siculo had received in the cloister. Nevertheless the work deviates from this teaching, though these deviations were slight, as might be expected since Siculo was writing under the eye of Ottoni and others, who as his teachers and translators of his work were in a position to modify any excesses of their articulate but unscho-

---

[25] *Espositione* 22ʳ–22ᵛ: '. . . apertamente, senza divin timore, negano la gratia misericordia e verità la qual esso vivente Iddio promette per la sue divine scritture senza alcune eccettione di persone . . .' See also 24ʳ.

[26] Ibid. 13ᵛ–14ʳ: 'Gli predestinatori non intendendo la mente del Apostolo dicono . . . Dio haver fatto gratia a una parte, e lassato l'altra nella sua mortalità e corruttione.'

[27] Ibid. 15ʳ–15ᵛ: 'Dal qual divino libro faremo cassi noi adulti, secondo ci testificano le divine scritture, non per il peccato del nostro padre Adamo, né per mancamento della divina gratia, ma per la nostra propria impenitenza, incredulità, e per gli attuali peccati, i quali senza divino timore commettiamo contro la sua divina volontà.'

larly protégé.[28] It was only in Siculo's next work that mere distortion developed into full-blown Pelagian heresy. Therefore we must regard this hitherto unexamined tract as providing proof that the heresy of Siculo and 'la setta dei Georgiani' had its roots in monastic patristic theology, and also as being the first step in his development from Cassinese monk to Pelagian heretic. The next stage in this metamorphosis emerged in his second work, the *Epistola*.

The *Epistola* was another attack on predestination, but more detailed than the *Espositione*. It was written against the folly of Francesco Spiera who had embraced justification by grace alone, but under interrogation had abjured his Protestantism. From a state of joy Spiera had been cast down into despair, believing that he was no longer one of the elect. He remained in a black depression, certain that he was 'one of the reprobate, placed beyond all hope of divine grace and Christian redemption',[29] refusing all comfort until he died.[30] Siculo attacked the doctrine of special election and the corollary that the reprobate are predestined to damnation, because these doctrines denied the total efficacy of divine grace, lacked trust in God's providence, and denied that Christ's blood was shed for all men.[31] This is a basic theme of Siculo's work, and one that corresponds exactly with the arguments against predestination put forward by other Cassinese writers, notably in Ottoni's commentary of 1538 upon Chrysostom's *Homilies on Romans*. Thus Siculo's basic theme is simply a reiteration of common Cassinese teaching.

[28] There are two other points made by Siculo which resemble passages in Cassinese writings. The first was the recognition that only a few men accept salvation: Siculo called them 'that small part', and 'those few believers' (26^v, 27^r, 30^r). The second was that the recipient of God's grace should manifest gratitude for this gift by his charity towards others (6^v–7^r, 28^{r-v}).

[29] *Epistola* 7^v: '. . . uno delli reprobi fuora d'ogni speranza delle divina gratia et Christiana Redentione'; 2^v: 'ha . . . denegato et sprezzato il fidel patto della clementia . . . ' Siculo said that Spiera fell into 'rabbiosa desperatione', 13^r.

[30] *Historia Francescae Spierae, qui, quod susceptam semel evangelicae veritatis professionem abnegasset damnassetque, in horrendam incidit damnationem* (Basle, 1550).

[31] *Epistola* 4^v: 'disconfidentia della divina gratia . . .' Also 51^r: 'negano la divine gratia non essere generale'. 8^r–14^r contains lengthy denunciations of 'quel mendatio e biastema di Francesco Spiera che dice, Maior est iniquitas mea quam misericordia Dei', and repeated assertions that all men are invited to the banquet of grace, 'al suo divino convito'. Also 2^r: salvation is available to anyone 'si voglia impio e peccatore, il quale ex corde tornare voglia alla vera penitentia e obedienta delli suoi commandamenti'.

However, we may go further than this particular observation. From the pages of the *Epistola* it is possible to reconstruct fully Siculo's pattern of salvation. As we do so, we shall be in a position to discover how far his pattern of salvation still corresponded to that of other Cassinese writers, and at which points he distorted or deviated from their teaching. In this way we shall be able more clearly to determine the relationship between Siculo's heresy and the theology of the Congregation in which he was trained.

In the *Epistola* Siculo's teaching was rather more developed than in the *Espositione*. His doctrine of salvation began with the notion of *imago Dei*, common to most Cassinese writers. He employed the customary language of the Congregation: God made man 'con le anime alla immagine, e similitudine divina'.[32] More specifically, Siculo employed the Augustinian notion, which Faucher had earlier expounded, that the *imago Dei* was threefold, that is, man's memory, intellect, and will were made in the mould of the 'divina e trina deità.[33] However, Siculo introduced one highly significant change in the Cassinese use of the exemplarist theme. Whilst Faucher, Benedetto, Chiari, and others emphasized the will—in accordance with Greek notions of the *imago Dei*—Siculo singled out reason as the prime element of the soul, because it was by reason that men understood scripture, comprehended their duty, and obeyed the Lord. Because man is created in the image of God, he said, he is a rational creature.[34] More explicitly, when he discussed the divine similitude, he declared that the divine element in man is rationality.[35]

At the next stage to be found in Congregational writers, namely the fall of man, Siculo's description of sin again reflected Cassinese doctrines drawn from Chrysostom. He said that men have lost their original likeness to God:[36] they are now 'mortal and full of corruption', damaged by the 'mortal poison' that is in

---

[32] *Epistola*, 52ʳ–58ʳ.

[33] Ibid. 39ᵛ, also 43ʳ.

[34] Ibid. 96ᵛ '. . . ad imaginem Dei creatus, in qual si voglia creatura rationalis scilicet.' Also 69ʳ–70ᵛ.

[35] Ibid. 99ᵛ, 'la raggione che cosa è essa divinità in l'huomo.' For Calvin's comment see Calvin *De aeterna Dei*, 340–1. Siculo had said (*Epistola* 99ᵛ–100ʳ) that the Protestant treatment of free will degraded human nature and made men like horses.

[36] Ibid. 99ᵛ.

human nature.[37] This imagery, often linked with that of Christ as the divine physician, was common to Cassinese writers. In this work Siculo said that the 'mortifero veneno' was the reason why men were subject to mortality, concupiscence, iniquity, and the tyranny of the devil.[38] In this state men were quite unable to obey the old law of Moses, with the result that 'through their imperfections they stood constantly in fear of the threats of the Law'.[39] Moreover this impotence was exacerbated by the natural desire of men to reject the constraints of the Law and to seek what the Law forbade,[40] an argument identical with the second office of the Law in the *Beneficio di Cristo*. Thus men are cursed and condemned to death under the Law.[41] His argument closely follows similar arguments we have seen in Ottoni's translation of Chrysostom's homily on Romans and in the *Beneficio*: clearly it was at the hands of his monastic teachers that Siculo received his understanding of man's predicament under the Law.[42] Nevertheless Siculo's version has a different flavour from that of his colleagues. There is much more emphasis upon guilt, condemnation, and the punishment— which he calls the 'first death'—due to fallen man, than is to be found in ordinary Cassinese writing. Whereas Cassinese doctrine followed the Greeks, who saw the fall of man to be manifest in the sickness of human nature, Siculo placed much more emphasis upon individual guilt.

The next step in Siculo's pattern of salvation was similarly taken from Cassinese teaching but expounded with an emphasis upon guilt and justice. The Congregation's writers had taught the Pauline doctrine that man was rescued from his predicament by God's initiative, by grace through the Cross of Christ, that is, the 'benefit' of Christ's death.[43] Siculo, too, refers on several

---

[37] Ibid. 15^r: 'mortali, e pieno di corrutioni'; 98^v: 'il mortal veneno, che per natura è in essa humana natura.'

[38] Ibid. 107^v, 98^v, 20^v.

[39] Ibid. 95^r: 'per la loro imperfettione sempre stavano in timore delle minaccie di essa legge.'

[40] Ibid. 96.

[41] Ibid. 19^r–20^v.

[42] See above, ch. 6, for a discussion of Ottoni's views. There is a passage of Siculo's on 124^r which closely resembles the treatment given in the *Beneficio*, 'Commendat charitatem suam deus erga nos, cum essemus mortui delictis et peccatis nostris . . . eramus natura filii irae.'

[43] The idea of 'Christ's benefit', like that of *imago Dei*, did not occur in the *Espositione*, but was introduced in the *Epistola*.

occasions to 'the bloody death of Jesus Christ' as the means by which God reconciled fallen man to himself,[44] and frequently he referred to this as the 'benignità' or the 'immensa bontà' of God's mercy.[45] Siculo spoke very little of Christ's benefit as the conquest of death and the gift of life; instead, his overriding theme was that the Cross had brought about the remission of guilt and punishment, and enabled a fresh start under obedience to new law.[46] Therefore he looked upon the 'beneficio di Cristo' merely as liberation from the penalty of the old law.

Like his former colleagues of the Congregation, Siculo argued that the doctrine of predestination was inconsistent with the love of a father towards his children.[47] Because it denied that the benefits of Christ's passion extended to the whole human race, therefore it denied God's paternal love and 'his mercy, goodness, forgiveness, tenderness, and his fatherly love towards us all'.[48] Moreover, Paul had said quite plainly that nothing can separate men from the love of God.[49] This argument was characteristic of the Congregation's teaching, and in using it Siculo was writing as a child of the Congregation, reiterating the arguments which his more scholarly colleagues had drawn from the Greek Fathers and expounded in the cloisters.

Indeed, Siculo's use of 'benignitas Dei' against the Protestants is an illustration of the way in which Cassinese teaching propounded the doctrine. At first sight the occurrence of the term may be taken as evidence of crypto-Protestantism, espe-

---

[44] *Epistola*, 14[r]: 'la morte sanguinolenta di Iesu Christo'; 88[v]: 'reconciliavit nos in corpore carnis suae per mortem.' In view of the Pelagian character of Siculo's teaching it should be noted that he was strictly Pauline in his belief that it was God who performed the act of reconciliation, not man. Also 20[v].

[45] e.g. the term occurs on almost every page, sometimes twice per page, between 34[v] and 45[r].

[46] 14[r], 20[v]. There are also brief allusions to liberation 'from the fear of death', 124[r], 126[r]. We must qualify the conclusion of Caponetto, *Beneficio*, 492 n. 107, that Siculo contradicted Benedetto's doctrine of the 'beneficio di Cristo': Siculo did not deny it, but merely restricted its effects to the juridical benefit of the remission of guilt.

[47] Ibid. 39[r], 43[r], 55[v].

[48] Ibid. 52[r]: 'misericordia eius, benignitas clemenza [*sic*] pietas et paterna eius charitas adversus omnes', '. . . negant [sc. Protestants] Dei misericordiam, Dei clementiam, Dei bonitatem, Dei benignitatem . . .' See also 2[v].

[49] Ibid. 58[r]. The reference is to Rom. 8: 34. In the course of his argument against the doctrine of election, Siculo agreed that the term 'election' and its cognates did appear in scripture, but he argued that the word referred only to God's choice of particular men to particular tasks, such as David to kingship, but not election to salvation or damnation. Calvin's reply to this point was brief: see *De aeterna Dei praedestinatione* 333.

cially since Cassinese writers appear to have been familiar with the writings of Luther, Melanchthon, and Calvin in which they found much which accorded with their own monastic Pauline studies. That Siculo himself was familiar with the Protestant theologians is obvious from his ability to summarize Luther's arguments on justification with remarkable sympathy and lucidity.[50] However, these passages of Siculo remind us that the Cassinese concept of 'benignitas', despite resemblances to Protestant doctrine, was not a product of the Reformation.

Whilst Siculo followed his former brethren in using 'benignitas' to deny predestination, his own exposition was characteristically forensic. The Cassinese scholars had argued the universal efficacy of grace from God's paternal love but Siculo went on to speak more of justice than of love, saying that a just father would not arbitrarily condemn some of his children. 'How unjust and fraudulent for some of his innocent children to be condemned for the offence of their father [Adam].' And how 'wrong and cruel to deprive some of his legitimate sons of their patrimony and punish them.' Moreover, if God, out of his grace, wanted to save Adam, how much more would he wish to save his descendants, who were not actually guilty of that original sin.[51] Siculo's legalistic approach to the application of 'benignitas Dei' was matched by his equally legalistic understanding of its purpose. The Cassinese scholars taught that the 'beneficio' was the conquest of death and the restoration of health, but Siculo described the 'benignitas Dei' as a remission of the guilt of the condemned human race, which wiped clean the slate so that men could henceforth by freely willed works attain a state of justice and thereby merit salvation.[52] '. . . by his bloody death we have all been redeemed and cleansed of every taint and stain of sin, so that we are able to believe and obey him . . . to be really and essentially just, holy, and living sons of his majesty through

---

[50] *Epistola* 49^r–50^r: '. . . tanto grande il beneficio di Christo a salvarci etc.' Siculo's perceptive summary of Protestant teaching was followed, 50^v–52^r, by general abuse of the Protestants, through his only specific argument was directed against predestination.

[51] Ibid. 55^r: '. . . tanto ingiusto, e dishonesto . . . condemnasse per il peccato di esso padre una parte delli suoi figlivolini innocenti'; '. . . impio e crudele . . . privare della heredità, e dare nelle mani della giustitia una parte delli suoi leggittimi figliuoli.' Of the lesser guilt of Adam's descendants he says '. . . i quali non sono stati consentienti attualmente a quell'originale peccato.'

[52] Ibid. 58^v, 14^v, 25^r.

the grace and strength of his holy spirit of sanctification.'[53] We shall now turn to this next step in Siculo's pattern of salvation.

From the preceding discussion of Siculo's teaching it will be clear that he highly esteemed the efficacy of free will. His strongest argument against predestination was that it denied the ability of Christian men to become righteous through freely willed works:

They [who teach predestination] deny the truth of the divine promises made to us and set forth in his most true scripture, concerning the real sanctification of those who believe and are obedient to the new testament . . . with heartfelt penitence and obedience to his command- ments, to be able to attain Christian justification . . . with discipline and mortification. They adulterate the divine scriptures in order to sustain the fallacies of their opinions . . .[54]

Siculo argued that free will was alive and vigorous in mankind, despite the fall. Indeed the fall of man itself gave to the human race its knowledge of good and evil, and therefore the ability to recognize good and evil.[55] Moreover the fact that man has the power to choose good is attested by the existence of God's commandments to live righteously: were this not possible God would never have commanded it.[56] It was 'diabolical' of the Protestants to suggest that fallen man did not possess free will 'able to obey the Holy Gospel'. Therefore, since fallen man 'retained his free will to be able to choose good and eschew evil',

---

[53] *Epistola* 123^r: '. . . nella sua sanguinose morte siamo stati tutti redenti e purificati d'ogni corrottione e machia di peccato, per poter noi suoi obedienti e credenti essere . . . realmente e essentialmente giusti, santi e vivi figliuoli di sua maiestà per gratia e virtù del suo santo spirito di santificatione.'

[54] Ibid. 51^v–52^r: '. . . negano la verità delle divine promissioni promesse e noniate per le sue veracissime scritture in real santificatione delli credenti, e obedienti del nuovo testamento . . . cordial penitenza e obedienza delli suoi commandamenti, a potere conseguire la sua christiana giustificatione . . . in disciplina e mortificatione . . . Adul- terano le divine scritture per mantenere le fallaci loro opinioni . . .' See also 49^r, 59^v. On 8^r–10^r there is a litany of scriptural passages to the same effect. See 103^r for his criticism of the doctrine that 'l'uomo ha libero arbitrio solamente nelle cose civili e naturali e non nelle cose pertinente alla salute'. See also 17^r, 19^v–20^r, 59^r, 66^v–67^r. For a catena of biblical exhortations on belief, obedience, good works, and the reward of salvation, see 52^r, 113^r, and 67^r.

[55] Ibid. 66^v–68^r: '. . . dopo il peccato del nostro primo padre Adamo non è stato perso il libero arbitrio. . .'; also 68^r: '. . . immo esso peccato ci a(c)quisto la scienza del bene e del male, con quale potiamo eleggere il bene e lassare il male.' See also 49^v–50^v.

[56] Ibid. 67^{r-v}; 68^v–70^r: 'Ma perchè Dio ci commanda . . . se in noi non è il potere fare?' See also 105^r–106^r for an exposition of 'i divini segni' made to all men.

he could rationally choose to obey the laws of God and thereby gain his reward in heaven.[57]

Historians have generally ascribed this kind of emphasis upon human free will to the influence of Renaissance optimism. Delio Cantimori explained Siculo's strong sense of human potential as an expression of contemporary faith in the power of the human mind, or rather, as a mixture of this rational element and mysticism.[58] In an earlier chapter we considered similar explanations of the teaching of the abbot Luciano degli Ottoni and found them to be unsatisfactory.[59] The preceding discussion of Siculo's writings suggests that they too were not an expression of optimistic rationalism but of monastic teaching which defended free will on specific theological grounds, drawn—as Ottoni's work of 1538 on Chrysostom shows—from Greek patristic thought.

However, once again Siculo distorted the original Cassinese argument. Whereas his scholarly colleagues had retained the original Greek sense of free will as an instrument of reconstruction, of vivification and restoration of the *imago Dei*, Siculo saw the will as the instrument of the obedience and human righteousness which merited the reward of heaven.[60] Siculo derived this forensic emphasis upon the will from his distortion of the familiar Cassinese teaching that man is made in the image of God. Siculo's treatment of this doctrine was discussed earlier in this chapter, and it was noted that of the soul's three qualities he gave priority to reason, as the faculty of the soul by which one determines or chooses obedience to the divine precepts. This emphasis upon human reason rather than will as an instrument of obedience and righteousness was a distortion of the teaching received within his own Congregation.

---

[57] Ibid. 69ʳ: '... restato il libero arbitrio a potere eleggere il bene e lassare il male.' The argument was based upon Cain's sin and condemnation in Genesis 4. Also 79ᵛ: 'veramente gli protestanti hanno grandissamente errato a predicare la giustificazione senza l'osservanza e obedienza del santo Evangelio'. See also 99ᵛ–100ʳ. Siculo also denied predestination in the sense of election out of God's infallible foreknowledge of each person's actions: see 111ʳ (misprinted as 109)–113ᵛ.

[58] Cantimori, *Eretici italiani*, p. 62. Cantimori thought Siculo's mystical themes were Valdesian because of his faith in divine grace and the infinite efficacy of the benefits of Christ.

[59] See above, ch. 6.

[60] Siculo did speak of vivification, but in vague terms. *Epistola* 107ʳ⁻ᵛ, also 25ʳ and 84ᵛ–85ᵛ.

By the strength of free will men were now enabled to fulfil the 'new law' of the Gospel. Men could not fulfil the justice of the old law, but now they were given a new law and the strength to obey it. Men, hitherto impotent, were now liberated and freely able to become just:

Human reason . . . is a power given by God to human nature so that man may control and govern himself according to the ways of God by whom he is created, so that reason is one of the virtues from God from whom derives our soul in the image and divine similitude. And because that divine power of reason is in man, in all things God deals with man according to reason. And therefore all his holy scriptures speak to us according to reason and not irrationally . . . O how very blind and ignorant are those who say that man does not have to conduct himself according to reason where salvation is concerned, because all the holy scriptures tell us that it is the case that our salvation or damnation is by the way of our reason . . . and what more precious attribute could man have than reason? Take away reason and where is the divinity in man . . . the holy scriptures greatly extol human nature and make us aware of its greatness and divine dignity so that when man realizes his greatness and divine status he is led to live and walk in accordance with his status and divine condition.[61]

Under this pattern of salvation, obedience was the essence of salvation. Man was fully responsible for his righteous behaviour, and salvation was the just heavenly reward for that righteousness.

Thus Siculo set up a thoroughgoing theology of salvation by works. Each Christian man, he said, shall be justly judged by his obedience to the precepts of the Bible.[62] The Bible was a book of

---

[61] *Epistola* 99[r]–100[r]: 'L'humana raggione . . . è una virtù da esso Iddio data ad essa humana natura acciò che ella si reggesse et governasse secundum Deum a quo creata est, per essere la raggione una della virtù da esso Dio da qual descende l'anima nostra all'imagine, et alla sua divina similitudine. Et perchè nel huomo è essa divina virtù della raggione, Iddio ogni cosa tratta con raggione con essa umana natura. Et perho tutte le sue divine scritture ci parlano a noi con ragione, e non senza raggione . . . O gran cecità et ignoranza de quelli, i quali dicono che l'huomo non si deve reggere secondo la raggione nelle cose della salute. Cum sit che le divine scritture tutte ci annontiano la nostra salute, et infernale dannatione per via di essa raggione . . . Et che più pretiosa cosa può avere in se l'huomo della raggione? Tolta via la raggione che cosa è essa divinità in l'huomo . . . le divine scritture . . . grandemente magnificano l'humana natura et ci fanno conoscere la sua grandezza et dignità, acciò che conoscendo l'huomo la sua grandezza et dignità divina sia constretto vivere et camminare secondo il suo stato et divina conditione.'

[62] Ibid 39[v]. Also 66[r]; 70[r]: 'credere, obedire e pentirsi, e caminare nella via della virtù e volontà di sua divina maiestà.'

rules of the 'new law', in which the 'works of faith' were laid down, namely mortification of the flesh, avoidance of wrongdoing, humility and godly conversation; only men who performed those 'works of faith' would be saved.[63] He attacked Protestants again because they taught that the Gospel brought justification by grace alone and without fearful obedience to religious laws.[64] He acknowledged that the old law was now abrogated, but it had been replaced by the new law which demanded equal obedience. Obedience was possible because it was written in men's hearts so that they could understand and obey. Moreover God gave them assistance in understanding and obeying his new law.[65]

Siculo was certain that his doctrine of salvation through obedience was not at variance with St. Paul's repudiation of salvation by works because the Apostle was speaking of 'opera della legge' and not of 'opera fidei'. Therefore, according to Siculo, the epistles of Paul and that of James do not clash, for whilst the former rejected the saving value of works of the Mosaic Law, the latter taught salvation through works of the new law.[66] He was using a distinction which had been made from time to time by Ottoni, and we may presume that Siculo was taught it as a novice. However, Siculo invested the 'new law' and 'opera fidei' with juridical merit which the Cassinese scholars never did.

Siculo's legalistic view of salvation permeated his description of the life of piety and faith. At times his language resembled the doctrine of faith that we have seen expounded by his former colleagues:

Let us embrace his goodness and divine mercy and let us walk in the obedience of his holy Gospel.[67]

---

[63] Ibid. 54^r, 82^r–83^r. Although the sense is wider than the English cognate, I have translated 'conversatio' as 'conversation'. The phrase in question is '. . . ut et nos in omni conversatione sancti simus', 83^r: a better, though somewhat lugubrious, translation might be 'walking and dwelling with the Lord'. On 79^r, in contrast with his list of 'opera fidei', Siculo set out a list of 'open sins of kings, states, cities, castles of Christendom, full of pomp and worldly vanity'.

[64] Ibid. 94^v–95^r. There is another lengthy diatribe against justification by grace alone and predestination on 59^r–61^v.

[65] Ibid. 95^{r-v}: '. . . aiuto . . . virtù per poterlo fare . . . la divina legge del santo spirito di Jesu Cristo scritta nel centro delli cuori propri delli obedienti e credenti. . .'

[66] Ibid. 76^r–78^v, 87^r–88^r.

[67] Ibid. 36^r: 'Abbracciamo la sua bontà e divina misericordia, e cammiamo nella obedienza dal suo Santo Evangelio.'

Turn yourselves to your God because he is kind and merciful, and long-suffering because of his great pity, and forgiving of the sin of men.[68]

It is necessary first of all for us to repent of our past sins with all of our heart and to believe and to obey his holy Gospel.[69]

This obedience that we shall give to his holy Gospel . . . is not the faith that we repeat when we mouth: I believe, I believe, I believe, I believe . . .[70]

In these phrases we observe a characteristic Cassinese emphasis upon the inward fervour of living faith. Nevertheless, despite similarities, Siculo did not possess the Cassinese doctrine of faith as the copula between divine and human life and the instrument of healing and restoration. Instead he spoke of 'faith' almost entirely as obedience which merits salvation—obedience first of all to the beliefs given by God and then obedience to the works demanded by God: 'through the faith that we give to the holy Gospel, we obtain the spirit of sanctification, through which we have living faith and hope in things eternal . . . through the faith that gives itself to the holy Gospel we attain that sanctity which God himself promised to give to his believers.[71] Even the assent to God's grace, which Ottoni, following Chrysostom, had seen as the first step in the restoration of disintegrated man, Siculo saw simply as a work of obedience, and moreover, gave its exposition a ferocious forensic twist: ' . . . he wishes that we accept our Christian redemption, and that we believe in him concerning our holy redemption, under the penalty, I say, of his displeasure and the punishment of hell.'[72] Siculo recognized that

[68] *Epistola* 34^v: 'Convertimini ad dominum deum vestrum, quia benignus et misericors et patiens e multae [*sic*] misericordia et placabilis super malitia hominum.'

[69] Ibid. 74^r: 'de necessitate a noi conviene primamente, pentirci cordialmente dalli nostri peccati passati, e credere, e obedire il suo santo Evangelio.' Also 'pentirci, credere e obedire', 75^r.

[70] Ibid. 92^r: 'E questa obedienza che noi daremo al suo santo Evangelio . . . non è quella che noi con la bocca diciamo Credo, credo, credo, credo . . . ' See also 92^v–94^r. There is a similar sentiment in Caponetto, *Beneficio* 41–2.

[71] Ibid. 64^r–64^v: ' . . . per la fede che si dà al santo Evangelio, si conseguisse il spirito de sanctificatione, per il quale si ha quella viva fede, viva speranza delle cose eterne . . . per la fede laquale si dà al santo Evangelio, si conseguisse quella santità, laqual Dio per sè promesse dare alli suoi credenti.' See also 60^{r-v}, 62^v.

[72] Ibid. 62^r: 'nostra Chistiana redentione . . . lui vuole che noi l'accettiamo, e gli crediamo in nostra divina redentione sotto la pena dico della sua disgratia e pene infernale'. Also 107^v: 'credere oportet, e(t) sine fide impossibile est placere Dio'. On

divine assistance was needed in order to live the life of faithful obedience, 'God-fearing and walking in the way of the divine commandments'.[73] This help, he said, was given by the Holy Spirit, who brought illumination.[74] The idea that the Spirit illuminated the understanding and strengthened perseverance was to be found in other Cassinese writers who treated it briefly and generally, in the manner of Chrysostom. At times, Siculo's description of the work of the Spirit was in the same restrained vein, but there were other passages in which Siculo described the work of the Spirit as a compelling definition of the laws of God—'la scienza di Dio'—so that men might know what must be done. Armed with that kind of knowledge a man of faith, disdaining 'worldly knowledge', was led to make freely willed decisions which merited either salvation or 'damnation, should we not wish to accept nor obey that which he has illuminated within us and taught us'.[75]

Siculo believed that the Spirit not only illuminated true believers, but also strengthened them to persevere in the ways of righteous living. Obviously, the monastic theme of perseverance was a valuable adjunct to his theology of obedience and easily adapted to the purpose. Siculo urged his readers to 'perseveranza et obedienza' like the Israelites in the wilderness, calling upon the Spirit to give them strength to persevere.[76] Repeatedly Siculo called the Spirit 'il spirito di sanctificatione', by which he meant the Spirit which confirmed righteous living: 'the apostle Peter says that God gave his holy Spirit of justification and sanctity to all his followers since they were obedient to his divine commandments and his holy will, and then they obtained his

---

64^v–65^r there is the charming parable of the king of France's decision to adopt Messer Barone of Riva. The point of the tale is that Messer Barone is obliged to place complete trust in the king's summons in order to journey to France and take up the inheritance offered to him. There is a similar story in the *Beneficio*, ch. 4, and in Considerations 13 and 38 of Valdés's *110 Divine Considerations*.

[73] Ibid. 45^r, 70^r.

[74] Ibid. 5^v; see also 64^r and 84^r: '. . . questo spirito di sanctificatione . . . per il quale [Dio] si dava in terra dalli suoi credenti vivo testimonio.'

[75] Ibid. 50^v, 72^v–73^r: 'era il spirito santo il quale gli faceva volere operare e pensare simili celesti pensieri . . .' For the contrast between 'Mondana sapienza' and 'superna scienza', see 113^v, 115^r, 119^v, 39^r: 'la causa della nostra perditione è perché noi non vogliamo consentire, né obedire a quello che lui dentro ci illumina e ci insegna', 'siamo illuminati da quel sole . . .'

[76] Ibid. 70^r; also 5^v–8^v.

holy spirit of sanctification.'[77] It seems that obedient Christians were given the visitation of the Spirit as a gift and a reward which would strengthen them to become even more just and sanctified. These allusions to the Spirit appear to be another aspect of Congregational teaching developed by Siculo along the lines of legalistic religion.

Similarly Siculo's teaching on the certitude which belongs to faith was coloured by his legalistic thinking. For Siculo certitude was the self-assurance of a man confident that he would be saved if he obeyed the set of precepts given in the Bible. It was 'the certainty that we, his believers, ought to have in his most true promises'.[78] Indeed, it was this kind of certainty, he argued, which could have saved the wretched Spiera from his despair. Had Spiera only possessed 'true understanding' he need never have doubted that God desired his salvation and offered it to him, and with calm confidence he could have set out fulfilling God's commands in order to attain that salvation.[79]

Siculo's obsession with God's commandments and man's obedience also shaped his idea of the relationship between God and man. Amongst Cassinese writers God was described as healing physician and affectionate father. But in the *Epistola* God appeared not as physician or a father, but almost everywhere as the stern ruler and lawgiver, rewarding those who obey him but wrathful to the disobedient. Man, for his part, was bound to God less by filial affection than by the fear of punishment, which was the 'living instrument to make the sinner turn to heartfelt penitence and observance of the divine commands and to have trust in the heavenly promises'.[80]

---

[77] *Epistola* 73ʳ: '. . . il suo santo Spirito di giustificatione, e santità . . . dedit Deus, dice l'apostolo Pietro, omnibus obedientibus sibi perocchè costoro obbedivano alli suoi divini commandamenti, e santa volontà, e doppoi conseguivano il suo santo spirito di sanctificatione.'

[78] Ibid. 5ᵛ: '. . . la certezza che noi suoi credenti dovemo havere delle suoi veracissime promissioni'; 3ʳ: '. . . quanto importa alla salute la vera cognitione e intelligentia delle divine scritture'.

[79] Ibid. 5ʳ: '. . . né dubitare che Dio mi habbia . . . a provedere e governare de ogni mia necessità'; 5ᵛ: 'la vera intelligentia'.

[80] Ibid. 89ʳ–89ᵛ: 'Non è, dico, il divin timore de non cadere in disgratia di sua divina maiestà vivo instromento da far tornare il peccatore alla cordial penitenza e osservanza delli suoi divini commandamenti e alla confidenza delle sue celeste promissioni? . . . qui timent dominum inquirent quae beneplacita sunt ei e non erunt incredibiles verbis illius . . .' Also 90ʳ⁻ᵛ, 94ᵛ, 102ᵛ, 113ᵛ.

Of course, in the details of good works, as distinct from their interpretation, he followed the Cassinese more closely. The principal example in the *Epistola* was the detailed preaching of brotherly love and peace amongst Christians which we have seen in several Cassinese writings. Siculo dwelt on the theme at some length. He condemned the immoral behaviour of rulers and the clergy, not only the most powerful, but also the least of them. Even the Jews and the barbarians, he said, fear and honour God more than those Christians who prevaricate shamelessly against the precepts of God: they lust, steal, blaspheme, and murder, and they are guilty of fornication, adultery, gambling, gluttony, drunkeness, false witness, and usury.[81] The French, Italian, Spanish, and German princes and prelates were at each other's throat's, and in open disobedience to the Gospel; their enmity, hate, and destruction replaced reverence, honesty, 'fraternal love', and 'zeal for the Christian religion'. Such conflict, he said, was the behaviour of the devil, not of members of Christ's body.[82]

The passage has an Erasmian flavour, but there is no evidence that Siculo ever read or heard of Erasmus.[83] The most probable source of Siculo's teaching is, once again, the cloisters of the Cassinese Congregation, where the social virtues had been for a long time a favourite theme of Cassinese writers. Siculo's passage may therefore be seen as a reflection of the Pauline exhortations to peace and concord which had been expounded vigorously by Chrysostom and studied and repeated by monks of the Congregation.

Siculo's religion was one of obedience and reward. Salvation was the reward of eternal life in heaven given to those men who

---

[81] Ibid. 90^{r-v}.

[82] Ibid. 92^v–94^r. On 93^v he said that concord was like the mystical union between Christ and believers in the eucharistic meal, '. . . unus panis e(t) unum corpus multi sumus, omnes qui de uno pane et de uno calice participamus . . .' This Augustinian simile, based upon 2 Cor. 10, occurred also in the *Beneficio*, ch. 6. Siculo went on to say that disunity means that men are of the body and members of the devil.

[83] It is possible that Siculo read Erasmus under the disguise of a patristic anthology published by the Mantuan, Marsilio Andreasi, in 1542, under the title *Trattato divoto et utilissimo della Divina Misericordia*, see S. Seidel Menchi, 'La circolazione clandestina di Erasmo in Italia: i casi di Antonio Brucioli e di Marsilio Andreasi, *Annali della Scuola Normale Superiore di Pisa*, Lettere e Filosofia, S.II, ix (1979), 573–601. Chiari was familiar with the books of Erasmus, but showed little enthusiasm for his doctrines. This was probably true of other Cassinese monks also, since Erasmus is rarely mentioned in Congregational writings.

had obeyed the divine precepts, whilst those men who had
disobeyed were to be cast aside and punished by the fires of hell.
It was a view of Christianity and salvation quite different from
that of the Cassinese monks for whom the notion of judgement,
though not entirely absent, was rather secondary to their vision
of human nature being healed and restored. In contrast, for
Siculo the heart of man's fulfilment turned upon the heavenly
tribunal which, at the end of a man's life 'in die irae et
revelationis' judged him according to his works with punishment
or reward. The day of judgement and the displeasure of God
dominated Siculo's theology. Before the tribunal each man must
present himself, truly pure, 'in order to be able to enter into his
heavenly inheritance'.[84] There he shall give an account of the
good and evil he has done, and he shall be judged according to
his works:[85] 'in the day of wrath and revelation . . . to each man
according to his works . . . equally we all shall have to give
account before his tribunal of our actions and sins that we
commit against his divine law and will.'[86] Those who have
laboured to attain the divine promises will be 'accepted by His
Divine Majesty and rewarded'.[87] But those who have gone
against the divine will and committed adultery, fornication,
usury, robbery, murder, and other 'nefandi e mortali peccati',[88]
will be condemned for their impenitence and disobedience to
the holy Gospel and for their carnal and dissolute lives: 'In
accordance with this pact and condition we must be obedient to
His Divine Majesty and walk in the path of virtue . . . if we do
otherwise we are cancelled and scratched out from the book of
life and condemned to the torments of hell by his dreadful and
exact justice.'[89]

---

[84] *Epistola*, 88[r]: 'per potere intrare nella celeste heredità'. Siculo referred to John
3: 13 ff., and Acts 22: 28. 67[r–v]: 'sua tremenda disgratia e pene infernali, se non obedire al
santo Evangelio . . .'

[85] Ibid. 54[r], 80[r]. Siculo said this was affirmed 'by all the scriptures'.

[86] Ibid. 27[v]–28[r]: 'in die irae et revelationis . . . unicuique secundum opera sua . . .
tutti egualmente havaremo dare ragione innanzi il suo tribunale delle nostre attioni, e
peccati, che contra la sua divina legge e voluntà commettemo.'

[87] Ibid. 80[r]: 'tutte sono accette a sua divina maiestà, e remuneratorie.'

[88] Ibid. 53[v].

[89] Ibid. 15[v]: ' . . . con questo patto e conditione, che dovemo obedire alla sua divina
maiestà e camminare per la via delle virtuti . . . altrimenti facendo siamo cassati e
annullati del libro della vita e condannati nelli cruciati infernali dalla sua horrenda e
giusta giustitia.' See also 16[r], 23r: ' . . . delebo eum de libro vitae', 27[r].

Here we have a contrast between two kinds of piety. The Cassinese monks, drawing upon the Greek Fathers, understood the life of sanctity to be a process of healing and reintegration of the human spirit, but their former colleague, Siculo, used their teachings and the vocabulary of his Cassinese background to expound a legalistic religion. The profound and subtle insights into human nature which the Cassinese had learned from their studies of St. Paul and John Chrysostom had been replaced by a demand for righteous behaviour. Within Siculo's religion there was little of the Cassinese doctrine of faith and the healing of human nature. Instead, his pattern of salvation was a life of obedience to God, concupiscence denied, sobriety, prayer, peace, and good works, which, done by men 'fearful of God and obedient to him, were all pleasing, worth while, and most sweet in the eyes of God'. It was a crude doctrine of good works by which human righteousness merited salvation *coram Deo*.[90] Even when Siculo spoke of love 'nelle viscere', he spoke of it as a 'praeceptum' to which obedience had been ordered and commanded—almost as if, drawing the scholastic distinction between uncreated and created charity, he looked upon love for God as being meritorious and justifying.[91] There is a gulf between that kind of piety, devoted to order, discipline, and obedience, and that which sees human salvation in terms of healing and restoration. Siculo, who had imperfectly digested the Greek Fathers from whom the Cassinese took their teaching, had moved to the far side of that gulf, trying unsuccessfully to use the Greek theology he had learned in the cloisters to expound his Pelagian version of juridical Latin theology.

Siculo completed the *Epistola* just before he left Riva in May 1550, and the closing pages of the book were a farewell to that city. He exhorted the people of Riva to keep continually in their memory the doctrines he had preached 'faithfully and sincerely' in the principal church during the forty days of Lent. He thanked them for their enthusiastic response to his preaching and begged them to beware lest some 'mendace maestro', by

90 Ibid., 101^v–102^r: 'buona opera, fatta da uomini di Iddio timorati e obedienti sono tutte grate e fruttiferi e soavissime avanti sua divina maiestà.'

91 Ibid. 122^r, 92^v: '. . . qual fraterna dilettione Christo sopra ogn'altra cosa ci ordina e commanda, che noi suoi discepoli doviamo osservare.'

preaching the Lutheran denial of works, should try to seduce them from obedience to the divine laws. Finally, he apologized for his abrupt departure from Riva. He would have liked to embrace each one as Christian love would require, but that was not possible. He assured them that 'questa tal partenza mia' did not mean tht he was ungrateful for their kindness to him: it was simply that he did have it in him to go through the business of making farewells, because departure 'was a sharp and piercing knife that cut me to the heart'.[92] At the same time, in case they were wondering, he assured them that he had not left because of some scandal, and that whilst at Riva he had been faithful, sincere, true in heart, spotless in behaviour, without even a thought of sin, but only giving thanks and praise to God.[93]

When he left Riva, in April or May, he went in the first place to Bologna, where he delivered his two manuscripts to the printer Anselmo Giaccarello. In Bologna he hoped that the Council would reconvene so that he could address it, but in the meantime he lived amongst the students of the Collegio di Spagna where he had been in 1548 or 1549, and to them he expounded the Pauline texts. The *processo* conducted subsequently by the Inquisition makes it clear that Siculo had been preaching his familiar themes of obedience and perfection.[94] He said that the apostles had been perfect, but the church had lost that perfection during the time of Augustine, Thomas, and other sophists. However, men were about to attain again that apostolic perfection in which they were not able to sin even

[92] *Epistola*, 121ᵛ–122ʳ: 'il mio tenere cuore non mi dava animo a potere fare simile ufficio di separatione'. '. . . il che a me era un pungente e talgente coltello che mi passava al cuore.'

[93] Ibid. 122ᵛ. Siculo did not say why he left Riva, but since he had preached in the main church throughout Lent it is probable that his doctrines had attracted the attention of the authorities: in the earlier part of the *Epistola* he said that he had been called before the magistrate.

[94] There is a detailed account of the sect's early days in Prosperi, 'Un gruppo ereticale', pp. 344 ff. Prosperi has worked from newly found material (see p. 341, n. 7). Also see Rotondò, 'Per la storia', pp. 141–2. Rotondò has based his conclusions upon the MS B. 1857 in the Biblioteca dell'Archiginnasio di Bologna, '1553 Processo (per eresia) contra quosdam Collegiales S. Clementis Maioris vulgo Collegio di Spagna.' This document of 100 folios, written in 1553, was the result of an investigation by the Holy Office. Rotondò's work supersedes an earlier study by A. Battistella, *Processi d'eresia nel Collegio di Spagna (1553–1554), Episidio della storia della Riforma in Bologna* (Bologna, 1901).

if they wished: he believed himself to have reached that level of perfection. All this he would reveal to the Council when he addressed it. He would tell them of his vision of Christ and Christ himself would speak through his mouth, and when the Fathers heard that apostolic perfection was imminent they would be amazed, and he would close the Council.[95]

The Council did not meet again at Bologna, but after some delay returned to Trent a few months later, in November. Siculo did not follow it all the way, probably because by now the authorities were asking questions about him. Instead he stopped at Ferrara, where there was some measure of tolerance for suspected heretics. In Ferrara he lived in the house of Nascimbene Nascimbeni, lecturer at the Studio.[96] It is not clear what happened during the next few months. The easy-going inquisitor of Ferrara actually praised Siculo for his vigorous attacks upon the Lutherans and this reputation was, for the time being, enhanced by the story of his vision, his revelations to be delivered to the Council, and the promise of great things to come, though what others, particularly the straightforward duke of Ferrara, made of him at close quarters has not been recorded.[97] Neither is it probable that Siculo found favour with the duchess. Renée's own religious inclinations—at the time

---

[95] Bibl. Arch. Bologna, MS B. 1857: 'credidit et dixit ipsum sanctum et iustum, sed non post damnationem' (8ᵛ); '. . . dictum Georgium fuisse sic et sanctum qualem post Petrum et Paulum non habuerit Ecclesia, praeferendo ipsum Augustino Thomae et coeteris doctoribus appellando ipsos trapacistos' (45ᵛ); 'homo . . . esset venturus ad tantam perfectionem ad quam devenerant Sancti Apostoli Petrus et Paulus, ita ut non possent peccare etiam si vellent' (45ᵛ); '. . . statim ut pote doctus a Spiritu Sancto interpretaretur' (48ᵛ): quoted in Rotondò, 'Per la Storia', pp. 141–3. The same pages include references to Siculo's hope to speak to the Council.

[96] B. Fontana, *Renata di Francia duchessa di Ferrara* (Rome, 1889–99), iii. 186. Fontana took his material from Archivio Secreto Vaticano, arm. xlvii. 12. Also see Caponetto, *Beneficio* 462–3.

[97] The inquisitor of Ferrara was the Dominican Girolamo Papino. See Fontana, *Renata di Francia*, ii. 421–2. Pietro Bresciani, a doctor and ex-Lutheran, said of Siculo 'vedendo in alcune cose impugnare lutherani gagliardamente et essendomi laudato dal padre inquisitor di Ferrara, io ne hebbi ottimo concetto et aspettava da lui gran cose, come prometteva, in susidio de la Giesia, per una visione et revellatione qual diceva haver havuto da Christo Signor Nostro, la qual doveva publicar nel concilio di Trento': F. Chabod, *Per la storia religiosa dello stato di Milano durante il dominio di Carlo V. Note e documenti* (Rome, 1936), 244. Chabod quoted from Archivio di Stato, Milano, MS Documenti Diplomatici, 142. At Ferrara Siculo was very probably in touch with Tiziano and his disciples who arrived there after a bizarre

under the half-hearted investigation of the inquisitor of Ferrara—were Calvinistic and directly contrary to Siculo's teachings. Certainly, she would have been well informed about the ex-monk: she had in her possession one of his books,[98] and it seems probable that it was through Renée that Calvin received the fairly detailed information used in his vehement attack upon Siculo. Neither she nor anyone else at Court attempted to assist him or intervene on his behalf at the time of his subsequent imprisonment and trial.[99]

Some time after his arrival in Ferrara Siculo wrote another book—his third—*Il libro grande*, which is no longer extant. Judging from a contemporary summary of the book, it appears to have contained his usual Pelagian doctrines, notably that a person in a state of grace cannot sin. However, Siculo also inserted some Protestant beliefs—denying the efficacy of sacramental grace and the existence of purgatory: these doctrines of secondary importance in Reformation theology and not incompatible with Siculo's Pelagian criticisms of the Protestants, were perhaps inserted in an attempt to please the duchess. The book also included denials of the doctrine of the trinity and the supernatural creation of the soul.[100] When *Il libro grande* appeared, these Protestant and anti-trinitarian additions, although incidental to his teachings, were so easily recognized as heretical that probably they stirred even the lax inquisitor of Ferrara to action in a way that Siculo's earlier writings had not. In September 1550 he was arrested and taken from the house of Nascimbeni to the prison of Ercole II. Under interrogation he claimed to be called by Christ to expound the obscure passages of Scripture and to address the Council of Trent. As for his book, his interrogators regarded it as the work of a man who had once been anti-Lutheran, but now, 'tutto il contrario', denied

attempt to convert Julius III to anabaptism about the time of his accession in February 1550: see Ginzburg, *Il Nicodemismo*, pp. 177–8. Ginzburg comments drily that the endeavour to convert the Pope 'dovette assumere necessariamente forme nicodemitiche.'

[98] Fontana, *Renata di Francia*, ii. 421–2. Fontana has used Archivio di Stato, Modena, minuta di lettera ducale, 18 Feb. 1557, letter to Battista Saracho. It is not clear which book had been in Renée's possession. For the details of Calvin's criticisms of Siculo see below.

[99] Ibid. ii. 279.

[100] Ibid. iii. 187.

purgatory and transubstantiation.[101] It seemed as if Siculo was then considered to be a Lutheran, at least in official eyes, though it must have been obvious to others that there was more to his heterodoxy than a touch of Protestantism.

Whilst Siculo was under arrest the abbot Luciano degli Ottoni intervened on his behalf, an episode which has been recently taken as evidence that Ottoni (and Benedetto da Mantova) were 'seguaci' of Siculo.[102] However, this conclusion is not borne out by the letter which the abbot wrote to the duke, from Bologna, on 23 November. The abbot had in his possession a letter which Siculo had written to the duke, but he hesitated to forward it because it contained 'some things unusual and out of the ordinary'.[103] He begged the duke to suspend judgement on the man: if things happened as Siculo prophesied then he was genuine, if not, he would be discarded, not the least by Ottoni himself. Siculo had prophesied that he would address the Council at Trent (deliberations had reopened at Trent on 14 November 1550, more than three years after the move to Bologna in 1547), where he would be introduced by 'quello grande uomo che si sa'. He also promised that when certain unspecified things happened 'the whole world would be set straight'. Ottoni reminded the duke how remarkable it was that these things were being said by a man who understood no Latin except for biblical passages and short, simple phrases, and whose Italian was 'molto obscura'. For the time being, said Ottoni, it would be better to wait and see, and 'not to run the risk of transgressing God's will'.[104]

---

[101] Ibid. iii. 186; '. . . in questo maggio [1550] avendo composto due libri contro uno Spiera luterano, vene a Ferrara et in casa d'un don Nasimbene prete a S. Clementi, compose uno libro tutto il contrario del primo nel qual negave il purgatorio e diceva non osservi cristo nel'hostia consecrata . . .

[102] See below, p. 244, n. 118. In his memorial of 1570 Nascimbeni called Ottoni 'complice di Giorgio', Caponetto, *Beneficio* 462.

[103] Rotondò, 'Per la storia', p. 153: '. . . già molto tempo io haveva una lettera di quello D. Georgio Siculo diretta ad essa, ma mai li l'haveva voluta dare per alcune cose che vi erano dentro fora del ordinario e consueto commune.'

[104] Ibid., p. 153: '. . . come vederà a la vulgare è molto obscura . . . esso fu sempre et è ingnorantissimo di lettere humane . . . esso promette tante gran cose che, se le attenderà, tutto il mundo li correrà dreto . . . promette e sempre ha promesso che si farà il Concilio e che si farà in Trento, e che parlerà in Concilio, e che Christo parlerà per la bocca sua, e ch'el farà vedere che esso sarà quello che parlarà e non D. Georgio, e che sarà introdotto a parlare per meggio di quello grande homo che si sa . . . a me pare che meglio e più sicuro sarebbe a stare aspettare l'exito suo, maxime instando il Concilio, e non mettersi al periculo di contravenire al volere divino.' The 'grande homo' was probably Cardinal Pole, then protector of the Congregation.

The burden of the letter was the request for the duke to stay his hand—which in the event he did for six months—but it amounted to no more than that. In particular the letter gives the impression that the abbot was reluctant to discuss the monk's theology in writing, although he offered to do so in private conversation. The nearest he came to the matter was to assure the duke that Siculo had been persecuted in the Congregation 'not out of regard for the faith, but as a result of human and monkish quarrels'.[105] Ottoni seemed reluctant to send Siculo's own letter to the duke. First he forgot to send it, then he made a Latin translation 'to make it clearer and easier for Your Excellency', then he dropped the original, with some other things, into a bucket of water, so that it was now 'spoiled and smeared'. Then, in a postscript, he admitted that the letter he was dispatching was not an original, but a copy, though he thought it might be in Siculo's hand.[106] Ottoni was not a well-organized man at the best of times, and his handling of the correspondence might be taken for his usual incompetence but for the fact that he was theologically very competent, and must have been quite well aware of the origins and implications of what Siculo was teaching.

Certainly, there is nothing in this letter to justify the conclusion that Ottoni was a 'follower' of Siculo: in any case it is most unlikely that the biblical and patristic scholar and the Congregation's chief spokesman at Trent should be the disciple of the unlearned, erratic and rather crude ex-monk nearly twenty-seven years younger than himself.[107] A more reasonable interpretation of Ottoni's actions and letter would be that the abbot, in his own bumbling way, on the one hand wished to conceal the extent to which Siculo, who had been nurtured in the Congregation, had distorted Congregational teaching to the

---

[105] Rotondò, 'Per la storia', p. 154: 'Se fossi alla presentia di V. Ecc. a direi molte altre cose e li farei conoscere che D. Georgio non è perseguitato da nostri per zelo di fede ma per passioni humane e fratesche.' It is not at all improbable that Siculo should have been dismissed for reasons of personality: in 1542 Don Giovambatista Gaetano, who had been sent away 'perchè è stato di poca umilità ed alquanto inquieto' asked Pietro Bembo to intercede for his readmission to the Congregation; P. Bembo, *Opere del Cardinale Pietro Bembo* (Venice, 1729), iii. 87.

[106] Rotondò, 'Per la storia', p. 154.

[107] Ottoni was professed in 1507, Siculo in 1534. Ottoni was the usual age, seventeen years old, at the time of profession, and there is no reason to suppose that the same was not true of Siculo.

point of heresy, and on the other hand wanted to protect and act as a father-in-God to the young man—at one moment admiring his native intelligence, at another being prepared to discipline him. The abbot's support for Siculo thus suggests a pastoral concern for the unusual ex-monk, mingled with a desire to protect the reputation of the Congregation. In short, the letter to the duke does not permit the conclusion that Ottoni was Siculo's 'seguace' in any theological sense.

Proceedings remained in abeyance during the remainder of the year. In January 1551 Nascimbeni was put under house arrest. On 30 March Siculo said that he wished to recant, but then did not do so.[108] By now the matter had become serious for the ecclesiastical authorities. The Council had resumed at Trent and was working well without Siculo's revelations, his 'grandi cose' had not come to pass, but the man himself held a variety of heretical opinions, not only the Protestantism with which he had been charged: he remained unrepentant, and it was feared there that more people might join the tiny circle of his adherents. Cardinal Ercole Gonzaga wrote to the duke, his cousin, to urge no more delay in the matter of 'this scoundrel Don Georgio', and specifically requested the duke's collaboration with the Dominican inquisitor in order to emphasize that this was no mere conflict between orders, and that Siculo's errors were serious— although the precise nature of his offence was not stated. The duke acted immediately, and a week later the inspector-general of the Inquisition wrote on behalf of the cardinal-inquisitor to thank the duke for his action in the case of 'Don Georgio, impio heretico'.[109] Efforts were made to convert him but they failed. The end came for Giorgio Siculo six weeks later. Early in the morning of 23 May he was taken from his cell and brought to a window of the lawcourt: at 3 o'clock in the darkness of a spring morning he was hanged from the window. The event was recorded thus: '1551, 23 Maggio. Ad ore tre di notte fu impiccato ad una finestra della Raggione Domenico Giorgio uomo assai dotto ma Luterano ed Eretico, alcuno non potè rivolgerlo alle massime vere cristiane.'[110]

---

[108] Fontana, *Renata di Francia*, iii. 186.

[109] Extracts from both letters are quoted in Cantimori, *Eretici italiani*, p. 59.

[110] Quoted in Fontana, *Renata di Francia*, ii. 279. C. Cantù, *Gli eretici d'Italia* (Turin, 1866), ii. 98. Cantù says that Siculo was hanged from a window 'dicono senza forma di processo'.

The first published assessments of Siculo were those of John Calvin and Bartolomeo Camerario.[111] In a work on predestination, published in 1552, Calvin made it plain that he thought Siculo a foolish fellow whose teachings were shallow and unworthy of attention, but they had had to be answered because 'his books buzz about Italy, stirring up men and troubling the poor and weak'. Calvin paid no attention to any anti-trinitarian or 'Protestant' elements, but working from a copy of the *Epistola*. he directly attacked the doctrine of obedience and the unfailing salvation of all who persevere. He swept aside all Siculo's teaching: righteousness, said Calvin, was dependent upon salvation and not vice versa; otherwise men became the authors of their own salvation. Likewise faith, understanding, 'illumination of the Spirit' were gifts given to the elect and not the means of achieving salvation. When Siculo had offered salvation to all, whether God's chosen heirs or not, he had been impudently 'generous to strangers', inviting them to come into God's house, when in fact it was God who chose whom to invite. In short, Siculo had denied that salvation was a gift of grace and had encouraged men falsely to believe that they could earn their own salvation.[112]

The other critic was the Neapolitan humanist and lawyer Bartolomeo Camerario, who in 1556 published a Catholic polemic against Calvin, using the Bible and Augustine to deny

[111] Siculo referred to a Lutheran in Italy who had railed against his preaching and intended to publish a refutation of his doctrine, *Epistola* 113^v–114^r. The man had already written something against Siculo's 'trattato di giustificatione', i.e. the *Espositione*. The unknown antagonist may have been Giulio da Milano who was in Italy at that time, and who accused Siculo of mingling anti-trinitarian with papist teaching—presumably the latter term referred to justification by works: see Cantimori, *Eretici italiani*, p. 60. There remains no trace of these writings. In 1550 the 'Calvinist' community of Cremona, the 'ecclesia Cremonensis' commissioned Niccolò Fogliata, a follower of Siculo, to get a copy of *Epistola* to Giulio della Rovere (i.e. Giulio of Milano), who passed information to Calvin: see Rotondò, 'Atteggiamenti della vita morale Italiana del Cinquecento. La Pratica Nicodemitica', *Rivista storica italiana*, lxxix (1967), 991–1030: 1014–15 refer to Siculo.

[112] *De aeterna Dei praedestinatione* 258–9, where Calvin's invective is sparkling and fluent, also 331–47. The book was written between October 1551 and January 1552 with the purpose of refuting Albert Pighius and Jerome Bolsec. Calvin's references to the words of Siculo correspond to passages in the *Epistola* which had been published eighteen months earlier. Calvin's work has been translated by J. K. S. Reid under the title *Concerning the Eternal Predestination of God* (London, 1961), with footnotes from the French copy. Calvin consistently rejected the idea that man's repentance must precede God's forgiveness and that grace is a consequence of personal repentance. Such a theory of penal satisfaction is refuted in *Institutes*, II. xvi. 4.

Calvin's position on predestination, free will, and works.[113] Nevertheless he was in agreement with Calvin's condemnation of Siculo's theology. Camerario said that Siculo had misread and misunderstood the Scriptures in a number of places and that his doctrine was heterodox because he preached salvation through works alone; 'we work together in the power of God, who has liberated us and called us with his holy calling, not in the power of our own works, but according to his purpose and in the grace which he has given to us before the world began (let Giorgio hear that . . .)'[114] Thus two contemporary scholars, from two different viewpoints, considered the heresy of Siculo to lie in his Pelagian interpretation of scriputure, which was acceptable to neither Rome nor Geneva.[115] It has been the argument of this chapter that these Pelagian tendencies were drawn from the distortion of Cassinese patristic theology at the hands of this zealous, but ill-educated, monk.

What further conclusions may we draw from our study of Giorgio Siculo? The few studies made of him have explained his teachings in terms of contemporary heretical groups. Cantimori described Siculo's writings as a mixture of rationalism and mysticism analogous to that of Servetus, based upon strong faith in the power of reason then common in Italy; confident, like Servetus, that free will may attain holiness; trusting in divine grace and the infinite mercy of God, as did 'religiosità spirituale valdesiana'. Cantimori thought Siculo typical of the many contemporary Italian 'reformers' who, whilst they wanted reform of morals and quoted scripture freely and to that extent were hostile to Rome, at the same time were not sympathetic to the theology of the Reformation. For this reason, said Cantimori, Siculo was indifferent to confessional doctrines, possessed a vague doctrine of church authority and was able to advocate a Nicodemist position of outward conformity, but inward

---

[113] B. Camerarius, *Bartholomaei Camerarii, Beneventani, De Praedestinatione, Dialogi Tres* (Paris, 1556), ch. 8; pp. 285–91; pp. 238–61 deal with the case of Spiera from a Roman Catholic viewpoint. There is a lengthy biographical article on Camerario in *Dizionario biografico degli italiani*, xvii (Rome, 1974), 172–4.

[114] *De aeterna Dei praedestinatione* 288–9: '. . . collaboramus secundum virtutem Dei, qui nos liberavit, et vocavit vocatione sua sancta, non secundum opera nostra, sed secundum propositum suum, et gratiam quae data est nobis in Christo Iesu, ante tempora secularia (audiat Georgius . . .)'.

[115] It was probably the view of the Holy Office investigators too, but their findings are not available.

withdrawal.[116] Ginzburg has been more specific, holding that the *Epistola*, under the guise of anti-Protestant polemic, was really representative of Venetian Anabaptism, preaching imminent regeneration. According to Ginzburg, Siculo was convinced that the regeneration of the church was so imminent that he felt no need to separate from the unregenerate, and therefore counselled Nicodemism for the short time remaining.[117] Finally, Ginzburg, Caponetto, and Prosperi have argued that Siculo had followers amongst senior monks, notably Ottoni, Chiari, and Benedetto da Mantova.[118]

In this chapter it has been argued that the explanation of Siculo's teaching lies in his monastic background. He never entirely discarded his past; he maintained his monastic vows and practices, he kept up personal links with the monks and he even retained the use of the title Don Giorgio: his teachings emphasized traditional monastic virtues, utilized the biblical studies of the cloister, and followed the outline of his Congregation's traditional pattern of salvation. However, the Cassinese doctrine of salvation as rescue from mortality, and as healing through faith and good works, which serve as a therapeutic instrument of restoration, was distorted by his obsession with the need for obedience and perfection in order to avoid the wrath of God. The biblical studies that flourished in Cassinese cloisters were reflected in the unrelenting avalanche of quotations and paraphrases that poured down to validate every step of the argument, but in his hands the scholarly exegesis of the monks was narrowed down to the treatment of the Bible as a book of precepts of the 'new law': the search for insights into the human condition was subordinated by a search for rules and precepts, for supernatural illumination, and for visitations of the spirit to strengthen belief and obedience.

His was a religion of regiment, of rules, obedience, rewards, and punishments. It was Latin, legalistic, guilt-ridden and

[116] Cantimori, *Eretici italiani*, pp. 57, 63 ff.

[117] Ginzburg, *Il Nicodemismo*, pp. 171–4, 'un corpo di dottrine molto coerente, di carattere nettamente ereticale, sostanzialmente corrispondente a quelle sostenute negli stessi anni dai gruppi di anabattisti italiani, specialmente veneti'. The Anabaptists held that men could be spiritually regenerated by the direct action of divine grace upon the soul and therefore be justified 'in spirito'.

[118] Ginzburg, *Il Nicodemismo*, pp. 173, 178; Caponetto, *Dizionario biografico degli italiani*, viii (Rome, 1966), 438–9; Prosperi, 'Un gruppo ereticale', pp. 349–50.

puritanical. But its underlying theology was a simplified and shallow version of the quite different Greek patristic theology of the Congregation. Siculo took that traditional pattern and distorted and coarsened it, so that what was once Greek patristic theology became something which resembled the 'rationalist mysticism' or 'Anabaptism' of the mid-sixteenth century.

Aftermath: the 1550s and 1560s

AT the time of the Siculo affair Ottoni was a sick man and probably something of an embarrassment to his order. He was moved from Ferrara to Mantua, and shortly after, moved on again. In some distress he wrote to Cardinal Ercole Gonzaga, denying accusations that he had permitted the circulation of 'books' and tolerated disorders, and claiming that he was being persecuted by the president of the Congregation.[1] Whatever the truth of the matter, it is certain that Gonzaga was extemely annoyed at the way Ottoni was being pushed around, but it is possible that Ottoni's imprudent support for Siculo, and his bumbling obstinacy exacerbated by ill health, proved too much for the president and other abbots during troubled times. At the end of 1552 Ottoni died after forty-five years as a monk of Santa Giustina: his epitaph remembered not so much his learning as his capacity to forgive and to shepherd the wayward: '. . . pacem calumniatoribus indicens, injurias condonavit mortaleque mortalibus curandum dedit.'[2]

Ottoni's death was another step towards the passing of the brilliant generation of monks who had been professed in the early years of the century. Their scholarship, which had defined and given weight to the Congregation's teaching, had come to nought at the Council of Trent. After the definitions of 1546, although Cassinese abbots continued to attend the Council, Congregational theology became irrelevant in western Christendom, perhaps not to personal piety, but certainly to the great questions of confessional definitions and ecclesiastical politics.

We have seen that the failure of 1546 was followed by signs of new kinds of piety, less tied to biblical and patristic scholarship and more directed towards personal experience—the Pelagianism of Siculo and the affective raptures of Faucher. These

---

[1] Ginzburg and Prosperi, 'Le due redazioni . . .', p. 198. The letter was dated 16 May 1550.

[2] Cited by Faralli, 'Per una biografia . . .', p. 50.

exaggerations, unsupported by traditional teaching, were not isolated examples, but occurred elsewhere within the order, notably at the monastery of Montecassino, in the manuscript known as Codex 584, an anonymous collection of sermons, letters, poems, and prayers.[3] Some items are copies of earlier texts—for example, extracts from Augustine—but the greater number appear to have been of Cassinese origin; one may be dated perhaps as early as 1520, but most were written in the mid-sixteenth century, that is, within the period after the Congregation's defeat at Trent. The style of the various pieces seems to bear out this dating. On the one hand there are signs of traditional Cassinese theology, but on the other hand the codex lacks the careful biblical argument of the old tradition; instead its principal themes are those of divine love and spiritual ravishment already seen in Faucher, and of determined obedience to God, already seen in Siculo. It is this approach that places Codex 584 in the 1550s, at the turning-point in the history of the Congregation when the old biblical and Greek patristic theology begins to weaken.

The signs of underlying Cassinese teaching are scattered throughout the codex: the creation of man in the image of God, the fall of man, the incapacity of the will to achieve salvation, and the inadequacy of mere good works, despite the continued existence of the will and its ability to do good, the necessity of grace, the benign liberality of God who loves sinners and gives himself as a gift—the benefit of the Cross—man's knowledge of his own misery and need of God (reminiscent of the *Beneficio di Cristo*) liberation from the law, faith, vivification, the healing of free will, Christians being not fearful servants, but loving sons, the necessity of good works, especially in forgiveness, love, and the care of others, the value of the monastic life, and at length, perfection and union with God.[4]

However, despite these signs, Codex 584 clearly marked a departure from the order's traditional teaching. First, it contained strongly affective piety of the kind already observed in the later teachings of Faucher. Here the principal emphasis was

---

[3] There is a critical edition, with commentary, by T. Leccisotti, 'Tracce di Correnti Mistiche Cinquecentesche nel Codice Cassinese 584', *Archivio italiano per la storia della pietà*, iv (1965), 1–120.

[4] Ibid. 40–1, 36, 38–9 ('beneficium redemptionis' is listed with other benefits), 69, 72: also 43–6, 53–6, 64, 77, 81, 84, 87.

upon the utter submission of the human to the divine will, and
man losing himself as he begs God to 'lift me, heart and soul, and
consume me entirely in you, because in you I shall find you and
myself', reaching 'annihilation of all his will and strength and
knowing'. Thus man is engulfed in the great sea of divine love
until he is swept up into a spontaneous and violent passion,
responding with joy to the kiss of 'lo sposo', carried away by
'annihilation of self' and 'madness' ('pazia') of love. Such men,
'without constraint, without fear, and free of sin', are truly
possessed of the 'pazia' for which man is created.[5] This piety was
clearly different from the traditional Cassinese teachings, and
Tommaso Leccisotti was correct to detect in it the influence of
Catherine of Genoa, and was probably correct to see that of
Paolo Giustiniani and the Company of Divine Love.

A second difference is the very strong emphasis upon
obedience and perfection of life according to the precepts of the
Bible and the Benedictine Rule. Obedience is an important
element in the Rule, and was to be found in the pattern of
salvation expounded by earlier Congregational writers for
whom it had occupied an important place amongst the good
works which flow from grace and lead to the restoration of the
imago Dei. However, in Codex 584 we see obedience extended to
constitute almost alone the prior part of the pattern of salvation,
that is, the part that leads on to raptures and ecstatic union with
God, whilst the Cassinese doctrines of sin, mortality, and grace
are of little or no significance. Moreover, not only does
obedience—together with ecstasy—comprise virtually the
whole pattern of salvation, the nature of that obedience is
different from the old tradition. Here it has acquired a legalism
of a paternal kind. Adam's fall is seen in terms of disobedience
and the punishment of exile from a loving father, whilst the
obedience of the faithful soul is seen to remove that punishment
and restore men to their position as loving and obedient sons of
God, 'O good Jesus, who are your beloved, if not *the lovers and sons
of obedience*?'[6]

---

[5] Leccisotti, 'Tracce di Correnti', 36–9 41–3, 59–60, 63, 78, 110–11. There is a
collection of meditations with similar themes in Codex 418 I, see *Codicum Casinensium
Manuscriptorum Catalogus*, iii (1940–1), 22–6.

[6] Leccisotti, 'Tracce di Correnti', 43–6, 52, 70–6, 79–95. The quotation is from 73:
'Qui sunt dilecti tui, o bone Iesu, nisi *amatores et filii obedientie*? Nam, sicut inobedientia
Adam, et in Adam omnes homines de paradiso eiecit, et Dei inimicos constituit, ita
obedientia ad celum reducit et dilectos facit.'

The third departure from traditional Cassinese piety is the remarkable paucity in Codex 584 of biblical and patristic references. The few references that do occur are used merely for illustration: there is nothing of the closely reasoned arguments, using Paul and Chrysostom, which are found in Chiari, Ottoni, and Folengo. Consequently, although the piety of the authors of Codex 584 is exceptionally fervent, it is not grounded in the Bible, nor in the Fathers. These writings of Codex 584 were not adding an extra dimension of mysticism to the order's biblical and patristic scholarship; on the contrary their writings virtually discarded the Bible and the Fathers, using particular biblical themes, especially 'faith' and 'obedience', as a vehicle for mystical expression, but without any attempt at systematic exposition. Thus its piety was quite distinct from the biblical and patristic scholarship that underlay the teachings of the Congregation.

In Codex 584 we see how the elements of faith and love and obedience, which had always been present in the Congregation's monastic piety, were now exaggerated and at the same time separated from the biblical and patristic scholarship in which they had once been securely placed. In this sense it may be said that Cassinese piety was beginning to disintegrate into three strands—one strongly affective, another emphasizing obedience and perfection, and the third the surviving old traditional piety based on Paul and Chrysostom. There is an explanation for these changes. The theological decrees of the first sessions of the Council of Trent excluded the Antiochene theology at the heart of the Congregation's teachings and devotion. Suddenly the monks found that the pattern of salvation which they had expounded with increasing determination and skill was now barely acceptable in the Catholic world: in turn this can only have shaken confidence in the biblical and patristic exegesis from which they had drawn their doctrine of salvation. In these circumstances it is hardly surprising that there was a tendency for monks to concentrate upon inward and personal features of the old pattern of salvation, especially 'love' and 'good works'. These two emphases, which are clearly recognizable as two elements of the earlier doctrine of 'faith', were perfectly acceptable in the climate of Roman Catholic spiritually after Trent—provided they were not pushed to extremes as Siculo had done. Nor is it surprising, considering the manner in which they were expounded, that the two elements became detached from biblical scholarship.

The same separation from theological scholarship is evident in the poetry of Don Leonardo Oddi of Perugia. About 1550 he composed several epic poems which clearly alluded to Cassinese teachings on sin, grace, and faith, but which avoided any theological treatment of those themes. Instead, Don Leonardo described his Dante-like journey out of the wickedness and turmoil of this world, through the Benedictine way of virtue and perfection, to a state of bliss, delight, and sweetness of faith 'apud benignissimum Deum'. In 1552 Oddi was imprisoned by his order for reasons which are not clear. It is possible that he carried to excess either his ecstatic raptures and visions, or his zeal for virtue and perfection (as was the case with Siculo, who had been hanged less than a year earlier).[7]

Meanwhile Chiari continued to carry out his episcopal duties at Foligno, writing and preaching extensively and caring for the poor in the spirit of his 1540 *Oratio* to the citizens of Brescia. When he died in May 1555, for the forty hours of his lying in state, the people of Foligno covered his feet in tears and kisses; and when he was buried, his epitaph stated that 'nobody was more merciful in calamity, or more gentle in confrontation'.[8]

Teofilo Folengo had died in 1544, and now Ottoni and Chiari were gone. The Cassinese were subdued and their spirituality unsettled. Then, in 1556 the Congregation, already burdened

---

[7] *Miscellanea Cassinese ossia nuovi contributi alla storia, alle scienze e arti religiose*, ii (1897), Litteraria, 1–47. The principal poem is 'De Laudibus Montis Casini'. The poems were dedicated to Don Vincenzo of Naples, abbot of Montecassino and president of the Congregation. The MS of a rather more Christocentric poem is in Bibl. Univ. Padua, MS 439, fos. 1^r–46^r; the phrase quoted is taken from fo. 2^v. Oddi's biographical details are in Armellini, *Bibl. Bened.-Cas.* ii. 76. He was professed in 1536. The reference to his imprisonment is in Leccisotti, 'Tracce di Correnti', 115.

[8] F. Egger, *Idea Ordinis Hierarchico-Benedictini* (Constance, 1717), p. 263. There is a modern assessment of Chiari's pastoral work in B. Ulianich, 'Scrittura e Azione Pastorale nelle Prime Omelie Episcopali di Isodoro Chiari', *Reformata Reformanda: Festgabe für Hubert Jedin*, eds. E. Iserloh and K. Repgen (Münster, 1965), pp. 610–34. At this time, Chiari also wrote a work 'In Caput IX Epistolae ad Romanos Orationes Duae', addressed to his colleague Calvini, then President of the order; Ziegelbaur, *Historia*, iii. 334. The MS is lost. Another MS, 'De arte Amandi', listed in the 1789 catalogue of S. Giorgio Maggiore, was lost in 1807: G. Ravegnani, *Le biblioteche*, pp. 55, 82.

with its own failures, was nearly drawn into another lost cause. Its protector, Cardinal Pole, now back in England, wrote to the president of the Congregation, asking for his help in restoring Benedictine monks in Westminster Abbey. The plan was to recruit only the best monks and to have abbots elected for short terms. Pole asked that Giambattista Folengo and Eutychius of Placentia, then carrying out a visitation in Spain, be sent on to London as advisers.[9] But this plan was not put into effect, there were further delays, and in due course, after 1558, the proposals were overtaken by events in England.

Changes similar to those observed in Faucher, Siculo, and Codex 584 were also manifest in other writings of the Congregation. In 1556 Don Marco of Brescia published a tract which was part commentary and part meditation on the thirteenth chapter of the Gospel of St. John. Don Marco described the Last Supper as the promulgation of the new law, 'the law of life, the law of love', the 'sweet precepts' of which demanded love, humility, forgiveness, reconciliation, good works, and peace. Obedience to this law was to be achieved through the will, for God deals with men 'not as underlings or servants, but his friends and free men'—Judas, for example, had not been compelled to betray Jesus, but did so only because he first betrayed himself to the devil. Obedience to this law would bring the knowledge of divine love: moreover the sacrament, a 'holocaust of sweet love', would strengthen the heart and 'inebriate the soul' until the 'immense love' of Christ and its sweetness was utterly known.[10]

The following year Marco published another tract of three sermons on the eighteenth chapter of St. John, concerning the Passion. There were touches of the traditional Cassinese style, but these were few and the direction of the work was quite different in the style and content of its exegesis. Marco was not concerned to analyse, explain, or argue a pattern of salvation. Instead he took particular terms and elaborated them into quite extravagant physical descriptions: the garden was depicted as a sweet bower of vines, rosy apples, lilies, and fragrant aromas into

---

[9] *C.S.P. Venetian*, 1555–6, pp. 334, 403; *Epistolae Poli*, v, app., p. 346. In 1557, the year after Folengo's return to Italy, his *In Psalterium Davidis* of 1549 was republished at Basle.

[10] *In Dominicam Coenam a Capite Ioannis tertio decimo usque ad caput decimum nonum, coenae amoris octo* (Brescia, 1556), preface, A iii; A vi; B i; B v; B vi. The tract is discussed briefly by A. Pantoni, 'Asceti Penitenti e Mistici della Congregazione Cassinese nei Secoli xvi–xviii', *Benedictina*, xvi (1960), 250.

which Christ entered so that he could preach his law of love. For Marco the significance of the Passion was the teaching it exemplified, that is, love, even for enemies: 'This is truly the distinctive doctrine of Christ, the extraordinary philosophy of Christian doctrine—to pray for your enemies, teaching him who had to suffer, and showing him who has to die.'[11] Christ was thus a divine exemplar of love, piety, forgiveness, humility, and so forth, in contrast to the present condition of mankind. The sermons continue in this fashion, with particular terms being used as an opportunity to expound obedience to the new law and the search for freedom from sin, that is, true wisdom and love. Indeed the Cross is described solely in these terms, for the 'immensa Dei beneficia' meant for Marcus only liberty from the slavery of the devil and sin and a new life of obedience and love.[12] This was his pattern of salvation. The rest of the Congregation's old Antiochene theology had disappeared.

Similar changes are apparent in a manual of private meditation written at Montecassino in 1557 by Don Joannes Baptista Neapolitanus.[13] This tract contains very many allusions to the traditional Cassinese pattern of salvation: the inclination of fallen man to evils and perversity, the Cross as '. . . beneficium . . . [et] Christi charitatem erga genus humanum', the 'beneficium scilicet mortem eius' which cancels the 'chirograph' written by the fall, reconciles men to God, and offers salvation to the whole human race. Don Joannes employed the customary catena of biblical and patristic quotations, together with exhortations to be grateful and to bear tribulations with hope and perseverance.[14] However, the main theme of the work was meditation, and the ways in which meditation is able to stir up a condition of love in the heart of a Christian. In particular, meditation upon the wounds of Christ, he said, inflames the soul with love and joy, hope, penitence, and affection (the imagery of the Song of Songs and the story of Mary Magdalene were used to good effect).[15] This affective response led the devout man to

[11] *De Supplitio et Morte Domini Nostri Jesu Christi* (Brescia, 1557), fo. A4. The copy at Rome (Bibl. Aless. Fondo Antico T.M. 67) is bound with *In Dominican Coenam*.

[12] Ibid. fos. A4; A5; A8; B2; B5; C4; E6; E7.

[13] 'Tractatus de Commendatione Meditationis Passionis Christi', Bibl. Apost. Vat. Chigi. C V 146, fos. 226^r–294^v (modern pagination). The tract is followed by sundry prayers for the mass of St. John Chrysostom, fo. 295^r.

[14] Ibid. 229^r, 230^r–231^r, 234^r, 235^r, 237^r, 243^r, 245^v–248^r, 252^r–255^r.

[15] Ibid. 229^r, 232^v–233^r (the Song of Songs), 234^v–235^r ('gustare quam suavis est Dominus'), 243^r–244^r, 245^v–248^r, 249^v–255^r, 267^r–269^v.

imitate Christ and to change his life ('mutare vitam suam'). There were detailed instructions in the techniques of meditation and a prayer of adoration to recite, 'O Sacratissima, amantissima et dulcissima vulneraJesu'.[16] It is not surprising that, whilst there were some references to Augustine, Ambrose, and Chrysostom, by far the greatest of Don Joannes's sources were the writings on divine love of Bernard of Clairvaux. However, the affective language of Joannes had degenerated from the erotic strength of Bernard and Denis Faucher to mere sentimentality.

His emphasis upon ardent love was derived from the component of love in the concept of faith in earlier Cassinese writings. But, whereas other, earlier writers looked to theological clarity in speaking about God's grace and man's faith, this monk looked inwards to meditate upon the experience of God's love and our response to it, and, finally, to attain a passionate union with Christ. Such sentiments may have been in tune with Catholic piety after the Council of Trent, but it was quite different from the Pauline and Antiochene spirituality of the Congregation before Trent.

Alongside these signs of change in spirituality, the traditional studies continued. At the Badia the Florentine monk, Don Crisostomo Nicholini translated John Chrysostom from Greek to Italian, though the piety of even this scholarly man had a rich emotional streak, 'with many revelations and apparitions from God and divine conversations' inspired by his strong devotion to the Passion.[17] At the same time the abbot of Montecassino, Angelo de Faggiis, de Castro Sangri, commonly called Sangrino, was writing poetry which reveals a spirituality based strongly on the theme of ardent love, similar to that of Codex 584. In 1561 Sangrino published a *Psalterium* in which each psalm was paraphrased and given an *argumentum* which related the material of the psalm to the New Testament, especially the Pauline epistles.[18] Throughout his *argumenta* Sangrino pursued

---

[16] Ibid. 235^r, 237^r–240^v, 244^v, 270^r–281^v, 293^r.

[17] See 'Raggionamento di San Giovanni Chrisostomo', Bibl. Aless. Rome, MS 98, fos. 236^r–251^v. Nicholini was born in 1523, professed in 1538, aged fifteen years, and died in 1560, aged thirty-seven years. See also Pantoni, 'Asceti Penitenti', pp. 247–8.

[18] *In Psalterium Davidis Regis et Prophetae clarissimi. Paraphrasis . . . Angelo Sangrino Abbate Casinensi Auctore* (Basle, 1561). There is a full treatment of Sangrino in G. Minozzi, *Montecassino nella Storia del Rinascimento* (Rome, 1925), pp. 297–353 (*vita*), 356–400 (*opera*). His *Poesis Christiana* (Padua, 1565), was actually written before 1561. Some poems were also edited by A. Mirra, *La poesia di Montecassino* (Naples, 1929).

one dominant and persistent theme, that of the immense mercy and goodness of God towards the human race. Human life is miserable, he said, but through his son God shall liberate the human race from the bitter tyranny of the devil. This 'benefit' of God required faith to accept it and then to manifest good works towards others, but the principal emphasis was upon the immense grace of the Cross. Sangrino did not develop a pattern of salvation in his *argumenta* but he did convey, quite clearly, the traditional Cassinese teaching of the benefit of Christ's death.[19]

Other scholarly work continued. In 1562 Don Vincenzo Campanus published a work which was substantially his *Fasciculus Myrrhae* of forty years earlier, and he also produced an anthology of devotions to the Virgin.[20] Don Alexius Ugonius published a historical account of recent Greek and Italian troubles, together with an exhortation to civil concord in Brescia (shades of Chiari!), letters to the Fathers of Trent, to Cardinal Pole, and so on.[21] In 1563 Chrysostomus Calvini, who had been at Trent with Ottoni and Chiari, revised the translation of the sermons of St. Dorotheus which had been done by Don Hilarion of Verona about fifty years earlier.[22] The following year Calvini, who was a friend of Alvise Priuli and Lodovico Beccadelli, succeeded the latter as Archbishop of Ragusa.[23] Sometime during the 1560s the Belgian monk, Don Eutytius Cordes, professed in 1540, a scholar in Latin, Greek, and Hebrew, wrote a commentary on the epistles of Paul, a dictionary of the Bible, a tract on justification directed against Protestants, and a number of other works. His writings appear to have been lost, except for one manuscript at Padua. This manuscript has had one tract

---

[19] *In Psalterium* 47, 72–3, 77, 92, 98, 100, 107–8, 135, 146, 158–60, 177, 188, 200–2, 215, 222–3, 228, 233, 236, 255, 261, 266, 278, 285, 294, 300–3, 313–15, 318, 359, 374, 380, 397, 401–3. The poems of Sangrino, some of which are strongly affective, are on pp. 414–62; note especially the elegies *Ad Jesum*, pp. 442–62, based upon Luke 23.

[20] *Collyrium Mentis seu Commentaria de Nominibus Christi* (Naples, 1562): for his *Fasciculus Myrrhae* see above, ch. 3; *Ad Deiparam Virginem Salutationes Pulcherrimae ex Sacra Scriptura Delectae* (Naples, 1562).

[21] *Flavii Alexii Ugonii . . . De maximis Italiae atque Graeciae calamitatibus etc.* (Venice, 1559); Armellini, *Bibl. Bened.-Cas.* i. 5–8.

[22] Calvini's revised translation, *Sancti Dorothei Sermones XXI*, was published in Venice in 1564. For Don Hilarion of Verona see above, ch. 2.

[23] Armellini, *Bibl. Bened.-Cas.* i. 117–19; Beccadelli, *Monumenti di Varia Letteratura*, i. 56. The friendship of the three men is attested by the letters of Priuli to Beccadelli, 13 June 1559 from London, and 30 Dec. 1559 from Paris, Bodleian MS Ital. C. 25, fos. 306^v–7^r, 309^r–10^r.

removed, leaving only a work entitled *De Gratia*. Cordes was writing after the sixth session of the Council of Trent (January 1547), which he described as affirming salvation by faith which 'required personal consensus in order to be efficacious.' He is quite clear that men become sons of God out of grace and not out of works or merit. However, his exposition of grace is clearly in the Thomist style rather than in the tradition of his own Congregation: he speaks of sin being expelled and justice infused, and he distinguishes, in the scholastic manner between 'gratia gratis data' and 'gratia gratum faciens'.[24] Thus in Cordes we see the old teaching taking yet another direction—towards Thomist orthodoxy.

*

During the later 1560s there was a resurgence of the doctrines of obedience which Siculo had earlier carried to excess. Between 1565 and 1567 three volumes of Chiari's Foligno sermons were published posthumously. In 1973 Adriano Prosperi and Carlo Ginzburg discovered that embedded in these lengthy volumes was almost all the theological material of Giorgio Siculo's *Epistola*, rather poorly translated into Latin.[25] Prosperi and Ginzburg concluded that Chiari had read Siculo's *Epistola* after it was published and was so impressed by it that he incorporated it into his sermons, and that he (and his editors) were therefore able to achieve a 'cripto-ristampa' of the heretical work. However, the attempt of the two historians to portray Chiari as a follower of Siculo is based upon their tenuous observations of similarities between the interpolations and Chiari's own words concerning predestination, criticisms of the clergy, and the renewing work of the Spirit. But, as we have already seen, both Chiari and Siculo were schooled in a common doctrine and similarities are therefore to be expected, especially since in his early days Siculo probably conversed with Chiari and heard his

[24] Bibl. Univ. Padua, MS 812, fos. 113–55 (fos. 1–112 are missing). See 273ʳ, also 218ʳ, 221ᵛ, 224ʳ (modern pagination). Cordes is noted by Armellini, *Bibl. Bened.-Cas.* i. 160–1.

[25] A. Prosperi, 'Una cripto-ristampa dell'Epistola di Giorgio Siculo', *Bollettino della Società di Studi Valdesi*, cxxxiv (1973), 52–68. The works were *Isidorii Clarii . . . in Evangelium secundum Lucam orationes quinquaginta quatuor* (Venice, 1565); *Isidorii Clarii . . . in sermonem Domini in monte habitum secundum Matthaeum, orationes sexaginta novem ad populum* (Venice, 1566); *Isidorii Clarii Orationum quas extraordinarias appellavit volumen primum* (Venice, 1567).

sermons. Prosperi and Ginzurg also explain the poor quality of
the translation into Latin by Chiari's presumed haste—not a
convincing explanation for a scholar of Chiari's calibre and
diligence.

There is no doubt that Chiari's works were used to provide a
cover for the heretical text, and that the ruse succeeded because
the passages were mixed up with more or less commonplace
criticisms of clerical laxity, because they were not obviously
Protestant, and because Chiari's name diverted suspicion. (In
fact, the heterodox passages were noticed by at least one
theologian before Prosperi and Ginzburg made their discovery.[26]) Nevertheless, it is most unlikely that Chiari himself
had been involved in the matter. We have already seen that he
and Siculo were quite dissimilar in terms of scholarship,
theology, and personality. Moreover, we do not have to look far
to find others with both the motive and the opportunity for the
interpolations. The two men responsible for the publications
were the editor, Don Benedetto Guidi,[27] a relatively young man
who published the work *De Laudibus Mulierum* anonymously in
Venice, and Don Andrea da Asola, who, despite the fact that he
was elected president of the Congregation in 1567, was a
follower of the dead heretic Giorgio Siculo.

Don Andrea's election probably reflected the state of confusion into which Cassinese spirituality had passed, being divided
not only between the old piety based upon Pauline scholarship
and the new piety of affective devotion, but also, as was now
clear, the puritanical Pelagianism of Siculo. It was to the
Pelagian group that Andrea da Asola belonged. The existence of
the group was revealed by a certain Don Teofilo of Siena, a
young man, professed only in 1561, and a mathematician later
to be involved in the reform of the calendar in 1582—perhaps
himself an example of yet another group, more secular in
outlook. He wrote to Pope Pius V with the claim that there was
heresy in the Congregation. The pope discussed the matter with
Charles Cardinal Borromeo, who then conducted an investiga-

[26] Bibl. Apost. Vat., Vat. Lat. 6207, fos. 94^{r-v}, a single folio *censura*, unsigned and
undated, which refers to sermons 65–8 of the volume of 1566, described as being 'contra
catholicos doctores sanctosque patres ... et ad Pelagianorum haeresim acceduntur:
haec sunt in summa'.

[27] For Guidi, see Armellini, *Bibl. Bened.-Cas.* i. 97–8; *A. et C.* 24–5. His writings are in
MS at Bibl. Padua, MS 1379 I.

tion which discovered members of 'la setta dei georgiani' in the monasteries at Mantua, Brescia, and Milan.[28] On 30 April 1568 Don Andrea was arrested and relieved of the presidency. The Congregation carried out its own internal investigation and trial under Angelo de Faggiis, Sangrino, who was then abbot of Montecassino. At his trial Don Andrea admitted negligence, but denied culpability, after which he was freed, and returned to Mantua.[29]

The episode strongly suggests that between 1565 and 1567 Don Andrea was in a position to make the insertions into Chiari's works, with the connivance of Don Benedetto Guidi. Everything we know about Chiari goes against his being responsible, but Don Andrea had the motive, and presumably the influence, to make the fraudulent interpolations. As for 'la setta dei georgiani', how seriously did these monks adhere to the theology of Siculo? If the president and other senior monks were indeed whole-hearted followers of Siculo, then the Congregation must have experienced a serious breakdown of its theological traditions. On the other hand, our analysis of Siculo has shown that his teachings were based upon ill-educated misunderstanding and distortion of patristic teaching. But since the president and the senior monks in question were, presumably, well-educated men, they were probably not completely committed to Siculo's theology. Moreover, Andrea's plea of negligence, and the light punishment inflicted upon the offenders, suggests

---

[28] C. Margarini, *Bullarium Cassinense*, tome ii (Todi, 1670), 473; E. Gattola, *Historia Abbatiae Cassinensis* (Venice, 1733), ii. 689; D. Maselli, 'Per la storia religiosa dello stato di Milano durante il dominio di Filippo II: l'eresia e la sua repressione dal 1555 al 1584', *Nuova rivista storica*, liv, (1970), 317–73, esp. 348–9. L. N. Cittadella, *Notizie relative a Ferrara, per la maggior parte inedite, ricavate da documenti* (Ferrara, 1864), pp. 384–5. There were some supporters of Siculo known to the Holy Office in 1561, although it is not clear whether they were religious or laymen: see Cantimori, *Eretici italiani*, p. 59.

[29] Maselli, op. cit., p. 349. By 4 June 1568 Andrea was referred to as 'già presidente'; he was tried on 12 June. The other monks were Don Constantino, Don Teofilo, of Mantua, Don Lucillo Martinengo, prior of Brescia, Don Pietro da Brescia, of Milan (not to be confused with the devout physician of the same name). In the trials of 28 Aug. 1568 one 'don Antonio, frate di S. Benedetto' (probably Don Antonio da Bozzolo) was sent to the galleys and 'privato dell'abito': Cittadella, op. cit., 385. Altogether sixteen persons, including a woman and several laymen were investigated for their adherence to 'la setta georgiana' and punished by imprisonment, the galleys or death. See also A. Frizzi, *Memorie per la storia di Ferrara, raccolte da A.F.*, 2nd. ed. (Ferrara, 1847–50), iv, 394–5. There is a good account of the doctor Francesco Severi and other followers of Siculo by Renate Raffaeli in 'Notizie intorno a Francesco Severi, il medico d'Argenta', *Studi Urbinati*, fasc. B3 (1983), 91–136.

an undue zeal for good works and an imprudent reverence for the memory of a martyred colleague—in short, exaggerated piety rather than plain heresy.

The events of 1568 provoked a strong reaction within the order. Even as the 'setta' was being investigated, a defensive exposition of the Congregation's traditional teaching was being prepared by Don Vincenzo of Milan. The work, *De Maximis Christi Beneficiis Pia Gratiarum Actio, ex utroque Testamento Compendiose collecta, piis & Catholicis Christianis dedicata*, was completed at Naples on 31 May 1568, exactly a month after Don Andrea was arrested and a few days before his trial.[30] It is a narrative of the main events of creation and the incarnation, life, death, and resurrection of Christ, and the church and last judgement. The margins carry biblical references every few lines or so of text. The old themes and emphases of the Cassinese pattern of salvation recur from time to time—sin, grace, universal salvation, the putting on ('induere') of new life, and care for others—but it was not a complete exposition of Cassinese teaching.[31] Rather, its purpose seems to have been to reassure Rome by its tone of respectable piety, by its anti-Pelagian, Pauline emphasis on the inadequacy of works and the necessity of the Cross, and by its simple chronicle of God's acts in history and by its sober description of man's relationship to God in marked contrast to the excesses of ardent mystical piety.[32] The contents of the work, the fact that it appeared with the 'approbamus' of the vicar-general of Naples and the president and diffinitors of the chapter-general of the Congregation (something never before done with Cassinese writing), its timing, as the investigations were coming to a head, the pointed dedication in the title 'piis & Catholicis Christianis', the uncharacteristic phrase 'Pia Gratiarum Actio', all these things indicate that the book was intended to deal with the crisis by supporting traditionalists within the Congregation and by reassuring Rome of the Congregation's orthodoxy.

---

[30] Bibl. Apost. Vat. Chigi I IV 148, fos. 66ʳ–86ʳ (modern pagination). The tract is bound with other MS material: in giving references I have used the modern through-pagination. For Vincentius, see Armellini, *Bibl. Bened.-Cas.* ii. 24–5. He was professed in Pavia in 1524. Armellini has a list of his writings, one of which was a tract on scriptural consolation in time of tribulation.

[31] *De Maximis* 81ᵛ, 82ʳ, 84ᵛ.

[32] Ibid. 78ʳ–79ʳ.

The Congregation survived the crisis. The zealous men who favoured Siculo's piety disappeared back into the cloisters. Those of an affective turn of mind continued discreetly with their ardent devotions, and amongst them were frequent manifestations of piety based almost entirely upon emotional experience rather than biblical exegesis—the kind of piety which had been almost unknown at the height of the order's scholarship. Now, there were men like Don Agostino da Maratea, of Naples, who studied intensely, ate and slept very little, dedicated himself to virtual silence and when he did speak, spoke only of spiritual matters; and Don Placido Petrucci, whose life was one of fervour, tears, pious meditation, intense study, ardent longing for divine love, and speaking with tongues.[33]

The scholarly element, though it never regained the dominance and vivacity of pre-Tridentine days, remained strong within the order. Hilarion of Genoa, who had spent the 1560s translating the Fathers into Italian, launched out in his later years into biblical commentaries, a work on free will, notes on the Greek text of Chrysostom, and sundry sermons.[34] However, the tenor of the Congregation's scholarship was changing: some of the older writings were revised and purged, such as Bornato's tract of 1537 on free will, whilst in 1585 Giambattista Folengo's commentary on the Psalms was republished after being rewritten by Cassinese monks.[35] Ottoni's translation in 1538 of Chrysostom quietly disappeared, as did Chiari's bible of 1541–2. Other monks turned towards the scholastics who had been scorned by earlier generations of Cassinese monks: Eutytius Cordes mingled the old pattern of salvation with Thomist teaching on grace,[36] and in 1569 Paolo Gravina, abbot of Montecassino, produced a version of the

---

[33] Armellini, *Catalogus* 12; Gattola, *Historia* 680–1.

[34] Armellini, *Bibl. Bened.-Cas.* i. 226–7; *A. et C.* 49–50. His translations of Augustine, Basil, and Ephraim into Italian were published at Brescia in 1566, his commentary on the Gospels at Brescia in 1567; his work on free will was *De Amore Erga Deum* (Brescia, 1572); see Bibl. Apost. Vat., Vat. Lat. 6149, fos. 1ʳ–14ᵛ, 156ʳ–160ʳ, for his work on the translation of Chrysostom.

[35] Bornato's work is discussed above, chs. 4, 5. The revised version of Folengo's commentary was *Joannis Baptistae Folengii ... monachi Casinatis ... in omnes Davidicos Psalmos doctissima ... commentaria, nunc recens studio atque opera monachorum ejusdem congregationis ... expurgata* (Rome, 1585).

[36] 'De Gratia', Bibl. Univ. Padua, MS 812, fos. 217ʳ–344ᵛ, esp. 224ʳ, 273ʳ; Armellini, *Bibl. Bened.-Cas.* i. 160–1.

Summa of Aquinas 'in terza rima divisa in otti canti', with a dialogue—a kind of theological musical which serves to symbolize the decline in the monastic scholarship of these cloisters.[37]

[37] Bibl. Apost. Vat., Vat. Lat. 10736; Armellini describes this rhyming *Summa* in *Bibl. Bened.-Cas.* ii. 121 ff.

Epilogue

AFTER the débâcle at the Council of Trent in 1546, the wealth and administration of the Congregation remained intact, but its spirituality began to change. Earlier generations of the order had built up the Congregation's Pauline and Antiochene theology, and during the heady years of the Reformation, from 1520 to 1546, they had forged it into something which might have cut through the knots of Latin theology. They believed that they could bypass the theological presuppositions common to all sides in the debate between Catholicism and Protestantism: their instrument for doing this lay in Greek patristic teachings—of which they had a knowledge unrivalled in western Christendom.

However, it was not to be. After 1546, when Rome had spoken, and the boundaries were drawn, and the rival faiths of Latin Christendom were defined, the Benedictines of Santa Giustina found themselves out in the cold, and their teachings now rejected. Their efforts to cure western schism with Greek theology had failed. One consequence of that failure was the weakening and eventual disappearance of their distinctive theological tradition. Another consequence, much worse, was the loss at Trent of the last hopes of ideological reconciliation in Christian Europe.

Bibliography

A. MANUSCRIPT SOURCES

Florence, Biblioteca Laurenziana, (i) Fondo Ashburnhamiani, MSS 140; 269; 1397; 1826; 1833; 1835; 1917. (ii) Fondo Conventi Soppressi, MSS 177 (2594); 85 (2656); 53 (2708); 151 (2712); 10 (2718); 73 (2722); 27 (2727); 21 (2732).

——, Biblioteca Nazionale, (i) Fondo Magliabechiano-Strozziana, MSS X (144); XXXVII (315); XXXVII (317). (ii) Fondo Conventi Soppressi, MSS B.5. 2582; A.3. 2601; C.4. 2659; D.7. 2879; D.8. 2738; D.8. 2778; E.3. 2736; E.6. 2700. (iii) Fondo Conventi Soppressi da Ordinare, MSS Badia 4; Badia 5; Badia 27; Badia 28; Badia 29. (iv) Fondo Principale, II.II (406).

Mantua, Biblioteca Comunale, MSS 49; 51; 63; 194; 255; 280; 281; 282; 317; 329; 395; 1360; 1361.

Oxford, Bodleian Library, MSS Lyall 77; Italiano C.25.

Padua, Biblioteca Universitaria, MSS 152; 427; 439; 503; 765; 812; 833; 1135; 1379 I, II.

Rome, Biblioteca Alessandrina, MSS 90 IIA, fos. 410^r–452^r; 91, fos. 887^r–907^r; 98, fos. 236^r–251^v.

Vatican, Biblioteca Apostolica Vaticana, (i) Fondo Vaticano Latino, 3961; 4712; 6149; 6207; 7928; 10907. (ii) Fondo Chigi, A IV 83; B IV 53; C V 146; I IV 148. (iii) Fondo Ottoboniano Latino, 896.

Venice, Biblioteca Marciana, MS 1809.

B. PRIMARY SOURCES IN PRINT

Aliotti, G., *Hieronymi Aliotti . . . Epistolae & opuscula, Gabrielis Mariae Scarmallii . . . notis, & observationibus illustrata etc.*, ed. G. B. Scarmalli (2 vols., Arezzo, 1769).

Annales Camaldulenses Ordinis Sancti Benedicti, eds. G. B. Mittarelli and A. Costadini (9 vols., Venice, 1755–77).

Aretino, P., *Lettere di M. Pietro Aretino* (6 vols., Paris, 1609).

——, *The Works of Aretino: Letters and Sonnets*, trans. S. Putnam (New York, 1933).

Armellini, M., *Bibliotheca Benedictino–Casinensis, sive Scriptorum Casinensis Congregationis, alias S. Justinae Patavinae etc.* (2 parts, Assisi, 1731–2).

——, *Catalogi Tres Episcoporum, Reformatorum et Virorum Sanctitate Illustrium e Congregatione Casinensi etc.* (4 parts, Assisi and Rome, 1733–4).

——, *Additiones, et correctiones Bibliothecae Benedictino–Casinensis etc.* (2 parts, Foligno, 1735–6).

Augustine of Hippo, *Augustine: Bishop of Hippo: Later Works*, trans. J. Burnaby, Library of Christian Classics, x (London, 1955).

Barbo, L., *De Initiis Congregationis Sanctae Justinae de Padua*, ed. G. Campeis (Padua, 1908).

Bembo, P., *Petri Bembi . . . opera in unam corpus collecta*, ed. A. Curione (3 tomes, Basle, 1567).

Benedetto da Mantova, *Trattato utilissimo del Beneficio di Iesu Christo Crocifisso* (Venice, 1543).

——, *Il Beneficio di Cristo: con le versioni del secolo xvi, documenti e testimonianze*, ed. S. Caponetto, Corpus Reformatorum Italicorum (Northern Illinois University Press and The Newberry Library, 1972).

Benedetto da Mantova, 'The Beneficio di Cristo translated, with an introduction', by Ruth Prelowski, *Italian Reformation Studies*, ed. J. A. Tedeschi (Florence, 1965), pp. 21–102.

de'Bianchi, Tommasino (T. de'Lancellotti), *Cronica modense*, Monumenta di Storia Patria delle Provincie Modenesi, vi, vii (Parma, 1868).

Bona, Ottavio (Teofilo da Brescia), *De Vita Solitaria* and *De Vita et Moribus Sancti Bernardi*, printed in one volume (Brescia, 1496).

Bornato, G., *De Libero Hominis Arbitrio. Opus vere Aureum pium et Catholicum* (Brescia, 1571).

Brebia, G., *Religioso monacho et sapienti* (Milan, 1477).

Bucelinus, G., *Annalium Benedictorum* (Veldkirch, 1665).

Bullarium Casinense, seu constitutiones summorum pontificum, imperatorum regum, principum et decreta sacrarum congregationum pro congregatione Casinensi, ed. C. Margarinus, i (Venice, 1650); ii (Todi, 1670).

Cajetan, Thomas de Vio, *Opuscula Omnia* (3 vols., Lyons, 1562).

Calendar of State Papers and Manuscripts, Relating to English Affairs, existing in the Archives and Collections of Venice, i, ed. Rawdon Brown (London, 1864).

Calvin, J., *De aeterna Dei praedestinatione qua in salutem alios ex hominibus elegit, alios suo exitio reliquit, item de providentia qua res humanas gubernat* (Geneva, 1552), printed in *Opera Calvini*, viii (*Corpus Reformatorum*, xxxvi, Berlin, 1870).

Calvin: Institutes of the Christian Religion, trans. F. L. Battles. Library of Christian Classics, xxi, xxii (Philadelphia, 1960).

Calvini, C., trans., *Sancti Dorothei Sermones XXI* (Venice, 1564).

Campanus, V., *Fasciculus Myrrhae in quo vita Christi secundum literam novi testamenti describatur . . . cum nonnullis expositionibus* (Naples, 1521).

——, *Collyrium mentis seu Commentaria de nominibus Christi* (Naples, 1562).

Camerarius, B., *Bartholomaei Camerarii, Beneventani, De Praedestinatione, dialogi tre* (Paris, 1556).

Catalogi Codicum Casinensium Antique (saec. viii–xv), ed. M. Inguanez, Miscellanea Cassinese, xxi (Montecassino, 1941).

Cavacius, J., *Historiarum Coenobii D. Iustinae Patavinae libri sex* (Venice, 1606).

Chabod, F., *Per la storia religiosa dello stato di Milano durante il dominio di Carlo V. Note e documenti* (Rome, 1936).

Chiari, I., *Isidori Clarii . . . epistolae ad amicos, . . . ex autographo descriptos . . . accedunt duo opuscula alia*, ed. J. Olgiato (Modena, 1705).

——, *Isidori Clarii . . . ad eos, qui a communi Ecclesiae sententia discessere adhortatio ad concordiam* (Milan, 1540).

——, *De Modo Divitiis Adhibendo Homini Christiano ad Cives Brixianos Salutaris Oratio* (Milan, 1540).

——, *Novi Testamenti vulgata quidem aeditio; sed quae ad vetustissimorum utriusque linguae exemplarium fidem, nunc demum emendata est . . . adiectis scholiis etc.* (Venice, 1541).

——, *Aeditio Veteris ac Novi Testamenti, quorum alterum ad Hebraicam, alteram ad Graecam, veritatem emendatum est diligentissime* (Venice, 1542).

——, *Isidori Clarii Fulgin. Episcopi Sententia de Iustificatione hominis, in conventu Patrum Tridentini Concilii, dicta* (Venice, 1548).

——, *Voten des Abtes Isidor Clarius vom Trienter Konzil*, ed. J. Hefner (Würzburg, 1912).

——, *Isidori Clarii . . . in Evangelium secundum Lucam orationes quinquaginta quattor* (Venice, 1565).

——, *Isidori Clarii . . . in Sermonem Domini in Monte habitum secundum Matthaeum, orationes sexaginta novem ad populum* (Venice, 1566).

——, *Isidori Clarii Orationum quas extraordinarias appellavit volumen primum* (Venice, 1567).

Chrysostom, John, *Divi Ioannis Chrysostomi Episcopi Constantinopolitani Opera* (Basle, 1530).

——, *Divi Ioannis Chrysostomi Episcopi Constantinopolitani Homiliae XXX ad Populum Antiochenum potissimum habitae Bernardo Brixiano interprete* (Basle, 1539).

——, *The Homilies of St. John Chrysostom . . . on the Epistle . . . to the Romans*, trans. J. B. Morris, Select Library of the Nicene and Post-Nicene Fathers, xi (1889).

——, *Saint John Chrysostom. Six Books on the Priesthood*, trans. G. Neville (London, 1964).

Chronicon Casinese (Venice, 1513).

Cittadella, L. N., *Notizie relative a Ferrara, per la maggior parte inedite, ricavate da documenti ed illustrate* (Ferrara, 1864).

Codicum Casinensium Manuscriptorum Catalogus, iii, ed. M. Inguanez (Montecassino, 1940–1).

Concilium Basiliense: Studien und Quellen zur Geschichte des Concils von Basel, ed. J. Haller, viii (Basle, 1936).

Concilium Tridentinum: Diariorum, Actorum, Epistolarum, Tractatuum Nova Collectio, ed. S. Merkle *et al.* (Frieburg-im-Breisgau, 1901–).

Congregationis S. Justinae de Padua O.S.B.: Ordinationes Capitulorum Generalium, ed. T. Leccisotti (2 vols., Montecassino, 1939, 1970).

Cortese, G., *Gregorii Cortesii Card. Omnia quae huc usque colligi potuerunt, sive ab eo scripta, sive ad illum spectantia,* ed. A. Cominus (Padua, 1774).

——, *Gregorii Cortesii Mutinensis S.R. Ecclesiae Cardinalis Epistolarum Familiarum Liber* (Venice, 1573).

——, *Decreta Sacrosancti Oecumenici et generalis concilii Tridentini* (Bologna, 1548).

Erasmus, D., *Desiderii Erasmi Roterodami Opera Omnia* (10 vols., Leiden, 1703–6).

Egger, F., *Idea Ordinis Hierarchico–Benedictini* (Constance, 1717).

Fascitello, H., *Honorati Fascitelli Aeserniensis Opera,* ed. G. V. Meola (Naples, 1776).

Faucher, D., *Chronologia Sanctorum et aliorum Virorum Illustrium ac Abbatum Sacrae Insulae Lerensis,* ed. V. Barrali Salerno (Lyons, 1603), part (ii), 222–372.

Ferrai, L. A., 'La Biblioteca di Santa Giustina di Padova' in G. Mazzatinti, *Inventario dei Manoscritti Italiani delle Biblioteche di Francia* (Rome, 1887), ii. 549–661.

Folengo, G.-B. and T., *Ioan. Bapti. Chrysogoni Folengii Mantuani Anchoritae Varium Peoma, et IANUS* (n.p., 1534?).

Folengo, G.-B., *Ioan. Baptistae Folengii Mantuani, Monachi Divi Benedicti, in Psalmos Commentaria, quibus permulta quae hodie passim controversa sunt, tanta pietate gravitateq(ue) deciduntur, ut nullus tam iniquus esse volet, quin se ex harum lectione longe meliorem doctioremq(ue) factum agnoscat* (Basle, 1540).

——, *Commentaria in Primam, D. Ioannis Epistolam, Io. Baptista Folengio Monacho Mantuano Auctore* (Venice, 1546).

——, *In Psalterium Davidis Israelitarum Regis et Vatis Divinissimi Ioan. Baptistae Folengii Mantuani Monachi Cassinatis Commentarii . . . ex ipsa Hebraica Veritate Confecti et Absoluti* (Basle, 1549).

Folengo, T., *Le maccherone,* ed. A. Luzi (Bari, 1927–8).

——, *Folengo, Aretino, Doni: tome I, Opere di Teofilo Folengo,* ed. C. Cordié. La Letterature Italiana. Storie e Testi, xxvi, tome 1 (Milan and Naples, 1977).

——, *Opera italiane,* ed. U. Renda, i, ii (Bari, 1911–12).

Fontana, B., 'Documenti Vaticani contro l'eresia luterana in Italia', *Archivio della Reale Società Romana di Storia Patria,* xv (1892), 71–165, 364–474.

Giacone, F., and Bedouelle, G., 'Une lettre de Gilles de Viterbe

(1469–1532) à Jacques Lefèvre d'Étaples (c.1460–1536) au sujet de l'affair Reuchlin', *Bibliothèque d'Humanisme et Renaissance*, xxxvi (1974), 335–45.

Jedin, H., 'Contarini und Camaldoli', *Archivio italiano per la storia della pietà*, ii (1959), 51–117.

Kristeller, P. O., and Granz, F. E., *Catalogus Translationum et Commentariorum* (Catholic University Press of America, ii, 1971), 140–75.

Lauchert, F., *Die italienischen literarischen Gegner Luthers* (Freiburg-im-Breisgau, 1912).

Leccisotti, T., 'Tracce di correnti mistiche cinquecentesche nel codice cassinese 584', *Archivio italiano per la storia della pietà* iv (1965), 1–120.

——, 'Documenti per l'Annessione di Montecassino alla Congregazione di S. Giustina, *Benedictina*, xvii, (1970), 59–91.

de Leva, G., *Storia documentata di Carlo V* (5 vols., Venice, 1867).

Longolio, C., *Christophori Longolii Epistolarum* (Lyons, 1563).

Martene, R., and Durand, U., *Veterum Scriptorum et Monumentorum, Historicorum, Dogmaticorum, Moralium, amplissima Collectio*, ix (Paris, 1733).

Melanchthon and Bucer, ed. W. Pauck, The Library of Christian Classics, xix (London, 1969).

Minozzi, G., *Montecassino nella storia del Rinascimento* (Rome, 1925).

Miscellanea Cassinese, ossia nuovi contributi alla storia, alle scienze e arti religiose raccolti, e illustrati (Montecassino, 1897–).

Missale monasticum s(ecundu)m more(m) ritu(m) Casinensis Congregationis al(ias) Sanctae Justinae (Venice, 1515).

de Montfaucon, B., *Bibliotheca Bibliothecarum Manuscriptorum Nova* (2 vols., Paris, 1739), i.

Monumenta S. Patrum Orthodoxgrapha, ed. J. J. Grynaeus (Basle, n.d., but 1569).

Morris, H., *Cartulaire de L'Abbaye de Lérins* (2 vols., Paris, 1905).

Oberman, H. A., *Forerunners of the Reformation, The Shape of Late Medieval Thought* (London, 1967).

Ochino, B., *Responsio Bernardi Ochini senensis ad Marcum Brixiensem* (Geneva, 1543).

Opusculi e lettere riformatori italiani del Cinquecento, ed. G. Paladino, Scrittori d'Italia, 58, 99 (2 vols., Bari, 1913–27).

degli Ottoni, L., *Divi Ioannis Christostomi in Apostoli Pauli Epistolam ad Romanos Commentaria: Luciano mantuano divi Benedicti monacho interprete, et in eos, qui eundem Chrysostomum divinam extenuasse gratiam arbitriique libertatem supra modum extullise suspicantur, et accusant, defensore* (Brescia, 1538).

Pars Prima: Constitutionum Congregationis Casinensis, alias Sanctae Justinae per Directionem Regiminis et Regularis Observantiae dictae Congregationis (n.p., n.d. but probably Florence, 1515).

Pellikan, C., *Das Chronikon des Konrad Pellikan*, ed. B. Riggenbach (Basle, 1877).

Pole, R., *Epistolae Reginaldi Poli S.R.E. Cardinalis et Aliorum ad Ipsum* ed. A. M. Quirini (5 vols., Brescia, 1744–57).

Puccinelli, P., *Chronicon insignis monasterii DD. Petri et Pauli de Glaxiate Mediolani* (Milan, 1655).

——, *Cronica dell'Abbadia di Fiorenza* (Milan, 1664).

Raphael of Piacenza, *Armeniados* (Cremona, 1518).

I regesti dell'archivio: abbazia di Montecassino, Ministero dell'Interno. Pubblicazioni degli archivi di stato, ed. T. Leccisotti, viii (Rome, 1973).

Regula SS. Benedicti, Basilii, Augustini, Francisci, cum vitis, epistolis, expositionibus etc. Coll. et ordinata per Jo. F. Brixianum, monachum congregationis S. Justine O.S.B. de observantia (Venice, 1500, and Paris, 1514).

Sadoleto, J., *Opera quae extant, omnia ad Eloquentiam, Philosophiam ac Theologiam pertinentia* (2nd edn., Verona, 1737–8).

Sangrino, A., *In Psalterium Davidis Regis et Prophetae clarissimi. Paraphrasis . . . Angelo Sangrino Abbate Casinensi Autore* (Basle, 1561).

——, *Poesis Christiana* (Padua, 1565).

Savonarola, G. M., *Libellus de Magnificis Ornamentis Regie Civitatis Padue*, ed. A. Segarizzi, Rerum Italicorum Scriptores, xxiv, part 15 (Città di Castello, 1902).

Siculo, G., *Espositione nel nono, decimo e undecimo capo della Epistola di San Paolo al li Romani* (Bologna, 1550).

——, *Epistola di Giorgio Siculo servo fidele di Jesu Christo alli cittadini di Riva di Trento contra il mendatio di Francesco Spiera, e falsa dottrina di Protestanti* (Bologna, 1550).

Simon, R., *A Critical History of the Text of the New Testament* trans. R. Taylor (London, 1689).

——, *Bibliothèque critique ou recueil de diverses pièces critiques* (Amsterdam, 1708).

Sixtus Senensis, O.P., *Bibliotheca Sancta* (Lyons, 1575).

de Soto, D., *In Epistolam divi Pauli ad Romanos Commentarii* (Antwerp, 1550).

Tornabene, F., *Catalogo ragionato delle edizioni del secolo XV e de' manoscritti che si conservano nella biblioteca de' Benedittini Casinese in Catania* (Catania, 1846).

Ugonius, F., *Flavii Alexii Ugonii . . . De maximis Italiae atque Graeciae calamitatibus etc.* (Venice, 1559).

Valdés, J., *Divine Considerations*, trans. N. Ferrar (Oxford, 1638, repr. London, 1905–6?).

——, *Alfabeto Christiano*, ed. and trans. B. B. Wiffen (London, 1861).

Valdés, J., *Diálogo de Doctrina Christiana*, ed. B. F. Stockwell (Buenos Aires, Mexico, 1946).

Vincenzo of Milan, *De Maximis Christi Beneficiis Pia Gratiarum Actio, ex utroque Testamento Compendiose Collecta, Piis & Catholicis Dedicata* (Naples, 1568).

La vita del Beato Ieronomo Savonarola scritta da un anonimo del secolo XVI, ed. P. G. Conti (Florence, 1937).

Wion, A., *Lignum Vitae* (Venice, 1595).

Zabarella, F., *Consilia eminentissimi . . . interpretis D. Francisci Zabarellae Patritii Patavini Cardinalis Florentini* (Venice, 1581).

Ziegelbaur, M., *Centifolium Camaldulense* (Venice, 1750).

——, *Historia rei literariae ordinis S. Benedicti* (4 vols., Augsburg, 1754).

C. SECONDARY SOURCES

Anderson, M. W., 'Biblical Humanism and Catholic Reform: 1444–1563' (Aberdeen Univ. Ph.D. thesis, 1964).

——, 'Gregorio Cortese and Roman Catholic Reform', *Sixteenth Century Essays and Studies*, ed. C. S. Meyer, i (1970), 75–106.

——, *Peter Martyr: A Reformer in Exile (1542–1562). A Chronology of Biblical Writings in England and Europe*, Biblioteca Humanistica et Reformatorica, x (Nieuwkoop, 1975).

Avagliano, F., 'Inni dell'Abate Sangrino in Onore dei primi quattro Abati Cavenis', *Benedictina*, xvi (1969), 24–46.

Bainton, R. H., *Bernardino Ochino esule e riformatore senese del Cinquecento, 1487–1563* (Florence, 1940).

Bakhuizen van den Brink, J. N., *Juan de Valdés, réformateur en Espagne et en Italie* (Geneva, 1969).

Battistella, A., *Processi d'eresia nel Collegio di Spagna (1553–1554). Episodio della storia della riforma in Bologna* (Bologna, 1901).

Beccadelli, L., *Monumenti di varia letteratura tratti dai manoscritti di Monsignor Lodovico Beccadelli* (Bologna, 1797–9).

de Beer, K., *Studie over de spiritualiteit van Geert Groote* (Brussel Nijmegen, 1938).

Bellodi, R., *Il monastero di San Benedetto in Polirone nella storia e nell'arte* (Mantua, 1905).

Benedini, B., *I manoscritti polironiani della Biblioteca Comunale di Mantova*, Atti e memorie, nuova serie, xxx (Mantua, 1958).

Billanovich, G., *Tra Don Teofilo Folengo e Merlin Cocaio* (Naples, 1948).

Biondi, A., 'La giustificazione della simulazione nel Cinquecento', *Eresia e riforma nell'Italia del Cinquecento*, Biblioteca del Corpus Reformatorum Italicorum, Miscellanea I (1974), 5–68.

Blum, L., *La Biblioteca della Badia Fiorentina e i codici di Antonio Corbinelli*, Studi e Testi, clv (Biblioteca Apostolica Vaticana, 1951).

Bonora, E., and Chiesa, M. (eds.), *Cultura letteraria e tradizione popolare in Teofilo Folengo* (Milan, 1979).

Bozza, T., *Introduzione al Beneficio di Cristo* (privately printed, Rome, 1963).

——, *Nuovi studi sulla riforma in Italia, I, Il Beneficio di Cristo*, Uomini e Dottrine, xxii (Leiden, 1976).

Brotto, G., and Zonta, G., *La facoltà teologica dell'Università di Padova*, (Padua, 1922).

Buschbell, G., *Reformation und Inquisition in Italien um die Mitte des XVI Jahrhunderts*, Quellen und Forschungen aus dem Gebeite der Geschichte, xiii (Paderborn, 1910).

Butler, C., *Western Mysticism* (London, 1926).

Cantimori, D., *Eretici italiani del Cinquecento* (Florence, 1939).

——, *Prospettive di storia ereticale del Cinquecento* (Bari, 1960).

Cantoni Alzati, G., *La Biblioteca di S. Giustina di Padova. Libri e cultura presso i benedettini padovani in età umanistica*, Medioevo e Umanesimo, xlviii (Padua, 1982).

Cantù, C., *Gli eretici d'Italia* (3 vols., Turin, 1865–7).

Capelle, B., 'Le rôle theologique de Bède le Vénérable', *Studia Anselmiana*, vi (1936), 1–40.

Caponetto, S., 'Origini e caratteri della Riforma in Sicilia', *Rinascimento*, vii (1956), 219–341.

——, 'Benedetto da Mantova', *Dizionario biografico degli italiani*, viii (Rome, 1966), 437–41.

della Casa, G., *Gasparis Contarini Vita*, in *Opere di Monsig. Giovanni della Casa con una copiosa giunta di scritture non più stampate* (3 vols., Florence, 1707).

Casadei, A., 'Fanino Fanini da Faenza', *Nuova rivista storica*, xviii (1934), 168–99.

Cessi, R., 'Paolinismo preluterano', *Rendiconti dell'Accademia Nazionale dei Lincei. Classi di scienze morali, storiche e filologiche* Ser. VIII, xii (1957), 3–30.

Comba, E., *I nostri protestanti* (2 vols., Florence, 1897).

Continelli, G., *Il Baldus di Merlin Cocaio* (Città di Castello, 1904).

Cracco, G., 'La Fondazione dei Canonici Secolari di San Giorgio in Alga', *Rivista di storia della chiesa in Italia*, xiii (1959), 70–81.

Damerini, G., *L'Isola e il Cenobio di S. Giorgio Maggiore* (Venice, 1956; 2nd edn. 1969).

Daniélou, J., *Platonisme et théologie mystique* (Paris, 1944).

De la Mare, A., *Catalogue of the collection of medieval manuscripts bequeathed to the Bodleian Library, Oxford, by James P. R. Lyall, compiled by Albinia de la Mare* (Oxford, 1971).

Dittrich, F., *Gasparo Contarini, 1483–1542* (Braunsberg, 1885).

Douglas, R. W., *Jacopo Sadoleto (1477–1547): Humanist and Reformer* (Cambridge, Mass., 1959).

Eubel, C., *Hierarchia Catholica Medii Aevi*, ii, iii, iv (Münster, 1901–).

Evennett, H. O., 'Three Benedictine Abbots at the Council of Trent, 1545–1547', *Studia Monastica*, i (1959), 343–77.

——, *The Spirit of the Counter-Reformation* (Cambridge, 1968).

Faralli, C., 'Per una biografia di Luciano degli Ottoni', *Bollettino della Società di Studi Valdesi*, cxxxiv (1973), 34–51.

——, 'Una Polemica all'epoca del Concilio di Trento: il Teologo e Giurista Domingo de Soto censura un'opera del Benedettino Luciano degli Ottoni', *Studi senesi*, lxxxvii (3rd series, xxiv, 1975), 400–19.

Federici, F., *Della Biblioteca di S. Giustina di Padova, dissertazione storica con note biografiche* (Padua, 1815).

Fenlon, D., *Heresy and Obedience in Tridentine Italy* (Cambridge, 1972).

Fontana, B., *Renata di Francia, duchessa di Ferrara. Sui documenti dell'archivio Estense etc.* (3 vols., Rome, 1889–99).

Frizzi, A., *Memorie per la storia di Ferrara raccolte da A.F.* (5 vols., 2nd edn., Ferrara, 1847–50), iv.

Garin, E., *La cultura filosofica del Rinascimento Italiano* (Florence, 1954).

Garufi, C. A., 'Contributo alla storia dell'Inquisizione in Sicilia nei secoli XVI e XVII. Note e appunti degli Archivi di Spagna', *Archivio storico siciliano* (1914), 264–329; (1916), 304–89; (1917), 389–465.

Gattola, E., *Historia Abbatiae Cassinensis, per saeculorum seriem distributa* (Venice, 1733).

Gill, J., *Eugenius IV: Pope of Christian Union* (London, 1961).

Gilson, E. H., *Jean Duns Scotus: introduction à ses positions fondamentales* (Paris, 1952).

Ginzburg, C., 'Due Note sul Profetismo Cinquecentesco', *Rivista storica italiana*, lxxviii (1966), 184–207, 212–27.

——, *Il Nicodemismo: Simulazione e dissimulazione religiosa nell' Europa del'500* (Turin, 1970).

Ginzburg, C., and Prosperi, A., 'Le Due Redazioni del "Beneficio di Cristo"', *Eresia e riforma nell'Italia del Cinquecento*, Biblioteca del Corpus Reformatorum Italicorum, Miscellanea I (1974), 137–204.

——, *Giochi di Pazienza: un seminario sul Beneficio di Cristo* (Turin, 1975).

Goffis, C. F., *L'eterodossia dei Fratelli Folengo* (Genoa, 1950).

Gorce, D., 'La Patristique dans la Réforme d'Erasme', *Festgabe Joseph Lortz, I, Reformation, Schicksal und Auftrag*, eds. E. Iserloh and P. Manns (Baden-Baden, 1958), 233–76.

Gradenigo, G. A., 'Memorie Intorno a Giovanni Cornaro', *Nuova raccolta d'opusculi scientifici e filogici*, ed. A. Calogierà (Venice, 1755–84), ii. 262–95.

———, 'Memorie istorico-critiche intorno la vita e gli scritti di Dionysio Faucher monaco benedettino-cassinese', *Nuova raccolta d'opuscoli scientifici e filogici*, ed. A. Calogierà (Venice, 1755–84), v. 257–302.

Grendler, P. F., *The Roman Inquisition and the Venetian Press, 1540–1605* (Leiden, 1977).

Gussago, G. J., *Biblioteca Clarense* (2 vols., Chiari, 1832).

Heath, P., Review of T. N. Tentler, *Sin and Confession on the Eve of the Reformation*, *Journal of Ecclesiastical History*, xxx (1979), 103–4.

Inguanez, M., 'Il venerabile Beda nei codici e negli scrittori cassinese medievali', *Studia Anselmiana*, vi (1936), 41–50.

Intra, G. B., 'Il Museo, statuario e la Biblioteca di Mantova', *Archivio Storico Lombardo*, a. (1881), fasc. i, pp. 123 ff.

Jacobilli, L., *Vite de' santi e beati di Foligno* (Foligno, 1628).

Jedin, H., *Papal Legate at the Council of Trent: Cardinal Seripando* (London, 1947).

———, *A History of the Council of Trent* (2 vols., London, 1957 and 1961).

———, 'Gasparo Contarini e il Contributo Veneziano alla Riforma Cattolica', *La civiltà veneziana del Rinascimento* (Florence, 1958), 103–24.

Jones, P. J., 'From Manor to Mezzadria: a Tuscan Case Study in the Medieval Origins of Modern Agrarian Society', *Florentine Studies: Politics and Society in Renaissance Florence*, ed. N. Rubinstein (London, 1968), 193–241.

Jung, E. M., 'On the Nature of Evangelism in Sixteenth-Century Italy', *Journal of the History of Ideas*, xiv (1953), 511–27.

Kaulen, F., *Geschichte der Vulgata* (Mainz, 1868).

Knowles, D., *Christian Monasticism* (New York, 1969).

Kristeller, P. O., *Supplementum Ficinianum* (2 vols., Florence, 1937), ii.

———, Studies on Renaissance Humanism During the Last Twenty Years', *Studies in the Renaissance*, ix (1962), 7–30.

———, 'The Humanist Bartolomeo Facio and his Unknown Correspondence', *From the Renaissance to the Counter-Reformation: Essays in Honor of Garrett Mattingly*, ed. C. H. Carter (New York, 1965), 56–74.

———, 'Augustine and the Early Renaissance', *Studies in Renaissance Thought and Letters* (Rome, 1956 and 1959), 355–72.

———, 'The Contribution of the Religious Orders to Renaissance Thought and Learning', *American Benedictine Review*, xxi (1970), 1–55.

———, *Medieval Aspects of Renaissance Learning* (Duke University Press, 1974).

———, *Iter Italicum* (London, 1963–).

Lauchert, F., 'Der italienische Benedictiner Isodorus Clarius und seine schrift für den religiosen Frieden', *Studien und Mittheilungen aus dem Benediktiner-Orden*, xxviii (1908), 613–17.

Labalme, P. H., *Bernardo Giustiniani: A Venetian of the Quattrocento*, Uomini e dottrine, xiii (Leiden, 1969).

Laprat, R., 'Commenda', *Dictionnaire de droit canonique* (Paris, 1924–35), fasc. xvii, pp. 1029–85.

Leccisotti, T., 'La congregazione benedettina di S. Giustina e la riforma della chiesa', *Archivo della Società Romana di Storia Patria*, lxvii, (1944), 451–69.

——, 'Montecassino agli inizi del Cinquecento', *Benedictina*, anno ii (1948), 75–94.

——, 'Sull'organizzazione della Congregazione "De Unitate"', *Benedictina*, ii (1948), 237–43.

Leclercq, J., *Un Humaniste ermite: le Bienheureux Paul Giustiniani (1476–1528)* (Rome, 1951).

——, *The Love of Learning and the Desire for God*, trans. C. Misrahi (New York, 1974).

Levi, A. H. T., Introduction to *Praise of Folly and Letter to Martin Dorp* (Penguin Books, 1971).

Logan, O. M. T., 'Grace and justification: some Italian views of the sixteenth and early seventeenth centuries', *Journal of Ecclesiastical History*, xx (1969), 67–78.

——, 'The Ideal of the Bishop and the Venetian Patriarcate: c1430–c1630', *Journal of Ecclesiastical History*, xxix (1978), 415–50.

Luzio, A., *Studi folenghiani* (Florence, 1899).

McConica, J. K., 'Erasmus and the Grammar of Consent', *Scrinium Erasmianum* (Leiden, 1969), ii, 77–99.

McNair, P., *Peter Martyr in Italy: an anatomy of apostasy* (Oxford, 1967).

de Maio, R., *Savonarola e la curia romana*, Uomini e dottrina, xv (Rome, 1969).

Marani, A., 'Il Clario e la Residenza dei Vescovi', *Brixia Sacra, Memorie Storiche della Diocese di Brescia*, a. vii (1972), 114–21.

Marchetti, V., 'Bartolomeo Camerario', *Dizionario biografico degli italiani*, xvii (1974), 172–4.

Martin, F. X., 'Egidio di Viterbo, 1469–1518' (Cambridge Ph.D. thesis, 1958).

——, 'The Augustinian Order on the eve of the Reformation', *Miscellanea Historiae Ecclesiasticae*, ii, Bibliothèque de la Revue d'histoire ecclésiastique, fasc. 44 (Louvain, 1967), pp. 71–104.

Maselli, D., 'Per la storia religiosa dello stato di Milano durante il dominio di Filippo II: l'eresia e la sua repressione dal 1555 al 1584', *Nuova rivista storica*, liv (1970), 317–73.

Matheson, P., *Cardinal Contarini at Regensburg* (Oxford, 1972).

Menegazzo, E., 'Contributo alla biografia del Folengo', *Italia medioevale e umanistica*, ii (1959), 367–408.

——, 'Pomposa nella Congregazione Benedettina Riformata di Santa Giustina, poi Cassinese', *Analecta Pomposiana*, i (1965).

——, 'Per la Conoscenza della Riforma in Italia. Note d'Archivio', *Atti e memori dell'Accademia Patavina di Scienze, Lettere ed Arti*, xc, part 3 (1977–8), 193–216.

Meneghin, V., *S. Michele in Isola di Venezia* (2 vols., Venice, 1962).

Mercati, G., *Ultimi contributi alla storia degli umanisti: fasc. I: Traversariana*, Studi e Testi, xc (Vatican, 1939).

Messedaglia, L., 'Varietà e curiosità folenghiane', *Atti della Accademia Pontaniana*, new series, ii (1948–9), 153–78; iii (1949–50), 267–95; iv (1950–2), 165–94.

Meyendorff, J., *Byzantine Theology: Historical trends and doctrinal themes* (New York, 1974).

Meyvaert, P., *Benedict, Gregory, Bede and Others* (London, 1977).

Moorman, J., *A History of the Franciscan Order from its Origins to the Year 1517* (Oxford, 1968).

di Napoli, G., *Giovanni Pico della Mirandola e la problematica dottrinale del suo tempo*, Collectio Philosophica Lateranensis, viii (Rome, 1965).

——, *Studi sul Rinascimento* (Naples, 1973).

New Catholic Encyclopedia (17 vols., New York, 1967–79).

Nieto, J. C., *Juan de Valdés and the Origins of the Spanish and Italian Reformation* (Geneva, 1970).

Novelli, L., 'La Badia del Monte prima e durante il passaggio nella Congregazione di S. Giustina di Padova', *Benedictina*, xv (1968), 240–86.

O'Malley, J. W., *Giles of Viterbo on Church and Reform: a Study in Renaissance Thought*, Studies in Medieval and Reformation Thought, v (Leiden, 1968).

Oberman, H. A., *The Harvest of Medieval Theology. Gabriel Biel and Late Medieval Nominalism* (Harvard, 1963).

Ossola, C., 'Tradizione e traduzione dell'"Evangelio di San Matteo" di Juan de Valdés, *Eresia e Riforma nell'Italia del Cinquecento*, Biblioteca del Corpus Reformatorum Italicorum, Miscellanea I (1974), 7–68.

Pantoni, A., 'Asceti Penitenti e Mistici della Congregazione Cassinese nei Secoli xvi–xviii', *Benedictina*, xvi (1969), 244–82.

Pantoni, A., ed., *Le Vicende della Basilica di Montecassino*, Miscellanea Cassinese xxxvi (Montecassino, 1973).

Paoli, C., and Enrico, R., *I codici Ashburnhamiani della Biblioteca Medicea Laurenziana di Firenze*, Indici e Cataloghi, viii (Rome, 1887).

Paquier, J., 'Un essai de théologie platonicienne à la renaissance: le commentaire de Giles de Viterbe sur le premier livre des Sentences', *Recherches de science religieuse*, xiii (1923), 293–312, 419–36.

Paschini, P., *Pier Paolo Vergerio il giovane e la sua apostasia* (Rome, 1925).

Pastor, L., *The History of the Popes*, xii, ed. R. F. Kerr (London, 1912).
Penco, G., *Storia del monachesimo in Italia dalle origini alla fine del Medio Evo* (Rome, 1961).
——, 'Il Primo Monastero Cassinese di Genova: S. Niccolò del Boschetto', *Benedictina*, xix (1972), 415–30.
——, *Storia della chiesa in Italia* (Milan, 1977).
Pepi, R., *La Basilica di S. Giustina in Padova, storia e arte* (Padua, 1970).
Pergamo, B., 'I Francescani alla Facoltà Teologica di Bologna (1364–1500)', *Archivum Franciscanum Historicum*, liii (1960), 361–441.
Perini, L., 'Ancora sul libraio-tipografico Pietro Perna e su alcune figure di eretici italiani in rapporto con lui negli anni 1549–1555', *Nuova rivista storica*, li (1967), 363–404.
Pesce, L., *Ludovico Barbo, vescovo di Treviso, 1437–1443*, Italia Sacra, ix, x (Padua, 1969).
Picasso, G. M., 'Gli Studi nella Riforma di Ludovico Barbo', *Los monjes y los estudios* (Abadia di Poblet, 1963), 295–324.
——, 'L'Imitazione di Cristo nell'Epoca della "Devotio Moderna" e nella Spiritualità Monastica del Secolo XV in Italia', *Rivista di storia e letteratura religiosa*, iv (1968), 11–32.
Piovene, G., 'Anacronismo della Venezia quattrocentesca', *La civiltà veneziana del Quattrocento*, ed. G. C. Sansoni (Florence, 1956), 3–21.
Pitigliani, R., *Il Venerabile Ludovico Barbo e la diffusione dell' Imitazione di Cristo per opera della Congregazione di Santa Giustina* (Padua, 1943).
Post, R. R., *The Modern Devotion*, Studies in Medieval and Reformation Thought, iii (Leiden, 1968).
Pratesi, A., 'Ludovico Barbo', *Dizionario Biografico degli Italiani*, vi (1964), 244–9.
Prevedello, G., *Santa Giustina Martire de Padova: note biografiche* (Padua, 1972).
Primiani, L., *Note storiche-critiche su Onorato Fascitelli* (Campobosso, 1897).
Prosperi, A., *Tra evangelismo e controriforma: G.M. Giberti (1495–1543)*, Uomini e Dottrine, xvi (Rome, 1969).
——, 'Una cripto-ristampa dell'Epistola di Giorgio Siculo', *Bollettino della Società di Studi Valdesi*, cxxxiv (1973), 52–68.
——, 'Un gruppo ereticale italo-spagnolo: la setta di Giorgio Siculo', *Critica storica*, anno 9, iii (1982), 337–51.
——, 'Lutero al Concilio di Trento', *Lutero in Italia*, ed. L. Perrone (Turin, 1983), 97–114.
(For A. Prosperi, also see C. Ginzburg)
Ragni, L., 'La proprietà fondiaria del monastero di San Benedetto in Polirone nei secoli xii–xiii' *Nuova rivista storica*, liv (1970), 561–80.
Raitt, J., 'Calvin's Use of Bernard of Clairvaux' *Archiv für Reformationsgeschichte*, lxxii (1981), 98–121.

Ravegnani, G., *Le biblioteche del monastero di San Giorgio Maggiore*, Civiltà Veneziana Saggi, xix (Venice, 1976).

Reusch, H., *Der Index der verbotenen Bücher* (2 vols., Bonn, 1983).

Rodocanachi, E., *La Réforme en Italie* (2 vols., Paris, 1920).

Rogness, M., *Philip Melanchthon, Reformer Without Honor* (Minneapolis, 1969).

Rosa, M., 'Il Beneficio di Christo: Interpretazioni a Confronto', *Bibliothèque d'humanisme et renaissance*, xl (1978), 609–20.

Rossi, P., 'The Legacy of Raymond Lull in the 16th century', *Medieval and Renaissance Studies* (The Warburg Institute, London, 1961), 182–213.

Rotondò, A., 'Per la storia dell'eresia a Bologna nel secolo XVI', *Rinascimento*, ser. 2, ii (1962), 107–54.

——, 'Atteggiamenti della vita morale italiana del Cinquecento: la pratica nicodemitica', *Rivista storica Italiana*, lxxix (1967), 991–1030.

Rovira Belloso, J. M., *Trento: una interpretacion Teologica* (Colectanea San Paciano, xxv (Barcelona, 1979).

Sambin, P., 'Sulla Riforma dell'Ordine Benedettino promossa da S. Giustina di Padova', with 'Schede per la Biografia di Ludovico Barbo', *Ricerche di storia monastica medioevale* (Padua, 1959), 61–122.

——, 'Marginalia su Ludovico Barbo', *Rivista di storia della chiesa in Italia*, ix (1955), 249–58.

Sarpo, P., *Istoria del Concilio Tridentino*, ed. G. Gambarin (Bari, 1935).

Scarinci, L., *Giustizia primitiva e peccato originale secondo Ambrogio Catarino*, *O.P.*, Studia Anselmiana, xvii (Vatican, 1947).

Schiapparelli, L., *Le carte del monastero di S. Maria di Fiorenze (Badia)* (Rome, 1913).

Schmitz, P., *Histoire de l'Ordre de Saint Benoît* (7 vols., Gemblous, 1942–56), iv, v.

Schnitzer, J., *Peter Delfin: General des Camaldulenserordens (1444–1525)* (Munich, 1926).

——, *Savonarola* (Milan, 1931).

Schutte, A. J., *Pier Paolo Vergerio: the making of an Italian Reformer*, Travaux d'Humanisme et Renaissance, clx (Geneva, 1977).

Simoncelli, P., 'Nuove Ipotesi e studi sull'Beneficio di Cristo', *Critica Storica*, new series, ii–iv (1975), 144–212.

——, *Il caso Reginald Pole*, Uomini e Dottrine, xxiii (Rome, 1977).

Somigli, C., *Un amico dei greci: Ambrogio Traversari* (Arezzo, 1964).

Steinmetz, D. C., *Misericordia Dei*, Studies in Medieval and Reformation Thought, iv (Leiden, 1968).

Stella, A., 'La lettera del Cardinale Contarini sulla Predestinazione', *Rivista di storia della chiesa in Italia*, xv (1961), 411–441.

Stinger, C. L., *Humanism and the Church Fathers: Ambrogio Traversari*

(1386–1439), and the Revival of Patristic Theology in the Early Italian Renaissance (New York, 1977).

Tassi, I., 'La crisi della Congregazione di S. Giustina tra il 1419 e il 1431', *Benedictina*, v (1951), 95–111.

——, *Ludovico Barbo (1381–1443)* (Rome, 1952).

Tentler, T. N., *Sin and Confession on the Eve of the Reformation* (Princeton, 1977).

Tiraboschi, G., *Storia della letteratura italiana*, vii (Modena, 1791), 346–9.

Tommasini, G. F., *Bibliotheca Patavina MS Publicae ac Privatae quibus diversi scriptores hactenus Incogniti Recensentur ac Illustrantur Studio et Opera* (Utini, 1639).

Trifone, B., *Annales Ordinis Sancti Benedicti, 1909* (Subiaco, 1910).

Trolese, F. G., 'Ludovico Barbo, 1381–1443, e la Congregazione Monastica Riformata di Santa Giustina: un Settantennio di Studi', *Fonti e ricerche di storia ecclesiastica padovana*, vii (1976), 35–134; ix (1977–8), 79–188.

Ulianich, B., 'Scrittura e azione pastorale nelle prime omilie episcopali di Isidor Chiari', *Reformata Reformanda: Festgabe für Hubert Jedin*, eds. E. Iserloh and K. Repgen (Münster, 1965), i, 610–34.

Vinay, V., 'Die Schrift "Il Beneficio di Giesu Cristo" nach der neusten Forschung', *Archiv für Reformationsgeschichte*, lxv (1974).

Walsh, K., 'The Observant Congregations of the Augustinian Friars in Italy c.1385–c.1465' (Oxford D. Phil. thesis, 1972).

Williams, G. H., 'Camillo Renato (c.1500–?1575)', *Italian Reformation Studies in Honor of Laelius Socinus*, ed. J. A. Tedeschi (Florence, 1965), 105–83.

Witters, W., 'La Rédaction Primitive des Déclarations et Constitutions de la Congrégation de Sainte Justine de Padue (xvᶜs.)', *Studia Monastica*, vii (1965), 127–46.

Zanetti, A. M., *Latina et Italica D. Marci Biblioteca Codicum Manuscriptorum*, v (Venice, 1740).

Zonta, G., 'Francesco Negri l'eretico e la sua tragedia "Il libero arbitrio"', *Giornale storico della letteratura italiana*, lxvii (1916), 265–324; lxviii (1917), 108–60.

Theological Names and Terms

Antiochene: The teachings of the early Christian theologians in Antioch, in Syria, notably St. John Chrysostom (*c.*347–407) (q.v.). The Antiochene school held to a literal exegesis of Scripture, expounding texts in their historical context, and according to the plain meaning of the words rather than any allegorical meaning. They emphasized the humanity of Christ and its implications for mankind, especially the conquest of death and the restoration of wholeness and perfection through divine grace and human moral effort.

Augustinian: This term refers to the teachings of St. Augustine (354–430), bishop of Hippo in North Africa, and also to the various medieval developments of his doctrine. In respect of salvation, Augustine taught that fallen man has inherited from Adam both the legal liability of sin and a fundamental moral weakness which makes salvation impossible except through divine grace.

Cassian: John Cassian (*c.*360–435) was a monk from the Middle East, who settled near Marseilles. His 'Institutes' set out rules for the monastic life and discussed the chief hindrances to achieving perfection. In opposition to Augustine (q.v. under **Augustinian**), he held that salvation is accomplished not solely through the grace of God, but also through the efforts of the human will.

Chrysostom: St. John Chrysostom (*c.*347–407), Bishop of Constantinople, was educated in law and theology at Antioch, and was there ordained priest. John's powerful preaching later brought him the name 'Chrysostom' (golden-mouthed). From 386 to 398 he set out to stimulate moral and social reform in Antioch by a series of homilies on the Bible. His method was to expound theological meaning in a straightforward literal manner, avoiding allegorical interpretations, and then to draw practical applications from the text. In common with other Antiochene (q.v.) theologians he saw physical and spiritual decay and death as the prime problem of mankind, and the Christian life to be the rescue from death by Christ, followed by the restoration of human nature to health and wholeness.

Dionysian: Pertaining to the mystical theologian Dionysius (*c*.500) who combined Platonist (q.v.) ideas with Christian doctrine. He described the spiritual life in terms of ascent through an elaborate hierarchy of angelic beings: the soul is purged of its attachment to the senses, then receives illumination and understanding of divine realities, and finally reaches an intimate mystical union with God.

Duplex Iustitia (**Double Justification**): A compromise doctrine of justification (q.v.) between the Reformed view (that man, despite remaining sinful, is justified in the eyes of God out of grace alone, being acquitted of guilt because the righteousness of God is ascribed to him), and the Catholic view (that man is justified because, with God's grace, he actually becomes sanctified). Double justification combined the two differing doctrines. It held that salvation begins as the development of inherent justice (q.v., under *Iustitia Inhaerens*) with the help of grace, but because of its human element, this inherent justice is imperfect. Whatever is lacking in the person's state of justice is then made up by the gift of God's own righteousness, which is imputed to man by grace alone, so that he is now acceptable to God. The doctrine, held by Contarini, Seripando, and other Italian *spirituali* and a few Protestants, was unacceptable to both Rome and the Reformers. It was brushed aside, though not formally condemned, by the Council of Trent.

Forensic Justification: The doctrine that salvation is primarily to do with the cancellation of human guilt—this being wrought by Jesus Christ having himself taken the punishment for human guilt.

Greek Fathers: The authoritative early Christian teachers in the regions of predominantly Greek culture, including not only Greece, but also Turkey, Syria, and Egypt. Their theology comprises three main schools—the Alexandrian, the Cappadocian, the Antiochene. The more influential theologians include Clement and Athanasius (of Alexandria), Basil of Caesarea, Gregory of Nazianzus (q.v.), and Gregory of Nyssa (all of Cappadocia, in central Turkey) and John Chrysostom (q.v.) of Antioch (Syria). The Greek Fathers were deeply involved in disputations with various fundamental heresies and in the task of defining the nature of the Trinity. They reveal a strong sense of both the majestic transcendence of God and the dignity of human nature which can be restored to perfection and participate in the divine nature. At the same time, almost all Greek Fathers were obliged to come to terms with the complex and despotic politics of the age and with contemporary social problems.

Gregory of Nazianzus: Gregory (329–89), one of the Greek Fathers (q.v.), was born in Cappadocia and educated in Athens. He successfully opposed the Arian teaching that Christ was the greatest of men but not God, and expounded the doctrine that the three persons of the Trinity are distinct, but undivided in honour and substance.

Imago Dei: The 'image of God', in which human beings are made. Augustine (q.v., under 'Augustinian'), believed this image to consist in the mind's three qualities of memory, intellect and will. Some theologians argued that the fundamental (or original) sin entirely corrupted this image of God in man, so that grace alone can rescue man; others held that the image is merely obscured and that sufficient of the image remains for man to co-operate with God's grace. The Greek Fathers also emphasized the notion that the *imago Dei* can be restored to its original perfection.

Iustitia Inhaerens (**Inherent Justice**): The condition of justice, or righteousness, which develops as a component part of a person's character: Inherent justice may be distinguished from the justice (or righteousness) of God which is imputed to—and which justifies—a person, but is not really inherent in the person.

Justification: The attainment of a state of righteousness, or justice, which is acceptable to God in his judgement of man. Theologians are agreed that this cannot take place without the action of God's grace, but the precise role of that grace is a matter of dispute. Some theologians have held that grace first wipes out the guilt of original sin, and then gives man divine strength to discard sin and become a just person. Others regard grace as the act by which God, out of love, acquits man of guilt ('cloaking' him with God's own righteousness) prior to the development of any personal condition of justice.

Occamist: The teachings of William of Occam (*c.*1285–1347), and later Gabriel Biel (*c.*1420–1495), emphasized the unlimited omnipotence and freedom of God, whose will was therefore unknowable through experience, reason, or natural knowledge. Consequently, God's judgement of man must remain fundamentally inscrutable, and the working of divine grace, in accepting sinful man as justified (q.v., under **Justification**), could only be known through faith and revelation.

Pauline: Paul of Tarsus (d. *c.*67) taught that Jesus Christ was not only the Messiah of the Old Testament, but also the eternal son of God, and head of the human race which is now redeemed—as an act of grace—by his blood. The human race, because it is redeemed by Christ, is to live a new life, in accordance with God's spirit, in union with Christ, and within the communion of the church. Throughout Christian history there have been disputes about the meaning of these concepts, especially the role of grace and human effort in salvation (see **Justification**).

Pelagianism: The teaching that human beings may initiate the process of salvation and carry it through by the exercise of free will in choosing the path of righteousness and justice. Pelagianism was condemned as a heresy in the fifth and sixth centuries.

Platonist: This term may be applied to the teachings of Plato (*c.*429–347 BC); or to the incorporation of his ideas into Christianity by the early Christian Platonists; or to the Florentine Neoplatonists of the fifteenth century, who revived their own version of Plato's teachings. All have in common a sharp distinction between the material world, including the human body, and the higher spiritual world. The soul, which is a spirit, rises above the changing world of observation to the higher world of the unchanging essence of things (the Forms), whose perfect beauty and goodness is known by the soul.

Predestination: The doctrine that since salvation is entirely a divine gift, and does not arise out of any human merit at all, it can only be God's decision who is to be saved. Therefore which particular persons are chosen and guided into salvation lies in God's will alone. The doctrine is most clearly expounded in Romans 8: 28–30; Ephesians 1: 3–14; 2 Timothy 1: 9, and was developed by St Augustine (q.v., under **Augustinian**).

Restoration: The teaching that human nature, now shattered by sin, suffering, and death, may again be restored to its original health, wholeness, and perfection as a result of Christ's conquest of death—the original and fundamental enemy of the human race.

Scotist: Duns Scotus (*c.*1265–1308) emphasized the will rather than the intellect in the plan of salvation. He taught that natural law is not primarily a product of God's intellect, but of his will, and, being dependent upon his will, is therefore not immutable. Also, man's prime relationship with God is not reached through intellectual understanding, but through love—which is an activity of the will.

Semi-Pelagianism: The doctrine that the process of salvation is initiated by the human will, and that only later does grace become necessary in completing the process of salvation. The doctrine lies between the Augustinian (q.v.) belief in grace alone and the Pelagian (q.v.) emphasis on human free will and good works. The sixteenth-century doctrine of *duplex iustitia* (q.v.) is similar.

Thomism: The teachings of Thomas Aquinas (*c.*1225–1274). Aquinas drew a sharp distinction between the realm of natural reason (dominated by the intellect) and the realm of faith (in which assent is controlled by the will). However, he laid great emphasis upon the role of the human intellect in exploring the path of salvation and in assisting the will to follow that path.

Index